Confronting Gun Violence in America

Thomas Gabor

Confronting Gun Violence in America

palgrave
macmillan

Thomas Gabor
Independent scholar
Lake Worth, Florida, USA

ISBN 978-3-319-33722-7   ISBN 978-3-319-33723-4   (eBook)
DOI 10.1007/978-3-319-33723-4

Library of Congress Control Number: 2016951862

Cover image © Kevkhiev Yury / Alamy Stock Photo

Printed on acid-free paper

This Palgrave Macmillan imprint is published by Springer Nature
The registered company is Springer International Publishing AG Switzerland

To Trayvon Martin and the many other victims of gun violence who paid the ultimate price for the belief that gun violence is a solution rather than a problem
And
To my dear friend, Charlie Ezra Rabie, a gentle soul who always sought to resolve problems in an amicable way, with all parties winning.

Acknowledgments

Over the 30 years in which I have worked in the area of gun violence and policy, the list of people with whom I have exchanged views and the experiences I have had the privilege to accumulate are far too long to enumerate. I had the opportunity to work on the United Nations study on firearm regulation in 1998, in close collaboration with the Canadian delegation, including Mr Tony Dittenhoffer, then with the Department of Justice, Canada. It was also a privilege to work on that project with Joseph Vince, then Chief of the Firearms Division of the Bureau of Alcohol, Tobacco, Firearms and Explosives and still one of America's leading authorities on gun violence, trafficking, and training of law enforcement officers.

In 1996, I was asked by attorneys representing the families of the primary school children who were murdered in Dunblane, Scotland, in 1996 to submit an expert report to Lord Cullen's Inquiry. This horrific event impressed upon me what is at stake in the debates on gun policy. This inquiry ultimately led to major policy changes in the UK.

In the mid-1980s, I had the opportunity to collaborate with five colleagues at the University of Montreal on *Armed Robbery: Cops, Robbers and Victims*, a book that has been judged to be the most comprehensive on the subject. I appreciated the opportunity to testify in front of the Legal Affairs Committee of the Canadian Senate in 1995 on the matter of establishing a long gun registry for the entire country. In addition, editing the special section on the subject for the *Canadian Journal of*

Criminology and Criminal Justice was highly informative. I have further benefitted from the collaboration with colleagues at Public Safety Canada and at Lansdowne Technologies in Ottawa in a study of firearm licensing systems around the world.

My friend Lt. Bob Wright of the Martin County (FL) Sheriff's Office always listened with a respectful bewilderment to my perspective. I appreciate that he insisted I join him at the firing range and experience guns first hand. My debates in the print media with Marion Hammer of the National Rifle Association have certainly been enlightening.

Conversations and collaboration with Patti Brigham, Chair of Gun Safety with The League of Women Voters, Florida, and other League members have been very informative and have compelled me to examine the implications on the ground of policies such as Stand Your Ground, campus-carry, and open-carry. My work as an Expert Witness for the Canada Border Services Agency in cases involving the initiative to arm all officers has provided an important perspective with regard to the new threats and priorities of agencies patrolling the borders of countries around the world.

Cases in which I have been retained by the Attorney General of Ontario (Canada) have compelled me to reflect on the benefits and downsides of the imposition of mandatory minimum sentences for offences involving firearms. My stint as a Visiting Scholar at the Research and Statistics Division of Justice, Canada, allowed me, among other things, to explore the scholarly evidence on the impact of mandatory sentences on gun-related crime and to determine that the conventional wisdom that these sentences do not work was not always correct. This experience brought me in contact with many promising young researchers who are now firmly established in academic or senior government positions.

Several cases in which I was retained by the Correctional Service of Canada have underscored the value, as well as the incendiary impact and limitations, of weapons in an institutional environment. Conversations with Mike Ryan, former head of security of CSC, and attorneys such as Bruce Hughson of the Department of Justice, Canada, as well as site visits to a variety of institutions were especially informative.

Many prominent people and groups involved in gun violence and security issues have offered their encouragement following the release of one of my reports or op-ed commentaries, including: Ladd Everitt, Director of Communications, Coalition to Stop Gun Violence & Educational Fund to Stop Gun Violence; Andy Pelosi, Executive Director of Campaign to Keep Guns off Campus and of GunFreeKids.org; Aria Duax, of the Wisconsin Anti-Violence Effort Educational Fund; David Hemenway, Director of Harvard University's Injury Control Research Center; Anna Eskamani, Director of Public Policy and Field Operations, Planned Parenthood of Southwest and Central Florida; Leslie Cole, Leslie Cole Associates security firm; Barry Freedman, FCS Consulting Services; Arlene Ustin, Karen Wilkerson, Geoff Kashdan, Rosalie Almborg, and MJ Range of the League of Women Voters of Palm Beach County, Florida; Linda Geller-Schwartz, National Council for Jewish Women (Palm Beach Section); Cathie Whittenberg, States United to Prevent Gun Violence; Dan Antonowicz, Criminology, Wilfrid Laurier University; Damir Kukec, Criminal Justice Commission of Palm Beach County; John Kiedrowski, Compliance Strategy Group; Daniel Vice, Brady Center to Prevent Gun Violence; and Lyse St. Jacques-Ayoub, Medical Council of Canada.

Among the most gratifying experiences have been my interactions with thousands of students who enrolled in my courses on violence and seminars on gun violence. Their enthusiasm and thirst for knowledge were contagious.

I am deeply indebted to Julia Willan, Senior Commissioning Editor at Palgrave Macmillan, who displayed enthusiasm for my project and provided encouragement right from the outset. I am also grateful to Dominic Walker for his support in getting the manuscript ready for publication. The entire team at Palgrave Macmillan has been highly professional. I am also grateful for the invaluable feedback provided by the external reviewers.

My greatest debt is owed to my wife, Christene, who provided a non-expert's perspective on each chapter of the book and was supportive throughout this project. Thank you, love, for believing in me and for putting up with my reclusive tendencies during the drafting of this book.

Contents

List of Tables

Part I

The Scale of America's Gun Problem

1

America's Gun Violence Problem

America is at a crossroads. The USA is experiencing levels of gun violence that are dramatically higher than those of other affluent countries.
The USA also leads the world when it comes to mass murder. Over the
last few years, our country has witnessed mass shootings in schools and
on college campuses, in workplaces, movie theaters, places of worship,
nightclubs, and shopping malls. Many Americans report being concerned
about being a victim of a mass shooting or of gun violence.[1] As citizens
become more vulnerable, there are growing calls for government action,
including reforms to gun laws.

At the same time, an increasingly unyielding gun lobby has opposed
federal legislation, including seemingly inoffensive laws that have had
the support of many gun owners. The power of this lobby was illustrated
in the aftermath of the mass murder in December 2012 of 20 school
children and 6 staff members at Sandy Hook Elementary School in
Newtown, Connecticut. Even on the heels of such a horrific incident,
Congress failed to pass a law that would have expanded background
checks to all gun sales, including private sales through the Internet and
at gun shows.

© The Author(s) 2016

T. Gabor, *Confronting Gun Violence in America*,
DOI 10.1007/978-3-319-33723-4_1

Aside from impeding gun law reform, the gun lobby has promoted many state laws over the last 30 years that have expanded the rights of gun owners. These laws have included those that allow gun carrying (both in a concealed and open manner), broadened the circumstances in which lethal force can be used in self-defense (e.g., Stand Your Ground laws), and increased the settings in which guns can be introduced, such as bars, colleges, churches, and even polling stations. The expansion of gun owners' rights has continued in some states even after the massacre at Sandy Hook.[2]

Expressing indignation about the lack of a national response to the continuing parade of mass shootings and the daily toll taken by gun violence, *The New York Times* published its first front page editorial in nearly a hundred years on December 4, 2015, two days after the slaughter of 14 people and serious wounding of another 22 in San Bernardino, California. The editors did not mince their words:

> *It is a moral outrage and a national disgrace that civilians can legally purchase weapons designed specifically to kill people with brutal speed and efficiency. These are weapons of war, barely modified and deliberately marketed as tools of macho vigilantism and even insurrection. America's elected leaders offer prayers for gun victims and then, callously and without fear of consequence, reject the most basic restrictions on weapons of mass killing.*[3]

Other countries have responded to mass murders far more decisively. In Canada, a gunman, in 1989, entered the School of Engineering at the University of Montreal, separated the men from the women, and murdered 14 women while screaming, "I hate feminists." This incident was followed by national laws that banned various military-style weapons and high-capacity ammunition magazines, introduced gun storage requirements, enhanced screening of gun license applicants, and created a national registry for long guns.[4]

In 1996, a gunman murdered 16 primary school children and a teacher in Dunblane, Scotland. This event resulted in the prohibition of virtually all handguns in the UK.[5] In the same year, 35 people were killed and 23 were wounded by a shooter in Port Arthur, Australia. Following this mass shooting, Australia's federal government forged an agreement with the states that called for restricted legal possession of automatic and semiautomatic firearms and further restricted the legal importation of nonmilitary centerfire self-loading firearms to those with a maximum magazine capacity of five rounds. The country literally melted down up to a third of its firearms as banned weapons were bought back from the public.[6] In Germany, mass shootings in Erfurt (2002) and Winnenden (2009) led to several reforms, including an increase in the age requirements for weapons purchases, psychological assessment of gun owners under the age of 25, and unannounced random inspections of gun owners' homes to ensure compliance with gun storage requirements.[7]

The muted response of the USA to the many mass casualty incidents that have occurred over the last few years is a glaring contrast to the experience of these countries. While a powerful gun lobby, spearheaded by the National Rifle Association, has actively resisted efforts to expand background checks and to impose other changes in federal regulations, the countries just mentioned overcame influential gun lobbies of their own to achieve their significant reforms. While other countries have increased restrictions on and banned certain guns, many American states continue to expand the rights of gun owners. One Canadian journalist has referred to America's affinity for guns as a form of "collective suicide pact."[8]

Our nation has displayed a profound ambivalence toward gun regulation. Aside from the impact on gun policy of the Second Amendment to the Constitution and its contentious reference to the "right of the people to keep and to bear Arms," public opinion is fairly evenly divided on the issue of the relative importance of gun rights versus gun safety. This said, the vast majority of Americans favor sensible gun laws. This book will examine the Second Amendment and public opinion, although the focus will be on research addressing the impact of guns on public safety and on the most effective solutions to the gun violence problem.

The Toll Taken by Guns

As for the human costs of gun violence, mass shootings have a higher profile, but it is the daily toll of incidents involving fewer casualties that account for most of America's gun-related deaths and injuries.

On an average day, more than 90 people are killed in gun homicides, suicides, and accidents.[9] In 2013, 117,894 Americans were either killed or treated for firearm-related injuries.[10,11] Every month, the number of American civilians who die from gunfire exceed the number of deaths of US military personnel in the first ten years of the war in Afghanistan.[12] Nicholas Kristof of *The New York Times* has reported that, since 1970, there have been 1.45 million gun deaths in the USA, a figure that exceeds all the deaths in wars throughout US history, including the Civil War, the two World Wars, and the conflicts in Korea, Vietnam, Afghanistan, and Iraq.[13]

According to the group Everytown for Gun Safety, there were nearly two mass shootings (at least four people are killed, excluding the shooter) a month between 2009 and 2015.[14] While mass murders occur elsewhere, they are far more commonplace in the USA than in other developed countries.

The statistics on gun ownership and on firearm-related mortality and injuries in the USA can help us understand why so many serious incidents can occur within such a narrow time frame. As of 2007, Americans owned 270 million or 31 % of the world's estimated 875 million privately owned guns, while accounting for less than 5 % of the world's population.[15] The Violence Policy Center in Washington, DC, has reported that, in 2014, 21 states and the District of Columbia had more deaths due to gunfire than due to car accidents. Data released at the end of 2015 by the Centers for Disease Control and Prevention show that, nationally, gun deaths are now as numerous as motor vehicle deaths.[16] This is the case despite the fact that owners drive cars far more often than typical gun owners use their guns.[17] While little headway has been made with regard to regulating guns, cars are subject to licensing and registration, car technologies continue to advance (e.g., rear-view cameras), and road laws governing speeding, texting while driving, and other behaviors that compromise safety keep evolving.

A 2011 study conducted at Harvard University's Injury Control Research Center analyzed gun death statistics for 2003 from the World Health Organization Mortality Database.[18] The study found that 80 % of all firearm deaths in 23 industrialized countries occurred in the USA. More recent research indicates that the gap between the USA and these countries is growing even wider.[19] Firearm homicide rates for 15-year-olds to 24-year-olds were nearly 43 times those of the other countries. In addition, 86 % of the women killed by firearms and 87 % of children under 15 years of age were Americans. On an average day, 20 US children and adolescents are hospitalized due to firearm injuries.[20]

American children and teenagers are 4 times more likely to die by gunfire than their Canadian counterparts, 7 times more likely to die by gunfire than young people in Israel, and 65 times more likely to be killed with a gun than children and teenagers in the UK.[21] Guns are used in approximately half a million violent crimes a year.[22] Figures such as these have led many medical and other professionals to view the number of firearm injuries and deaths as a public health epidemic or catastrophe.

Table 1.1 illustrates the dramatic difference in the number of firearm homicides in the USA when compared with other high-income countries. The odds of being murdered with a firearm are at least three times that of any other country. While one in every 29,000 Americans is murdered each year with a firearm, less than one in a million Germans and residents of the UK meet the same fate, and less than one in ten million residents of Japan are murdered with a gun each year. The odds of being murdered by any means (with or without guns) are also greater in the USA, but the differences are not as great. Consider a comparison with Finland. The odds of being murdered with a firearm in the USA are 11 times that of incurring the same fate in Finland; however, the odds of being murdered by any means are just over three times that of Finland. In the USA, 69.2 % of homicides involve a gun, whereas in Finland just 19.1 % involve a gun. The odds of being murdered by a means other than a firearm (not shown in the table) are virtually identical in the two countries, showing that it is the enormous difference in gun homicides that makes the overall odds of being murdered higher in the USA. We can observe that the percentage of homicides in which a firearm is used is much higher in the USA than in the other countries. Higher gun availability in the USA is likely an important factor in the choice of guns over other means of killing.

Professor David Hemenway of Harvard's Injury Control Research Center points out that, when compared with all other first world countries, we have average rates of assault, burglary, and robbery, but we have

Table 1.1 Comparison of firearm homicides and odds of being murdered in elected high-income countries

Country and most recent year of data used in the UN's data tables	# of Firearm homicides	Odds of being murdered with a firearm	Odds of being murdered by any means	% of homicides involving a firearm
USA (2014)	10,945	1 in 29,000[a]	1 in 20,000	69.2
Israel (2011)	81	1 in 95,000	1 in 51,000	53.6
Canada (2013 and 2014)	131	1 in 271,000	1 in 69,000	25.4
Finland (2012)	17	1 in 319,000	1 in 61,000	19.1
Switzerland (2013)	18	1 in 452,000	1 in 140,000	31.0
Australia (2013)	35	1 in 655,000	1 in 106,000	16.2
Spain (2012)	51	1 in 918,000	1 in 129,000	14.0
Germany (2011)	61	<1 in 1,000,000	1 in 121,000	9.2
UK (2011/12)	38	<1 in 1,000,000	1 in 97,000	5.8
Japan (2008)	11	<1 in 10,000,000	1 in 197,000	1.7

Sources: National Center for Injury Prevention and Control. Injury mortality reports 1999 and onward (USA). Web-based Injury Statistics Query and Reporting System/CDC WISQARS. Atlanta: Centers for Disease Control and Prevention; 2015; Police Crime Statistics Annual Report. Sections of the Criminal Code and selected offences: elucidations and evolution of offences 2012, 2009–2013. Neuchâtel, Switzerland: Office Fédéral de la Statistique; Switzerland.2014; CANSIM Database. Homicide Survey, homicides involving firearms, by type of firearm, Canada, 1998 to 2013. Ottawa: Statistics Canada, 2015. Police-Reported Crime Statistics in Canada. Homicide in Canada 1983 to 2014. Ottawa: Statistics Canada, 2014; Homicides and gun homicides in Finland. Vienna: UNODC Global Study on Homicide; 2013; Homicides and gun homicides in Spain. Vienna: UNODC Global Study on Homicide; 2013; Homicide in 207 countries—Germany. Vienna: Global Study on Homicide; 2011; Homicides in Israel. Vienna: UNODC Global Study on Homicide; 2013; World Health Organization. HO.2014. Inter-country Comparison of Mortality for Selected Cause of Death—Gun Homicide in Israel. Copenhagen: World Health Organisation Regional Office for Europe; 2014; Underlying cause of death, all causes, year of occurrence, Australia, 2004–2013—assault. Canberra: Australian Bureau of Statistics; 2013; UK. 2012. Deaths: external causes of morbidity and mortality—underlying cause, sex and age group, 2011. Mortality Statistics: Deaths Registered in England and Wales, 2011. London: Office for National Statistics; UK. 2013; Table 2.01: Offences initially recorded as homicide by current classification, 1961 to 2011/12. Crime Statistics, Focus on: Violent Crime and Sexual Offences, 2011/12. London: Office for National Statistics; Homicide in 207 Countries—Japan: Trends, Context, Data. Vienna: UNODC Global Study on Homicide 2011; 2013
[a]Odds are rounded to the nearest thousand

the most guns, the weakest gun laws, and by far the highest rates of gun homicide, gun suicide, and accidental gun death.[23] We are therefore an outlier in our levels of lethal violence, not violence overall, suggesting that it is the dramatically higher prevalence of guns that accounts for the differences in lethal violence, including suicide, between the USA and other advanced countries. In fact, our nonfirearm suicide rates are much lower than those for the 23 high-income countries overall. However, the enormous difference in gun suicides brings our rates close to the level of these countries.

Gun violence does not touch all segments of American society uniformly. African-Americans are ten times as likely to die of gun violence as are whites.[24] States in the South tend to have the highest gun death rates, and states in the Northeast tend to have the lowest firearm death rates.[25] While men are more likely to be homicide victims, women are especially at risk from guns in the home, as most women are killed by intimate partners or close relatives rather than by strangers.[26] For example, in 2005, 40 % of female homicide victims in the USA were killed by a current or former intimate partner and guns were used in over half of those murders.[27]

Gun violence is not just something abstract; it is very personal to many Americans. A poll by *Huffington Post* found that 40 % of Americans know someone who has been killed or committed suicide with a gun. Almost half of all African-Americans know someone killed with a gun, and one in five know a family member who has been killed with a gun.[28]

Another consequence of widespread gun ownership and carrying is the killing of civilians by police officers. An analysis by the *Washington Post* found that the final tally for 2015 will approach a thousand civilians killed by law enforcement.[29] While the circumstances of these incidents vary and many factors are at play, it is noteworthy that in nearly six in ten cases, the individual shot possessed a firearm. While police body cameras and photos from smart phones are revealing many questionable shootings by police, the widespread availability of guns in the USA is also likely contributing to genuine errors in which police mistakenly believe a suspect is armed. Former Seattle Police Chief Norm Stamper writes: "Guns make police officers hyper vigilant. And a scared cop is a dangerous cop."[30]

The Cost of Gun Violence

Consider also the economic costs of firearm-related injuries. One study conducted in the 1990s estimated that the annual cost of firearm injuries was over $20 billion.[31] This figure, thought by the authors to be a low estimate, included the direct medical expenditures, as well as the costs due to lost productivity arising from illness, disability, and premature death. Lost productivity refers to the loss of paid and unpaid work for the victims and others affected by an incident, including employers. Researchers Ted Miller and Mark Cohen analyzed the cost of firearm injuries for 1992 and, apart from medical costs and lost productivity, included such items as emergency transport, administrative costs (e.g., processing and investigation of insurance claims), and the costs of pain, suffering, and lost quality of life. For 1992, they arrived at a total cost of $112 billion for gunshot injuries and deaths.[32]

In the late 1990s, Professors Philip Cook of Duke University and Jens Ludwig of Georgetown University undertook a calculation that added other items, such as personal efforts to manage risk, preventive measures by public agencies, and security costs (e.g., at airports and schools).[33] They arrived at an annual cost of $100 billion for firearm injuries and deaths. In a more recent estimate, *Mother Jones* magazine turned to Ted Miller, who has been studying the societal cost of violence from the 1980s.[34] Based on data for 2012, Miller tallied the direct and indirect costs of gun violence. Direct costs include emergency services, medical care, and the cost of police investigations. Indirect costs made up the bulk of the costs and included lost wages and the overall impact on the quality of victims' lives. Quality-of-life costs were estimated using amounts awarded by juries for pain and suffering in wrongful death and injury cases. This analysis found the total annual cost of gun violence in America to exceed $229 billion.

Even this enormous number may underestimate the full costs. Consider the costs associated with highly traumatic shootings in public places. When a gunman killed two people, wounded another, and took his own life at the Clackamas Town Center near Portland, Oregon, in December 2012, more than 150 officers from at least 13 law enforcement agencies responded. The investigation lasted more than three months and produced a report nearly 1000 pages in length. Following the incident, the 1.5-million-square-foot mall shut down for three days during the height of the holiday shopping season in order to calm the public, undertake repairs, and to ramp up security. As a result, 188 stores lost revenue while the mall was closed.[35]

When it comes to children, the effect of gunshot wounds is far more catastrophic than are health hazards such as tobacco. While the adverse effects of smoking tend to surface later in life, children who are struck by a bullet and killed or injured are usually robbed of their childhood immediately. Aside from the early loss of a life or the quality of life as they grow up, the medical and related costs of caring for an individual who has been disabled as a child or teen are astronomical.

To be fair, we must balance the costs associated with firearm injuries and mortality with the potential benefits of guns as protective tools that may save lives. The current scholarly debate is more sophisticated than it was 25 years ago when people argued that guns were either wholly harmful or beneficial. Today, most of us recognize that there are both criminal uses and defensive or lawful uses. The key question is: Overall, do firearms provide more harms or benefits to society? The net costs or benefits of owning and carrying guns for self-protection are discussed in Chaps. 9 and 10 and the analysis conducted in this book comes to a clear conclusion on this issue.

A Historical Note

The catastrophic mass shootings in Newtown, Aurora, Charleston, San Bernardino, and Orlando, as well as the daily deaths, injuries, and costs associated with firearms, have justifiably opened a national conversation about the role of guns in American life in the twenty-first century. We are no longer a frontier country and, increasingly, we live at close quarters in urban communities rather than in remote rural areas. Most of us no longer hunt as our primary means of obtaining food or need guns to protect ourselves from wildlife. There is a legal system to settle disputes, so gunfights and other duels are no longer necessary to settle scores. There are fewer legitimate reasons for gun possession by private citizens in the twenty-first century than there may have been in the earlier years of our Republic, although there are groups that are actively lobbying for the widespread arming of our population and the ability to carry firearms across state lines and to introduce them into virtually all settings, including college campuses, government buildings, and schools.[36]

While a great deal of American literature and many Hollywood films portrayed American frontier towns as free of virtually any restrictions on guns, this picture of the Old West is not accurate. Adam Winkler, a professor of constitutional law at the University of California in Los Angeles (UCLA) has written that gun control in frontier towns was quite strict.[37] In notorious Dodge City, Kansas, for example, people were required to turn in their guns when they entered the town. Contrary to the mythology of violence-ridden Western towns beset by shootouts, an average of just one to two murders per year occurred in Dodge City during the cattle era.[38] Winkler also notes that the epic gunfight at the OK Corral in Tombstone, Arizona, occurred when Wyatt Earp and his brothers tried to enforce a gun ordinance by disarming a semi-outlaw group called the Cowboys.

Ray Allen Billington, a historian specializing in the study of the American frontier and West, noted that businesspeople and the other leaders of the Western cattle towns were quick to establish local police forces and to enforce prohibitions against carrying guns. Disarmament was routinely practiced in newly established Western towns and was generally understood as a means of improving public safety. According to Billington, the shootouts glorified in countless books and movies were "unheard of."[39]

Professor Winkler of UCLA adds that the Revolutionary Era was marked by strict gun laws in which all free men were mandated to acquire militarily useful firearms and to attend periodic gatherings during which the guns were inspected and recorded by officials—an early variation of gun registration.[40] In some states (e.g., New Hampshire), officials conducted door-to-door inventories of guns available in the community and the states could seize guns if they were needed for military purposes. Gun control was also prevalent in the South, a region with some of the most restrictive gun laws in the nineteenth century. These laws were designed to prevent gunfights and to disarm blacks following the Civil War. Laws banning the carrying of concealed weapons were widespread and generally believed to be an essential part of preventing violence.[41] Therefore, contrary to a prevalent belief, gun control is not a twentieth century phenomenon.

What does the future hold for those who view the gun as a venerated object and who embrace the mythology around its role in the formation of this country? Professor Winkler conjectures that their influence and that of the gun lobby will wane over time.[42] He notes that the core support for the National Rifle Association comes from white, rural, and less educated voters. He argues that the changing composition of the US population, specifically a surge in the proportion of Hispanic and Asian Americans, along with continuing urbanization, will turn the country against uncompromising gun rights advocates. In Chap. 13, these and other trends in public opinion are discussed.

Participants in the Great American Gun Debate

Historical facts notwithstanding, conversations about guns are increasingly joining politics, sex, and religion as taboo at the dinner table, as the issue is so volatile and elicits so much passion or revulsion. It is very difficult to bridge the divide between the activists on both sides of the gun control debate and then between the activists and the research community. While it is somewhat oversimplified to place the participants in the debate into a number of distinct groups, to do so helps illustrate why the issue of guns in American society appears so intractable.

Activists and members of the public who favor the close regulation of firearms and the outright banning of certain categories (e.g., "junk" guns, assault weapons) believe that it is simply foolish to seek an armed society, to allow people to carry concealed weapons, to possess military-style weapons, to carry firearms into public buildings, colleges, and parks, to store guns within easy reach of children, and to allow the sale of guns without carefully screening buyers. To this group, more regulation of firearms simply makes sense and is the prudent thing to do in protecting people from lethal instruments. People from other countries often share this view and just shake their heads with regard to the volume and accessibility of guns in American society and at what they consider to be our lax gun laws.

The activists on the other side of the debate speak a different language. While arguing that owning and carrying guns affords them protection, many of their arguments revolve around their personal rights and the historical significance and role of guns, rather than their practical merits. Tom Diaz, formerly a senior policy analyst with the Washington-based Violence Policy Center and a former National Rifle Association (NRA) member, put it this way: "To many, guns are repulsive and exceedingly dangerous, even evil. But to others, guns are venerated objects of craftsmanship and tangible symbols of such fundamental American values as independence, self-reliance, and freedom from governmental interference."[43] People adopting this perspective view gun ownership as a sovereign right and usually invoke the much-debated Second Amendment of the US Constitution to support this position.

Members of the research community, while not unanimous in their conclusions, appear to be reaching some degree of consensus. Scholars generally undertake statistical studies to document the extent of firearm-related injuries and deaths, to determine the contribution of gun ownership, carrying, and storage, and to calculate the impact of different policies, be these policies to impose restrictions and bans or those expanding gun rights (e.g., right-to-carry laws).

In addition to the above-mentioned three groups or communities, there are those with strong commercial interests in manufacturing, importing, and selling firearms, ammunition, and accessories to as many Americans as possible. Their views are usually closely aligned with the gun lobby as this sector has an economic interest in ensuring that regulations will be minimized. Restrictions on gun ownership and prohibitions relating to certain types of firearms and ammunition are seen by these interests as impeding sales. Furthermore, John Donohue, a Stanford University law professor, makes the point that allowing felons and the mentally ill to purchase guns on the private market fuels crime, fear, and more gun sales.[44]

Issues Addressed in This Book

As a researcher, my role is to present the evidence as I see it on a variety of policy questions relating to firearms. My aim is to share research findings with nonexperts, scholars, and activists who are interested in understanding the impact of guns and gun legislation on American society. My goal is not to be neutral but to be guided by the evidence. I do not hesitate to draw strong conclusions where I believe the evidence warrants it.

Below are some questions that have prompted me to conduct research on the firearms–violence issue for 25 years and to write this book. These questions are the basis for the discussion ahead and, hopefully, will stimulate enlightened discussion on the role of guns in American society:

- If more guns make our society safer, shouldn't the homicide rates in the USA be lower, not higher, than countries with fewer gun owners and less guns?
- Do methods/weapons matter in homicide and suicide, or is the intent of the shooter all we need to know in understanding the outcomes of attacks and suicide attempts?
- Are fatal gun accidents simply due to catastrophic human errors and gun defects that are unavoidable or are these deaths preventable?
- Does it make sense to believe that greater access to guns by teenagers and young children does not lead to more impulsive suicides and lethal accidents?
- Is it reasonable to believe that mass murders, large-scale school shootings, and killings of police officers would remain at the same level if fewer guns were available, there was more intensive screening of gun owners, and guns were less accessible to unauthorized users?
- Do guns in the home provide protection from an intruder or are they more likely to be used to harm a family member in a domestic dispute, suicide, or accidental shooting?
- Do laws that encourage more people to carry firearms, whether in a concealed or open fashion, foil and deter crime or do these laws increase levels of violence?

- Do laws that expand the circumstances in which people can use lethal force (e.g., Stand Your Ground) when they feel threatened reduce or increase the homicide rate?
- Do states with more guns in private hands have higher homicide rates than states with fewer guns in private hands?
- How can the screening of gun owners and buyers be improved?
- Are gun manufacturers and dealers subject to adequate federal regulations and enforcement?
- Is the public more concerned about protecting gun rights or about controlling gun ownership?
- Are there gun laws or regulations that have been shown to reduce violence?

Notes

1. McClatchy-Marist Poll. Domestic issues key to 2016 Presidential campaign [Internet]. Poughkeepsie, NY: Marist College Institute for Public Opinion; 2015 Nov. 11. Available from: http://maristpoll.marist.edu/wp-content/misc/usapolls/us151029/Immigration_Guns_Campaign%20 Issues/McClatchy_Marist%20Poll_Immigration_Guns_2016%20 Campaign%20Issues_Survey%20Findings_Nature%20of%20the%20 Sample%20and%20Tables_November%202015.pdf
2. Foley R. States expanded gun rights after Sandy Hook school massacre [Internet]. Miami Herald. 2015 Dec 13. Available from: http://www. miamiherald.com/news/nation-world/article49550275.html
3. Editorial. End the gun epidemic in America [Internet]. The New York Times. 2015 Dec 4. Available from: http://www.nytimes.com/2015/12/05/ opinion/end-the-gun-epidemic-in-america.html
4. Royal Canadian Mounted Police (CA). History of firearms control in Canada: up to and including the Firearms Act [Internet]. Ottawa: Royal Canadian Mounted Police; 2012. Available from: http://www.rcmp-grc. gc.ca/cfp-pcaf/pol-leg/hist/con-eng.htm
5. Firearms (Amendment) Act of 1997, United Kingdom. Available from: http://www.legislation.gov.uk/ukpga/1997/5
6. Alpert P. The big melt: how one democracy changed after scrapping a third of its firearms. In: Webster D, Vernick J, editors. Reducing gun vio-

lence in America: informing policy with evidence and analysis. Baltimore: Johns Hopkins University Press; 2013. P. 205–211.

7. Gabor T. International firearm licensing regimes: a study of six countries. Ottawa: Public Safety Canada; 2013.

8. Kay J. More guns aren't the answer: For Canadians, America's gun cult looks like a collective suicide cult [Internet]. National Post. 2016 Jan 8. Available from: http://news.nationalpost.com/full-comment/jonathan-kay-more-guns-arent-the-answer-americans-are-likelier-to-wet-their-pants-facing-a-mass-shooter

9. Centers for Disease Control and Prevention (US), National Vital Statistics Report. Deaths, Final Data for 2013. Table 10. Hyattsville, MD: National Center for Health Statistics; 2016.

10. Centers for Disease Control and Prevention (US). Overall firearm gunshot nonfatal injuries and rates per 100,000 (2013) [Internet]. WISQARS. Available from: http://webappa.cdc.gov/cgi-bin/broker.exc CDC, FastStats, Mortality (2013), http://www.cdc.gov/nchs/fastats/injury.htm

11. Centers for Disease Control and Prevention (US). Mortality (2013) [Internet]. FastStats. Available from: http://www.cdc.gov/nchs/fastats/injury.htm

12. Operation Enduring Freedom. Coalition military fatalities by year [Internet]. Available from: http://www.icasualties.org/oef/

13. Kristof N. A new way to tackle gun deaths [Internet]. The New York Times. 2015 Oct. 3. Available from: http://www.nytimes.com/2015/10/04/opinion/sunday/nicholas-kristof-a-new-way-to-tackle-gun-deaths.html?emc=eta1&_r=0

14. Everytown for Gun Safety. Analysis of Recent Mass Shootings. New York: Everytown for Gun Safety; 2015.

15. Karp A. Completing the count: civilian firearms. Small Arms Survey, 2007. Geneva: Graduate Institute of International Studies; 2007.

16. Ingraham C. Guns are now killing as many people as cars in the US [Internet]. The Washington Post. 2015 Dec 17. Available from: https://www.washingtonpost.com/news/wonk/wp/2015/12/17/guns-are-now-killing-as-many-people-as-cars-in-the-u-s/

17. Rand K. Gun Deaths Outpace Motor Vehicle Deaths in 21 States and the District of Columbia in 2014. Washington, DC: Violence Policy Center; 2016.

18. Richardson E, Hemenway D. Homicide, suicide, and unintentional firearm fatality: Comparing the United States with other high-income countries, 2003. J Trauma. 2011; 70(1): 238–243.

19. E. Grinshteyn and D. Hemenway, Violent death rates: The US compared with other high-income OECD countries. The Am. J. Med. 2015; 129(3): in press.

20. Leventhal J, Gaither J, Sege R. Hospitalizations due to firearm injuries in children and adolescents. Pediatr. 2014; 133(2): 219–225.

21. Parsons C, Johnson A. Young guns: how gun violence is devastating the millenial generation. Washington, DC: Center for American Progress; 2014. P. 2.

22. National Institute of Justice (US). Gun Violence [Internet]. Washington, DC: Department of Justice; 2013. Available from: http://www.nij.gov/topics/crime/gun-violence/

23. Richardson E, Hemenway, D. Homicide, suicide, and unintentional firearm fatality.

24. Keating D. Gun deaths shaped by race in America [Internet]. The Washington Post. 2013 Mar 22. Available from: http://www.washingtonpost.com/sf/feature/wp/2013/03/22/gun-deaths-shaped-by-race-in-america/

25. Centers for Disease Control and Prevention (US). Violence-related firearm deaths among residents of metropolitan areas and cities, United States, 2006–2007 [Internet]. Morbidity and Mortality Weekly Report. 2011 May 13. Available from: http://www.cdc.gov/mmwr/preview/mmwrhtml/mm6018a1.htm

26. Hemenway D. Private guns, public health. Ann Arbor: University of Michigan Press; 2004. P. 122–123.

27. Stachelberg W, Gerney A, Parsons C, Knauss M. Preventing domestic abusers and stalkers from accessing guns. Washington, DC: Center for American Progress; 2013. P. 1.

28. Edwards-Levy A., 40 percent of Americans know someone who was killed with a gun [Internet]. Huffington Post. 2015 Oct 8. Available from: http://www.huffingtonpost.com/entry/americans-know-gun-violence-victims_56169834e4b0e66ad4c6bd2b

29. Kindy K. Fatal police shootings in 2015 approaching 400 nationwide [Internet]. The Washington Post. 2015 May 30. Available from: https://www.washingtonpost.com/national/fatal-police-shootings-in-2015-approaching-400-nationwide/2015/05/30/d322256a-058e-11e5-a428-c984eb077d4e_story.html

30. Norm Stamper, I Ran a Big City Police Department. The Way We Train Cops to Use Lethal Force is Broken [Internet]. The Trace. 2016 Jul 12. Available at: https://www.thetrace.org/2016/07/seattle-former-top-cop-guns-america-policing-problem/

31. Max W, Rice D. Shooting in the dark: the cost of firearm injuries. Health Aff. 1993; 12(4): 171–185.
32. Miller T, Cohen M. Costs. In: R. Ivatory R, Cayten C, editors. The textbook of penetrating trauma. Baltimore: Williams and Wilkins; 1996. P. 49–59.
33. Cook P, Ludwig J. Gun violence: the real costs. New York: Oxford University Press; 2000.
34. Follman M, Lurie J, Lee J, West J. What does gun violence really cost [Internet]? Mother Jones. 2015 May/Jun. Available from: http://www. motherjones.com/politics/2015/04/true-cost-of-gun-violence-in-america
35. Cook P, Ludwig, J. Gun violence.
36. The Brady Center to Prevent Gun Violence. No gun left behind: the gun lobby's campaign to push guns into colleges and schools. Washington, DC: The Brady Center to Prevent Gun Violence; 2007.
37. Winkler A. Gunfight: The battle over the right to bear arms in America. New York: W.W. Norton; 2011.
38. Wills G. A necessary evil: a history of American distrust of government. New York: Simon and Schuster; 1999.
39. Billington R. Westward expansion: A history of the American frontier. New York: Macmillan, 1974. P. 587.
40. Winkler A. Gunfight. P. 113.
41. Winkler A. Gunfight. P. 13, 135, 167.
42. Winkler A. The NRA will fall. it's inevitable [Internet]. The Washington Post. 2015 Oct 19. Available from: https://www.washingtonpost. com/posteverything/wp/2015/10/19/the-nra-will-fall-its-inevitable/? tid=sm_fb
43. Diaz T. Making a killing: the business of guns in America. New York: The New Press; 1999. P. 3.
44. Donohue J. Why the NRA fights background checks [Internet]. CNN. com. 2013 Apr 10. Available from: http://www.cnn.com/2013/04/10/ opinion/donohue-background-checks/index.html?iid=article_sidebar

2

Gun Ownership in the USA

Americans are viewed as having a national gun fetish. Whether it is Western movies, the gangsters in the 1920s, or the permissive gun laws relative to other countries, we are viewed as having a love affair with guns. How prominent is the so-called "gun culture"? Does this image of a gun-crazy society have any basis in fact?

When compared with other countries, the USA is certainly an outlier with regard to its arsenal of privately owned firearms. The USA surpasses other nations by a wide margin both in terms of the absolute number of guns and in the number of guns relative to its population. When population differences are taken into account, Americans own three or more times as many firearms than residents of the vast majority of nations. Estimates of the number of firearms in the hands of Americans vary, and no government agency is charged with collecting data on gun ownership on a routine basis. The Congressional Research Service reported that the civilian gun stock was about one gun per person, or about 310 million guns in 2009.[1] The International Small Arms Survey put the US

© The Author(s) 2016
T. Gabor, *Confronting Gun Violence in America*,
DOI 10.1007/978-3-319-33723-4_2

gun stock in 2007 at 270 million.[2] Philip Cook and Kristin Goss of Duke University prefer a range of 200–300 million due to the unknown number of firearms that become unusable or that are imported or exported illegally each year.[3]

International Comparison

According to the 2007 Small Arms Survey conducted by the Geneva, Switzerland-based Graduate Institute of International Studies, Americans owned 270 million of the world's 650 million privately owned firearms.[4] This represented about 90 guns for every 100 residents of the USA. This international report stressed the uniqueness of Americans' gun-buying habits and the "gun culture" in the USA:

> With less than 5 per cent of the world's population, the United States is home to roughly 35–50 per cent of the world's civilian-owned guns, heavily skewing the global geography of firearms and any relative comparison.... Of some eight million new firearms manufactured annually around the world, roughly 4.5 million are bought by the people of the United States.... With this sustained and unsurpassed level of routine gun-buying, American civilians will become even more dominant in global gun ownership. Therefore, any discussion of civilian gun ownership must devote disproportionate attention to the United States, if only because of the scale of its gun culture. Exceptional civilian gun habits in the United States distort impressions of global trends. Without the US share, the global civilian total falls from 570–730 million to roughly 320–440 million civilian firearms...[5]

Table 2.1 illustrates the range of civilian gun ownership levels for selected countries. Table 2.1 shows that Americans own three or more times as many guns per 100 people as civilians own in most countries. Americans own 10 times as many guns per 100 people as residents of Russia or Brazil, 15 times as many guns as residents of England and Wales, and 30 times as many guns per 100 people as residents of China.

Table 2.1 Privately owned guns in selected countries

Country	Private gun ownership per 100 people
USA	90
Yemen	61
Finland	55
Switzerland	46
Iraq	39
Serbia	38
France	32
Canada	32
Sweden	32
Germany	30
Australia	16
Mexico	15
Argentina	13
Italy	12
Spain	11
Russia	9
Brazil	9
England and Wales	6
India	4
China	3

Source: Small Arms Survey. Geneva, Switzerland: Graduate Institute of International Studies; 2007

Gun Ownership Levels and Trends

Table 2.2 displays some of the most recent and significant gun ownership figures for the USA. While the figures from Gallup tend to be somewhat higher than those yielded by other surveys, recent polls tend to show that about a third of all households own one or more firearms. About a quarter of adults own a gun. While long guns (shotguns and rifles) make up about 60 % of the gun stock, about one of six adults owns a handgun.[6] While there have been some spikes in gun ownership over the last few decades, the overall trend is clearly heading downward. The General Social Survey of the University of Chicago's National Opinion Research Center, which has been tracking gun ownership for over 40 years, shows

Table 2.2 Household and personal gun ownership levels and trends

Survey	Households owning one or more guns	Adults owning one or more guns	Trend in household gun ownership	Respondent, spouse, or both hunt	Multiple gun owners
General Social Survey (2014)	31 %	22 %	Decline from 47 % in 1973; Peak year— 50 % in 1977	Decline from 32 % in 1976 to 15 % in 2014	
Pew Research Center (Feb./2013)	37 %	24 %	Decline from 45 % in 1993		
Gallup (Oct./2015)	41 %	28 %	Decline from 49 % in 1959; Peak year— 51 % in 1993		
Quinnipiac University (Dec./2015	37 %	25 %			
Harvard School of Pub. Health (2015)		22 %			8 % of gun owners (2 % of all adults) own 10+ guns
Harvard School of Pub. Health (2004)	38 %	26 % (16 % own a handgun)			48 % of gun owners own 4+ guns (average of 6.6 guns per owner)

(*continued*)

Table 2.2 (continued)

Survey	Households owning one or more guns	Adults owning one or more guns	Trend in household gun ownership	Respondent, spouse, or both hunt	Multiple gun owners
Johns Hopkins and GfK KN (Jan./13)	33 %	22 %			
Police Foundation (1994)	35 %	25 % (16 % own a handgun)			74 % of owners possessed 2+ guns

Sources: Smith T, Son J. Trends in gun ownership in the United States, 1972–2014. Chicago: National Opinion Research Center, University of Chicago; 2015; Pew Research Center. Why own a gun: protection is now top reason. Washington, DC: Pew Research Center; 2013 Mar 12; Gallup. Guns [Internet]. Available at: http://www.gallup.com/poll/1645/Guns.aspx; Masters K. Over 6 Million Americans own 10 or more guns: A forthcoming Harvard survey suggests that more Americans own a sizable stockpile of firearms than there are residents of Denmark [Internet]. The Trace. 2015 Oct 6. Available from: http://www.thetrace.org/2015/10/gun-ownership-america-hemenway-survey-harvard/; Hepburn L, Miller M, Azrael D, Hemenway D. The US gun stock: results from the 2004 national firearms survey. Inj Prev. 2007; 13: 15–19; Barry C, McGinty E, Vernick J, Webster D. After Newtown: public opinion on gun policy and mental illness. N Engl J Med. 2013; 368: 1077–1081; Cook P, Ludwig J. Guns in America: results of a comprehensive national survey on firearms ownership and use. Washington, DC: Police Foundation; 1996; Quinnipiac University Poll. Hamden, CT: Quinnipiac University. December 16–20, 2015

that the percentage of households owning a gun is just over half of what it was in 1977 (31 % vs. 50 %).

Recent surveys have begun to document an increasing concentration of guns in the possession of a smaller number of owners. The size of the gun stock does not seem to be declining, as indicated by the number of guns manufactured and imported.[7] However, the number of owners as a percentage of the population is going down. This situation suggests that guns are becoming more concentrated among a core group of owners. Recent polls have found support for this trend. A Harvard poll conducted in 2004 found that nearly half of all gun owners had four or more guns and averaged 12 firearms per person.[8] A 2015 Harvard poll showed a continuation of this concentration of ownership, as close to a tenth of all gun owners possessed 10 or more guns.[9]

The table illustrates that, contrary to popular belief, the vast majority of Americans are not gun owners. Rather, ownership is concentrated among a declining group of Americans that is more armed than before. A CNN analysis found that the most armed group of American gun owners own about a third of the planet's privately owned guns while making up about 1 % of its population.[10]

Table 2.2 provides clues as to one reason for a decline in the percentage of households with guns. According to the General Social Survey, the proportion of households involved in hunting is half of what it was in the mid-1970s. The decline in hunting, in turn, is a result of declining rural populations and changes in social attitudes in relation to hunting.[11] Changing demographics and the end of conscription into military service in 1973 are other reasons given for the decline in household ownership. Specifically, the growing Hispanic and Asian population has lower gun ownership levels, and the lack of a draft means that fewer Americans are introduced to firearms through military service.[12]

The Pew Research Center, however, has found that while hunting has been in decline, one factor has become more salient as a reason for purchasing guns—self-protection. Pew has found that the proportion of those citing protection as the reason for buying a gun has risen from 26 % to 48 % from 1999 to 2013.[13] In addition, major events that instill fear in the population tend to increase gun purchases or firearm permit applications. In 1992, there was a 46 % increase in applications in the four-week period following the Los Angeles riots.[14] The mass shooting in an Aurora, Colorado, movie theater in the summer of 2012 was followed by a dramatic jump in firearms applications and enrollments in firearms classes. Similar increases in applications were observed following the shootings on the Virginia Tech campus in 2007 and the near assassination of Congresswoman Gabrielle Giffords of Arizona in 2011.[15] The FBI has also documented spikes in background checks following high-profile mass shootings, such as the events in Newtown,

Connecticut, and San Bernardino, California, indicating an increase in gun purchases.[16]

The impact of these high-profile shootings and episodes of disorder is in sharp contrast with the reaction in other countries. Australia, for example, placed increased restrictions on automatic and semi-automatic firearms and firearm magazines and introduced a national firearms registration system following the 1996 massacre of 35 people in Port Arthur, Tasmania.[17] These measures may have reduced the country's entire gun stock by up to a third.[18]

National surveys in the USA have shown that handgun owners were more likely to say that they acquired their firearm for self-protection than long gun owners. Long guns are usually obtained for target shooting.[19,20] In many countries, the acquisition of guns for self-protection is allowed in exceptional circumstances only. In Canada, for example, permits to carry by those not undertaking law enforcement functions are very rare and only granted when people have received verified threats to their lives and law enforcement agencies cannot protect them. Anonymous surveys of the general public do indicate that no more than 5 % of owners obtain guns for self-protection.[21]

In the USA, over 40 states require no permit to carry guns or are "shall issue" states, making it a right of residents (and in some cases nonresidents) to be issued concealed carry permits, unless they are convicted felons or have a history of mental illness. As of 2014, there were approximately 11 million Americans with permits to carry guns, about 3 % of the nation's population.[22]

One can only speculate that guns have a special significance to some Americans, and that they are not merely practical tools but important symbols of self-reliance. This segment of American society so fears the increasing regulation of firearms that they often go on a gun-buying spree following high-profile shootings. To this segment of America, guns are "venerated objects" that have been described as "symbols of such American values as independence, self-reliance, and freedom from governmental interference."[23] On the other hand, of the majority of households without a gun, six in ten say they would feel uncomfortable having a firearm in their home.[24]

Demographics of Gun Ownership

Gun ownership varies considerably across demographic groups and geographic regions, another indication that the idea of an all-encompassing gun culture is a fiction. The following description of gun ownership demographics is based primarily on the 2014 General Social Survey and polling by the Pew Research Center in 2013.[25,26]

- *Gender*—37 % of men and 12 % of women personally own a gun. The gender gap is between 23 % and 25 %.
- *Race*—31 % of whites, 15 % of blacks, and 11 % of Hispanics personally own a gun.
- *Age*—The peak ages for gun ownership are 50–64, followed by age 65 years and over. An indication of a generational divide is that 16 % under age 30 own a gun, whereas 27 % over age 30 are gun owners.
- *Education*—Those with some college education, but without a degree, are more likely to own a gun than are college graduates or those with no college education.
- *Region*—Personal gun ownership in the South (29 %) and Midwest (27 %) is considerably higher than in the West (21 %) and Northeast (17 %).
- *Communities*—Gun ownership tends to decline considerably in larger communities. Personal gun ownership is 39 % for rural residents, 24 % for suburban residents, and 18 % for urban residents. Some urban areas in Texas, Arizona, and Florida are exceptions (e.g., Phoenix, Dallas-Fort Worth, and Tampa-St. Petersburg).[27]
- *Household Income*—Gun ownership increases with household income. Household ownership is 18 % for households earning less than $25,000 per year, 32 % for households earning $25,000–$49,999, 42 % for households earning $50,000–$89,999, and 44 % for households earning $90,000 and over.
- *Parental Gun Ownership*—Individuals growing up in a home with a gun were more than three times as likely to own a gun as those with no family history of gun ownership.[28]
- *Military Service*—Veterans were over twice as likely to own a gun as those with no military service.[29]

- *Political Views*—Those self-identifying as conservatives were twice as likely to be gun owners as were those self-identifying as liberals.

Are Gun Owners "Good Guys with Guns?"

The number of gun owners is just one consideration when we examine the potential hazard to Americans. Aside from the number of guns, we need to look at who owns them and how guns are handled by those owning them. We often hear that the vast majority of gun owners are responsible and that those who misuse firearms are a small, criminal minority.

However, some studies have found that "at-risk" groups may be over-represented among gun owners. One national survey has found that individuals who have been arrested for other than a traffic offense are more likely to be gun owners than are those who state that they have never been arrested (37 % vs. 24 %).[30] A survey of gun owners revealed that those with automatic or semi-automatic firearms were more likely to report binge drinking than were other gun owners.[31] In addition, a survey of American college students by Harvard University researchers found that those possessing a working firearm at college were more likely to engage in binge drinking, to drink and drive, and to engage in other alcohol-related risky behavior than those not possessing a gun on campus.[32] Furthermore, a study of patients in a Veterans Affairs Hospital revealed that those with post-traumatic stress disorder (PTSD) were more likely to own firearms than were other patients. A significant number of these patients exhibited threatening behavior with a firearm and reported being at risk of self-destructive behavior.[33]

While much attention has focused on the mental health issues of those who have displayed extreme violence, a study led by Jeffery Swanson, a professor of psychiatry at Duke University, is disturbing.[34] The investigators used a national sample of 5,600 adults to estimate the number of people who both display impulsive angry behavior and possess or carry guns. Many of these people did not otherwise exhibit severe mental disorders that would disqualify them from gun ownership. These individuals are short-tempered, break things, and get into fights when they get angry. The study found that nearly 9 % of the adult population—over 20 million people when extrapolated to the entire population—self-reported patterns of impulsive angry behavior coupled with guns in the home and 1.5 % carried guns outside the home. In addition, study participants who owned six or more firearms were far more likely than people with only one or two firearms to carry guns outside the home and to have a history of impulsive, angry behavior.

Studies in Europe support these findings. There is some evidence that handgun owners are more likely to be crime victims and to admit to committing violent offences than those not owning handguns. The researchers indicate that gun ownership may reflect a more risky lifestyle. Swiss researchers found that handgun owners displayed more serious psychiatric symptoms than nonowners.[35]

There is also evidence that concealed gun permit holders commit their share of crimes and may even pose a greater risk to the public than those not holding permits. This would be ironic as these permit holders purportedly obtain guns to defend themselves and to foil crimes rather than to commit them. Data on this issue are presented in Chap. 10, which deals with the risks and benefits of gun ownership for the purpose of self-defense.

How much knowledge do owners have of their guns and what is their understanding of gun safety? In the 1990s, Russ Thurman, a firearms expert and contributor to the magazine *Shooting Industry*, made the following observation about shooting ranges: "Unfortunately, I've found most safety standards at shooting ranges to be extremely casual. On a number of occasions, I've cut short a range visit because of how carelessly other shooters handled firearms."[36] A reader of *Gun & Ammo* magazine described a situation in which a shooter at a range did not even know how to load his brand new handgun. This prompted him to conduct an informal survey over the period of a month. He found that 80 % of the shooters came to the range for the first time, had recently purchased their firearm, and knew little about the firearm or about gun safety.[37]

In 1992, the *American Rifleman*, the National Rifle Association's own publication, carried a story detailing the closing of a shooting range due to gross abuses by patrons. John Scull, an official with the Federal Bureau of Land Management, described abuses such as drinking while shooting at the range, using automatic weapons, people setting off fires while using illegal tracer bullets, and acts harmful to the environment (e.g., shooting car batteries so that acid flows into streams).[38] He estimated that, rather than the work of a few rotten apples, 30–40 % of the patrons at that range were involved in these abuses.

The Boston-based Strategic Planning Institute has found that "a large majority of shooting facilities in the country are not professionally managed commercial operations."[39] It has been reported that many ranges are operating on a shoestring and cutting corners with regard to safety and environmental concerns.[40]

How do gun owners in America typically store their guns? It is important to note that a gun acquired for self-defense, as opposed to, say, target shooting, is more likely to be loaded when it is stored or carried by the owner.[41] If guns are not loaded and accessible to the owner, they will not be available when a threat arises. In theory, the defensive use of guns is made possible when loaded weapons are accessible. This accessibility of guns, however, also carries with it the risk of theft, an accidental discharge, the possibility of an impulsive suicide, or spontaneous firing in a dispute.

The importance of the safe storage of firearms has been emphasized by Gary Kleck of Florida State University, who observed that none of the studies he reviewed showed a child who was killed in a gun accident when guns were locked up.[42] However, national surveys have found that about 20 % of owners kept a loaded firearm unlocked in the home.[43,44] A study of 242 family heads in Philadelphia revealed that just 21 % of the families owning firearms stored them locked, unloaded, and out of the reach of children.[45]

People, especially children, involved in tragic gun accidents often mistakenly believed that guns in the home were unloaded. A survey conducted on behalf of the Harvard Injury Control Research Center found that women may be unaware of the presence of a gun in the household or they may incorrectly believe that it is stored unloaded and locked up.[46] A survey of households with firearms and children under 18 found that 22 % of the households had a loaded gun in the home and 8 % had a loaded and unlocked gun there.[47] Households with adolescents were somewhat more likely than those with young children to store guns loaded, unlocked, or both. Ten percent of the households with adolescents and 8 % of those with younger children (0–12 years of age) kept loaded firearms unlocked.

Another issue is that of young people carrying guns in their neighborhoods or in school. A common question is: "Where do kids obtain guns?" A national survey of male students in 10th and 11th grade conducted for the National Institute of Justice sought to answer this question. The survey found that 52 % of students who carried handguns obtained them from a family member or friend and another 19 % bought them from a family member or friend.[48] The vast majority of students did not rely on street purchases to obtain their guns.

Bottom Line

The USA surpasses all other countries with regard to the number of privately owned firearms. It is also unique, relative to other high-income countries, in terms of the number of civilians who own guns for self-protection and carry concealed guns. This said, civilians with concealed carry permits make up just 3 % of the population, and the proportion of households owning guns is declining. Gun ownership is increasingly concentrated in the hands of a minority of Americans who are passionate about the right to own and carry firearms. There is evidence that owners may also be disproportionately prone to risky behaviors. Legislators must contend with this passionate minority of gun owners who resist regulation while confronting the risks associated with gun ownership.

This is the delicate balance between gun rights and gun safety. However, the two are not incompatible. For example, people can keep guns at home without leaving loaded guns within reach of children and other family members. Gun ownership can be a right while every effort is made to ensure that those who would pose a risk to public safety cannot easily obtain them. People can be encouraged to engage in shooting sports while the reckless uses of firearms at sporting venues (e.g., firing ranges) can be subject to tight regulation. The belief that it is all or nothing—we support either gun rights or gun safety—maintains the policy stalemate in America. On one side are the passionate owners, the gun lobby, and the Second Amendment. On the other side the annual carnage (over

100,000 gun deaths and injuries), the determined survivors, the mass murders, and school massacres. Neither side will disappear.

It remains to be seen whether the nation will move forward toward achievable compromises or whether the following pessimistic observation by the magazine, *The Economist*, is prophetic:

> *Those who live in America, or visit it, might do best to regard [mass killings] the way one regards air pollution in China: an endemic local health hazard which, for deep-rooted cultural, social, economic and political reasons, the country is incapable of addressing.*[49]

Notes

1. Krouse W. Gun Control Legislation. Washington, DC: Congressional Research Service; 2012. P. 9.
2. Karp A. Completing the count: civilian firearms. Small Arms Survey, 2007. Geneva: Graduate Institute of International Studies; 2007.
3. Cook P, Goss K. The gun debate: what everyone needs to know. New York: Oxford University Press; 2014. P. 3–4.
4. Karp A. Completing the count.
5. Karp A. Completing the count. P. 46.
6. Hepburn L, Miller M, Azrael D, Hemenway D. The US gun stock: results from the 2004 national firearms survey. Inj Prev. 2007; 13(1): 15–19.
7. Cook P, Goss K. The gun debate. P. 7.
8. Hepburn et al. The US gun stock. P. 17.
9. Masters K. Over 6 million Americans own 10 or more guns: A forthcoming Harvard survey suggest that more Americans own a sizable stockpile of firearms than there are residents of Denmark [Internet]. The Trace. 2015 Oct 6. Available from: http://www.thetrace.org/2015/10/gun-ownership-america-hemenway-survey-harvard/
10. Brennan A., Analysis: Fewer US gun owners own more guns [Internet]. CNN.com. 2012 Jul 31. Available from: http://www.cnn.com/2012/07/31/politics/gun-ownership-declining/index.html
11. Spitzer R. The politics of gun control. 3rd ed. Washington, DC: CQ Press; 2004. P. 9.

12. Tavernise S, Gebeloff R. Share of homes with guns show 4-decade decline [Internet]. The New York Times. 2013 Mar 9. Available from: http://www.nytimes.com/2013/03/10/us/rate-of-gun-ownership-is-down-survey-shows.html?pagewanted=all

13. Pew Research Center. Why own a gun: protection is now top reason. Washington, DC: Pew Research Center; 2013 Mar 12.

14. O'Neill M. No longer gun shy, Californians discover a new status symbol [Internet]. Chicago Tribune. 1993 Feb 19. Available from: http://articles.chicagotribune.com/1993-02-19/features/9303183042_1_gun-world-gary-kleck-target-range

15. Burnett S. Aurora theater shooting: gun sales up since tragedy [Internet]. The Denver Post. 2012 Jul 25. Available from: http://www.denverpost.com/news/ci_21142159/gun-sales-up-since-tragedy

16. Federal Bureau of Investigation. NICS firearm background checks: month/year [Internet]. Washington, DC: US Department of Justice; 2015. Available from: https://www.fbi.gov/about-us/cjis/nics/reports/nics_firearm_checks_-_month_year.pdf

17. Australian Institute of Criminology. Legislative Reforms [Internet]. Canberra: AIC; 2012. Available from: http://aic.gov.au/publications/current%20series/rpp/100-120/rpp116/06_reforms.html

18. Alpert P. The big melt: How one democracy changed after scrapping a third of its firearms. In: Webster D, Vernick J, editors. Reducing gun violence in America: informing policy with evidence and analysis. Baltimore: Johns Hopkins University Press; 2013. P. 205–211.

19. Karp A. Completing the count.

20. Cook P, Ludwig J. Guns in America: results of a comprehensive national survey on firearms ownership and use. Washington, DC: Police Foundation; 1996.

21. Gabor T. Firearms and self-defence: a comparison of Canada and the United States. Ottawa: Department of Justice Canada; 1997.

22. CBS DC. Report: number of concealed carry permits surges as violent crime rate drops [Internet]. CBS DC. 2014 Jul 10. Available from: http://washington.cbslocal.com/2014/07/10/report-number-of-concealed-carry-permits-surges-as-violent-crime-rate-drops/

23. Diaz T. Making a killing: the business of guns in America. New York: New Press; 1999. P. 3.

24. Pew Research Center. Why own a gun.

25. Pew Research Center. Why own a gun.

26. Smith T, Son J. General Social Survey Final Report: Trends in Gun Ownership in the United States, 1972–2014. Chicago: National Opinion Research Center, University of Chicago; 2015.

27. Cook P, Goss K. The gun debate. P. 5.

28. Cook P, Goss, K. The gun debate. P. 4.

29. Hepburn L, Miller M, Azrael D, Hemenway D. The US gun stock.

30. Cook P, Ludwig J. Guns in America.

31. Hemenway D, Richardson E. Characteristics of automatic or semiautomatic firearm ownership in the United States. Am J Public Health. 1997; 87(2): 286–288.

32. Miller M, Hemenway D, Wechsler H. Guns and gun threats at college. J Am Coll Health. 2002; 51: 57–65.

33. Freeman T, Roca V, Kimbrell T. A survey of gun collection and use among three groups of veteran patients admitted to veteran affairs hospital treatment programs. South Med J. 2003; 96: 240–243.

34. Swanson J, Sampson N, Petukhova M, Zavslavsky A, Applebaum P, Swartz M, et al. Guns, impulsive angry behavior, and mental disorders: results from the National Comorbidity Survey Replication (NCS-R). Behav Sci Law. 2015; 33: 199–212.

35. Killias M, Haas, H. Waffen—Wievielehabensie,wiegefährlichsindsie? [Firearms—how many own them, how dangerous are they?]. Crimiscope. 2001; 16/17, 1 10.

36. Thurman R. Not in harm's way. Shooting Industry. 1994; P. 70.

37. Diaz T. Making a killing. P. 181.

38. Scull J. Another range gone. American Rifleman. 1992; Feb. P. 12.

39. Diaz T. Making a killing. P. 182.

40. Rupp J. Franchising the indoor range. American Rifleman. 1989; May. P. 36–37.

41. Cook P, Ludwig J. Guns in America. P. 7.

42. Kleck G. Point blank: guns and violence in America. Hawthorne, NY: Aldine de Gruyter; 1991. P. 279.

43. Cook P, Ludwig J. Guns in America. P. 7.

44. Hemenway D, Solnick S, Azrael D. Firearm training and storage. JAMA. 1995; 27: 46–50.

45. Wiley C, Casey R. Family experiences, attitudes, and household safety practices regarding firearms. Clin Pediatr. 1993; 32(2): 71–76.

46. Azrael D, Miller M, Hemenway D. Are firearms stored safely in households with children? It depends on whom you ask. Pediatr. 2000; 106(3): e31.

47. Johnson R, Miller M, Vriniotis M, Azrael D, Hemenway D. Are household firearms stored less safely in homes with adolescents?: Analysis of a national random sample of parents. Arch Pediatr Adolesc Med. 2006; 160(8): 788–92.

48. Sheley J, Wright J. High school youth, weapons, and guns: a national survey. Washington, DC: National Institute of Justice; 1998.

49. Editorial. Charleston massacre: The latest American mass killing [Internet]. The Economist. 2015 Jun 18. Available from: http://www.economist.com/blogs/democracyinamerica/2015/06/charleston-massacre

Part II

Harms Associated with Firearms

3

Gun Deaths: The USA versus the World

Chapter 2 showed that, depending on the estimate, the size of the civilian gun stock in the USA ranges between 200 million to well over 300 million firearms. Regardless of the precise count, the USA has the largest number of private arms in absolute terms and as a percentage of its population—perhaps as many as one gun for every American. Are we safer as a result of the presence of such a large number of guns relative to other countries?

Comparisons with Other High-Income Countries

Data from the United Nations Office on Drugs and Crime has shown that, when compared with 31 other high-income Organisation for Economic Co-operation and Development (OECD) countries (as defined by the World Bank),[1] the USA, ranked #1 in gun availability by the International Small Arms Survey, had the highest gun homicide rate by a considerable margin, and was second to the very small country of Estonia in its overall (gun and nongun) homicide rate (see Table 3.1). Specifically, in 2011–2012, it had three and a half times the gun homicide rate of Chile

© The Author(s) 2016
T. Gabor, *Confronting Gun Violence in America*,
DOI 10.1007/978-3-319-33723-4_3

Table 3.1 Homicide rates for 32 high-income countries (2011–2012)

Nation	Homicide rate per 100,000	Gun homicide rate per 100,000	Ranking on gun availability for 178 countries (2007)
USA	4.7	3.6	1
Switzerland	.6	.2	3
Finland	1.6	.3	4
Sweden	.7	.2	10
Norway	2.2	.1	11
France	1.0	.2	12
Canada	1.6	.4	13
Austria	.9	.1	14
Germany	.8	.1	15
Iceland	.3	.0	15
New Zealand	.9	.2	22
Belgium	1.6	.3	34
Czech Republic	1.0	.2	38
Luxembourg	.8	.0	41
Australia	1.1	.2	42
Slovenia	.7	.2	47
Denmark	.8	.2	54
Italy	.9	.4	55
Chile	3.1	1.0	59
Spain	.8	.1	61
Estonia	5.0	.2	65
Ireland	1.2	.3	70
Portugal	1.2	.4	72
Slovakia	1.4	.3	73
Israel	1.8	1.0	79
UK	1.0	.1	88
Hungary	1.3	.1	93
Netherlands	.9	.3	112
Poland	1.2	.0	142
Republic of Korea	.9	.0	149
Japan	.3	.0	164
Singapore	.2	.0	169

Source: United Nations Office on Drugs and Crime. Global Study on Homicide. Vienna: UNODC; 2013, Statistical Annex; Karp A. Small Arms Survey 2007. Geneva: Graduate Institute of International Studies; Gun facts, figures and the law [Internet]. gunpolicy.org; Geneva, Switzerland: Available from: http://www. smallarmssurvey.org/fileadmin/docs/A-Yearbook/2007/en/Small-Arms-Survey-2007-Chapter-02-annexe-4-EN.pdf

and Israel, the countries with the next highest rates. When an average gun homicide rate was computed for the other high-income countries, the USA had *18 times* the rate of the other countries combined (3.6 vs. 0.2 per 100,000). The gap was smaller for homicides overall, but the USA still had nearly four times the combined rate for the other countries (4.7 vs. 1.2 per 100,000)

To put this in perspective, there were 16,121 homicides in the USA in 2013.[2] If the USA had a homicide rate similar to that of the average high-income country—that is, a quarter of its actual rate—there would have been approximately 4000 homicides a year, about 12,000 fewer murders than we actually had. On the other extreme, each of the four countries with the lowest gun homicide rates, Poland, South Korea, Japan, and Singapore, had fewer than one gun homicide for every million people. Poland had a total of 16 gun homicides in 2011, South Korea had 9 in 2011, Japan (with a population of about 125 million people) had 11 in 2008, and Singapore had not even one gun homicide in 2011. Note that these four countries also had the lowest levels of gun availability among high-income countries, meaning they had the fewest privately held guns in relation to their populations.

While many factors influence a country's homicide rate (e.g., the degree of economic development and economic inequality),[3] Table 3.1 shows that countries with the highest gun availability rankings have higher homicide rates than those with the lowest gun availability rankings. The 10 countries ranking in the top 15 in the world on gun availability had 2.5 times the gun homicide rates, on average, as the countries ranking 72nd in the world or lower on gun availability (.5 vs. .2 per 100,000). The difference in overall homicide between the two groups of countries still held but the gap was narrower (1.4 vs. 1.1 homicides per 100,000). The correlation between homicide rates and gun availability is far from perfect, but it is hard to ignore the pattern that higher homicide rates, especially firearm homicides, are associated with more civilian-held guns.

Sripal Bangalore of New York University's School of Medicine and Franz Messerli of Columbia University's College of Physicians and Surgeons examined the relationship between gun ownership, firearm-related deaths, and the mental illness burden in 27 developed countries.[4] They found that there was a strong positive correlation between guns per capita and gun deaths, meaning that gun deaths rose consistently with the volume of guns in a country. Mental illness and gun deaths were also related, but the link was not as strong. There was no statistical link between the volume of guns and the crime rate across the 27 countries, leading the investigators to conclude that the study "debunks the widely quoted hypothesis that guns make a nation safer."

A study by David Hemenway and Matthew Miller of Harvard University examined homicide rates for 26 of the 27 high-income countries with greater than one million population.[5] Using two measures of gun availability, the researchers found that there was a strong, statistically significant association between gun availability and homicide rates. Thus, where there are more guns, there are usually more homicides. It is important to note that such a statistical link simply indicates that homicides increase with gun availability. The link does not demonstrate that higher gun ownership levels *cause* higher rates of homicide. The findings do not rule out the possibility that other factors, such as a high national propensity for violence, are responsible for both higher gun availability and higher homicide rates.

The gap between the USA and other countries widens when firearm homicides only are considered. In 2003, the Harvard team of Hemenway and Erin Richardson compared the USA with 23 other high-income countries and found that the USA had an overall homicide rate that was 6.9 times that of the average for the other countries. The nongun homicide rate was just 2.9 times that of the average rate for the other countries, but the gun homicide rate was approximately 20 times that of the other countries.[6] More recent data (2010) analyzed by these two researchers show the gap has grown wider and the USA now has 25 times the combined firearm homicide rate of the other high-income countries.[7] For 15- to 24-year-olds, the firearm homicide rate in the USA was an astounding 49 times higher than in the comparison countries.

The much greater gap in the gun homicide rate than the nongun rate reflects the fact that a much higher percentage of homicides in the USA are committed with guns than in other countries. It is in relation to gun homicides that the USA is truly an anomaly among developed countries. Gun deaths overall are over seven times higher in the USA than in these other countries. While these figures alone are insufficient to draw conclusions about cause and effect, they do suggest that more liberal gun laws and higher ownership levels in this country do not seem to enhance public safety, as often asserted by gun rights activists and gun lobby groups.

In the early 1990s, Martin Killias, a Swiss criminologist, used telephone survey data on gun ownership to examine the relationship between household gun ownership and homicide and suicide rates for 11 European countries, Australia, Canada, and the USA. His study found that national firearm homicide and suicide rates tended to rise with rates of gun ownership and that there was no compensating increase in non-gun homicides in countries with lower levels of gun ownership. Thus, people in countries with fewer gun owners did not appear to switch to other methods to commit homicides and suicides. Killias concluded that the link between gun ownership and homicide and suicide rates suggested that the presence of a gun in the home increases the likelihood of homicide or suicide. This said, he acknowledged that larger studies were needed to examine the possible influence of such factors as the national tendency toward violent solutions, as such a tendency could be responsible for both gun ownership and homicide or suicide.

A subsequent study by Killias and his colleagues yielded mixed results. Using International Crime Survey results from 1989 to 1996 for 21 countries, the researchers found a strong link between civilian firearm ownership and the firearm suicide and homicide rates of women.[8] For men, the link between gun ownership and gun homicide was weak, but stronger for gun-related assault and robbery. Thus, for women, gun homicide and suicide rates tended to rise with a nation's gun ownership rates. For men, there was no clear pattern for homicide but gun assaults and robberies did tend to increase with higher gun ownership rates.

A Harvard study of 25 high-income countries supported the notion that women are at greater risk in countries with higher firearm availability levels.[9] That study found a very strong link between gun availability and female homicide rates. During the study period (1994–1999), the USA had the highest level of household firearm ownership and the highest female homicide rate of the 25 countries. The USA accounted for 32 % of the female population in these high-income countries, but 70 % of all female homicides and 84 % of all female firearm homicides.

The Killias and Harvard studies suggest that the connection between gun ownership and homicide may be stronger for women than for men. Researchers believe that this situation may be due to the fact that women are often murdered in the home and guns are more likely to be kept there. Also, personal crises are more likely to come to a head in the home than in public places. Therefore, civilian gun ownership may pose an even greater threat to women than to men.

The differences between the USA and other countries in firearm-related mortality for children are also dramatic. When compared with children in other high-income countries, American children and youth between the ages of five and fourteen were 13 times as likely to die as a result of a gun homicide, 8 times as likely to be a gun suicide victim, and 11 times as likely to die from an unintentional gun discharge.[10]

The scale of gun-related deaths of American children and teens is further illustrated by the Children's Defense Fund (CDF), a child advocacy group. In their publication, *Protect Children, Not Guns 2012*, the CDF reports the following findings from research:[11]

- A total of 5740 American children and teens died from gunfire in 2008 and 2009, a toll that exceeded the number of US military personnel who were killed in Iraq and Afghanistan during those two years (5013).
- The number of preschoolers killed by guns in 2008 and 2009 was nearly double that of police officers killed in the line of duty during that same period.
- Gun homicide was the leading cause of death of black teens (15–19 years of age) in 2008 and 2009. For white teens, gun homicide in 2008 and gun suicide in 2009 followed motor vehicle accidents as the leading causes of death.
- An analysis of data from 23 industrialized countries found that 87 % of children under 15 years of age who were killed by guns in these countries lived in the USA.
- During the 30-year period from 1979 to 2008, 116, 385 children and teens were killed by firearm, far in excess of the number of military personnel who died in the more than decadelong Vietnam War.

Despite these dramatic figures, the CDF asks:

Where is our anti-war movement here at home? Why does a nation with the largest military budget in the world refuse to protect its children from relentless gun violence and terrorism at home? No external enemy ever killed thousands of children in their neighborhoods, streets and schools year in and year out. By any standards of human and moral decency, children in America are under assault, and by international standards, America remains an unparalleled world leader in gun deaths of children and teens—a distinction we shamefully and immorally choose![12]

Is It Guns or Is the USA a More Violent Society?

Those opposing most gun regulations often ignore the enormous difference in gun-related death between the USA and other high-income countries. Others opposed to most regulations often attribute the gap to the idea that the USA is simply more crime prone than these countries. They say that Americans also commit more property crimes and violent crimes that do not involve guns. The evidence, however, does not support this position.

The International Crime Victims Survey of 2004–2005 compared the extent of criminal victimization in 30 countries, including the USA, Canada, Mexico, Australia, New Zealand, many European countries, and several Asian, African, and Latin American countries. National surveys were conducted in each country, and respondents answered a series of questions on criminal victimizations they had experienced over the previous year.[13] Overall, the USA ranked somewhere in the middle in terms of crime overall, just above average for car theft, burglary, theft of personal property, and assaults and threats and below average for robbery. Sexual assault was the one offense in which the USA ranked high relative to other countries. The International Crime Victims Survey of 2000 found that, for 11 crimes (excluding homicide), the USA had an overall victimization rate that was slightly below the average for 17 other industrialized nations.[14]

Therefore, the much higher levels of lethal violence and firearm homicide in the USA cannot be explained by a general tendency of Americans to commit more crime or to be more violent than citizens of other developed nations. It is in relation to homicide, especially gun homicide, where the USA stands apart when compared with other high-income countries.

Finding a statistical link or correlation between gun ownership levels and homicide does not mean that there is a simple cause and effect relationship between the two. Many factors may influence a nation's homicide rate. However, a strong statistical link may mean that gun ownership is one factor shaping national homicide rates. The fact that there may be countries that may have a relatively high homicide rate despite having relatively few civilian-owned guns (e.g., Estonia) or a low homicide rate with fairly high gun availability (e.g., Germany) does not negate an overall tendency of homicide to increase with higher gun ownership levels. Such exceptions simply show that, in these countries, other factors may exert a greater influence on homicide rates than does the presence of guns.

Skeptics also point to countries that have high gun ownership levels and low levels of violence to make the point that gun availability is not an important factor in the violence observed in a country. We may find nations with high gun ownership and low levels of violence or low gun ownership and high violence. A few exceptions do not negate an overall pattern showing a relationship between two factors, such as ownership levels and rates of violence. As an example from the health field, a small percentage of heavy smokers or highly obese people who live long and healthy lives does not invalidate the research finding that, in most cases, heavy smoking and obesity will increase a person's risk of experiencing a number of serious illnesses. In the same way, studies finding that there is a link between gun availability and homicide are not invalidated by a few exceptions.

Switzerland and Israel: Are They Really Exceptions?

Gun rights activists point to Switzerland and Israel as demonstrating that relaxed gun laws can lower crime. For example, Wayne LaPierre of the National Rifle Association (NRA) has written that Switzerland has a higher rate of firearms possession than the USA and very few gun homicides. LaPierre argues that this demonstrates "that there is no causal effect between firearms possession and crime. Indeed, just the opposite seems to be the case: a thoroughly armed people is relatively crime free; it is the ultimate deterrent to crime."[15]

LaPierre and other opponents of tighter gun regulations misrepresent the role of guns in both Switzerland and Israel. First, the USA has more guns per capita than either country (Table 3.1). In both countries, firearms are usually kept for military purposes or in relation to security functions rather than for hunting, collecting, or self-protection as in America. Switzerland and Israel have a system of military conscription. In Switzerland, all males are required to undertake military service from the age of 19, beginning with a five-month stint and continuing with annual refresher courses for at least another ten years.[16] In Israel, with the exception of conscientious objectors, all men and women must perform military service from the age of 18. Men serve for three years and then participate in the reserves until the age of 51, and women serve for 21 months.[17]

Regulations are very strict. In Switzerland, guns must be stored unloaded and kept in a locked cabinet. Citizens are subject to regular inspections of their guns. The purchase of a handgun requires a license in Switzerland, and just 4 % of national survey respondents have indicated they keep their guns for self-protection.[18] The Swiss military has downsized considerably since the end of the Cold War, and currently just 23 % of former soldiers are electing to keep their weapons once their military service has been completed.[19]

In Israel, civilian gun ownership levels are 1/13th those in the USA, despite the fact that most adults have served in the military.[20] Almost half of gun permit applicants are rejected, and licenses are confined to security personnel, those transporting valuables and explosives, hunters, and West Bank residents. Handgun purchases require psychological checks and an extended waiting period. Neither country provides a good example of permissive gun laws as they are, in fact, examples of the opposite and gun ownership in both countries is declining.[21,22]

Following the massacre at Sandy Hook Elementary School in Newtown, Connecticut, the NRA called for the arming of school personnel as their primary response to such incidents. Bans on assault-style guns, limits on high-capacity magazines, and even universal background checks were dismissed by the NRA as ineffective and a violation of owners' Second Amendment rights. The NRA's vision for America seems to be the arming of the entire population as well as the use of armed guards to secure "soft" targets, such as schools, shopping malls, and movie theaters.

Elizabeth Rosenthal of *The New York Times* has written that this is already the reality in some Latin American countries and that the ubiquitous presence of "good guys" with guns has not made these countries safer. In fact, countries adopting this approach—Guatemala, Honduras, El Salvador, Colombia, and Venezuela—have some of the highest homicide rates in the world.[23]

Rosenthal quotes Rebecca Peters, former director of the International Action Network on Small Arms, as saying: "A society that is relying on guys with guns to stop violence is a sign of a society where institutions have broken down. It's shocking to hear anyone in the United States considering a solution that would make it seem more like Colombia."

Rosenthal notes that as guns proliferate, innocent people often seem more terrorized than protected. She cites Guatemala to illustrate this point. In that country, there are numerous bus robberies, resulting in the death of not only a large number of bus drivers but assistants and passengers who have been caught in the crossfire. Arming a large number of people for security work creates another problem in Guatemala and elsewhere: A large private security force is created, with inadequate training and accountability. The result is that lethal force is often used in a disproportionate fashion, such as to deter minor offenses like theft.

Bottom Line

Most international studies show that countries with higher gun ownership levels tend to have higher gun and overall homicide rates than those with lower ownership levels. There is an enormous gap in gun-related mortality between the USA, the country with the largest stock of privately owned firearms in the world, and other high-income countries. This wide gap applies to gun homicide, suicide, and lethal accidents.

American children are at a substantially higher risk of dying by gunshot than children in comparable countries.

While many factors can be responsible for America's elevated gun homicide rate, international surveys show that this is not due to a higher overall rate of crime or violence. It is in the case of *lethal* violence that there is a marked gap between the USA and similar countries. The gap in gun homicide is nearly five times greater than the gap in the non-gun homicide rate. These findings point to the role of guns in creating more lethal outcomes when violence occurs. The proliferation of guns and homicide found in a number of Latin American countries supports the findings from research that arming a society to the teeth is likely to be counterproductive.

Notes

1. The World Bank. Country and lending groups [Internet]. Washington, DC: The World Bank Group; 2016. Available from: http://data.worldbank.org/about/country-and-lending-groups#High_income
2. Centers for Disease Control and Prevention. FastStats (2013): assault or homicide. Hyattsville, MD: National Center for Health Statistics. Available from: http://www.cdc.gov/nchs/fastats/homicide.htm
3. United Nations Office on Drugs and Crime. Global Study on Homicide. Vienna, Austria: UNODC; 2011.
4. Bangalore S, Messerli F. Gun ownership and firearm-related deaths. Am J Med. 2013; 126: 873–876.
5. Hemenway D, Miller M. Firearm availability and homicide rates across 26 high-income countries. J Trauma. 2000; 49(6): 985–988.
6. Richardson E, Hemenway D. Homicide, suicide, and unintentional firearm fatality: comparing the United States with other high-income countries, 2003. J Trauma. 2011; 70(1): 238–243.
7. Grinshteyn E, Hemenway D, Violent death rates: The US compared with other high-income OECD countries. Am J Med. (in press).
8. Killias M, vanKesteren J, Rindlisbacher M. Guns, violent crime, and suicide in 21 countries. Can J Crim. 2001; 43(4): 429–448.
9. Hemenway D, Shinoda-Tagawa T, Miller M. Firearm availability and female homicide victimization rates across 25 populous high-income countries. J Am Med Wom Assoc. 2002; 57(2): 100–104.

10. Richardson E, Hemenway D. Homicide, suicide, and unintentional firearm fatality. P. 241, Table 3.

11. Children's Defense Fund. Protect children, not guns. Washington, DC: Children's Defense Fund; 2012.

12. Children's Defense Fund. Protect children. P. 4–5.

13. Van Dyk J, van Kesteren J, Smit P. Criminal victimization in international perspective. Vienna: United Nations Office on Drugs and Crime; 2007.

14. Van Kesteren J, Mayhew P, Nieuwbeerta P. Criminal victimisation in seventeen industrialized countries: findings from the 2000 International Crime Victims Survey. The Hague: Ministry of Justice; 2000.

15. LaPierre W. Guns, crime and freedom. Washington, DC: Regnery Publishing Inc.; 1994. P. 171.

16. Foulkes I. Knives out for conscription into Swiss army [Internet]. BBC News. 2011 Jan 11. Available from: http://www.bbc.co.uk/news/world-europe-12083427

17. Israel Defence Forces. Military [Internet]. Globalsecurity.org. Available from: http://www.globalsecurity.org/military/world/israel/idf.htm

18. Killias M, Markwalder N. Firearms and homicide in Europe. In: Liem M, Pridemore WA, editors. Handbook of European homicide research. New York: Springer; 2012; P. 264.

19. Killias M, Markwalder N. Firearms and homicide in Europe. P. 269.

20. Fisher M. Israeli gun laws are much stricter than US gun advocates suggest [Internet]. Washington Post. 2012 Dec 26. Available from: http://www.washingtonpost.com/blogs/worldviews/wp/2012/12/28/israeli-gun-laws-are-much-stricter-than-some-u-s-gun-advocates-suggest/

21. Henigan D. Lethal logic: exploding the myths that paralyze American gun policy. Washington, DC: Potomac Books; 2009. P. 108–110.

22. Hartman B. Israeli gun control regulations opposite of US [Internet]. The Jerusalem Post. 2012 Dec 18. Available from: http://www.jpost.com/National-News/Israeli-gun-control-regulations-opposite-of-US

23. Rosenthal E. More guns = more killing [Internet]. *The New York Times*. 2013 Jan 5. Available from: http://www.nytimes.com/2013/01/06/sunday-review/more-guns-more-killing.html?partner=rss&emc=rss&_r=0

4

Homicide and the Instrumentality Effect

Perhaps the most critical question in the gun violence debate is: Are firearm homicides and injuries primarily due to an intention to kill or maim, or does the weapon itself play the key role in these outcomes? The latter possibility is referred to as the "instrumentality effect." The gun lobby and gun rights advocates argue that gun violence and suicides simply reflect the motives and inclinations of the shooter. This view is expressed by the slogan, "Guns don't kill people, people kill people." To them, the type of instrument is irrelevant and easily replaced by those determined to harm others or themselves. Conversely, public health researchers argue that while intentions and personal traits are important, the tool used in attacks on others or in self-harm will also affect outcomes. They do not feel that one has to choose between the role of an individual's intent and weapons-related risk factors.

Gun rights advocates display a contradiction when it comes to the role of guns in violence. On one hand, they claim that guns do not facilitate violence as a determined attacker will succeed regardless of their availability. Hence, in their view, restricting the availability of guns is an exercise in futility as individuals will merely substitute other means to achieve their desired ends. To them, gun regulations merely trample on the rights

© The Author(s) 2016   **51**
T. Gabor, *Confronting Gun Violence in America*,
DOI 10.1007/978-3-319-33723-4_4

of responsible gun owners. However, when it comes to self-defense, guns take on a quasi-religious status, and they are viewed as revered objects that protect law-abiding Americans from depraved predators who lurk in every corner of our society and are ready to pounce at a moment's notice.

Consider a familiar pitch by Marion Hammer, the main Florida lobbyist for and former head of the National Rifle Association. She wrote the following as part of her effort to promote gun carrying on Florida's college campuses:

> It is a fact that college campuses in Florida are gun-free zones where murderers, rapists and other violent criminals can commit their crimes without fear of being harmed by their victims. It is a fact that … sexual offenders live in very close proximity to Florida's college and university campuses … police do the best job they can, but they are not there when the attack occurs … only the victim has a chance to actually stop it. Denying the tools of self-defense creates more victims.[1]

Ms. Hammer leaves the impression that college campuses are hunting grounds for predators. In fact, studies by the US Department of Education and the Department of Justice show that campuses are safer than the surrounding community and that more than 90 % of attacks on students occur off campus.[2,3] Aside from presenting an inaccurate picture of crime on college and university campuses, Ms. Hammer argues that guns are a critical tool in empowering potential victims. At the same time, gun-rights advocates like her oppose all forms of regulation, including enhanced background checks that would make guns less accessible to those who would be most likely to misuse them. It is an obvious contradiction to argue that guns can empower potential victims by deterring and neutralizing would-be attackers, but are of little use to offenders and domestic abusers in intimidating and harming victims of crime. One cannot argue that guns are a powerful defensive tool but inconsequential in the hands of aggressors.

How Guns Facilitate Homicide

This section shows that the instrument does make a difference and that guns may facilitate killing in a number of ways even where there is no prior intention to kill.

Gun Attacks are More Lethal than Attacks with other Weapons

The most obvious way guns can facilitate killing is that they are more lethal than other weapons. The presence of firearms may make disputes, assaults, or robberies more deadly. Whether the offense is committed by a calculating, cold-blooded killer or by an individual exhibiting rage, there is strong evidence showing that firearms are more lethal than other weapons.

Professionals in the medical field have shown the damage to humans produced by high-velocity weapons that fire larger bullets designed to cause severe injuries. Researchers specializing in the care of patients with traumatic brain injuries at the University of Alabama have described what happens to the brain when a person is shot in the head:

> *Passage of a bullet can cause laceration (tearing) injuries to the brain, as well as shock waves with cavitation (temporary stretching). ... This creates an area of disrupted tissue surrounding the path of the bullet. The area of disrupted tissue can be as much as 30 times larger than the missile diameter and can cause injury to parts of the brain a considerable distance from the actual bullet path. Sometimes there are multiple paths of injury in the brain caused by a bullet fragmenting after entering the brain.*[4]

Back in the 1960s, surgeons Robert Richter and Mahfouz Zaki from Brooklyn, New York, compared the damage inflicted by guns as opposed to knives:

> *If the velocity of a knife at the moment of stabbing is estimated at 30 miles per hour (the actual figure may be lower), that value is 18 times smaller than the muzzle velocity of a 25-caliber pistol bullet used in commercially available guns. ... One must simply expect that a far greater proportion of bullet wounds inflict serious damage than do stab wounds.*[5]

One can add that firearms today are far more lethal than they were when the above passage was written. Attorney Tom Diaz has documented in great detail the gun industry's quest for increasingly lethal products over the last 30 years.[6] He has done so using the gun industry's and the gun press' own publications and ads. Diaz writes:

Just as tobacco industry executives loaded cigarettes up with addictive nicotine and flavor enhancing additives, so have gun industry executives steadily increased the lethality of guns and ammunition. They have made guns to hold more rounds, increased the power of those rounds, and made guns smaller and more concealable. They have developed ammunition to cause ghastly wounds rivaling the worst carnage seen on battlefields.[7]

In fact, the *American Rifleman*, the National Rifle Association's own publication, regularly provides reviews of the "stopping power" of different models of guns and ammunition. In one issue of the magazine, Field Editor Richard Mann reports on tests he conducted on the damage caused by 100 different handgun loads that were fired into ballistic gelatin.[8] He measured the extent to which different firearm models and types of ammunition penetrated the gelatin and the extent to which the bullets expanded. Such expansion produces a wider wound channel when humans are shot.

Mann writes:

A bullet that expands creates a larger wound cavity. The more expansion, the more tissue that is damaged, destroyed or traumatized. However, over-expansion and/or fragmentation to the point the bullet loses a lot of weight limits penetration and penetration is important. ... And then there's impact velocity. When you combine high impact velocity with expansion, wound cavities get very large.

Mann's observations and research results in the American Rifleman support what emergency room doctors and surgeons have known for a long time: Different firearms and ammunition vary greatly in terms of the injuries they produce and in their lethality. If different guns and ammunition vary so widely in terms of their injuriousness and lethality, how can anybody credibly argue that the instrument used in an attack is inconsequential? If guns and ammunition vary in their lethality, it is hardly credible to argue that entirely different categories of weapons (guns vs. knives or clubs) will cause the same damage.

Consider an influential study of robberies (holdups, muggings) in 43 US cities by Philip Cook of Duke University.[9] His study found a strong link between the weapon used and the likelihood of a fatal outcome. In gun robberies, there was a fatality in one in every 250 incidents.

This was three times greater than the likelihood of death in a knife robbery and nine times greater than the likelihood of death where other weapons were used. The lowest death rates were found in unarmed robberies (one in every 5000 incidents). Firearm robberies were 20 times more likely to result in a death than were unarmed robberies.

Are these significant differences in lethality due to the more lethal intent of gun robbers or due to the differential dangerousness of the weapons used—the *instrumentality* effect? Robbery (holdups or muggings) provides an excellent opportunity to examine this question because robbers almost never set out to kill their victims. Deaths in robberies, even gun robberies, are rare. Rather than using guns to kill their victims, robbers tend to choose guns to gain the quick compliance of their victims and to *avoid* violence. Their aim is to obtain cash and exit the crime scene as quickly as possible, as delay will lead to their arrest and a possible confrontation with police or witnesses. As most robberies involve minimal planning, the choice of a weapon has less to do with personality or intent and more to do with the availability of guns when the decision is taken to commit a robbery.[10]

Violence is actually more likely to occur when robbers are unarmed as the victim is more likely to resist the robber.[11] Even so, fatalities are far more likely when guns are used as the slightest hesitation of a victim or the intervention of a bystander may lead a nervous armed robber to take the irrevocable decision to discharge his weapon.

Cook found that the weapon used was a determining factor in the outcome of a robbery. He argued that:

> *The relatively high death rate in gun robbery is the direct consequence of the fact that a loaded gun provides the assailant with the means to kill quickly at a distance and without much skill, strength, or danger of a counterattack. A passing whim or even the accidental twitch of a trigger finger is sufficient. Thus, a gun is intrinsically more dangerous than other types of weapons.*[12]

In a classic study conducted in the late 1960s, Franklin Zimring, then a University of Chicago law professor, used an innovative methodology to isolate the impact of the weapon on the outcome of assaults. Reviewing Chicago Police data for 1967, he found that assaults with firearms were five times as likely to result in the victim's death as knife attacks.[13] He anticipated that critics would attribute this finding to a greater intent to kill on the part of those attacking with guns, rather than the greater lethality of guns versus knives. However, Zimring showed that the type of people involved in the attacks, as well as their motives and circumstances of the assaults, were very similar in gun and knife attacks.

To further dispel the idea that knife assailants are less determined to kill, he examined the location of all the knife and gun wounds and, in fact, found that a higher percentage of knife as opposed to gunshot wounds were in vital regions of the body (head, chest, abdomen, back, and neck). He further found that those using knives were more likely to inflict multiple wounds than those attacking with guns. When he compared gun attacks with only the most serious knife attacks (those directed to the victim's vital regions), he found that gun attacks were still two and a half times as likely to kill as knife attacks. Therefore, the study strongly pointed to the conclusion that the difference in lethality between gun and knife attacks was due to the greater dangerousness of guns rather than to the more lethal intent of those using guns.

Richard Block of Loyola University in Chicago has uncovered additional compelling evidence on the lethality of guns relative to knives. He found that over three times as many aggravated assaults and three times as many robberies resulted in death when guns rather than knives were used.[14] In order to isolate the lethality of the weapons used, he only looked at serious incidents in which assaults and robberies resulted in injuries. Thus, one could assume that the offenders in these cases all intended to do serious harm to the victim. Block pointed to the research of Zimring, Cook, and others, as well as his own findings, and concluded that firearms are three times as likely to be lethal than knives, suggesting that this difference in lethality held up regardless of the jurisdiction or type of crime. In his view, this was the instrumentality (weapons) effect. Gary Kleck of Florida State University, generally a skeptic regarding the idea of an instrumentality effect, has conceded that police-based and medical studies show that gun wounding death rates are three or four times the death rates of knife wounding.[15]

Guns Enable Mass Casualty Incidents

It is hard to envision the murder of large numbers of people with knives, clubs, fists, and other instruments that are not firearms. While such events have been known to occur, the vast majority of mass killings, high-profile school killings, and workplace killings in the USA are committed by firearms and nearly all are committed by one person.[16] The lack of accomplices in most incidents, the speedy response by law enforcement agencies, and the possible intervention of bystanders make it almost imperative for a perpetrator bent on inflicting mass casualties to use firearms capable of discharging a large number of rounds of ammunition in a short period of time.

Self-loading firearms (whether automatic or semiautomatic), in particular, allow just one individual to kill and seriously injure dozens of people even where the police respond within minutes. For example, on July 20, 2012, one shooter using as one of his weapons an AR-15 magazine-fed, semiautomatic rifle, shot 71 people in less than five minutes in a Colorado movie theater. The same make and model of rifle was used to kill 26 elementary school children and teachers in Newtown, Connecticut, in December 2012.[17] A review of the most notorious school mass killings in the late 1990s shows that they all were committed with firearms and that the capabilities of the firearms (caliber and rapid-fire capability) used influenced the number of victims who were shot and killed.[18]

Firearms Are Needed to Kill or Rob Armed or Protected Targets

The killing of political figures or police officers without firearms will likely leave the assailant outgunned. Similarly, robberies targeting well-guarded facilities, such as armored trucks, are not likely to be successful without firearms or replica firearms. Most political assassinations and all presidential assassinations (Lincoln, Garfield, McKinley, and Kennedy) have involved firearms. Police officers almost always are killed with a gun. In 2011, 63 of 72 officers killed feloniously while on duty were shot.[19] In Chap. 8, we see that police officers are at greater risk in states with higher gun ownership levels. The lesson learned here is that guns are difficult to replace in the commission of certain crimes.

Guns Allow Killing by the Physically Vulnerable or the Squeamish

Guns may facilitate killing by minors, the disabled, or others who would otherwise be incapable of inflicting serious damage upon others. In this way, they can be viewed as an equalizer.[20] Guns can also provide an impersonal means of killing for those who are too squeamish to severe another's arteries with a sharp instrument or fracture a skull with a heavy, blunt instrument.[21]

Guns Facilitate Killing from a Distance

Guns allow killing and wounding from a distance, such as drive-by killings and those killed by snipers. Drive-by stabbings are hard to envision. In 2002, Beltway snipers John Allen Muhammad and Lee Boyd Malvo killed ten people and terrorized residents of Washington, DC, Maryland, and Virginia with a crime spree.[22] They equipped their Chevrolet Caprice with a firing port through which they could shoot people at random without being detected. Their crimes could not be committed without a firearm. Both, Bushmaster, the manufacturer of the weapon used, and the gun store that sold it without maintaining records were sued by some of the victims' families and eventually paid out a sum of money to settle the case out of court.[23]

There have also been a number of cases in which individuals have been shot randomly on freeways or have been shot in road rage incidents. In August and September 2015, ten shootings occurred on the I-10 highway and one on the I-17 highway in Phoenix, Arizona. Eight of the vehicles were struck by bullets and three by unspecified projectiles.[24] While other objects can be hurled at other vehicles, none have the range and lethality of firearms.

Guns Can Endanger Innocent Bystanders

Innocent bystanders are far more likely to be hurt or killed in a firearm attack than an attack involving other types of weapons.[25] In a 2015 road rage incident in Albuquerque, New Mexico, two vehicles cut each other off on the I-40 highway. One driver pulled alongside the other and opened fire. The second driver's four-year-old daughter was killed.[26] In another example, a man driving in Orlando, Florida, was caught in the crossfire as some form of shooting was taking place in that neighborhood. Two individuals were detained by police for questioning.[27]

Guns May Encourage Law Breaking

The availability of lethal weapons may support the careers in crime of robbers, as such weapons allow offenders to attack more lucrative targets, thereby increasing their profits. Firearms also increase the success rates of holdups, as victim compliance is more likely and injuries to both parties are less likely as victim resistance is lower. Therefore, firearms may enable armed robberies, some of which result in the death of the victim.[28]

Guns Facilitate Impulsive Killings

In the case of attacks that have been carefully planned, the perpetrator is likely to proceed, regardless of whether a specific type of weapon is available. Where an attack is more impulsive, guns are unique in the sense that, unlike other weapons, once the trigger is pulled, guns do not allow users to change their minds. Serious harm may occur within seconds. With knives, blunt instruments, or fists, the user may reconsider and pull back from the brink by aborting an attack or softening a punch, blow, or stabbing movement.

Some researchers have noted that the outcome of domestic violence is especially influenced by the availability of lethal weapons. While spousal abuse is often repetitive, abusers tend to be impulsive and volatile.[29] The presence of a firearm during violent episodes has been found to increase the chances that an assault against a partner will result in a fatality.[30] Youth homicide, too, is strongly influenced by the presence of guns as much youth violence is impulsive in nature.[31]

Guns May Precipitate Aggression: The Weapons Effect

An interesting line of inquiry suggests that, by their mere presence, guns may "trigger" aggressive actions when people are mildly angered. In pioneering work in the 1960s, the social psychologist Leonard Berkowitz tested the question of whether "the trigger pulls the finger" in addition to the reverse. His work was based on earlier observations that children who were exposed to aggressive stories and toys displayed more antisocial behavior than children exposed to neutral stories.[32]

Berkowitz and his colleague conducted an experiment in which each male subject was brought together with another student (really an accomplice of the researcher), and the two men were told they were participating in a study of reactions to stress.[33] They were told that they would work on assigned problems and take turns evaluating the other's work by administering one or seven shocks (all fairly mild). The accomplice was placed in front of a shock board and administered either one or seven shocks to the real subject, supposedly reflecting his partner's judgment of his work. Most of the men receiving seven shocks became angry with the other person for the unfavorable and mildly painful evaluation.

Then it was the subject's turn to evaluate his partner. He was taken to the shock apparatus and given his partner's answers to the assigned problems. Some of the subjects saw a revolver and a shotgun lying on a table next to the shock key, while others saw two badminton rackets on the table. A third group of subjects saw nothing but the shock key on the table. The study found that the angered men—those who had received seven shocks—who saw firearms on the table struck back harder at their partners than did the angered men who saw neutral objects or no objects at all on the table next to the shock apparatus. Berkowitz believed that the mere sight of the guns stimulated the angered men to give their antagonists more shocks. In his view, visual cues such as firearms can evoke a conditioned aggressive response because they have been associated previously with aggression.

Subsequent studies have been mixed in terms of whether they demonstrated a "weapons effect." Recent work by Jennifer Klinesmith and her colleagues at Knox College in Illinois found another explanation for such an effect. Male students had their testosterone levels measured prior to the experiment. One set of students then were encouraged to handle a gun, while the other group played a game. Subsequent measurement of their testosterone levels found that those handling the gun had a greater increase in their testosterone levels. They were then given an opportunity to engage in aggressive behavior, and those who had handled the gun displayed more aggression. Furthermore, those showing greater increases in testosterone level showed more aggressive behavior. The study suggests that the presence of guns may produce hormonal changes in males that then elicit aggressive behavior.[34]

Guns in the Home Increase the Risk of Homicide

Researchers in the public health field have used a method called the case-control study to examine the impact of guns on homicide and other harms. These studies have had enormous influence on understanding the importance of the presence of guns on fatalities. In the field of medicine, a case-control study identifies a sample of people who have a disease, say lung cancer, and then identifies a sample of people as closely matched as possible who do not have the disease. The goal is to determine whether a factor believed to be a cause (e.g., smoking) is more present in the group with the disease than in the control group.

Especially noteworthy in this context, due to its influence and the attacks it elicited from those opposed to gun regulation, was a study led by Arthur Kellermann in 1993. An emergency room doctor and professor who grew up around guns, Kellermann and his colleagues conducted a case-control study to determine whether gun ownership increased the risk of homicide in the home.[35] The investigators studied 388 homicides occurring in the home in three counties located in three different states (Ohio, Tennessee, and Washington). A control group of 388 individuals was matched with these victims on sex, race, age, education, economic status, and type of residence. In their statistical analysis, the researchers also took into account factors such as previous violence and the use of drugs in the home.

The study found that firearms were more likely to be kept in the home of the homicide victims than the control group. The presence of firearms was found to significantly increase the risk of homicide in the home once the groups were matched on the all the above-mentioned factors. Therefore, rather than serving as a source of protection, firearms were associated with an increased risk of homicide independent of other factors. Other case-control studies have generally yielded support for the idea that guns in the home elevate the risk of homicide.

Bottom Line

The crime of homicide provides a good illustration of the instrumentality effect; the notion that the means used is one key factor in the outcome of violent incidents. It is, of course, not the only factor as the strength of a perpetrator's intent to kill is also important.

Guns facilitate killing in a number of ways. They facilitate mass murder, killing at a distance, the killing of armed or well-protected targets, impulsive homicides, and the killing of innocent bystanders. Research consistently shows that attacks with guns are more often lethal than attacks involving other weapons, even where assailants with guns are no more determined to kill than are those using knives. Case-control studies show that the presence of guns in the home raises the risk of homicide in that residence. Surgeons provide firsthand clinical support for the idea that, while guns themselves vary in their lethality, bullet wounds tend to produce more severe damage to the body than do other weapons. Gun industry advertising and research by gun experts also acknowledge that guns and ammunition vary in their lethality. Thus, multiple sources indicate that guns enable certain types of crime and play an important role in the outcome of an attack, independent of the intent of the perpetrator.

Notes

1. Hammer M. The real experts say Campus Carry is not a problem [Internet]. Sun-Sentinel. 2015 Feb 27. Available from: http://www.sun-sentinel.com/opinion/commentary/sfl-florida-guns-on-campus-20150227-story.html

2. The US Department of Education. The incidence of crime on the campuses of U.S. postsecondary education institutions. Washington, DC: US Department of Education; 2001 [Internet]. Available from: http://www2.ed.gov/finaid/prof/resources/finresp/ReportToCongress.pdf

3. U.S. Department of Justice. Violent victimization of college students, 1995–2002. Washington, DC: Bureau of Justice Statistics; 2005. Available from: http://www.bjs.gov/content/pub/pdf/vvcs02.pdf

4. Salisbury D, Novack T, Brunner R. Traumatic brain injury caused by violence [Internet]. Birmingham: University of Alabama Traumatic Brain Injury Model System. Available from: http://main.uab.edu/tbi/show.asp?durki=85704

5. Richter R, Zaki M., Selective conservative management of penetrating abdominal wounds. Ann Surg. 1967; 166(2): 238–244.

6. Diaz T. Making a killing: the business of guns in America. New York: The New Press; 1999.

7. Diaz T. Making a killing. P. 95–96.

8. Mann R. Handgun stopping power: Sizing up your options [Internet]. American Rifleman. 2012 Aug 29. Available from: http://www.american-rifleman.org/articles/handgun-stopping-power/

9. Cook P. Robbery violence. J Crim L & Criminology. 1987; 78(2): 357–376.
10. Gabor T, Baril M, Cusson M, Elie D, Leblanc M, Normandeau A. Armed robbery: cops, robbers, and victims. Springfield, IL: Charles C Thomas; 1987.
11. T. Gabor et al. Armed robbery. P. 103–104.
12. Cook P. Robbery violence. P. 372.
13. Zimring F. Is gun control likely to reduce violent killings? U Chi L Review. 1968; 35(4): 721–737.
14. Block R. Violent crime. Lexington, MA: Lexington Books; 1977.
15. Kleck G. Targeting guns. NY: Aldine de Gruyter; 1997. P. 227.
16. Sugarmann J. Every handgun is aimed at you. New York: The New Press; 2001. P. 156–163.
17. CBS News. Popular AR-15 rifle at center of gun control debate [Internet]. 2012 Dec 18. Available from: http://www.cbsnews.com/8301-505263_162-57559725/popular-ar-15-rifle-at-center-of-gun-control-debate/
18. Hemenway D. Private guns, public health. Ann Arbor: University of Michigan Press; 2004. P. 91–92.
19. Federal Bureau of Investigation. Uniform Crime Reports: law enforcement officers killed and assaulted 2011. Washington, DC: US Department of Justice. Available from: http://www.fbi.gov/about-us/cjis/ucr/leoka/2011/officers-feloniously-killed/officers-feloniously-killed
20. Cook P. The effect of gun availability on violent crime patterns. Ann Am Acad Pol Soc Sci. 1981; 455(1): 63–79.
21. Kleck G, McElrath K. The effects of weaponry on human violence. Soc Forces. 1991; 69(3): 669–692.
22. Kantor S. Sniper killings grip Maryland [Internet]. Chicago Tribune. 2002 Oct 4. Available from: http://articles.chicagotribune.com/2002-10-04/news/0210040287_1_shootings-dealership-al-briggs
23. Manning S. Families of sniper victims reach settlement [Internet]. Washington Times. 2004 Sep 10. Available from: http://www.washingtontimes.com/news/2004/sep/9/20040909-095944-5026r/
24. Sayers J. Pheonix freeway shootings: what you need to know. The Arizona Republic [Internet]. 2015 Sep 25. Available from: http://www.azcentral.com/story/news/local/phoenix/breaking/2015/09/10/phoenix-freeway-shootings-what-you-need-know/72029778/
25. Larson E. The story of a gun: the maker, the dealer, the murderer—inside the out-of-control world of American firearms. The Atlantic. 1993; 27(1): 48–78.

26. Martinez M, Cabrera A, Weisfeldt S, Criss D. Albuquerque road rage: man in custody after 4-year-old shot, killed [Internet]. CNN.com. 2015 Oct 21. Available from: http://www.cnn.com/2015/10/21/us/child-road-rage-death/index.html

27. Allen S. Innocent bystander shot while driving on OBT, cops say [Internet]. Orlando Sentinel. 2015 Sep 14. Available from: http://www.orlandosentinel.com/news/breaking-news/os-shooting-stolen-vehicle-obt-408-20150914-story.html

28. Skogan W. Weapon use in robbery. In: Inciardi J, Pottieger A, editors. Violent crime. Beverly Hills: Sage: 1978. P. 61–74.

29. Hastings J, Hamberger L. Personality characteristics of spouse abusers: a controlled comparison. Violence Vict. 1988; 3(5): 31–48.

30. Saltzman L, Mercy J, O'Carroll P, Rosenberg M, Rhodes P. Weapon involvement and injury outcomes in family and intimate assaults. JAMA. 1992; 267(22): 3043–3047.

31. Hemenway D. Private guns. P. 48.

32. Feshbach S. The catharsis hypothesis and some consequences of interaction with aggressive and neutral play objects. J Pers. 1956; 24: 449–462.

33. Berkowitz L, LePage A. Weapons as aggression-eliciting stimuli. J Pers Soc Psychol. 1967; 7(2): 202–207.

34. Klinesmith J, Kasser T, McAndrew F. Guns, testosterone, and aggression. Psychol Sci. 2006; 17(7): 568–571.

35. Kellermann A, Rivara F, Rushforth N, Banton J, Reay D, Francisco J. et al. Gun ownership as a risk factor for homicide in the home. New Engl J Med. 1993; 329(15): 1084–1091.

5

Mass Shootings: An Escalating Threat

The USA has one-third of the world's civilian mass shootings and five times as many of these incidents as the second-ranked country.[1] While mass murders in public account for less than 1 % of all gun murder victims,[2] they receive a great deal of media coverage and can leave the public feeling far more vulnerable than other types of killings, such as those occurring in the family, among acquaintances, or even gang-related killings. People feel they can avoid these other categories of homicide by avoiding those who are prone to extreme violence. Public mass shootings, on the other hand, are viewed as involving strangers and as occurring in places we or family members frequently use or visit—workplaces, schools, restaurants, shopping malls, and movie theaters. Mass murders, such as those at Virginia Tech, Sandy Hook Elementary School, or the Century movie theater in Aurora, Colorado, can leave a community severely traumatized and fearful. They can even produce economic damage as residents may avoid crowded public spaces that may attract the next individual contemplating a massacre.

© The Author(s) 2016

T. Gabor, *Confronting Gun Violence in America*,
DOI 10.1007/978-3-319-33723-4_5

Are US Mass Murders Increasing?

Most mass murders involve firearms. Although there are exceptions, it is hard to conceive of one or two individuals inflicting mass casualties in public with knives, clubs, or their bare hands. Mass murders are defined by the FBI as killings in which an individual intentionally kills four or more people (not including himself) in a single incident, usually at one location. According to the *Washington Post*'s Ezra Klein, 15 of the 25 or 60 % of the worst mass shootings over the last 50 years have occurred in the USA, despite the fact that the USA accounts for less than 5 % of the world's population.[3]

Klein also notes that mass shootings are getting worse, as half of the 12 deadliest shootings as of December 15, 2012, have occurred since 2007. Data compiled by CNN support Klein's observation that the toll taken by mass murders is increasing. The network compiled data on the 28 deadliest US mass shootings from 1949 through October 2015. With the attacks in San Bernardino (December 2015) and Orlando (June 2016) added to that list, 15 (50 %) of the 30 deadliest mass shootings have occurred since 2007. An analysis by the Congressional Research Service found that 7 of the 13 incidents with the highest number of fatalities over the last half century occurred in a seven-year period from 2007 to 2013.[4] Table 5.1 lists the 17 deadliest mass shootings since 1949.

There is some debate as to whether the number of mass murders has been on the rise. Professor James Alan Fox of Northeastern University, who has researched the subject for three decades, states that there have been just under 20 per year over the last 35 years if we use the FBI's definition of four or more individuals killed (excluding the killer). He has found that there has not been a trend in the direction of more mass murders.[5] An investigation by Mark Follman, a senior editor of *Mother Jones* magazine, focused on a subset of these incidents that were more "random," excluded gang killings and robberies, and concluded that mass shootings are increasing.[6]

A study of 160 "active shooter" incidents by the FBI, occurring from 2000 to 2013, lends support to the idea that mass casualty incidents may

Table 5.1 Deadliest US mass shootings since 1949

49 killed—June 12, 2016—Orlando, Florida. Omar Mateen, 29, opened fire at the Pulse nightclub, killing 49 people and injuring 53 in the deadliest civilian (non-military) mass shooting in US history. There is some dispute as to whether this was a hate crime as the club has many gay patrons. In a call to 9-1-1 during the attack, Mateen pledged his allegiance to the Islamic State. He took hostages when the police arrived at the scene and was shot by them in a gunfight.
32 killed—April 16, 2007—Virginia Tech in Blacksburg, Virginia. A 23-year-old student, Seung-Hui Cho, went on a shooting spree, killing 32 people in two locations and wounding an undetermined number of others on campus. The shooter then committed suicide.
27 killed—December 14, 2012—Sandy Hook Elementary School, Newtown, Connecticut. Adam Lanza, 20, killed 20 children (ages six and seven) and 6 adults, school staff and faculty, before turning the gun on himself. Nancy Lanza, his mother, was also dead from a gunshot wound.
23 killed—October 16, 1991—In Killeen, Texas, 35-year-old George Hennard crashed his pickup truck into Luby's Cafeteria. After exiting the truck, he killed 23 people and then committed suicide.
21 killed—July 18, 1984—In San Ysidro, California, 41-year-old James Huberty, armed with a long-barreled Uzi, a pump action shotgun, and a handgun killed 21 adults and children at a local McDonald's. He was killed by a police sharpshooter.
18 killed—August 1, 1966—University of Texas. Charles Joseph Whitman, a former US Marine, killed 16 and wounded at least 30 from a university tower. Police officers killed Whitman in the tower. Whitman had also killed his mother and wife earlier in the day.
14 killed—December 2, 2015—San Bernardino, California. Syed Farook and his wife Tashfeen Malik killed 14 people and injured 21 at the Inland Regional Center in what has been characterized as a terrorist attack. The couple targeted a San Bernardino County Department of Public Health training event and holiday party of about 80 employees in a rented banquet room. Several hours later, police pursued their vehicle and killed them in a shootout.
14 killed—August 20, 1986—In Edmond, Oklahoma, part-time mail carrier, Patrick Henry Sherrill, armed with three handguns, killed 14 postal workers in 10 minutes and then took his own life with a bullet to the head.
13 killed—November 5, 2009—At Fort Hood, Texas, Major Nidal Malik Hasan killed 13 people and injured 32. He was convicted and sentenced to death.
13 killed—April 3, 2009—In Binghamton, New York, Jiverly Wong killed 13 people and injured 4 at an immigrant community center. He then committed suicide.
13 killed—April 20, 1999—Columbine High School—Littleton, Colorado. 18-year-old Eric Harris and 17-year-old Dylan Klebold killed 12 fellow students and 1 teacher before committing suicide.

(continued)

Table 5.1 (continued)

---

13 killed—February 18, 1983—In Seattle, three men entered the Wah Mee gambling and social club, robbed the 14 occupants, and then shot each in the head, killing 13. Two of the men, Kwan Fai Mak and Benjamin Ng, were convicted of murder in August 1983. Both are serving life in prison. The third man, Wai-Chiu "Tony" Ng, after years on the run in Canada, was eventually convicted of first-degree robbery and second-degree assault. He was deported to Hong Kong in 2014.

13 killed—September 25, 1982—In Wilkes-Barre, Pennsylvania, 40-year-old George Banks, a prison guard, killed 13 people, including 5 of his own children.

13 killed—September 5, 1949—In Camden, New Jersey, 28-year-old Howard Unruh, a veteran of World War II, shot and killed 13 people as he walked down Camden's 32nd Street. His weapon of choice was a German-crafted Luger pistol. He was found insane and was committed to a state mental institution.

12 killed—September 16, 2013—In Washington, DC, Aaron Alexis killed 12 people inside the US Navy Yard. The shooter was also killed.

12 killed—July 20, 2012—In Aurora, Colorado, 12 people were killed and 58 were wounded at a movie theater screening of the new Batman film. James E. Holmes, 24, was taken into custody outside the theater. Dressed in full tactical gear, he set off two devices of some kind before spraying the theater with bullets from an AR-15 rifle, a 12-gauge shotgun, and at least one of two .40-caliber handguns police recovered at the scene.

12 killed—July 29, 1999—In Atlanta, Georgia, 44-year-old Mark Barton killed his wife and two children at his home. He then opened fire in two different brokerage houses, killing 9 people and wounding 12. He later committed suicide.

Source: CNN. 28 deadliest mass shootings in US history fast facts [Internet]. 2015 October 29. Available from: http://www.cnn.com/2015/10/29/us/28-deadliest-mass-shootings-in-u-s-history-fast-facts/index.html

be increasing.[7] These incidents are defined as those in which an individual is actively engaged in killing or attempting to kill in a confined and populated area. While fewer than half (40 %) of these incidents became mass murders, they shared many attributes of mass murders and all had the potential of turning into one. The study found that these active shooter incidents more than doubled from 2000–2006 to 2007–2013.

I used Follman's updated list of mass shootings for 1982–2015, in order to determine whether we are seeing more fatalities and casualties from these incidents than we did two or three decades ago.[8] His dataset focused on public shootings rather than those that were family-, felony-, or gang-related. I compared four time periods: the 1980s, 1990s, 2000–2009, and 2010–2015 (Table 5.2). The table shows that the number of incidents per year has more than doubled from the 1980s to the 1990s and 2000s. Between 2010 and 2015, the number of incidents per year has again increased sharply, at over four times the frequency observed in the 1980s.

The average number of deaths per year resulting from mass public shootings also has increased and, in the most recent period, was almost four times that of the 1980s. The number of fatalities per case increased from the 1990s to the post-2000 periods; however, cases in the 1980s yielded a larger number of fatalities per case. This situation was due to the impact of two very large mass killings on the relatively small number of incidents in the 1980s. Total casualties per incident in the earliest period also exceeded those observed in the three subsequent periods. The number of fatalities as a percentage of all casualties increased by about 10 % from the 2000s. As discussed below, this finding might point to the impact of more lethal weapons and ammunition used from 2000 on.

A different dataset of mass public shootings analyzed by the Congressional Research Service investigators, spanning 44 years from 1970 to 2013, also found a steady increase in incidents per year from the 1970s to the 2010–2013 time period.[9] That study also found that the number of victims murdered per incident increased over time, with the exception of the 1990s. There was no discernible pattern with regard to the percentage of victims who died.

Table 5.2 Public mass shootings and casualties, 1980–2015

Period	# of cases	Cases per year	Fatalities	Fatalities per Year	Fatalities per case	Total victims	% of victims who died	Total victims per incident
1980–1989	8	.8	79	7.9	9.9	167	47.3	20.9
1990–1999	23	2.3	161	16.1	7.0	337	47.8	14.7
2000–2009	20	2.0	173	17.3	8.7	302	57.3	15.1
2010–2015	22	3.7	182	30.3	8.3	322	56.5	14.6

Source: Follman M, Aronsen G, Pan D, Caldwell M. US Mass Shootings, 1982–2015. Data from Mother Jones' investigation. Mother Jones. 2012 Dec. 28. Updated cases through 2015 available from: http://www.motherjones.com/politics/2012/12/mass-shootings-mother-jones-full-data

The increasing number of overall incidents, fatalities, and casualties arising from mass public shootings can be attributed to a host of factors, including changing motives, weapons, and medical responses over time. While a more definitive analysis awaits more complete data on these incidents, newer and more lethal weapons are likely part of the explanation. Suppose we accept Professor Fox's conclusion that the number of mass murders has basically remained about the same over the last 35 years. A compelling argument can then be made that the dramatically improved medical response over the last three decades is masking what would have otherwise been a major increase in incidents and fatalities. Improvements in the medical system are driving down the number of people who die of gunshot wounds. As an illustration from an earlier era, an Indiana study conducted in the 1970s found that mortality rates declined sharply over time for gunshot wounds to the abdomen. These rates fell from 60 % in the 1930s to 36 % from 1938 to 1946, 16 % from 1955 to 1962, and 13 % from 1962 to 1970.[10] Survival rates during that time more than doubled (from 40 % to 87 %).

More recently, emergency room doctors who treat individuals with gunshot and knife wounds indicated that survival rates have risen due to the spread of hospital trauma centers, the increased use of helicopters to transport patients, improved training of first responders, and lessons learned from the battlefields of Iraq and Afghanistan. C. William Schwab, a surgeon and director of the Firearm and Injury Center at the University of Pennsylvania, states that many more people are being saved than was the case just ten years ago.[11]

To illustrate, data from the Centers for Disease Control and Prevention's (CDC's) National Electronic Injury Surveillance System-All Injury Program show that serious assaults by gunfire, requiring a hospital stay, rose by 47 % to 30,759 in 2011 from 20,844 in 2001.[12] In those same years, homicides in the USA declined by about 20 % from 15,980 in 2001 to 12,664 in 2011.[13] Thus, despite a large increase in serious injuries by firearm, the mortality rate and, hence, homicide rate declined. There has been a 5 % increase—from 78 % to 83 %—in the survival rate from gunshot wounds from 2001 to 2011. Research performed for *The Wall Street Journal* by the Howard-Hopkins Surgical Outcomes Research Center, a collaboration between Howard University and Johns Hopkins

University, reveals that the percentage of shooting victims in the USA who have died declined by almost 2 % from 2007 and 2010. One reason for the lowering of mortality rates comes from military doctors who have learned to deal better with blood loss, a major cause of death arising from gunshot wounds. Less fluids are now being administered by first responders to slow down the bleeding, and patients are instead pumped full of platelets and plasma to aid in clotting.

Bellal Joseph and his colleagues at the Division of Trauma, Critical Care, Emergency Surgery and Burns, Department of Surgery, University of Arizona, examined the impact of aggressively managing patients with gunshot wounds to the brain at a level one trauma facility. Aggressive management was defined as resuscitation with blood products, therapy to reduce intracranial pressure, and/or the use of concentrated products to promote blood clotting. Gunshot wounds to the brain typically have survival rates of 10 % to 15 %. Over a five-year period, the surgeons found that, with the adoption of aggressive management, survival rates increased incrementally every year, from 10 % in 2008 to 46 % in 2011![14]

Andrew Peitzman, chief of general surgery and trauma services at the University of Pittsburgh Medical Center, notes that trauma doctors have revolutionized the care of gunshot wounds over the last 30 years.[15] Peitzman adds that the typical shooting of 30 years ago often involved a .22-caliber Saturday Night Special, while the common shooting today involves a 9 mm semiautomatic pistol, which has larger bullets and can fire more quickly. The typical shooting victim today has at least three bullet wounds.

If the number of motivated shooters has remained the same from the 1980s, both the number of mass murders and overall death toll from mass murders should have declined due to advances in emergency medicine and surgery. There is no evidence of such a decline. This means that there are more motivated shooters, and/or the firepower of weapons has increased. The CDC data cited above indicate that homicide rates were declining when assaults by gunfire were increasing. The present analysis, as well as that of the Congressional Research Service, shows that public mass murders by gunfire have increased over the last three decades and fatalities overall have increased. Our analysis has also found that the percentage of victims of mass shootings who die has increased, despite improvements in emergency response and treatment.

Taken together, these findings suggest that the weapons available to mass killers today have played a significant role in increasing the number of incidents that qualify as mass murders (four or more persons killed), as well as the overall number of fatalities and other casualties. The ability of weapons today to discharge rounds quickly and accurately can also facilitate the achievement of the perpetrator's aims before law enforcement arrives at the scene. The next section provides data on the weapons used in mass shootings.

Weapons Used in Mass Shootings

The Everytown for Gun Safety Group, formerly Mayors Against Illegal Guns, conducted an analysis of 133 mass shootings of all types that occurred between 2009 and 2015.[16] Just 11 % involved assault weapons and/or high-capacity magazines. These incidents resulted in an average of 13.3 people shot, 155 % more people than in incidents involving other weapons (5.2). The use of weapons with these features resulted in 47 % more deaths on average than other incidents—7.5 deaths versus 5.1 deaths.

Mark Follman's study of mass public shootings for *Mother Jones* magazine showed that more than half of all the shooters possessed assault-style weapons and/or high-capacity magazines. About 80 % of the weapons in the shootings analyzed by Follman and his colleagues were obtained legally, a fact that ought to lead one to pause about the ease with which perpetrators of these slaughters obtain their weapons.[17] As shown by the Everytown analysis, assault-style weapons do not merely look intimidating. Casualties increase when they are used by shooters, further evidence of an instrumentality effect, the notion that the weapon itself has an impact on casualties, aside from the intent of the shooter.

The Role of Mental Illness

While some high-profile mass murders have involved individuals with a clear mental illness, many cases do not fall in this category. The majority of mass murders are not random killings but involve family members. James Fox of Northeastern University states that the most common description of the mass murderer is "a white male who has a history of frustration and failure, who is socially isolated and lacking support systems, who externalizes blame onto others, who suffers some loss or disappointment perceived to be catastrophic, and has access to a powerful enough weapon."[18] He notes that these are very determined individuals who are often very composed when they commit mass murder because they have thought about the act for a long time.

On the subject of the mental state of mass killers, including those not committed in public, Fox states:

> [*mass killers*]*typically plan their crimes in advance, often weeks or months in advance. They are calm, deliberate and determined to get justice for what they perceive to be unfair treatment. The idea that they suddenly snap actually makes little sense. They snap and just so happen to have 2 AK-47's and 2000 rounds of ammunition around. … Most of the time, the motive is to get even with those they hold responsible for their misfortunes. Usually people at work or at home, or sometimes a class of people. … And do you ever notice how often witnesses say "he was smiling, and looked so calm." That's because they had been through this in their mind for so long.*[19]

The analysis by Everytown examined 133 incidents and in just one was there evidence that the shooter was prohibited by federal law from possessing guns as a result of a severe mental illness.[20] In 15 (11 %) of the incidents, concerns about the shooter's mental health had been brought to the attention of a medical practitioner, school official, or other authority prior to the shooting. In close to two-thirds of the cases in which sufficient information was available, the shooter did not fall in a category that would prohibit him from possessing firearms, as a result of a felony conviction, history of domestic abuse, or mental illness.

Can Arming Civilians Protect Us?

Those who believe that the solution to mass murder is more guns should note that the majority of these killings occur among family members inside private residences.[21] According to Everytown's study, just 17 (13 %) of all mass shootings over an eight-year period occurred in so-called gun-free zones. Advocates of arming more of the population say that if more people were armed, there would be a better chance of stopping these atrocities. Mark Follman's original study of mass shootings over 30 years did not find a single incident in which the killing was stopped by a civilian using a gun.[22] Follman notes that this is the case despite the fact that America has been flooded with millions of additional firearms and a barrage of new laws has made it easier than ever to carry them in public.

Consider the mass murder at the Century movie theater in Aurora, Colorado, on July 20, 2012. Could the carnage have been prevented if guns were allowed into the theater? While there is no certain answer, consider the following:

At the end of 2011, approximately 90,000 Colorado residents had active carry permits, approximately 2.5 % of the adult population at that time.[23] The majority of the moviegoers were under 40, as indicated by the age of the victims, and as this was a midnight screening of the movie *The Dark Knight Rises*. Available data from Texas and Florida indicate that the peak age of permit holders is over 50.[24,25] In addition, many permit holders only carry their weapons when they feel they are at risk and just 10 % carry their weapons on a daily basis.[26] Given these facts, it is likely that, at most, 1 % of the patrons—4 of the 400 people in the theater—would have been armed during a midnight showing attended mostly by young adults. It is incorrect to assert that the theater would have been full of armed patrons had guns been permitted on the premises.

A number of timely actions would have been required for an effective response. In Aurora, as in most mass shootings, the casualties occurred within a few minutes as victims were initially seated.[27] Many present believed that the shooter was part of the performance. An armed patron would need to recognize the threat was real, take the decision to intervene as opposed to leaving the scene, move to a protected position within range of the assailant, draw a weapon, and wait until an opportunity to shoot was present and no one else was in the line of fire. Then, the patron would have had to hit the mark.

Studies show that the average officer hits the mark in one out of every six shots during combat situations.[28] Civilians would likely do much worse. In addition, the shooter released some form of smoke bomb, which would have the effect of obscuring the audience's vision and cause irritation to the eyes and throat. With the armor worn by the alleged shooter in Aurora, greater precision would be required if the aim was to hit exposed parts of his body. The speed of the event, the element of surprise, the level of stress—there was panic in the theater—the protective armor of the shooter, and the poor visibility would have all lowered the odds that one of the small number of permit holders could have intervened successfully before many of the casualties were inflicted and before police arrived—one minute after being called and three minutes after the shooting began. (It is not known whether, in fact, there were armed patrons in the theater in violation of the prohibition in Aurora and they were unable or unwilling to act.). In addition, a shootout with the perpetrator presents obvious dangers for bystanders and may produce catastrophic errors by responding officers.

The increasing annual death toll from mass shootings suggests that the continuing proliferation of firearms and laws permitting gun carrying have not reduced the bloodshed. Dr. Stephen Hargarten, a leading expert in emergency medicine and gun violence at the Medical College of Wisconsin, has noted that the intervention of armed civilians is more likely to make matters worse.[29] The shootout between police and a gunman outside the Empire State Building in August 2012 is a case in point as nine bystanders were wounded.[30] One wonders about the toll if armed civilians with substantially less training than police officers routinely engaged aggressors in crowded movie theaters, malls, and schools.

Consider the murder of 5 Dallas police officers and the wounding of 9 others on July 7, 2016. The shooter ambushed the police officers who were on duty during a protest of police killings of African-American civilians. Dallas's Police Chief, David Brown, stated that the state's laws permitting the open carrying of long guns confused officers responding to the shooting as they thought they were under attack by multiple shooters. Such a situation can divert the attention of responding officers and may impede the response to such shootings. None of the armed civilians engaged the perpetrator.[31]

Attacks on Schools

School-based attacks provide some clues as to the prevention of certain mass shootings. The combined efforts of the US Secret Service and the Department of Education identified 37 incidents of targeted school-based attacks, committed by 41 individuals between 1974 and 2000.[32]

For the purposes of this study, an incident of targeted school violence was defined as any incident where (i) a current student or recent former student attacked someone at his or her school with lethal means (e.g., a gun and knife) and (ii) where the student attacker purposefully chose his or her school as the location of the attack.

Here are some of the key findings of the study and their implications for the development of strategies to address the problem of targeted school violence:

- *Incidents of targeted violence at school rarely are sudden, impulsive acts.*

The attacks examined appeared to be the outcome of a comprehensible process of thinking and behavior—behavior that typically began with an idea, progressed to a plan, moved on to securing the means to execute the plan, and culminated in an attack. This process is potentially knowable or discernible from the perpetrator's behaviors and communications.

- *Prior to most incidents, other people knew about the attacker's idea and/or plan to attack.*

Schools can encourage students to report information relevant to an impending attack and can identify and remove barriers in the school environment that may discourage students from sharing this information.

- *There is no accurate or useful profile of students who engaged in targeted school violence.*

Rather than trying to determine the "type" of student who may engage in targeted attacks on schools, attention should focus on a student's behaviors and communications to determine if he or she appears to be planning an attack. If an attack is likely, the focus should be on how fast the student is moving toward attack and where intervention may be possible.

- *Most attackers engaged in some behavior prior to the incident that caused others concern or indicated a need for help.*

A student's family, teachers, and friends may have information regarding actions that have raised concern. Again, open communications are vital and educators, as well as other adults, can learn how to detect these signals and make appropriate referrals.

- *Most attackers had difficulty coping with significant losses or personal failures. Moreover, many had considered or attempted suicide.*

Attention should be given to any sign that a student is having difficulty coping with major losses or perceived failures, particularly where these losses or failures seem to have prompted feelings of desperation and hopelessness.

- *Many attackers felt bullied, persecuted, or injured by others prior to the attack.*

The analysis supports initiatives to prevent bullying in schools. Educators can play a key role in these efforts and schools should prohibit bullying and empower students to report cases of bullying.

- *Most attackers had access to and had used weapons prior to the attack.*

The idea of an attack, coupled with an effort to acquire, prepare, or use a weapon, may signal a significant move in the attacker's progression from idea to action. Attention should focus on weapon access and use or any efforts by a student to build a bomb or acquire bomb-making components.

- *In many cases, other students were involved in some capacity.*

Any investigation of potential targeted school violence should include attention to the role that a student's peers may be playing in that student's thinking about and preparations for an attack.

- *Despite prompt law enforcement responses, most shooting incidents were stopped by means other than law enforcement intervention.*

The short duration of most targeted school attacks underscores the need to develop preventive measures for a school or school district. These measures should include protocols and procedures for responding to and managing threats.

The report concludes by advocating a threat assessment approach in the prevention of school-based attacks. Threat assessment is a fact-based investigative and analytical approach that focuses on what a particular student is doing and saying, rather than on any similarity to those who have attacked schools in the past. Threat assessment emphasizes the importance of such behavior and communications for identifying, evaluating, and reducing the risk posed by a student who may be thinking about or planning a school-based attack. To implement a threat assessment approach, school officials and police will require training on what information to gather, how to gather and evaluate it, and how they might try to intervene in cases where the information collected indicates that a student may be planning a school-based attack.

The final chapter of this book provides additional ideas as to what our society can do to detect an individual's preparation for a school-based or other mass casualty incident.

Bottom Line

Studies of mass public shootings by the Congressional Research Service and by this writer (using data collected by reporters at *Mother Jones* magazine), as well as the FBI's analysis of active shooter incidents, have shown an increase in these incidents over the last few decades and again over the last five to ten years. Over the past 65 years, half of the incidents involving the largest number of fatalities have occurred since 2007. The number of fatalities per year has increased steadily from the 1980s to the 2010s. The Congressional study also found that the number of victims murdered per incident increased over time, with the exception of the 1990s. My analysis did show an elevated number of fatalities per case in the 1980s; however, this situation was due to the impact of two very large mass killings due to the smaller number of incidents during that decade.

The overall increase in mass public shootings, in fatalities per year, and in casualties from the 1980s does not follow the trends in homicide in general. Homicides in general have declined sharply during this period.

In the 1980s, the overall homicide rate ranged between about 8 and 10 per 100,000 people. In the 2000s, the rate has been under 6 per 100,000. The rate in 2010 was less than half of what it was in 1980.[33]

Thus, the drop in the homicide rate would suggest that the USA was not becoming more violent. Improved medical care, declines in intimate partner homicides, and aging of the population are some of the reasons generally given for the reduction in homicide from the 1980s.[34] Was the increase in mass public shootings due to the presence of more unstable individuals motivated to kill people in large numbers or did the lethality of the weaponry available to shooters a factor?

While there is no definitive answer to this question, the role played by more lethal weapons and ammunition appears to provide at least a partial answer. Studies show that incidents involving assault weapons and high-capacity ammunition magazines produce more casualties and deaths.[35] Chapter 11 discusses how a slowdown in gun sales prompted the gun industry to develop products that appealed to core consumers, such as those that were more lethal and more capable of producing mass casualties. Thus, despite advances in emergency medicine and surgery that have increased survival rates substantially, the products available today have continued to increase the toll resulting from mass killings. The medical advances have likely kept this toll from increasing far more dramatically and have therefore masked what would have otherwise been a far more disturbing trend in mass murder.

Other findings relating to mass public shootings have implications for how they may be prevented. Weapons are usually obtained legally by the perpetrators; therefore, background checks and other screening of purchasers need to be examined. Although most shooters did not have a severe mental illness, family members and associates, who often pick up troubling signs, can be part of screening processes. Few shootings occur in so-called gun-free zones, and there is no evidence that arming more of the public would provide a net benefit in foiling attacks in public. The study of targeted school attacks by the US Secret Service and the Department of Education revealed that there is no useful profile of perpetrators, as their characteristics varied in terms of their age, race, family background, social relationships, school performance, and disciplinary record.

These findings point to the need for a comprehensive strategy in dealing with mass shootings, both inside schools and in the community. Simplistic approaches, such as arming the population and relying on profiles, are not useful and may even be counterproductive. Further study is required to identify the factors that make the USA so susceptible to mass murder. The final chapter of this book addresses this issue and offers a comprehensive approach to reducing gun violence, including mass shootings.

Notes

1. Timberg S. Mass shootings and the dark side of American exceptionalism [Internet].Salon.com. 2015 Aug 27. Available from: http://www.salon.com/2015/08/27/mass_shootings_and_the_dark_side_of_american_exceptionalism_they_happen_because_theres_a_large_gap_between_what_people_are_aspiring_to_and_what_they_can_realistically_achieve/
2. Everytown for Gun Safety. Analysis of recent mass shootings. New York: Everytown for Gun Safety; 2015.
3. Klein E. Twelve facts about guns and mass shootings in the United States [Internet]. Washington Post. 2012 Dec 14. Available from: http://www.washingtonpost.com/blogs/wonkblog/wp/2012/12/14/nine-facts-about-guns-and-mass-shootings-in-the-united-states/
4. Krouse W, Richardson D. Mass murder with firearms: incidents and victims, 1999–2013. Washington, DC: Congressional Research Office; 2015. P. 15.
5. McArdle M. Forget what you've heard: mass shootings aren't rising. But they probably aren't going away [Internet]. The Daily Beast. 2013 Feb 1. Available from: http://www.thedailybeast.com/articles/2013/02/01/forget-what-you-ve-heard-mass-shootings-aren-t-rising-but-they-probably-aren-t-going-away.html
6. Follman M. More guns, more mass shootings—coincidence? Mother Jones. 2012 Sep 26. Available from: http://www.motherjones.com/politics/2012/09/mass-shootings-investigation
7. Federal Bureau of Investigation. A study of active shooter incidents in the United States between 2000 and 2013. Washington, DC: US Department of Justice; 2014.

8. Follman M, Aronsen G D, Pan D, Caldwell M. US mass shootings, 1982–2015: data from Mother Jones' investigation. Mother Jones. 2012 Dec 28. Available from: http://www.motherjones.com/politics/2012/12/mass-shootings-mother-jones-full-data

9. Krouse W, Richardson D. Mass murder with firearms. P. 14–15.

10. Taylor F. Gunshot wounds of the abdomen. Ann Surg. 1973; 177(2): 174–177.

11. Fields G, McWhirter C. In medical triumph, homicides fall despite soaring gun violence [Internet]. The Wall Street Journal. 2012 Dec 8. Available from: http://online.wsj.com/news/articles/SB10001424127887324712504578131360684277812

12. Fields G, McWhirter C. In medical triumph.

13. Federal Bureau of Investigation. Crime in the United States, 2001, 2011. Washington, DC: Department of Justice.

14. Joseph B, Aziz H, Pandit V, Kulvatunyou N, Wynne J et al. Improving survival rates after civilian gunshot wounds to the brain. J Am Coll Surg 2013; 218(1): 58–65.

15. Roth M. Gunshot wound care has improved dramatically [Internet]. Pittsburgh Post-Gazette. 2012 Jul. 23. Available from: http://www.post-gazette.com/stories/news/health/gunshot-wound-care-has-improved-dramatically-645837/#ixzz2hnldZnfn

16. Everytown for Gun Safety. Analysis of Recent Mass Shootings.

17. Follman M, Aronsen G, Pan D. A guide to mass shootings in America [Internet]. Mother Jones. Updated 2015 Oct 2. Available from: http://www.motherjones.com/politics/2012/07/mass-shootings-map

18. McArdle M., Forget what you've heard.

19. McArdle M., Forget what you've heard.

20. Everytown for Gun Safety. Analysis of recent mass shootings. P. 5.

21. Everytown for Gun Safety. Analysis of recent mass shootings. P. 6.

22. Follman M. The NRA myth of arming the good guys [Internet]. Mother Jones. 2012 Dec 28. Available from: http://www.motherjones.com/politics/2012/12/nra-mass-shootings-myth

23. United States Government Accountability Office. Gun control: state laws and requirements for concealed carry permits vary across the nation. Washington, DC: GAO; 2012. Appendix V.

24. Texas Department of Public Safety. Concealed handgun licensing [Internet]. 2013; Jan 25. Available from: http://www.txdps.state.tx.us/RSD/CHL/Reports/2012Calendar/byAge/9LicenseApplicationsIssued.pdf

25. Florida Department of Agriculture and Consumer Services. Concealed weapon or firearm license holder profile [Internet]. Updated 2015 Oct 31. Available from: http://www.freshfromflorida.com/content/download/7500/118857/cw_holders.pdf

26. Smith T. 2001 National Gun Policy Survey of the National Opinion Research Center: research findings. Chicago: NORC; 2001. Table 14.

27. Witt A. Timeline: Colorado theater shooting [Internet]. CNN.com. Available from: http://www.cnn.com/interactive/2012/07/us/aurora.shooting/index.html

28. Dahl J. Empire State Building shooting sparks questions about NYPD shot accuracy [Internet]. CBS News. 2012 Aug 29. http://www.cbsnews.com/8301-504083_162-57502545-504083/empire-state-building-shooting-sparks-questions-about-nypd-shot-accuracy/

29. Follman M. More guns, more mass shootings.

30. Ariosto D. 2 dead nine wounded in Empire State Building shooting, police say [Internet]. CNN.com. 2012 Aug 25. Available from: http://www.cnn.com/2012/08/24/justice/new-york-empire-state/

31. Sheyder E., Dallas police chief says armed civilians in Texas "increasingly challenging" [Internet]. Yahoo News. 2016 Jul 12. Available from: https://www.yahoo.com/news/dallas-police-chief-expresses-worry-armed-civilians-texas-013819002--finance.html

32. Vossekuil B, Fine R, Reddy M, Borum R, Modzeleski W. The final report and findings of the safe school initiative. Washington, DC: US Secret Service and US Department of Education; 2004.

33. Cooper A, Smith E. Homicide trends in the United States, 1980–2008: annual rates for 2009 and 2010. Washington, DC: Bureau of Justice Statistics; 2011.

34. Dugan L, Nagin D, Rosenfeld R. Explaining the decline in intimate partner homicide: the effects of changing domesticity, women's status and domestic violence resources. Homicide Stud. 1999; 3: 187–214.

35. Everytown for Gun Safety. Analysis of recent mass shootings. P. 4.

6

Suicide: Impact of Lethal Methods

Each year, over 20,000 Americans die of a suicide by firearm.[1] Firearm suicides account for two-thirds of all gun-related deaths. Half of all suicides in the USA involve firearms, making it the most common suicide method.

This chapter tests the idea of whether methods make a difference in suicide. Is a gun merely an expendable tool that can easily be replaced by someone bent on suicide? Or, alternatively, can a reduction in the availability of guns prevent some suicides from occurring?

Extent of Planning and Ambivalence

[Ken]Baldwin was twenty-eight and severely depressed on the August day in 1985 when he told his wife not to expect him home till late. ...On the [Golden Gate] bridge, Baldwin counted to ten and stayed frozen. He counted to ten again, then vaulted over. Baldwin recalls, "I instantly realized that everything in my life that I'd thought was unfixable was totally fixable—except for having just jumped."

© The Author(s) 2016
T. Gabor, *Confronting Gun Violence in America*,
DOI 10.1007/978-3-319-33723-4_6

> *Kevin Hines was eighteen when he took a municipal bus to the bridge ... he paced back and forth and sobbed on the bridge walkway for half an hour. No one asked him what was wrong. ... "So I jumped ... my first thought was What the hell did I just do? I don't want to die."*[2]

Many people seem to believe that suicide is the result of a long-standing mental illness and that the individual who takes his or her life has contemplated doing so for a long time. Consider a national survey in which close to 3000 respondents were asked to estimate how many of the more than 1000 people who had jumped from the Golden Gate Bridge would have committed suicide some other way if an effective barrier had been installed on the bridge.[3] More than a third of respondents estimated that none of the suicides could have been prevented as, in their view, every single jumper would have found another way to complete suicide. An additional 40 % of the respondents believed that most of the jumpers would have completed suicide using other means. Thus, over seven out of ten survey respondents believed that the suicide of all or most of the jumpers was inevitable and that limiting access to one suicide method was completely or most likely to be futile.

According to this view, an individual, at some point, makes an irrevocable decision to end it all, selects a method, and takes the steps necessary to complete the act. If most suicides fit this profile of a rational act by a highly determined individual, it might be logical to argue that if guns were the chosen method, the lack of availability of a firearm would be irrelevant, as an alternative method would be selected with the same result. According to this line of reasoning, the method chosen is irrelevant, as the lack of availability of any single method, including guns, will not stop a determined individual from succeeding. With this scenario, the presence or absence of guns is unimportant due to their easy substitution.

Two assumptions must be examined. First, is the determination to kill oneself always so clear and the act always premeditated? Such a view of suicide rules out impulsive actions, self-destructive behavior under the influence of drugs or alcohol, and suicides prompted by personal crises. This more rational view of suicide also fails to distinguish between suicide victims of different ages. Thus, a teenager committing suicide may be more impulsive and commit suicide for reasons that may be different from adults. Impulsive suicide is where the availability of more lethal methods can especially make a difference.

Even assuming that people substitute methods when their preferred method is unavailable, the issue of method lethality needs to be addressed. A second assumption to test is whether all suicide methods are equally lethal. Where guns are the preferred method and they are unavailable, will their substitution with an overdose of medication or some other method achieve the same result?

Some suicides are indeed carefully planned. However, contrary to the popular view described above, there is a substantial body of evidence showing that many suicides have an impulsive component. Keith Hawton, a psychiatrist who heads Oxford University's Center for Suicide Research, has written the following in relation to the issue of planning versus impulsivity of this ultimate act of self-harm:

> For most people who become suicidal, the period of real risk is relatively brief, lasting in some individuals for even just a few minutes or a few hours. In others it may last days, but rarely longer. … In some people, a lesser degree of risk is present for a much longer period of time, possibly years, and during that time they may go through periods of added and very high risk.[4] The concept of periods of risk is very important in understanding the role of altering the availability of methods in prevention, in that if access to a dangerous means of suicide is restricted at such times, then survival until the end of these periods is more likely.[5]

The Brady Center to Prevent Gun Violence reports:

> Various studies of survivors of suicide have calculated that as many as two-thirds of those who reported suicidal behavior did not plan their attempt. Interviews with survivors of near-lethal suicide attempts revealed that a quarter made the attempt less than five minutes after making the decision. About half of those did so within 20 minutes, and three-quarters of suicide attempts occurred within an hour. In a separate study, survivor interviews found that many made their attempt within 24 hours of a crisis, particularly interpersonal crises and physical fights.[6]

In 1978, Richard Seiden, a researcher at the University of California at Berkeley published a study in which he followed up over 500 people who were prevented from attempting suicide at the Golden Gate Bridge between 1937 and 1971.[7] An average of 26 years after the aborted attempt, 94 % of these individuals were either still alive or had died of natural causes. To Seiden, this finding supported the view that suicidal behavior is crisis oriented and acute in nature. He concluded that if suicidal people can get through this crisis, they would be unlikely to commit suicide later. Seiden believed the high-risk period was 90 days.

A Texas study in the 1980s showed that suicidal thinking can be transient. The study examined the cases of 30 people who were treated for gunshot wounds to the head, chest, or abdomen.[8] Most, if not all, would have perished had a helicopter service and urban trauma center not been available. These were therefore very serious attempts. Interviews revealed that half of these patients had been drinking within 24 hours of the suicide attempt and 18 of the 30 had experienced a significant interpersonal conflict during that period. Most had no long-standing psychiatric disorders, only two had a history of suicides, and none of the 30 left a suicide note. Half the patients reported having suicidal thoughts for less than 24 hours. Many expected to die from their attempt, but indicated that they were glad to have survived. A follow-up two years later indicated that none had attempted suicide up to that point. This study showed that suicidal motivation can be fleeting but very serious at the same time.

An Alaskan study of survivors of self-inflicted gunshot wounds (mostly to the head or trunk) came to a similar conclusion.[9] More than half of the individuals reported drinking at the time of the shooting, and many attributed the incident to the drinking. Most had no history of depression or psychiatric disorders. Many of the incidents were precipitated by a conflict with a family member or girlfriend.

A Houston study of 153 survivors of nearly lethal suicide attempts by individuals between 13 and 34 years of age also supports the view that most attempts do not involve extensive planning or deliberation.[10] These individuals were asked: "How much time passed between the time you decided to complete suicide and when you actually attempted suicide?" Twenty-four percent said that less than five minutes elapsed between the decision to commit suicide and the actual attempt. Seventy percent made the attempt within an hour of the decision. Just 13 % of the survivors said that they had deliberated on committing suicide for one day or more.

Research in Australia supports the findings from American research on the impulsivity of many suicides. One study of emergency department visits found that close to half of the individuals attempted suicide within five minutes of taking the decision to do so.[11] The investigators reviewed previous research and concluded that one-third to four-fifths of attempts were impulsive. In another Australian study, close to two-thirds of survivors of suicide attempts by firearm reported that their attempt was prompted by a conflict with a partner or family member.[12] The majority of these survivors were young men who did not have a history of depression or other mental disorder. Most of these attempts were described as impulsive.

Another indication that suicide often does not involve careful deliberation or mental illness is the phenomenon of cluster suicides. It is not uncommon for a cluster or series of suicides or suicide attempts to occur in a limited geographic area within a relatively short time frame. A suicidal act by an adolescent may trigger copycat acts by peers who have been profoundly affected by the first act. One documented case of suicide clustering occurred in Chappaqua, New York. In 1978, the community's high school experienced two suicide deaths separated by three months.[13] These deaths were followed by five attempts and one serious suicide threat within seven weeks of the second death. The last six students not only knew each other but had visited each other when they were hospitalized for their suicide attempts. During the previous year, no students from this high school were hospitalized for suicide attempts.

More recently, two suicide clusters were reported in the two public high schools in Palo Alto, California.[14] The ten-year suicide rate for these schools has been four to five times the national average. While there are unique pressures on youth in these Silicon Valley schools, smartphones and social media bring them almost immediate and regular updates of each tragedy. Such saturated coverage of each event may trigger suicidal thoughts and surveys do show that a significant number of students in these schools have seriously contemplated suicide over the previous 12 months.

That suicide by adolescents is often impulsive is also shown by the number of cases—as many as 75 %—in which no notes have been left. In addition, there is often an absence of previous attempts and lack of communication about the intention to commit suicide.[15,16]

Dr. David Brent, an adolescent psychiatrist at the University of Pittsburgh, found that 40 % of children younger than 16 who died by suicide did not have a clearly definable psychiatric disorder. What they did have was a loaded gun in the home. Brent notes that for those under the age of 16, the availability of a gun is more important than psychiatric disorder. Brent states: "They're not suicidal one minute, then they are. Or they're mad and they have a gun available."[17]

How determined are people who attempt suicide? David Owens and his colleagues at the University of Leeds in the UK sought to answer this question by conducting a rigorous review of 90 research studies in which individuals who had attempted suicide and received medical care were followed up for one or more years.[18] The aim was to see how many people repeated their attempts and the number who ultimately committed suicide. The studies as a whole indicated that over two-thirds of suicide attempters were not known to have further attempts. Another 23 % had another nonfatal attempt within four years. Two percent of the subjects across all the studies actually committed suicide within one year, and 7 % of those monitored for nine years or more eventually committed suicide. Thus, while suicide attempters are more likely to commit suicide than the rest of the population, about 1 in every 14 actually goes on to take his or her life.

We might even conclude from the Leeds study that it is just the 2 % who complete suicide within a year of the initial attempt are absolutely determined to commit suicide. It might be assumed that those who do so several years later have been motivated by events that have arisen long after the initial attempt occurred. These results hardly support the idea that most people attempting suicide have taken an irrevocable decision to end their lives.

Kay R. Jamison, a specialist in mood disorders at Johns Hopkins University, comments on the ambivalence of the majority of those who are suicidal. She believes that, at most, 10–15 % of suicide cases are characterized by an unwavering determination to die on the part of the victim.[19] For other suicidal people, the risk is transient.

A publication of the National Alliance on Mental Illness states the following about the determination to commit suicide:

Even the most severely depressed person has mixed feelings about death, waver-
ing until the very last moment between wanting to live and wanting to die.
Most suicidal people do not want death; they want the pain to stop. The impulse
to end it all, however overpowering, does not last forever.[20]

Suicidal intent is not uniform for those who contemplate ending their lives. Intent likely falls along some form of continuum or scale. While some attempters are at the low end with little intent to die, others are at the high end, and still others may be ambivalent and fall somewhere in between the extremes. Furthermore, some have high intent but only for brief periods. Some scholars believe that reducing easy access to highly lethal suicide methods may be most effective in the case of the last two groups.[21]

Hawton of Oxford notes that the method chosen to attempt suicide may be more important to the outcome than the individual's intent:

Availability of a method may be the key factor that leads to translation of sui-
cidal thoughts into an actual suicidal act.[22] *Most importantly, the nature of the*
method that is available may have a vital influence on the outcome, particu-
larly where an act is impulsive—then the person engaging in suicidal behavior
is likely to use the means most easily available to them. If the method has a high
risk of being fatal (e.g. firearms, dangerous chemical substances), then there is a
strong possibility that the act will result in death.

Gun Availability and Suicide

Survivors of near-fatal suicide attempts have confirmed that availability of a method is an important factor in its selection. For example, in the above-mentioned Texas study of survivors of serious self-inflicted gun-shot wounds, the answer most often given by the subjects for selecting a firearm was its availability in their homes.[23] There is additional evidence that method availability is critical in its selection. Men are more likely to be gun owners and to select guns in suicide attempts than are women.[24] People who live in communities with more firearms are more likely to select them than those residing in communities with fewer guns.

Researchers affiliated with the Israeli Defense Forces assessed the impact on suicide of a simple policy change.[25] In that small country, many soldiers—usually conscripts 18–21 years of age—go home on weekends and used to take their weapons with them. A policy change in 2006 instructed them to leave their weapons on the base when they took their weekend leaves. After the policy change occurred, annual suicide rates decreased by 40 %. Most of this decrease was in firearm suicides over the weekend. There were no significant changes in rates of suicide during weekdays and no evidence of a compensating increase in suicides by other means. The authors concluded that a relatively simple policy change that reduced access to firearms had a major impact on suicide rates.

Consider the case of Canada, where gun ownership is greater in smaller communities. A study in the Province of Ontario in 1989 found that firearm suicides increased with decreasing urbanization.[26] In cities with a population of over 50,000, 22 % of male suicides involved firearms compared to 43 % in cities between 10,000 and 50,000, and over 50 % in communities under 10,000. This pattern was also found in other parts of Canada. The researchers further found that this pattern only held for long guns. The selection of handguns in male suicides was almost identical in communities of varying size, reflecting the fact that handgun ownership is more even across communities of different size.[27]

The psychologist David Lester, author of numerous works on suicide, undertook a novel analysis to determine the extent to which the availability of a suicide method plays a role in its selection. Lester examined the rates of suicide using three methods for the 48 continental states.[28] These methods were firearm suicides, poisoning by solids and liquids, and poisoning by gases. He then examined the rates of accidental death stemming from the same causes. He found that states with high rates of accidental death by firearms also tended to have high rates of suicide by firearms. He also found that states with high rates of accidental death by some form of poisoning also tended to have high rates of suicide by that form of poisoning. These findings support the idea that accidental death rates from particular methods provide a measure of the availability of those means of death and indicate that opportunity is influential in the suicide method used in an area.

Other research comparing the states lends further support to the link between the availability of firearms and suicide. For example, one study using survey-based measures of state household firearm ownership obtained from the CDC found that males, females, and people of all age groups were at an elevated risk for suicide if they lived in a state with high firearm ownership levels.[29] These findings held up even after accounting statistically for state levels of mental illness, substance abuse rates, poverty, and other factors that may increase suicide rates in a state. The authors also compared the 40 million people living in the states with the lowest firearm ownership levels (15 % were gun owners) to the 40 million or so people living in the states with the highest gun ownership levels (47 % were gun owners). There were almost four times as many firearm suicides in the high-ownership states but slightly more nonfirearm suicides in the low-ownership states. Thus, there was no evidence of a major shift to other methods in states with lower firearm availability. Looking at overall suicide (firearm and nonfirearm suicide combined), the high-ownership states had nearly double the number of suicides of the low-ownership states.

A number of case-control studies have supported the notion that firearm availability increases the risk of suicide. These studies have focused on the impact of gun availability in the home. For example, David Brent of the University of Pittsburgh's School of Psychiatry and his associates compared a group of 47 adolescent suicide victims in Western Pennsylvania with a matched group of hospitalized suicide attempters and another control group of 47 psychiatric patients who had never attempted suicide.[30] The three groups were matched on age, race, gender, and social class. The researchers found that the majority of the suicide victims had used a gun, whereas none of the attempters had used a firearm. Firearms were twice as likely to have been present in the homes of suicide victims as in the homes of either the attempters or the group that never attempted suicide. Firearms in the homes of the suicide victims also tended to be stored less securely (loaded and unlocked) than were those in the homes of the control groups. The researchers concluded, based on comparisons with the control groups, that the presence of a firearm in the home increases the likelihood of both suicide attempts and their lethality.

Douglas Wiebe of the University of California, Los Angeles, School of Public Health conducted a very large case-control study to examine the risk of firearm suicide for those living in homes with guns.[31] He matched over 13,000 control subjects to 1959 individuals who had committed suicide. His study showed that people who had a firearm in the home were about 17 times more likely to commit suicide with a gun than people not living in homes with guns. He did find that people without guns in the home were more likely to commit suicide by other means, but this elevated risk of nongun suicide was far more modest than the elevated risk of gun suicide by those living with guns. Thus, many people without access to guns did not switch to other methods.

Justin Mason and Alexander Tabarrok of George Mason University investigated the relationship between firearm availability and suicide in all US states over the years 2000–2009.[32] They used several measures of gun possession and controlled statistically for several factors that could affect suicide rates aside from gun availability. They found strong evidence that increases in gun prevalence cause an increase in firearm suicides. Despite substantial substitution of methods, they observed that increased gun prevalence causes an increase in total suicide. They concluded that if all states were to reduce the rates of gun ownership by 10 percentage points, the expected result would be between 1640 and 2960 fewer deaths by suicide, annually.

Consider the link between gun ownership and firearm suicide across all the states. Table 6.1 shows that the five states with the highest firearm suicide rates are Wyoming, Alaska, Montana, Idaho, and Oklahoma. Collectively, they have nearly six times the firearm suicide rates of the five states with the lowest gun suicide rates—Connecticut, Hawaii, New York, New Jersey, and Massachusetts. The second column shows that the five states with the highest firearm suicide rates on average have over four times the household gun ownership levels as the states with the lowest rates. Consequently, while this analysis does not demonstrate cause and effect, among these ten states there is a consistent and strong tendency for firearm suicide rates to increase with gun ownership levels.

Many studies have examined the link between gun availability and suicide. Researchers at Harvard's Injury Control Research Center have tried to make sense of the entire body of research and have concluded that:

Table 6.1 Gun ownership in the states with the highest and lowest firearm suicide rates

State	Gun ownership/% of households	Firearm suicides per 100,000
Wyoming	62.8	15.01
Alaska	60.6	13.94
Montana	61.4	13.87
Idaho	56.8	11.50
Oklahoma	44.6	10.56
Average	**57.24**	**12.98**
Connecticut	16.2	2.73
Hawaii	9.7	2.54
New York	18.1	2.27
New Jersey	11.3	1.88
Massachusetts	12.8	1.72
Average	**13.62**	**2.23**

Sources: Okoro, C, Nelson A, Mercy, J.A., Balluz A, Crosby, A. Mokdad, A. (2002). Prevalence of household firearms and firearm-storage practices in the 50 states and the District of Columbia: findings from the Behavioral Risk Factor Surveillance System, 2002. Pediatr. 2002; 116(3): 370–376; Centers for Disease Control and Prevention. (2015). National Centers for Injury Prevention and Control, Web-based Injury Statistics Query and Reporting System (WISQARS). Available from: http://www.cdc.gov/injury/wisqars/index.html

The preponderance of current evidence indicates that gun availability is a risk factor for youth suicide in the United States. The evidence that gun availability increases the suicide rates of adults is credible, but is currently less compelling.[33]

Studies in general show that gun suicides are lower where gun availability is lower but do not consistently find that suicide rates overall (all methods) are lower. Therefore, we cannot rule out the possibility that some people do switch to more available methods. This issue of substitution is explored later in this chapter.

Researchers at Johns Hopkins Center for Gun Policy and Research examined the impact on suicide of a permit-to-purchase handgun law introduced in Connecticut in the mid-1990s. They found that the law may have contributed to a 15.4 % reduction in firearm suicide rates.[34] They argue that such a law makes it difficult for an individual at risk of suicide to purchase a gun when they experience a suicidal impulse as they must apply for a permit and pass an eight-hour safety course.

The American Association of Suicidology has issued a very strong consensus statement on the risks to which youth are exposed when guns are kept in the home:

> *The risk conferred by guns in the home is proportional to the accessibility (e.g., loaded and unsecured firearms) and the number of guns in the home. Guns in the home, particularly loaded guns, are associated with increased risk for suicide by youth, both with and without identifiable mental health problems or suicidal risk factors.*[35]

Method Lethality

Table 6.2 provides the fatality rate for some of the most common methods of suicide, according to some of the largest studies conducted in this area. The CDC study covered all US suicide deaths and a national sample of emergency room visits for suicide attempts for 2001.[36] The multistate study examined mortality and hospital data for eight states in the 1990s.[37] The Australian study used national mortality and hospital data covering a ten-year period (1993–2003).[38] The Canadian study used national mortality and sample hospital data.[39]

Table 6.2 Percent of suicide attempts that are fatal, by method

Method	CDC study (%)	Multistate study (%)	Australian study (%)	Canadian study (%)
Firearm	85	82.5	90	92
Suffocation/hanging	69	61	83	78
Poisoning/overdose	2	1.5	2.2	23
Fall	31	34.5	60	
Cut/pierce	1	1.2	2.6	
Drowning		66	80	67
Gases/vapors		41.5	61.5	78

Sources: Vyrostek S, Annest J, Ryan G. Surveillance for fatal and nonfatal injuries. MMWR. Atlanta: Centers for Disease Control and Prevention; 2004 Sep 3; Spicer R, Miller T. Suicide acts in eight states: incidents and case fatality rates by demographics and method. Am J Public Health. 2000; 90(12): 1885–1891; Elnour A, Harrison J. Lethality of suicide methods. Inj Prev. 2008; 14(1): 39–45; Chapdelaine A, Samson E, Kimberley M, Viau L. Firearm-related injuries in Canada: issues for prevention. CMAJ. 1991; 145(10): 1217–1223

All the studies found firearms to be the most lethal suicide method. The percentage of suicide attempts with a firearm that proved fatal ranged between 83 and 92 %. Next in line in terms of lethality were suffocation or hanging, with a lethality level ranging between 61 and 83 %, and drowning, ranging between 66 % and 80 %. With the exception of the Canadian study, which was based on a smaller sample than the others, the least fatal methods were poisonings/overdoses and cutting/piercing at around 1–2 %. Thus, a suicide attempt involving firearms appears to be about 40 times as likely to end in a fatality as one involving a cutting instrument.

Is this difference in lethality due to a greater determination to die on the part of those choosing firearms? The difference in lethality is likely a reflection of the method used and not due to a difference in intent. Research is inconclusive about the extent to which the choice of method relates to intent, as many survivors indicate that method availability and other factors are more important than the extent of the determination to die.[40,] [41] In addition, people are often misinformed about the methods that are most lethal.[42] Therefore, choosing a gun over a knife or poisoning may not reflect a highly serious determination to die as the person may not be aware that guns are so much more lethal than these other methods.

Aside from their differences in the physical damage they produce, methods vary in lethality due to the speed at which the attempt occurs. Attempters who take pills, inhale car fumes, or cut themselves with a sharp instrument can change their minds or be rescued once the attempt is underway. In the case of a firearm, once the trigger is pulled, there is no opportunity to reconsider or intervene and the odds of averting death or disabling injuries are long.

Method Substitution

Research shows that we cannot assume that when a lethal suicide method becomes less available, people will simply switch to another method with the same result. If we believed that method substitution is inevitable, reducing access to lethal methods (e.g., guns) in order to prevent suicide would be futile. However, a growing number of studies show that when lethal means are made less available or less deadly, suicide rates by that method decline and, often, suicide rates as a whole decline. Consider the following cases:

In certain regions of Asia and the Pacific Islands, pesticides are among the most common suicide methods. In some areas (e.g., Sri Lanka), controlling the availability of highly lethal pesticides, such as paraquat, has brought about dramatic reductions in the overall suicide rate, indicating that large-scale substitution of other lethal methods did not occur. The fatality rate of attempts using paraquat has been reported to be over 60 %, whereas it may be below 10 % for other pesticides that have replaced paraquat.[43]

In another example, Scott Anderson of *The New York Times* has reported on the case of the Ellington and Taft Bridges in Northwest Washington, DC.[44] Both bridges span Rock Creek and both have about a 125-foot drop into the gorge below. However, the Ellington Bridge has been viewed as Washington's "suicide bridge" as it accounted for half of the city's jumping deaths.

> *The adjacent Taft, by contrast, averaged less than two suicides per year. After three people leapt from the Ellington in a single 10-day period in 1985, a consortium of civic groups lobbied for a suicide barrier to be erected on the span. Opponents to the plan … countered with the same argument that is made whenever a suicide barrier on a bridge or landmark building is proposed: that such barriers don't really work, that those intent on killing themselves will merely go elsewhere. In the Ellington's case, opponents had the added ammunition of pointing to the equally lethal Taft standing just yards away: if a barrier were placed on the Ellington, it was not at all hard to see exactly where thwarted jumpers would head.*

The opponents, however, were wrong. Five years after the Ellington barrier went up, a study showed that suicides at the Ellington were eliminated completely, while the rate at the Taft had changed only marginally. In addition, over the five-year period, the total number of jumping suicides in Washington had decreased by 50 %, the precise percentage the Ellington had once accounted for.

Why did jumpers favor the Ellington Bridge over the Taft? Anderson speculates that this was due to the height of the concrete railing on the

Taft, which stands chest-high on an average man, while the pre-barrier Ellington came to just above the belt line. A jump from either was lethal, but one required more effort and time, both of which are obstacles to impulsive suicide attempts.

One of the best examples of what can be achieved when an easily available and highly lethal means of suicide is eliminated occurred when the domestic gas supply was changed in the UK. Before 1958, domestic gas was toxic, containing over 12 % carbon monoxide. People would commit suicide simply by putting their heads in the oven. In 1958, nontoxic natural gas was introduced region by region, and, by 1974, virtually all the gas supply in the UK was nontoxic.[45] Prior to the changeover, suicide by gas inhalation was the leading means of suicide in the UK.

Keith Hawton of Oxford University notes that as the carbon monoxide content of gas supplies decreased, there was a steady reduction in carbon monoxide suicides in England and Wales. While there was a modest increase in the use of other suicide methods, the overall suicide rate decreased by a third. A similar pattern was observed in Scotland. Hawton believes that thousands of lives were saved simply by detoxifying the domestic gas supply.[46]

One additional case, reported by Swiss researchers, illustrates the fact that large-scale substitution does not typically occur when a lethal means of suicide becomes less available.[47] In the early 1990s, there was a major downsizing of the Swiss Army. With more than 625,000 men in its ranks, the Swiss Army at the time was the largest army in Western Europe. Following the end of the Cold War, the army was reduced to about 400,000 men after 1996 and to some 220,000 in 2004. These changes reduced substantially the number of citizens who kept military weapons in their homes. While former soldiers may keep their guns following their service, fewer now do so—the percentage has dropped from a peak of 90 % to 23 % in 2007.

The effect on suicide was large in the 20–49 age group, as these men were particularly affected by the reduction of the maximum age of military duty from 50 to 30. In 1995, prior to the first downsizing of troops, 187 (or 38 % of all suicides by men aged 20–49) committed suicide with a firearm, and 311 (or 62 %) did so using some other method. By 2000, the number of firearm suicides had dropped among men aged 20–49 to

170 (36 % of all suicides for this age group), whereas other suicide methods remained at 300 (or 64 % of all suicides for the group). In 2004, the year following the second downsizing of the military, firearm suicides dropped to 116 (or 33 % of the group), and other suicides remained at 232 (67 % of the group). By 2008, gun-related suicides had dropped to 76 (or 24 %), whereas other suicides remained fairly stable in this age group (245, or 76 %). Over the entire period, firearm suicides decreased among men aged 20–49 by 59 %, whereas suicides by other methods decreased by 21 %. Also interesting was the finding that there was no reduction in suicide among men over 50, a group that was not affected by the downsizing of troops.

Bottom Line

While research has not resolved all the questions about the extent to which guns contribute to suicide rates, there is mounting evidence that guns enable suicide. There is a general belief that individuals who attempt suicide are a determined lot and will eventually find a way to kill themselves. Therefore, according to this belief, restricting the availability of any given method (e.g., guns) is futile as people will simply find another way to end their lives.

In fact, many studies show that suicides are often impulsive, as the decision to attempt suicide often occurs just a few minutes or hours prior to the attempt. Also, there is frequently great ambivalence about suicide, rather than a single-minded determination to die. Many individuals who make serious attempts but survive do not repeat their attempts and most do not eventually kill themselves. The frequent impulsivity, ambivalence, and regret mean that the presence of lethal methods when an attempt is made may be all important in whether an individual succeeds in taking his or her life. There are enormous differences in lethality of methods, with firearms consistently found to be the most lethal of them all.

There is abundant evidence that suicide methods are often chosen on the basis of their availability. Many cases show that we cannot assume that people will switch to similarly lethal methods when their chosen method becomes unavailable. Therefore, much of what we know about suicide indicates that reducing access to highly lethal methods, such as firearms, is likely to lead to a reduction in suicides. Men and other groups, such as soldiers, are more likely to have access to firearms and, hence, may be more likely to experience lower suicide rates with reduced access to guns.

Notes

1. Centers for Disease Control and Prevention. Suicide and self-inflicted injury [Internet]. FastStats. Available from: http://www.cdc.gov/nchs/fastats/suicide.htm
2. Friend T. Jumpers: the fatal grandeur of the Golden Gate Bridge [Internet]. The New Yorker. 2003 Oct 13. Available from: http://www.newyorker.com/magazine/2003/10/13/jumpers
3. Miller M, Azrael D, Hemenway D. Belief in the inevitability of suicide: results from a national survey. Suicide Life Threat Behav. 2006; 36(1): 1–11.
4. Hawton K. Restriction of access to methods of suicide as a means of suicide prevention. In: Hawton K, editor. Prevention and treatment of suicidal behavior: from science to practice. Oxford: Oxford University Press; 2005. P. 283.
5. Hawton K. Restriction of access to methods of suicide. P. 284.
6. The Brady Center to Prevent Gun Violence. The truth about suicide and guns. Washington, DC: The Brady Center to Prevent Gun Violence; 2015. P. 10.
7. Seiden R. Where are they now: a follow up study of suicide attempters from the Golden Gate Bridge. Suicide Life Threat Behav. 1978; 8(4): 203–216.
8. Peterson L, Peterson M, O'Shanick G, Swann A. Self-inflicted gunshot wounds: lethality of method versus intent. Am J Psychiat. 1985; 142(2): 228–231.
9. Kost-Grant B. Self-inflicted gunshot wounds among Alaska natives. Pub Health Rep. 1983; 98(1): 72–78.
10. Simon T, Swann A, Powell K , Potter L, Kresnow M , O'Carroll P. Characteristics of impulsive suicide attempts and attempters. Suicide Life Threat Behav. 2001; 32(1): 49–59.
11. Williams C, Davidson J, Montgomery I. Impulsive suicidal behavior. J Clin Psychol. 1980; 36(1): 90–94.

12. De Moore G, Plew J, Bray K, Snars J. Survivors of self-inflicted firearm injury. A liaison psychiatry perspective. Med J Aust. 1994; 160(7): 421–425.

13. Robbins D, Conroy R. A cluster of adolescent suicide attempts: Is suicide contagious? J Adolesc Health Care, 1983; 3(4): 253–255.

14. Rosin H. The Silicon Valley suicides: why are so many kids with bright prospects killing themselves in Palo Alto [Internet]? The Atlantic. 2015 Dec. Available from: http://www.theatlantic.com/magazine/archive/2015/12/the-silicon-valley-suicides/413140/

15. Tonkin R. Suicide methods in British Columbian adolescents. J Adolesc Health Care, 1984, 5(3): 172–177.

16. Poteet D. Adolescent suicide. The Am J Forensic Med Pathol. 1987; 8(1): 12–17.

17. Seupel C. Blocking the paths to suicide [Internet]. The New York Times. 2015 Mar 9. Available from: http://mobile.nytimes.com/2015/03/10/health/blocking-the-paths-to-suicide.html?_r=1

18. Owens D, Horrocks J, House A. Fatal and non-fatal repetition of self-harm: systematic review. Br J Psychiatr. 2002;181(3): 193–199.

19. Jamison K. Night falls fast: Understanding suicide. New York: Knopf; 1999. P. 47.

20. National Alliance on Mental Illness. Common misconceptions about suicide. National Alliance on Mental Illness; 1999.

21. Harvard Injury Control Research Center. Method choice and intent [Internet]. Available from: http://www.hsph.harvard.edu/means-matter/means-matter/intent/

22. Hawton K. Restriction of access to methods of suicide as a means of suicide prevention. P. 279.

23. Peterson L et al., Self-inflicted gunshot wounds: lethality of method versus intent.

24. Centers for Disease Control and Prevention. Suicide: facts at a glance [Internet]. P. 1. Available from: http://www.cdc.gov/ViolencePrevention/pdf/Suicide_DataSheet-a.pdf.

25. Lubin G, Werbeloff N, Halperin D, Shmushkevitch M, Weiser M, Knobler H. Decrease in suicide rates after a change of policy reducing access to firearms in adolescents: a naturalistic epidemiological study. Suicide Life Threat Behav. 2010; 40(5): 421–424.

26. Moyer S, Carrington P. Gun availability and firearms suicide. Ottawa: Department of Justice Canada; 1992.

27. Mauser G. Firearm ownership in British Columbia: an empirical test of alternative models. Burnaby: Faculty of Business Administration, Simon Fraser University; 1989.

28. Lester D. Specific agents of accidental and suicidal death: comparisons by state, 1970. Sociol Soc Research. 1989; 73(4): 182–184.

29. Miller M, Lippmann S, Azrael D, Hemenway D. Household firearm ownership and rates of suicide across the 50 United States. J Trauma. 2007; 62(4): 1029–1034.

30. Brent D, Perper J, Allman C, Moritz G, Wartella M, Zelenack J. The presence and accessibility of firearms in the homes of adolescent suicides: a case-control study. JAMA. 1991; 266(21): 2989–2995.

31. Wiebe D., Homicide and suicide risks associated with firearms in the home: A national case-control study. Ann Emerg Med. 2003; 41(6): 771–782.

32. Briggs J, Tabarrok A. Firearms and suicides in US states. Int'l Rev. L Econ. 2014; 37: 180–188.

33. Miller M, Hemenway D. Gun prevalence and the risk of suicide: a review. HHPR. 2001; 2(2): 29–37.

34. Crifasi C, Meyers J, Vernick J, Webster D. Effects of changes in permit-to-purchase handgun laws in Connecticut and Missouri on suicide rates. Prev Med. 2015; 79(3): 43–49.

35. Youth Suicide by Firearms Task Force. Consensus statement of youth suicide by firearms. Arch Suicide Res 1998; 4(1): 89 94.

36. Vyrostek S, Annest J, Ryan G. Surveillance for fatal and nonfatal Injuries. MMWR. Hyattsville, MD: Centers for Disease Control and Prevention; 2004 Sep 3.

37. Spicer R, Miller T. Suicide acts in eight states: Incidents and case fatality rates by demographics and method. Am J Pub Health. 2000; 90(12): 1885–1891.

38. Elnour A, Harrison J. Lethality of suicide methods. Inj Prev. 2008; 14(1): 39–45.

39. Chapdelaine A, Samson E, Kimberley M, Viau L. Firearm-related injuries in Canada: issues for prevention. CMAJ. 1991 ; 145(10): 1217–1223.

40. Peterson L et al. Self-inflicted gunshot wounds.

41. Plutchik R, van Praag H, Picard S, Conte H, Korn M. Is there a relation between the seriousness of suicidal intent and the lethality of the suicide attempt? Psychiatry Res. 1988; 27(1): 71–79.

42. Swahn M, Potter L. Factors associated with the medical severity of suicide attempts in youth and young adults. Suicide Life Threat Behav. 2001; 32(1): 21–29.

43. Bertolote J, Fleischmann A, Eddleston M, Gunnell D. Deaths from pesticide poisoning: a global response. Br J Psychiatr. 2006; 189(3): 201–203.
44. Anderson S. The urge to end it all [Internet]. The New York Times Magazine. 2008 Jul 6. Available from: http://www.nytimes.com/2008/07/06/magazine/06suicide-t.html?_r=0
45. Hawton K. Restriction of access to methods of suicide.
46. Hawton K. Restriction of access to methods of suicide. P. 281.
47. Killias M, Markwalder N. Firearms and homicide in Europe. In: Liem M, Pridemore W, editors. Handbook of European Homicide Research. New York: Springer; 2012. P. 343–354.

7

Unintentional Deaths: Unavoidable or Preventable?

Most of the attention of the public and of research into firearm-related harm has focused on intentional rather than unintentional injuries and fatalities. When thinking of harms involving guns, people envision murders, robberies, and other crimes with guns or the use of guns in suicide attempts.

Unintentional firearm deaths and injuries can take many forms. Children can shoot themselves, siblings, or friends believing a gun is a toy or is not loaded. Hunters can mistakenly believe that another hunter is game. A gun that is dropped may discharge. Another scenario underscores the tragedies that can occur when firearms are kept at home for self-protection and individuals display errors in judgment. Consider the following case in Ohio:

> *A Cincinnati father shot and killed his 14-year-old son when police said he mistook the teen for an intruder. Police told the Associated Press that the man thought his son had gone to school Tuesday morning, but the teen went back home. The man ... heard noise in the basement, grabbed his gun and went to check it out. Then, police said, he got spooked and shot his son—striking him in the neck.*[1]

© The Author(s) 2016

T. Gabor, *Confronting Gun Violence in America*,

DOI 10.1007/978-3-319-33723-4_7

Young People Are Disproportionately Affected

From 1999 to 2010, there was an average of about 700 recorded unintentional fatalities with firearms each year in the USA, or close to two a day.[2] In 2011, there were 14,675 nonfatal unintentional firearm injuries, or about 20 for every unintentional fatal firearm injury.[3] While the predominant image of a gun accident may be that of a hunter shooting a fellow hunter, the victims are often young people. In fact, children under 15 in the USA are nine times as likely to die from a gun accident than children in 25 other industrialized countries combined.[4]

Many victims of fatal unintentional shootings are under the age of 25. Those between 15 and 19 years of age have the highest rate of unintentional fatalities by firearm. Those under 15 are also well represented among the victims, accounting for over 10 % of fatal unintentional shootings and about a third of nonfatal unintentional shootings.[5,6] Victims of fatal gun accidents are usually shot by a family member or friend of roughly the same age.[7]

An investigation by Michael Luo and Mike McIntire of *The New York Times* has revealed that the accidental shootings of children are undercounted and that the total may be twice that of the official count.[8] This is the case because many coroners simply classify any death due to the shooting of one person by another as a homicide and avoid recording whether the killing was intentional or unintentional.

The Impact of Gun Ownership

A key question is whether gun accidents are just unfortunate and random events or whether they are due to the careless actions of high-risk individuals, as one academic has claimed.[9] Equally important is whether these incidents are unavoidable or whether they are preventable through measures to improve gun safety? Public health researchers prefer the term "unintentional" shootings over "accidents" so as to convey their view that these incidents, while not intended, can be lowered significantly through reducing the number of guns in homes, improving the training of owners, and adopting gun safety measures. The statistics on the youthfulness of many victims and of the shooters appear to invalidate the notion that gun accidents are due to the negligence and recklessness of a small proportion of gun owners.

A critical question is the extent to which gun accidents are simply a matter of numbers. Whether it is bicycles, cars, or guns, it would appear logical to presume that the more prevalent these products, the more accidents, injuries, and fatalities there will be. Unlike gun homicides and suicides, which may be driven by powerful social and psychological factors, accidents are by definition unintentional. Thus, the argument that people will switch to other methods to harm others or themselves if guns are less available does not apply in the case of these incidents as the shooters are not seeking to do harm to others or themselves. While, human error and mechanical failure are important considerations in gun or car accidents, it appears intuitive that these errors and failures occur more often where there are more rather than fewer guns or cars.

When we compare Japan and the USA, the impact of the difference in the prevalence of firearms is striking. Table 7.1 shows that the USA has about two and a half times Japan's population. However, according to the most recent data available from Japan, the USA has over *120 times* Japan's number of unintentional gun deaths (851 vs. 7). Adjusting for population differences, the USA has about 45 times more unintentional gun deaths than does Japan (2.7 vs. .06 deaths per million people). This is an astounding difference. Is this due to the enormous disparity in gun ownership or are Americans just much more accident prone and careless with guns than the Japanese?

As Table 7.1 shows, the USA has about 88 times the rate of gun owners per million people as Japan. Recent surveys show that in the USA about 22 % of the population are gun owners;[10] whereas, in Japan, there are about 2.5 licensed gun owners for every 1000 people, well under 1 % of the population.[11] Are Americans more prone to gun accidents due to carelessness or other factors? We calculated the fraction of gun owners who die from a gun accident and found that in Japan there is approximately one fatality for every 42,000 gun owners. In the USA, there is an unintentional gun fatality for every 81,000 gun owners. The lower fatality rate per owner in the USA can be due to a variety of reasons, from owner-related factors to differences in the uses and quality of guns in the

Table 7.1 Unintentional firearm deaths in Japan and the USA

	Japan	United States
Population	127 million (2013)	316 million (2013)
Unintentional firearm deaths	7 (1999)	851 (2011)
Unintentional firearm death rate per million people	.06	2.7
Gun owners per million people	2500	220,000
Ratio of unintentional gun deaths to gun owners	1:42,000	1:81,000

Sources: Statistics Japan, Statistics Bureau. January 1, 2013 (final estimates) [Internet]. Ministry of Internal Affairs and Communications. Monthly report. Available from: http://www.stat.go.jp/english/data/jinsui/tsuki/index.htm; United States Census Bureau. United States and world population clock. [Internet]. Available from: http://www.census.gov/popclock/; Japan: Guns, facts, figures and the law [Internet]. Gunpolicy.org. Available from: http://www. gunpolicy.org/firearms/region/japan; National Center for Injury Control and Prevention, Centers for Disease Control and Prevention. WISQARS 20 leading causes of nonfatal unintentional injury, United States 2011, All Races, Both Sexes, Disposition: All Cases [Internet]. Available from: http://webappa.cdc.gov/ cgi-bin/broker.exe

two countries. These data provide absolutely no support for the notion that American owners are more accident prone.

Regardless of the reasons for the lower fatality rate per owner in the USA, these figures illustrate that the massive gap in fatal gun accidents is very likely due to the much higher level of gun ownership in the USA. This is the case because the number of these fatalities is far higher—45 times higher adjusting for population differences—in the USA despite the fact that the average Japanese gun owners is about two times as likely to be the victim of a fatal gun accident. This comparison between the two countries illustrates the extent to which gun ownership levels can override other factors that may contribute to gun-related mortality.

There are very compelling findings about the importance of gun ownership levels when US states are compared. Researchers at Harvard University's School of Public Health examined the link between gun availability and state unintentional gun death rates over a 19-year period. For every age group, states with more guns tended to have more accidental gun deaths than states with fewer guns. The death rate was seven times higher in the four states with the most guns compared to the four states with the fewest guns.[12] In a more recent study, David Hemenway of Harvard compared high and low gun states and found that the average resident from the states with the highest gun ownership levels was six times more likely to die in a gun accident than the average resident from the six states with the lowest gun ownership levels.[13]

Douglas Wiebe of UCLA's School of Public Health used national data to estimate the risk of death by an unintentional gunshot associated with having firearms in the home.[14] A sample of 84 adults who died in the USA in 1993 from unintentional gunshot injuries was selected and compared with 1451 control subjects who were matched to the cases by sex, age group, race, and region of residence. The relative risk of death by an unintentional gunshot injury was nearly four times greater for subjects living in homes with guns than those living in homes without guns. Persons living in multiple gun households and homes with handguns were at greater risk than those residing in homes with one long gun. Wiebe concluded that firearms in the home appear to be a risk factor for an unintentional gunshot fatality among adults.

My collaborators and I conducted a Canadian study of the link between firearm ownership and unintentional firearm deaths. The study compared the provinces and territories of Canada over a ten-year period (1988–1997) and revealed a very strong link between the ownership levels of a province and its unintentional death rate due to gunshot.[15] While these findings do not demonstrate that higher ownership levels *cause* more of these unintentional gun deaths, the findings point to what may appear obvious to many. Everything else being equal, places with more guns will experience more fatal gun accidents than places with fewer guns.

The finding that locations (countries, states, homes) with higher levels of gun ownership have more fatal gun accidents strongly suggests that these accidents are a matter of numbers. In the case of homicide or suicide, there are many social, economic, and psychological factors that can produce high mortality rates. For example, area *A* may have higher gun ownership levels and homicide rates than *B*, but *A*'s higher ownership levels may not be a cause of its higher homicide rates. *A* may have higher levels of violence, including homicide, due to persistent poverty and an active gang situation and the high gun ownership levels in the area may be due to the violence rather than the reverse.

It is unlikely that there are deeply rooted social and economic reasons for unintentional gun deaths. Unless one can demonstrate that gun owners in one area are more accident prone, a link between gun ownership levels and fatal gun accidents may reflect a causal rather than a mere statistical link. For example, the large gap between the USA and other high-income countries in accidental shooting deaths is either due to the more widespread ownership and accessibility of guns in the USA or a much higher level of accident proneness of Americans. The case has not been made that Americans are more accident prone than citizens of other countries. It would be quite a stretch to attribute the enormous gap in unintentional firearm deaths between the USA and other high-income countries to anything but to factors such as the higher level of gun ownership, greater accessibility of loaded guns to children, and the prevalence of gun carrying in the USA.

In addition, when it comes to unintentional deaths by firearm, the substitution idea is irrelevant as, by definition, nobody intends to commit an unintentional act. While, in theory at least, those committing homicide and suicide may find other means to commit these acts where guns are their weapon/instrument of choice and are unavailable, this idea cannot be applied to unintentional deaths as, by definition, nobody plans to have an accident. Thus, with unintentional deaths by firearm, the case can be made more persuasively that lowering the availability of firearms in an area will reduce these fatalities. One would not expect accidental deaths from other sources to increase as a result.

Dennis Henigan, formerly a vice president of the Brady Campaign to Prevent Gun Violence, explains why guns are more dangerous than other weapons.[16] Henigan argues that, unlike knives, clubs, and other potential weapons that are designed for other purposes, guns are designed to kill humans or animals by expelling a projectile at a high speed. Whether, it is acquired for self-protection, to hunt, or for criminal purposes, a firearm is a tool that is designed primarily to kill or to immobilize a target. Henigan adds that, unlike other weapons and as an indication of their lethality, guns often kill and inflict serious injuries even when the user does not intend any harm.

In his book *Lethal Logic* Henigan recounts the story from his childhood of a neighbor who was shot accidentally by her husband while he was cleaning his handgun at the kitchen table. It is an obvious truth that people are rarely killed during the cleaning of knives, baseball bats, or other potential weapons. Henigan explains that, apart from their greater lethality, guns are more susceptible to accidentally injuring the user or others because they are more complex than these other weapons. For example, accidents often occur because people, often children, are unaware that a gun is real or loaded. In other cases, a gun discharges after it has been dropped. In still other cases, hunting accidents are enabled by the long range of rifles and shotguns as people are mistaken for game. Henigan notes that Americans are six times more likely to die from an accidental firearm discharge than from an accident involving a knife or other sharp object.[17] This is the case despite the fact that knives and other sharp objects are present in far more homes, are greater in number, and are used more frequently than are guns.

Accident Victims: Accident Prone or Genuine Victims?

Criminologist Gary Kleck of Florida State University has taken the unique position that gun accidents are often due to recklessness rather than being genuine accidents. Such a view is in conflict with the work of virtually every public health researcher who has studied gun accidents. Let's examine his statements and logic.

Kleck argues that males, African-Americans, and young persons between 15 and 24 years of age are overrepresented in fatal gun accidents. He then states, "These are the same groups that show the highest rates of intentional violence such as homicide, both as offenders and as victims, suggesting that there are some common predisposing factors shared by participants in accidents and participants in acts of intentional violence."[18] Further on he argues that "one can view the reckless behavior that precedes many accidents as deviant behavior" and then applies the theory that those involved in gun accidents are more likely to be risk-takers with low self-control.[19] He cites as evidence one study conducted in Vermont that found that individuals involved in gun accidents, whether shooters or victims, were more likely to be involved in a highway crash in the three previous years than other drivers.

It is interesting that *victims*—not just shooters—of homicide and of firearm accidents are also portrayed as persons with low self-control with a particular proneness to accidents. Also, showing that certain age and other groups may have a higher accident rate can be due to a host of reasons. Demonstrating, for example, that youth are more likely to be involved in an accident (when exposure to firearms is taken into account) than are adults falls far short of showing that they are reckless. Adults may be more knowledgeable about firearms, may use them for different purposes, and may be more prudent. None of this demonstrates that accidents involving youth, especially where the youth is a victim and not a shooter, proves that youth are reckless and to blame for accidents that befall them.

Kleck also claims that alcohol is frequently a factor in gun accidents. His primary source for this claim is a 1975 study in which *victims* of fatal gun accidents were examined for ethanol in the blood. Close to half of the victims had alcohol in their blood.[20] In self-inflicted gun accidents, the victim is also the shooter. However, there is no indication as to how many incidents were self-inflicted and how many cases involved actual impairment rather than simply alcohol consumption. No justification is provided by Kleck for looking at victim alcohol consumption where the victim was not also the shooter. Overall, he provides no proof that victims of gun accidents contribute to their victimization.

Kleck also refers to studies of fatal gun accidents by Metropolitan Life Insurance Company and states that "cases involving clearly reckless activities were common."[21] In fact, the MetLife studies he cited found that about 30 % of cases in which the circumstances were recorded involved playing with a weapon or Russian roulette. He claims that the cases that resulted from playing were clearly evidence of recklessness although he makes no mention of the significant number of cases involving children and other minors. Is he suggesting that a five-year old playing with a gun in the belief that it is a toy is engaging in reckless behavior? Is it not the role of parents and society to ensure that young children do not have access to loaded guns?

Most of the MetLife studies to which Kleck refers are over 50 years old. The habits of Americans have changed drastically since then, as there are fewer hunters today but more handguns being carried in public and kept in the home for self-defense. It is likely that there will be far more accidents involving children in the home today than in the 1940s and 1950s. Due to their age, these studies could not be located by the present author, and Kleck does not report the age breakdown of the subjects. If only the cases involving adults were examined, it may be safe to assume that the proportion of fatal accidents that occurred after careless handling of a gun would be well under the 30 % figure mentioned above. Kleck also does not address the fact that insurance companies have an incentive to show that accidents were the fault of the owner as this may permit them to deny claims. Insurance industry data may therefore be highly suspect, a point that Kleck acknowledges.[22]

Kleck concludes:

> *One cannot have a gun accident without a gun. The presence of a gun in the vicinity of risk-taking or reckless persons is a significant additional hazard in the environment of persons who need as few hazards around them as possible. At the same time, gun accidents are not an inevitable byproduct of routine gun ownership by ordinary people. They appear to most commonly be the result of reckless or aggressive behavior by the same kind of individuals responsible both for intentional violence and other types of accidents. … Gun accidents are but one part of a larger picture of their reckless disregard for their own safety and the safety of others.*[23]

While Kleck makes a passing reference to the importance of the presence of a gun and of gun ownership levels in gun accidents, his perspective is one that departs dramatically from conventional thinking on gun accidents and is based on important omissions and a questionable interpretation of the evidence. While the evidence points strongly to a link between gun ownership and fatal gun accidents—something he acknowledges—his narrative places the bulk of the blame for these events on certain categories of gun owners and even victims of unintentional shootings. In Kleck's narrative, children and youth are virtually ignored as participants in these tragedies despite the fact that 25 % of victims are under the age of 21.[24]This omission is serious as one cannot expect children and youth to demonstrate the same degree of maturity and responsibility expected of adults.

Kleck's own evidence does not support the view that most fatal gun accidents arise from reckless rather than routine handling. He minimizes the role of the prevalence of guns in favor of blaming shooters and victims of gun accidents for their fate.

In fact, public health researchers, using more recent and comprehensive data, have documented the fact that the majority of incidents involve routine handling, and it is for this reason that they argue that the focus with regard to gun accidents ought to be on the gun and its safety features, rather than on reckless behavior.

Researchers at the Centers for Disease Control and Prevention examined a national sample of unintentional, nonfatal firearm injuries requiring hospital care between 1992 and 1994.[25] The majority of patients were males between 15 and 34 years of age, and most of the injuries occurred as a result of routine, gun handling activities as opposed to playing with firearms or other careless activities. These routine activities included gun cleaning, loading/unloading, hunting, target shooting, and showing, handling, or carrying a firearm.

One study of fatal gun accidents involving children found that in 20 % of these incidents, the child shooting the firearm simply was not aware it was loaded.[26] Many adults are also uninformed about guns. One national survey of adults found that approximately 35 % of respondents incorrectly believed that a firearm with its ammunition magazine removed could not be shot, or said that they did not know whether this was the case.[27]

Several studies have sought to determine the number of unintentional firearm fatalities that could have been prevented through the use of one or more firearm safety devices. Such studies examine the specific circumstances of these gun accidents, and rules are established in determining whether an incident might have been prevented had a specific device(s) been required. These cases provide an idea as to the minimum number of genuine accidents that were due to such things as the mistaken belief that a firearm was not loaded. These cases do not include other types of genuine accidents that cannot be prevented through safety devices (e.g., hunters shooting fellow hunters). Therefore, the studies that follow provide a minimum figure of unintentional deaths by firearm that are genuine accidents.

The US General Accounting Office estimated that 23 % of a sample of unintentional deaths could have been prevented by a loaded chamber indicator and 8 % could have been prevented by a childproofing device.[28] The childproofing device referred to was one that can prevent the discharge of a firearm by young children.

Jon Vernick and his associates at the Johns Hopkins Bloomberg School of Public Health conducted a study to determine the proportion of unintentional and undetermined firearm-related deaths that were preventable by three safety devices: personalization devices, loaded chamber indicators (LCIs), and magazine safeties. A personalized gun operates only for an authorized user, an LCI indicates when the gun contains ammunition, and a magazine safety prevents the gun from firing when the ammunition magazine is removed.[29]

The researchers collected information on all unintentional and undetermined firearm deaths from 1991 to 98 from Maryland's Office of the Chief Medical Examiner and from the Wisconsin Firearm Injury Reporting System for Milwaukee. Out of a total of 117 firearm deaths in the sample, 37 % were classified as preventable by a personalized gun, 20 % by an LCI, and 4 % by a magazine safety. Overall, 44 % of the deaths were deemed to be preventable by at least one safety device. Nationally, the researchers estimated that 442 deaths might have been prevented in 2000 had all guns been equipped with these safety devices.

These two studies show that a third to almost a half of all fatal gun accidents might be prevented through simple gun safety devices and that, at a minimum, these incidents have nothing to do with reckless handling of firearms. These are instances of preventable human errors or of the access of children to loaded guns.

The improper storage of firearms is another issue that can contribute to gun accidents, especially among children who gain access to and play with loaded guns. A study of 88 fatal gun accidents involving children in California found that in over a third of the cases the child shooter did not know the gun was loaded or mistook it for a toy.[30] Incidents of careless playing with firearms that the children knew were loaded were unusual. Blood alcohol levels were normal in all victims and shooters.

Several American studies have found that many firearm owners keep guns loaded in the home and, in many cases, also keep loaded guns unlocked and within the reach of children. For example, a study of family heads in Philadelphia, Pennsylvania, found that just 21 % of the families owning a gun stored them safely—locked, unloaded, and out of the reach of children.[31] Data from the National Health Interview Survey have shown that 40 % of gun-owning households with children stored their guns unlocked.[32] Furthermore, a national study by Harvard University researchers found that states where loaded firearms were more likely to be stored unlocked had higher rates of unintentional firearm deaths.[33]

Bottom Line

The USA has high rates of fatal gun accidents relative to other countries. Many of the victims are children and youth. The comparison of the USA with Japan, a country with strict gun laws and very low ownership levels, illustrates the extent to which gun accidents are a numbers game: the more guns there are, the more fatal gun accidents there are likely to be. States with the highest gun ownership levels also tend to have more accidents than those with the lowest ownership levels.

Guns are especially dangerous because they are more lethal than other weapons and because they are more complex than knives or other weapons. Users are often unaware that a gun is loaded or that it can fire with the ammunition magazine removed. Children may tragically believe that a gun is a toy when this is not the case. The evidence does not support the position that most of those involved in gun accidents are reckless people rather than the victims of misfortune. The idea that the victims of fatal gun accidents are reckless individuals is both inaccurate and offensive. Many victims are children and youth, victims only rarely have been shown to be impaired by alcohol, and most fatal gun accidents occur during the routine handling of a firearm. The evidence suggests that a significant proportion of fatal gun accidents can be prevented through better gun storage practices, improved education, and training in gun safety, through the use of basic devices that can indicate when a gun is loaded, and features that can prevent the discharge of a firearm by a young child or other unauthorized user.

Notes

1. Bever L. Ohio father fatally shoots suspected intruder who turned out to be his teen son [Internet]. The Washington Post. 2016 Jan 12. Available from: https://www.washingtonpost.com/news/morning-mix/wp/2016/01/12/ohio-father-fatally-shoots-suspected-intruder-who-turned-out-to-be-his-teen-son/
2. National Center for Injury Prevention and Control (US). Unintentional injuries 1999–2010. Atlanta: National Vital Statistics System Web-Based Injury Statistics Query & Reporting System (WISQARS) Injury Mortality Reports; 2012 Dec.
3. National Center for Injury Prevention and Control (US). WISQARS 20 leading causes of nonfatal unintentional injury, United States 2011, all races, both sexes, disposition: all cases [Internet]. Atlanta: Centers for Disease Control and Prevention. Available from: http://webappa.cdc.gov/cgi-bin/broker.exe
4. Centers for Disease Control and Prevention (US). Rates of homicide, suicide, and firearm-related death among children in 26 industrialized countries. MMWR (Morbidity and Mortality Weekly Report). 1997 Feb 7; 46(5): 101–105.
5. Hemenway D. Private guns, public health. Ann Arbor: University of Michigan Press; 2004. P. 27–29.
6. National Center for Injury Control and Prevention (US). WISQARS 20 Leading causes of nonfatal unintentional injury.
7. Hemenway D, Barber C, Miller M. Unintentional firearm deaths: a comparison of other-inflicted and self-inflicted shootings. Accid Anal Prev. 2010; 42(4): 1184–1188.
8. Luo M, McIntire M. Children and guns: the hidden toll [Internet]. The New York Times. 2013 Sept 28. Available from: http://mobile.nytimes.com/2013/09/29/us/children-and-guns-the-hidden-toll.html?_r=0
9. Kleck G. Targeting guns: firearms and their control. New York: Aldine de Gruyter; 1997. P. 384.
10. McGinty E, Webster D, Vernick J, Barry C. Public opinion on proposals to strengthen US gun laws. In: Webster D, Vernick J, editors. Reducing gun violence in America. Baltimore: Johns Hopkins; 2013. P. 241.
11. Japan: Guns, Facts, Figures and the Law [Internet]. Gunpolicy.org. Available from: http://www.gunpolicy.org/firearms/region/japan
12. Miller M, Azrael D, Hemenway D. Firearm availability and unintentional firearm deaths. Accid Anal Prev. 2001; 33(4): 477–484.

13. Hemenway D. Risks and benefits of a gun in the home. Am J Lifestyle Med. 2011; 5(6): 1–10.

14. Wiebe D. Firearms in US homes as a risk factor for unintentional gunshot fatality. Accid Anal Prev. 2003; 35(5): 711–716.

15. Gabor T, Roberts J, Stein K, DiGiulio L. Unintentional firearm deaths: can they be reduced by lowering gun ownership levels? Can J Public Health. 2001; 92(5): 396–398.

16. Henigan D. Lethal logic: exploding the myths that paralyze American gun policy. Washington, DC: Potomac Books; 2009. P. 19, 27.

17. Henigan D., Lethal Logic. P. 28.

18. Kleck G. Targeting guns. P. 304.

19. Kleck G. Targeting guns. P. 307.

20. Rushforth N, Hirsch C, Ford A, Adelson L. Accidental firearm fatalities in a metropolitan county (1958–1975). Am J Epidemiology. 1975; 100: 499–505.

21. Kleck G. Targeting guns. P. 309.

22. Kleck G. Targeting guns. P. 309.

23. Kleck G. Targeting guns. P. 313–314.

24. National Center for Injury Prevention and Control (US). WISQARS, 2007, United States unintentional firearm deaths and rates per 100,000 [Internet]. Atlanta: Centers for Disease Control and Prevention. Available from: http://webappa.cdc.gov/cgi-bin/broker.exe

25. Sinauer N, Annest J, Mercy J. Unintentional, nonfatal firearm-related injuries. A preventable public health burden. JAMA. 1996; 275(22): 1740–1743.

26. Wintemute G, Teret S, Kraus J. When children shoot children: eighty-eight unintended deaths in California. JAMA. 1987; 257(22): 3107–3109.

27. Vernick J, Meisel Z, Teret S, Milne J, Hargarten S. "I didn't know the gun was loaded": an examination of two safety devices that can reduce the risk of unintentional firearm injuries. J Public Health Policy, 1999; 20(4): 427–440.

28. United States General Accounting Office. Accidental shootings: many deaths and injuries caused by firearms could be prevented. Washington, DC: United States General Accounting Office; 1991. P. 1–47.

29. Vernick J, O'Brien M, Hepburn L, Johnson S, Webster D, Hargarten S. Unintentional and undetermined firearm related deaths: a preventable death analysis for three safety devices. Inj Prev. 2003; 9(4): 307–311.

30. Wintemute G, Teret S, Kraus J. When children shoot children.

31. Wiley C, Casey R. Family experiences, attitudes, and household safety practices regarding firearms. Clin Pediatr. 1993; 32(2): 71–76.
32. Schuster M, Franke T, Bastian A, Sor S, Halfon N. Firearm storage patterns in U.S. homes with children. Am J Public Health, 2000; 90(4): 588–594.
33. Miller M, Azrael D, Hemenway D, Vriniotis M. Firearm storage practices and rates of unintentional firearm deaths in the United States. Accid Anal Prev. 2005; 37(4): 661–667.

8

The Deadliest States

America's 50 states provide a "natural" laboratory to assess the impact of gun ownership on public safety. Knowing which states have the most gun crimes and deaths provides clues as to whether guns afford overall protection to the public or whether they are a threat to public safety. A key question is: Do states with the highest gun ownership levels have the highest or lowest rates of gun violence? Also explored in this chapter is the impact of a state's gun laws on its levels of gun violence.

While gun deaths may be shaped by many factors, such as a state's levels of poverty, degree of urbanization, and the age of its population, statistical methods are available to take these factors into account and to isolate the impact of gun ownership. If guns overall serve to protect citizens from harm, as gun-rights advocates argue, we would expect states with higher levels of gun ownership to report fewer gun deaths than states with lower ownership levels. On the other hand, if states with higher levels of gun ownership tend to have more gun deaths than those with fewer gun owners, this finding would suggest that guns are having an adverse effect on public safety.

There is one other possibility. There may be no consistent link at all between gun ownership and gun death rates. While some states with high

© The Author(s) 2016
T. Gabor, *Confronting Gun Violence in America*,
DOI 10.1007/978-3-319-33723-4_8

gun ownership levels have high gun death rates, a comparable number of these states may have low gun death rates. Those states with low levels of gun ownership also may have varying gun death rates. If this lack of a pattern was found, one could neither argue that gun ownership was protective or harmful. Rather, such a finding would suggest that gun death rates and ownership levels are unrelated and that other factors likely account for the varying gun death rates across the states.

Comparing States with the Most and Least Gun Deaths

When we compare the states using a number of methods, a clear pattern emerges. One method is to compare the extremes: the states with the highest and lowest gun-related mortality rates. Information on gun deaths by state was obtained from the CDC's National Center for Injury Prevention and Control.[1] Data on gun ownership were obtained from the analysis of a very large national survey by CDC researchers.[2]

Table 8.1 Gun ownership levels in the states with the highest and lowest gun death rates (2014)

States with the five *highest* gun death rates			States with the five *lowest* gun death rates		
Rank	State	Gun death rate per 100,000	Household gun ownership (%)	Rank	State	Gun death rate per 100,000	Household gun ownership (%)
1	Alaska	19.2	60.6	50	Hawaii	2.6	9.7
2	Louisiana	19.0	45.6	49	Rhode Island	3.0	13.3
3	Mississippi	18.3	54.3	48	Massachusetts	3.2	12.8
4	Alabama	16.9	57.2	47	New York	4.2	18.1
5	Arkansas	16.6	58.3	46	Connecticut	5.0	16.2

Source: Centers for Disease Control and Prevention, National Center for Health Statistics. Underlying Cause of Death 1999–2014 on CDC WONDER Online Database, released 2015. Data are from the Multiple Cause of Death Files, 1999–2014; Okoro, C, Nelson, A, Mercy, JA, Balluz, A, Crosby, A, Mokdad, A. (2002). Prevalence of household firearms and firearm-storage practices in the 50 states and the District of Columbia: findings from the Behavioral Risk Factor Surveillance System, 2002. Pediatr. 2002; 116(3): 370–376

The findings presented in Table 8.1 are dramatic. In 2014, the five states with the highest gun death rates were Alaska, Louisiana, Mississippi, Alabama, and Arkansas. On average, these states experienced 18.0 gun deaths per 100,000 people. The five states with the lowest gun death rates were Hawaii, Rhode Island, Massachusetts, New York, and Connecticut. These states had an average of 3.6 gun deaths for every 100,000 people. Thus, when population differences were taken into account, the five states with the highest gun death rates had five times the gun deaths as the states with the lowest gun death rates.

This is an enormous difference in gun deaths when these two sets of states are compared. If guns served as a deterrent to gun violence and as a means of protection, one would expect the states with the lowest gun death rates to have the largest number of gun owners. In reality, the opposite is true. Nationally, as seen in Chap. 2, about a third of American households own one or more firearms. In the five states with the most gun deaths per 100,000, more than half of all households (55.2 %) own at least one gun. Conversely, in the states with the lowest gun death rates, just one in every seven households (14 %) owns a gun. This analysis indicates that, at the state level, higher gun ownership levels are associated with more rather than fewer gun deaths.

The Link Between State Gun Ownership and Homicide

Matthew Miller and his colleagues at Harvard University's School of Public Health examined the link between rates of household firearm ownership and homicide across the states over a ten-year period (1988–1997).[3] Using a measure of gun ownership that has been validated in previous research, the researchers found that, after accounting for the effects of poverty and urbanization, people in states with high gun ownership levels had elevated rates of homicide, particularly firearm homicide. This finding applied to every age group. The authors acknowledged that the study could not definitively determine causation as high levels of homicide could conceivably lead many people to acquire guns, rather than the reverse. This said, the ten-year time span of the study provided sufficient time for a crime deterrent effect to kick in if, in fact, the acquisition of guns on a large scale really did prevent crime.

In another study conducted in the early 2000s, the same Harvard research team used survey data to determine the levels of gun ownership in each state.[4] Once again, they found that states with higher gun ownership levels had higher rates of firearm homicide and total homicide. This study was powerful as the researchers sought to isolate the impact of gun ownership on homicide by statistically controlling the effects on homicide of other forms of violence (aggravated assault and robbery), unemployment, urbanization, poverty, and alcohol consumption.

A more recent study conducted by Michael Siegel of Boston University's School of Public Health and two associates analyzed data over a 30-year period (1981–2010).[5] The long study period allowed the authors to not only compare states with varying gun ownership levels over several decades but also observe the impact on homicide of changes in gun ownership levels over time. The study isolated the impact of gun ownership on firearm homicide by statistically controlling (accounting for) the impact of a host of social, economic, and demographic factors, such as urbanization, income inequality, alcohol consumption, and the proportion of young adults. The researchers found that gun ownership was a significant predictor of firearm homicide rates. Specifically, for each percentage point increase in gun ownership, the firearm homicide rate increased by almost 1 %. Over the 30-year period, states with higher rates of gun ownership experienced more gun homicides and total homicides.

As for the risks faced by women in different states, a Harvard study examined the link between firearm availability and homicide, suicide, and unintentional gun death for women across the 50 states over a ten-year period. The study found that women in states with high gun ownership levels have elevated rates of unintentional gun deaths, suicides, and homicide, particularly firearm suicides and homicides.[6] In another study by researchers at Harvard's School of Public Health, the 16 states with the highest rates of gun ownership were compared with the 6 states with the lowest ownership rates. The two groups of states each had a total of about 31 million adults in 2009. Collectively, the states with the high rates of gun ownership had over four times as many gun suicides as the states with the lowest ownership rates. The nongun suicide rates were almost identical in the two groups of states, indicating that there was no apparent shift to other methods in states with the lowest ownership rates.[7]

Anthony Hoskin of the University of Texas examined the link between gun availability and three types of violent crime across America's 120 most populous counties.[8] He found strong support for the view that easy access to guns raises the risk of serious violence, as homicide rates increased along with gun ownership rates. Nine variables that might affect homicide rates were statistically controlled in order to isolate the impact of ownership. The analysis ruled out the possibility that homicide rates increased gun ownership, rather than the reverse. Hoskin also looked at aggravated assault and robbery rates and found no support for the idea that widespread gun ownership lowers violent crime by deterring potential offenders.

State Gun Laws and Mortality Rates

Another way of assessing the impact of firearms on mortality is to compare states having very restrictive gun regulations with those that are highly permissive. First, we needed a system to rate states in terms of the strictness of their gun regulations. In 2011, the Brady Campaign Against Gun Violence scored each state on a number of measures to determine the extent to which each state exceeded federal regulations.[9] Using research conducted on each state by the San Francisco-based Law Center to Prevent Gun Violence, Brady scored states on such things as whether

- the state requires permits to purchase handguns;
- dealers require a state license;
- gun purchases are limited to one per month;
- background checks are enhanced;
- assault weapons are banned;
- gun magazine limits exist;
- child safety laws exist;
- guns are limited in certain public places; and

- state law enforcement had the discretion to deny applicants a concealed weapons permit.

Using the Brady Scorecard, we then identified the ten states with the highest scores and therefore the strictest gun regulations. According to the scorecard, California, with 81 of a maximum of 100 points, had the toughest laws in the country, as the state had introduced numerous measures that exceeded federal requirements. We then sought to identify the ten states with the weakest laws but, due to ties in the Brady scores, ended up with nine states that had 0–2 points on the Brady Scorecard. These very low scores indicate that these states had introduced few, if any, measures that tightened or expanded upon federal rules.

We then compared firearm mortality rates for the states with the strongest and weakest regulations. Table 8.2 shows that, collectively, the states with the weakest laws had almost *two and a half times* the average firearm mortality rate possessed by the strictest states—14.5 versus 6.3 firearm deaths per 100,000 people. There are obviously many factors, other than firearm regulations, that can contribute to lower mortality rates. One factor, other than gun laws, that could account for the differences between the two groups of states is the overall rate of violent crime (both gun and nongun violence). Could it be that the states with the weakest regulations also happened to have the highest rates of violence and this factor, rather than gun laws, accounted for the higher gun death rate? As the table shows, we looked at this possibility and found that, in 2010, violent crime rates were actually slightly higher in the states with the strongest gun regulations. Thus, these states had fewer gun deaths despite the fact that they had more violent crimes.

In the USA, there is a strong link between community size and homicide rates.[10] We therefore examined the possibility that the level of urbanization, rather than firearm regulations, was responsible for the differential mortality figures displayed in the table. Thus, if the strictest states had fewer urban residents, it could be this factor, rather than the regulations, that was responsible for their lower rates of firearm mortality.

In fact, Table 8.2 shows that, collectively, the states with the strictest regulations had a substantially higher level of urbanization than the states with the weakest rules—89.5 % of the population of the strictest states

Table 8.2 Firearm mortality rates in the most restrictive and permissive states

State	Brady score	Age-adjusted firearm mortality rate PER 100,000	Violent crime rate per 100,000	% Urban population	% Population living in poverty (2010)
California	81	7.7	440.6	95.0	15.8
New Jersey	72	5.2	307.7	94.7	10.3
Massachusetts	65	4.1	466.6	92.0	11.4
New York	62	5.1	392.1	87.9	14.9
Connecticut	58	5.9	281.4	88.0	10.1
Hawaii	50	3.2	262.7	91.9	10.7
Maryland	45	9.3	547.7	87.2	9.9
Rhode Island	44	4.6	256.6	90.7	14.0
Illinois	35	8.2	435.2	88.5	13.8
Pennsylvania	26	10.1	366.2	78.7	13.4
Average for the most restrictive states	**53.8**	**6.3**	**375.7**	**89.5**	**12.4**
Alaska	0	20.4	638.8	66.0	9.9
Arizona	0	14.6	408.1	89.8	17.4
Utah	0	12.2	212.7	90.6	13.2
Louisiana	2	19.2	549.0	73.2	18.7
Idaho	2	12.8	221.0	70.6	15.7
Kentucky	2	12.4	242.6	58.4	19.0
Oklahoma	2	14.4	479.5	66.2	16.9
Montana	2	15.4	272.2	55.9	14.6
North Dakota	2	9.5	225.0	59.9	13.0
Average for the most permissive states	**1.3**	**14.5**	**361.0**	**70.1**	**15.4**

Sources: Brady Campaign 2011 Scorecards [Internet]. Washington, DC: Brady Center to Prevent Gun Violence; 2011. Available from: http://www. bradycampaign.org/xshare/stateleg/scorecard/2011/2011_scoring_system.pdf; Centers for Disease Control and Prevention. National Vital Statistics System (2010); United States Census Bureau (2010). Urban and rural population by state [Internet]. Available from: http://www.census.gov/geo/reference/ua/ urban-rural-2010.html; Bishaw A. Poverty: 2010 and 2011, American Community Survey Briefs [Internet]. US Census Bureau. Available from: http:// www.census.gov/prod/2012pubs/acsbr11-01.pdf; Federal Bureau of Investigation. Uniform Crime Reports, Crime in the United States 2010, Table 4 [Internet]. Available from: http://www.fbi.gov/about-us/cjis/ucr/ crime-in-the-u.s/2010/crime-in-the-u.s.-2010/tables/10tbl04.xls

versus 70.1 % of the population of the most permissive states was urban as of 2010, the last census for which this information was available. This finding indicates that the firearm mortality rates of the strictest states were less than half of those in the more permissive states despite the fact that the strictest states were also more urbanized. It is likely that the differences in mortality might be even greater if the most permissive states became as heavily urbanized as the states with the toughest gun regulations.

Economic factors could also conceivably explain the higher firearm mortality rates in the states with the weakest regulations. In fact, poverty levels were higher in these states than in those with stronger regulations. However, as the table shows, the difference between the two groups of states in the proportion of the population living in poverty was 3 %. This modest difference could hardly explain the 134 % higher gun mortality rates in the states with the weakest regulations.

While our findings do not definitively show that stronger gun laws lower gun-related mortality, they do rule out three major competing explanations for the very substantial differences in gun deaths. The findings suggest that licensing requirements on owners and dealers, limiting child access to guns, and other regulations to promote safety may substantially reduce gun-related deaths.

Dr. Eric Fleegler, a Boston pediatric emergency physician, and his colleagues rated states on five categories of laws (e.g., laws dealing with gun trafficking, enhanced background checks, child safety laws) to develop a "legislative strength" score.[11] States were placed in four categories or quartiles, depending on the strength of their gun laws. The researchers calculated a firearm fatality rate for each state based on an average rate over a four-year period (2007–2010). When a number of socioeconomic and demographic factors were statistically controlled, the researchers found that the states with the weakest gun laws collectively had over six times more gun deaths per 100,000 people than did the states with the highest legislative strength scores—an enormous difference.

The Children's Defense Fund, a children's advocacy group, identified the states that were on the top ten lists for gun homicides and suicides for both children and adults.[12] Four states made both lists, indicating that they are leaders in the nation with regard to gun-related death, whether those deaths are homicides or are self-inflicted. These states are

Louisiana, New Mexico, Tennessee, and Oklahoma. According to the Brady Scorecard, all four of these states had scores of eight or less, placing them all among the states with the weakest gun laws.[13]

Another study divided states into those with strict and nonstrict firearm laws, based on the presence or absence of enhanced background checks, gun licensing requirements, and child safety measures.[14] Using the 2009 Nationwide Inpatient Sample, firearm pediatric injury rates were found to be higher in the states with nonstrict gun laws. The investigators concluded that children living in states with strict firearm legislation are safer.

State Gun Ownership and Homicides of Law Enforcement Officers

One would expect to find more killings of police officers in New Jersey, a state with some of America's most dangerous cities (e.g., Camden and Newark), than one would find in Montana, a state with a large rural population and pristine national parks. This is not the case and David Swedler, who teaches at the University of Illinois (Chicago) School of Public Health, states that the most powerful explanation for the location of police killings is the availability of guns.[15] More than nine in ten officers killed in the line of duty are killed with guns. Swedler and his colleagues examined cases of police officers killed between 1996 and 2010.[16] When they compared states with high and low gun ownership levels, the researchers found that police officers in the high ownership states were three times more likely to be killed than officers in the low gun ownership states. Officer deaths were more strongly linked to state gun ownership levels than to violent crime rates.

Bottom Line

Different research methods arrive at the same conclusion: States with high gun ownership levels and weak gun regulations tend to have substantially higher gun death rates than states with lower ownership levels and stronger regulations. These findings derive from studies that have taken into account other factors that may have an impact on firearm mortality, such as rates of violence, urbanization, and poverty. Studies that have examined death rates for population subgroups have found that women and children are at an elevated risk in states with high gun owner-ship levels. Police officers, too, seem to be at higher risk when working in states with higher rates of gun ownership. State gun ownership appears to put people at greater risk of gun violence than a state's overall levels of violence. All of these findings call into question the purported protective value of guns in a region or community.

Notes

1. National Center for Health Statistics (US). Underlying Cause of Death 1999–2014. Data are from the Multiple Cause of Death Files, 1999–2014. Hyattsville, MD: Centers for Disease Control and Prevention; 2015.
2. Okoro C, Nelson D, Mercy J, Balluz L, Crosby A, Mokdad A. Prevalence of household firearms and firearm storage practices in the 50 states and the District of Columbia: findings from the behavioral risk factor surveillance system, 2002. Pediatrics. 2005; 116(3): 370–376.
3. Miller M, Azrael D, Hemenway D. Household firearm ownership levels and homicide rates across U.S. regions and states, 1988–1997. Am J Public Health. 2002; 92(12): 1988–1993.
4. Miller M, Azrael D, Hemenway D. State-level homicide victimization rates in the U.S. in relation to survey measures of household firearm ownership, 2001–2003. Soc Sci Med. 2007; 64(3): 656–664.
5. Siegel M, Ross C, King C. The relationship between gun ownership and firearm homicide rates in the United States, 1981–2010. Am J Public Health. 2013; 103(11): 2098–2105.
6. Miller M, Matthew D, Azrael D, Hemenway D. Firearm Availability and unintentional firearm deaths, suicide, and homicide among women. J Urban Health. 2002; 79(2): 26–38.
7. Cook P, Goss K. The Gun Debate: What everyone needs to know. New York: Oxford University Press; 2014. P. 21.
8. Hoskin A. Household gun prevalence and rates of violent crime: a test of competing gun theories. Criminal Justice Studies, 2011; 24(1): 125–136.
9. Brady Campaign to Prevent Gun Violence. Brady Campaign 2011 Scorecards [Internet]. Washington, DC: Brady Campaign to Prevent Gun

Violence. Available from: http://www.bradycampaign.org/xshare/stateleg/scorecard/2011/2011_scoring_system.pdf

10. Federal Bureau of Investigation. Crime in the United States, 2011 [Internet]. Washington, DC: US Department of Justice. Available from: http://www.fbi.gov/about-us/cjis/ucr/crime-in-the-u.s/2011/crime-in-the-u.s.-2011/tables/table-2

11. Fleegler E, Lee L, Monuteaux M, Hemenway D, and Mannix R., Firearm legislation and firearm-related fatalities in the United States. JAMA Internal Medicine, 2013, 173: 732–740.

12. Children's Defense Fund. Protect children not guns, 2013. Washington, DC: CDF. P. 23.

13. Brady Campaign to Prevent Gun Violence. 2011 Scorecards, 2011 State Rankings.

14. Safavi A, Rhee P, Pandit V, Kulvatunyou N, Tang A, Aziz H et al. Children are safer in states with strict firearm laws: a National Inpatient Sample study. J Trauma Acute Care Surg. 2014; 76(1): 146–151.

15. Parmet S. Police homicides more likely in states with high gun ownership [Internet]. UIC News Center. 2015 Sept 1. Available from: https://news.uic.edu/police-homicide-higher-in-states-with-more-gun-ownership

16. Swedler D, Simmons M, Dominici F, Hemenway D. Firearm prevalence and homicides of law enforcement officers in the United States. Am J Public Health. 2015; 105(10): 2042–2048.

Part III

Guns as a Means of Self-Defense

9

Armed Self-Defense I: The Number of Defensive Gun Uses

Following the murder of 20 school children and 6 staff members at Sandy Hook Elementary School in Newtown, Connecticut, by a 20-year-old man with significant mental health issues, Wayne Lapierre, CEO of the National Rifle Association (NRA), stated: "The only thing that stops a bad guy with a gun is a good guy with a gun." His solution was predictable: Arm school staff throughout the country.

The above quote is not only cynical and insensitive, coming on the heels of this horrific event, but also misleading. It is but the latest of the bumper sticker slogans that has become the mantra of those who believe that the right of gun ownership supersedes all other rights, including the most basic right to life of those victimized by individuals who should never be in possession of lethal weapons. It is a cynical view because, according to the NRA's vision, arming individuals seems to be the only recourse our society has left in dealing with violence. And, it is misleading, because there are strategies that do not involve arming the population that have been demonstrated to work in reducing violence.

According to the gun lobby, gun ownership in America ought to be virtually unregulated and extended to almost everyone, including minors.[1] The NRA's vision of the bogeyman we should all arm ourselves against is

© The Author(s) 2016
T. Gabor, *Confronting Gun Violence in America*,
DOI 10.1007/978-3-319-33723-4_9

that of the stranger (the "bad guy") who may prey upon us at any time and location. Their view of the world casts the rest of us (the "good guys") as the righteous guardians of America, the last line of defense preventing the country from descending into complete chaos and disorder.

In his book on the firearms industry, Tom Diaz, a former NRA member, notes that the gun industry's primary marketing tactic involves the use of fear. Diaz writes:

> *The pitch to women is simple: You're a woman. Some stranger is going to try to rape you. You'd better buy a handgun. People buy handguns out of fear, and stranger rape—it is theorized—is what women fear most. As a result, the gun lobby has been relentless in its use of fear of rape to promote handguns as self-defense weapons.*[2]

The only problem with the gun lobby's narrative is that, while crimes by strangers can be devastating in the trauma they produce, the good guy–bad guy depiction is pure fantasy and totally distorts what is known about violence. Consider what we know about homicide from the FBI's Expanded Homicide Database.[3] In 2013, there were 12,253 known homicides in the USA. Among those homicides in which the relationship between the offender and victim was known, just 19 % (1281 of 6681) were committed by strangers. By far the largest group of victims was acquaintances of the offender, followed by wives and girlfriends. Attacks on women are even less likely to involve strangers.[4] For other forms of violence, the 2013 National Crime Victimization Survey (NCVS) indicates that about a third of reported and unreported acts of violence are committed by strangers.[5]

These statistics support what we have known about most violence, other than robbery, for over half a century; that most acts of violence arise from disputes or interactions between people known to one another. Most acts of violence are not premeditated acts by predators searching for innocent victims. They stem from conflicts and other interactions that may be more likely to result in death or serious injury when guns are present.

Even violence among strangers often fails to fit the NRA's simplistic scenario of a violent predator launching a planned attack on an innocent stranger. The interactions leading to a homicide can be quite complex, and personal beliefs and experiences may play a role in the events leading to a homicide or serious violent crime. Even weather and the time of day may affect the outcome when two individuals, previously unknown to one another, converge and feel threatened by the other.

Consider the events of the night of February 26, 2012, at the Retreat at Twin Lakes in Sanford, Florida. Twin Lakes is a diverse, gated community of townhomes to which police had been called more than 400 times in just over a year. Fear prevailed in the community following numerous burglaries, thefts, a shooting, and many reports of individuals casing homes and of people trespassing into the community during that period. In 2011, a neighborhood watch program was created, and George Zimmerman, a 28-year-old resident, was selected as program coordinator. Zimmerman, who was apparently liked within the community, was also a frequent caller to the police, making 46 calls in a 14-month period for disturbances, break-ins, and suspicious activities.[6] One neighbor referred to him as "strict."

February 26 was a rainy night, and Miami teenager Trayvon Martin, who was visiting his father and father's fiancée at Twin Lakes, was walking home from a nearby convenience store where he had purchased some candy and ice tea. Martin was wearing a hoodie to stay dry and the tall African-American teenager probably fit the profile of those Zimmerman considered to be a threat to the community. The armed Zimmerman, who was patrolling in a car, decided to pursue the unarmed Martin, first in his car and then on foot. An altercation ensued and the lack of eyewitnesses makes it unclear as to precisely what transpired once Zimmerman left the vehicle. Arguing that he feared for his life during the altercation, Zimmerman shot and killed the teenager.

The case drew national and international attention. The acquittal of Zimmerman on a second-degree murder charge on July 13, 2013, created an international uproar and led to a call to examine broad self-defense laws that allow an individual who has pursued another and instigated an encounter to later justify the use of lethal force when the altercation he has instigated turns in an unexpected direction.

This case, and many like it, does not match the gun lobby's portrayal of violence as involving a predatory criminal who has decided in advance to launch an attack against a complete stranger. The Martin case illustrates that homicide can be the tragic result of a combination of fear, racial stereotypes, the presence of firearms, and an aggressive style of policing (in this case by a private citizen) in which a confrontational approach was selected. While all these factors contributed to the tragic outcome, the presence of a gun made it more likely that one of the parties would die or suffer disabling injuries.

Even where strangers are involved, such as in the encounter between Trayvon Martin and George Zimmerman, cases are often complicated by the perceptions, fears, and preconceived ideas of the parties. In addition, the NRA's simplistic worldview of "good guys" and "bad guys" does not take into account the fact that most gun deaths are suicides and not the killing of attackers and intruders by their victims. There are almost twice as many children who die of gunfire each year than there are criminals killed by civilians in justifiable homicides.[7] The children and other victims of lethal and disabling gun accidents are not "bad guys" (see Chap. 7) but merely victims of a highly prevalent and largely unregulated lethal product.

The killing of Trayvon Martin by George Zimmerman naturally raised questions about self-defense laws, such as those in Florida, that justify the use of lethal force without the duty to retreat in a wide range of circumstances. This case and others like it also raised the issue of whether gun laws that allow a large number of civilians—close to 1.5 million in Florida—to carry concealed weapons contributes to or detracts from public safety. Also, there is evidence that the proliferation of guns makes us *feel* less rather than more safe.

In the aftermath of the acquittal of George Zimmerman, the criticism of Florida's self-defense laws in the international press was scathing. Nicolas Richter, a reporter with *Suddeutsch Zeitung*, Gemany's largest national newspaper, wrote:

> *In this case, the Americans argued so much over the influence of the color of a person's skin that another idea was mostly overlooked—that of the dangers and excesses of vigilante justice. Many Americans only feel secure if they are allowed to carry a loaded weapon. The Zimmerman case shows where this can lead: Amateurs with wild suspicions can patrol neighborhoods, overestimate every threat, and ultimately propagate the very insecurity they set out to contain.[8]*

Despite the fact that Zimmerman was armed and pursued the unarmed teenager, the jury in the case bought his argument that Martin attacked him and that he feared for his life, thereby justifying the use of lethal force against Martin. The case illustrates something criminologists have known for a long time: that homicides often arise from an altercation and that both parties may feel threatened. Homicides are often complex events rather than the Hollywood depiction of heroes and villains in which a "bad guy" preys on a "good guy." The Sanford case also illustrates the danger of broadening the concept of self-defense to allow armed pursuers to use lethal force against an unarmed individual who is just going about his business and has made no threats at all. Such a concept of self-defense may well enable homicide and other violence as it legitimizes the use of force in a wide range of circumstances and leads people to believe they will be immune from prosecution.

In the early days of the gun control debate, both pro- and antigun control sides would parade out cases supporting their position. Those favoring tighter gun regulations would point to people who have died or suffered serious injuries from the misuse of a firearm. Those opposed to most gun regulations would point to cases in which an individual saved one or more lives, including his own, through the defensive use of a firearm. The evidence on both sides tended to be anecdotal.

Some cases have been especially influential in shaping public policy. The 1991 mass killing (50 shot, 23 dead) in Luby's Cafeteria in Killeen, Texas, by George Hennard led gun-rights advocates to argue that if someone in Luby's had a gun, many deaths could have been averted. Following a campaign by Suzanna Hupp, the daughter of two of the shooting's victims, the Texas legislature passed a shall-issue gun law requiring the state to issue concealed weapon permits to qualifying applicants.[9] Ms. Hupp argued that the law at the time of the massacre prevented her from bringing her gun into the restaurant and that lives would have been saved had the gun been with her.

And what do we make of the argument that someone with a concealed firearm and some shooting skills could have saved lives in Luby's that afternoon? This may well be true. The mass casualties may have been reduced that day. However, it is also hard to dispute the idea that guns in the wrong hands—in this case the shooter's—also facilitate casualties and mass casualties by those seeking to harm others or themselves in criminal or suicidal actions. This is why we need to go beyond anecdotes as anyone can parade out cases of criminal, self-destructive, and defensive uses of firearms.

Fortunately, the debate took a more sophisticated and helpful turn in the 1990s, when scholars tried to document the net impact of firearms. Once it became obvious that guns can be used for both criminal and defensive purposes, research turned to the question of whether, overall, guns served mostly a positive or harmful role. In other words, what is more common, criminal and harmful uses or defensive uses?

The Link Between Gun Ownership and Gun Deaths

In previous chapters, we have seen that countries and states with higher levels of gun ownership tend to have more lethal gun violence, as well as more gun suicides and fatal gun accidents. For example, Chap. 8 ("The Deadliest States") showed that the five states with the highest gun death rates had four times the gun ownership levels as the five states with the lowest gun death rates. This finding indicated that gun deaths increase, rather than decline, with the presence of more guns. If guns provided a net or overall benefit in terms of public safety, we would expect to see less gun violence where there are more guns rather than the reverse.

Consider the regions of the USA. FBI data for 2014 show that the region with both the highest violent and property crime rates was the South and the region with the lowest violent and property crime rates was the Northeast.[10] A Pew Research Center poll in March 2013 showed that 42 % of households in the South owned a gun, while just 25 % of Northeastern households owned a gun.[11] These two regions accounted for over half of the population of the USA (175 million people), illustrating that the association between higher gun ownership levels and higher levels of both violent and property crime have a broad applicability. These regional comparisons provide no support for the idea that higher gun ownership levels serve as a net deterrent to crime.

A study conducted by Linda Dahlberg and her colleagues at the Centers for Disease Control and Prevention showed a strong association between guns in the home and the risk of dying from a firearm-related homicide.[12] Those persons with guns in the home were at greater risk than those without guns in the home of dying from a homicide in the home. The researchers also found that more than three-quarters of the homicide victims knew the person who killed them and that this person was often a family member. Thus, most homicide victims in homes with guns were not shot by unknown intruders.

In another study, Douglas Wiebe of the University of California-Los Angeles School of Public Health found that adults in homes with guns were about one and a half times as likely to be intentionally killed in the home as those without guns in the home.[13] Wiebe's results showed that women with guns in the home were about two to four times as likely to be intentionally killed as women without guns in the home. This study again showed that guns in the home do not have a net protective effect. Rather, they are more likely to pose a threat to residents of a home than to protect them from intruders.

Another study illustrating the threat faced by women was conducted by Emily Rothman of Boston University's School of Public Health and her collaborators at Harvard University's Injury Control Research Center.[14] The researchers analyzed interviews conducted with over 8000 men enrolled in a certified batterer intervention program between 1999 and 2003. The types of gun threats against partners were (a) threatening to shoot then, (b) threatening to shoot a pet or person the victim cares about, (c) cleaning, holding, or loading a gun during an argument, and (d) shooting a gun during an argument. Abusive men who were recent gun owners were found to be nearly eight times more likely to have threatened their partners with a gun than nongun owners. The researchers concluded that gun ownership among this population is strongly associated with using a gun to threaten an intimate partner.

Researcher David Hemenway of Harvard's Injury Control Research Center notes:

Batterers use guns in a variety of ways to control their victims. Not only do they threaten to kill the women, but they also sometimes threaten to kill themselves

or the children. Other methods of gun intimidation include, during an argu-
ment, cleaning, holding, or loading a gun; going outside and shooting the gun;
or threatening to shoot a pet. A national random survey found more hostile gun
displays against women in the home—primarily by intimate partners—than
self-defense gun uses in the home by women or anyone else.[15]

Anthony Hoskin of the University of Texas at Odessa examined the relationship between gun availability and three types of violent crime across the 120 most populous counties in the USA.[16] He used survey data from the Centers for Disease Control and Prevention's Behavioral Risk Factor Surveillance System to determine household gun ownership for each county. Hoskin found strong support for the view that greater access to guns raises the risks of serious violence by giving the perpetrator the power to inflict greater victim injury. The study revealed that increasing household gun ownership was associated with higher rates of homicide, independent of the influence of other factors, such as a county's unemployment rate, the age and racial distribution of its population, alcoholism rate, and educational attainment. Findings were mixed for aggravated assault and robbery rates. By contrast, the study found no support for the idea that widespread legal gun ownership lowers violent crime by deterring prospective offenders.

After reviewing the evidence relating to the costs and benefits of keeping a gun in the home, Harvard's Hemenway writes:

> *scientific studies suggest that the health risk of a gun in the home is greater than*
> *the benefit. … There is compelling evidence that a gun in the home is a risk*
> *factor for intimidation and for killing women in their homes, and it appears*
> *that a gun in the home may more likely be used to threaten intimates than to*
> *protect against intruders.*[17]

Number of Defensive Uses

One of the most contentious aspects of the debate on guns is that of the relative number of offensive (criminal) and defensive gun uses (DGUs). As guns can be used both for legitimate and criminal purposes, the question becomes one of the net benefits or harms associated with the use of firearms. Thus, do the benefits of firearms outweigh their harms? The FBI's annual crime reports and the Department of Justice's NCVS provide reasonably reliable, nonpartisan information on the number of criminal uses of firearms each year. The Centers for Disease Control and Prevention gather and compile credible data on gun-related homicides, suicides, and accidents.

It is the calculation of DGUs that is most problematic in determining the annual number of gun-related harms and benefits. Studies yield a wide range of figures, and research in this area is often highly partisan. The numbers yielded by the studies range from less than 100,000 to more than two million DGUs per year. These variations are due, in part at least, to differences in survey methodologies, sample size, and the definitions of what constitutes a DGU.

The use of guns by police officers is a good starting point in the debate about the benefits of guns as a protective tool. Television shows can lead us to believe that law enforcement officers are routinely involved in shootouts and often use guns to neutralize or subdue people. The police are armed and trained to use a gun and are engaged full time in the investigation of crime, the pursuit of suspects, and regularly deal with high-risk individuals. Despite these facts, most officers never fire their guns on duty. According to the late James Fyfe, an expert on the use of force by police, the average big-city cop is involved in a fatal shooting every 450 years.[18] This shows that firefights involving police are not commonplace and that they usually resort to other means to calm most disturbances. One calculation found that, in a given year, just 1 in every 170 police officers has been involved in some form of shooting incident.[19]

These numbers show that even police officers, who are armed and are more routinely involved in dangerous situations than the average citizen, rarely rely on guns when doing police work. Incidents of self-protection by police would be even fewer, as officers may shoot at fleeing suspects and may also engage in illegitimate uses of force. At the time this section is being written, there has been increasing concern around the USA regarding police shootings of unarmed suspects, especially young African-American men and teenagers (e.g., the fatal shooting of Michael Brown by a Ferguson, Missouri, police officer).

The New York City Police Department (NYPD) provides detailed data on intentional firearm discharges by police occurring in conflicts with civilians. The city's annual report on firearms discharges for 2011 notes:

While it must be acknowledged that the most serious category of discharges—shootings involving adversarial conflict with a subject—increased by 9 percent over last year's record low, it is also true that experiencing 36 adversarial-conflict incidents during a year makes for a remarkably infrequent rate. In context, the rarity is even more apparent: in a city of 8.2 million people, from a Department of nearly 35,000 uniformed members who interacted with citizens in approximately 23 million instances, 62 officers were involved in 36 incidents of intentional firearms discharges during an adversarial conflict.[20]

Thus, in the nation's largest city—a city which is no stranger to crime—there was just one incident involving intentional firearm discharges by police for every 1000 uniformed police officers. Even more striking was that there was just one such firearm discharge by police for every 639,000 recorded interactions with citizens. Such statistics hardly make the case for arming America's citizens as they go to far less dangerous jobs, attend college courses, buy groceries, watch sporting events and shows, and otherwise go about their daily business.

A survey conducted by the National Opinion Research Center (NORC) in 2001 found that about 10 % of Americans carried a gun for self-protection over the previous year.[21] A much smaller number carried guns on a regular basis. Less than 3 % of those carrying a firearm drew or displayed a gun during the previous year in response to a perceived threat in the previous year. Thus, assuming that all of these claimed instances of DGU were legitimate acts of self-defense, 3 % of the 10 % who carried a gun for self-protection or about 1 in every 300 citizens used a gun for a defensive purpose outside the home in 2001. These statistics are not directly comparable to the NYPD data as the NORC survey examined all types of purported defensive uses of firearms rather than merely firearm discharges. We will return to the issue of how many of these claims are actually legitimate acts of self-defense as many claims of DGUs by civilians have been questioned.

The Kleck and Gertz Survey

A critical study to which much of this chapter will be devoted was one conducted by Gary Kleck and Marc Gertz of Florida State University.[22] This national survey fueled the contention by gun-rights advocates that an armed population makes for a more peaceful and safe society. The survey asked the following question: "Within the past five *years*, have you yourself or another member of your household *used* a gun, even if it was not fired, for self-protection or for the protection of property at home, work, or elsewhere? Please do *not* include military service, police work, or work as a security guard."

Respondents were also asked to indicate whether an incident involving a DGU occurred in the previous 12 months. A total of 222 of 4,977 respondents reported one or more DGUs in the previous year, resulting in the authors' well-known estimate of 2.2–2.5 million DGUs per year when the sample results were applied to the entire population.

The authors acknowledged that their results should be treated with caution due to the small number of respondents who claim to have used their gun defensively over the study period. Of the 222 respondents claiming a DGU, just 213 respondents provided complete information. The authors noted that they had lower confidence with regard to 26 of the respondents as it was not clear that a crime had been committed or that an adversary was present. Removing these cases left 187 respondents reporting one or more DGUs.

Kleck and Gertz also acknowledged that the number of respondents claiming DGUs may have been inflated due to telescoping, a form of memory distortion in which an individual incorrectly believes that an event occurred within a certain time frame, when it appeared in the more distant past (e.g., 14 months ago rather than over the past 12 months). The authors indicated that telescoping may have inflated the figures by 21 %, meaning that 37 respondents may have committed this error in recall. This would leave just 150 respondents in the national sample who claimed a DGU without committing an error in recall due to telescoping. Kleck and Gertz acknowledged that with such small numbers (e.g., 150 respondents claiming a DGU), major errors can occur in arriving at national estimates if just a few individuals provide misleading or inaccurate information.

Major Problems with the Kleck and Gertz Survey

Perhaps the most significant error is in the interpretation of the claims by these respondents that their acts were truly defensive rather than offensive. The authors note: "We made no effort to assess either the lawfulness or morality of the Rs' (respondents') defensive actions."[23] By their own admission, in close to half the cases (46.8 %), respondents claiming the DGU were not threatened or attacked. In just a fifth (20.8 %) of the cases did they indicate that they were actually attacked. Furthermore, the individual claiming the DGU indicated that the offender was unarmed in over half (51.9 %) the cases and was armed with a gun in just 17.9 % of the cases. In more than half the cases, the adversary had no weapon whatsoever. Thus, it is important to note that many claimed acts of self-defense were cases in which the individual was not threatened or attacked and most adversaries were unarmed. Many of these alleged acts of self-defense may not stand up in court, and some may well have been instigated by the respondent. In addition, in some cases, the person claiming a DGU merely referred to a gun rather than brandishing or firing it.[24]

Therefore, just a fraction of the 150 respondents in the original sample of close to 5,000 Americans reported a DGU in which the adversary was armed and threatening or attacking the respondent and where the respondent actually wielded, pointed, or discharged the weapon. Such small numbers are susceptible to serious errors in estimating DGUs nationally if just a few of these respondents exaggerated or mistakenly viewed their actions as defensive. If only those cases are counted in which the adversary was armed and threatened or attacked the respondent, the DGUs would amount to perhaps a few hundred thousand rather than over two million DGUs, nationally. In fact, Kleck and Gertz found that just one in six of the respondents who claimed a DGU indicated that their lives were in serious danger and almost certainly would have been killed had they not taken protective action.[25]

In many countries, the use of lethal force to defend oneself would only be justified if a person had a reasonable belief that he or she would be killed by an assailant. In Canada, for example, a defensive response that is proportional to a threat is a major consideration in whether the response was reasonable.[26] Kleck and Gertz acknowledge that if only those cases are considered in which respondents believed their lives were in serious danger, the national estimates of DGUs would range between 340,000 and 400,000.[27] These numbers are less than a fifth of those usually associated with this study—2.2 to 2.5 million annual defensive uses of guns.

Table 9.1 below illustrates why the conclusions drawn from Kleck and Gertz's survey are highly suspect and appear to defy credibility. Comparing police and citizen firearm discharges arrived at by Kleck and Gertz produces results that are implausible. The NYPD carefully logs and investigates all firearm discharges by officers. In 2011, there were 36 incidents involving intentional firearm discharges against an adversary for 35,000 uniformed officers which equates to about one incident for every 1,000 officers in the Big Apple. The vast majority of these incidents (95 %) were those in which police were seeking out individuals or responding to crimes or dangerous situations (e.g., a report of a man with a gun).[28] In just 5 % of the incidents were officers attacked when they were not undertaking some form of enforcement action. If just these incidents were considered, the cases of intentional firearm discharges for NYPD officers for 2011 was in the order of 1 incident per 20,000 officers.

The NYPD figures show how rare police DGU really is, even in a large city and even where police-initiated enforcement actions are considered. By contrast, Kleck and Gertz's 1993 survey suggests that civilians use

Table 9.1 Comparing firearm discharges by police officers with those of civilians using NYPD data and the Kleck and Gertz 1993 survey

	NYPD uniformed officers	Civilians (according to Kleck and Gertz's study)
Intentional firearm discharges	1 incident annually per 1000 uniformed officers	1 incident for every 114 civilian gun owners
	1 incident per 20,000 officers when just attacks on officers are considered	1 incident for every 368 adults (gun owners and nonowners)

Sources: New York City Police Department. Annual firearm discharge report 2011. Executive Summary. August, 2012; Kleck G, Gertz M. Armed resistance to crime: the prevalence and nature of self-defense with a gun. J Crim Law Criminol. 1995; 86(2): 150–187; December 1993 Gallup poll cited in Kleck and Gertz, P. 167

guns for protection far more frequently than police officers, even when all civilians, including those who do not own guns, are considered. These findings suggest that the figures drawn from the Kleck and Gertz survey are seriously inflated.

The calculations in the table have been arrived at using population and gun ownership figures at the time the 1993 survey was conducted. The figures in the table are based on Kleck and Gertz's lower figure of approximately 2.2 million DGUs per year. Just under a quarter of those claiming a DGU indicated that they had actually fired a gun, yielding about half a million "defensive" firearm discharges. The US adult population in April 1993 was approximately 191 million, yielding one gun discharge for every 368 adults. As nonowners of guns are not likely to use guns defensively, it makes more sense to compare police officers with gun owners than all adults. In 1993, there were approximately 59 million gun owners (31 % of the adult population). Using Kleck and Gertz's data, there would have been 1 intentional firearm discharge for every 114 gun owners.

According to the Kleck and Gertz survey, gun owners, despite the fact that just a fraction carry guns at all and still fewer do so on a regular basis,[29] were almost 10 times as likely to fire a gun defensively than armed police officers, who regularly encountered dangerous situations as part of their job. Police not only encounter dangerous people routinely; they also seek them out in law enforcement operations. Furthermore, uniformed officers are trained in the use of firearms and carry them openly, making their weapons more accessible than civilians. While it is true that their training may lead officer to use other means to subdue suspects, the figures show that there is something seriously wrong with the fact that the Kleck and Gertz survey results show in excess of two million defensive uses.

Labeling Kleck and Gertz's figure of 2.5 million a "mythical number," researchers Philip Cook of Duke University, Jens Ludwig of the University of Chicago, and David Hemenway of Harvard University have suggested that number merits consideration as "the most outrageous number mentioned in a policy discussion."[30] These and other researchers point out that the figure of over two million DGUs lacks credibility, given what we know about the volume of different crimes.

Harvard's Hemenway notes that the above estimates of the frequency of armed self-defense were seriously inflated. According to the Kleck and Gertz survey, a third of DGUs (approximately 845,000) occurred during burglaries. This number exceeds the total number of burglaries occurring annually in the USA in which residents owned a gun and were home during a burglary. Thus, if we are to believe the Kleck and Gertz estimates, more than 100 % of burglary victims used guns to protect themselves from burglars.[31] Any number approaching, let alone exceeding, 100 % lacks credibility as even armed homeowners will not always have a gun handy or be in a position to use a gun or to scare off an intruder. Offenders have the benefit of choosing the time and location of their crimes, while victims are usually caught off guard and engaging in routine activities (including sleeping) when the offense occurs. In fact, one study of home invasions—incidents in which people are home—found that fewer than 2 % of victims used a firearm in self-defense.[32]

Dennis Henigan, formerly a vice president of the Brady Center to Prevent Gun Violence, adds that, according to Kleck's survey, 40 % of women use firearms to defend themselves in sexual assaults when data show that guns used for defense in sexual assaults have been utilized in less than 1 % of cases.[33]

Kleck and Gertz estimated that about 200,000 offenders were shot by victims in one year. One would expect that many of those shot would go to the emergency room for treatment as surveys of jail inmates show that even most of those committing crimes and getting shot go to the hospital.[34] Yet, Kleck and Gertz's estimated number of self-defense shootings is twice the total number of people who are treated for gunshot wounds in emergency rooms of American hospitals.[35] Most of those treated are not offenders who have attacked people but are the victims of assaults, suicide attempts, and firearm accidents.

The above figure of 200,000 shootings of offenders by victims per year is seriously inflated when we examine law enforcement data on justifiable homicides and data on the fatality rates stemming from firearm injuries. Researchers from the Centers for Disease Control and Prevention have found that, overall, close to a third of all persons who sustain a firearm injury ultimately die from their wounds.[36] Thus, if victims shot 200,000 offenders, there should be more than 60,000 justifiable homicides a year in the USA. Data from the FBI show that each year there are approximately 250 justifiable homicides a year by private citizens in the USA.[37] While the FBI figures for justifiable homicide may underestimate or overestimate the true figures, they suggest that, knowing the fatality rates for gunshot wounds, the real number of shootings of offenders by victims is well under 1,000 rather than 200,000 per year, an enormous difference.

Klecks telephone survey respondents claim to have saved 400,000 people from death each year, but just 27,000 homicides occurred that year in the country. For every murder, they claim to have saved 15 people (themselves and families) from certain death.[38]

Where do these inflated figures of DGUs come from? Many self-defense claims are, in fact, aggressive and often criminal actions by those provoking others or imagining threats. The fatal shooting in 2012 of teenager Jordan Davis by Michael Dunn in Jacksonville, Florida, is instructive. Dunn, a 47-year-old white computer engineer, parked in front of a convenience store and approached a van in which several black teenagers were playing what Dunn considered to be excessively loud hip-hop music. Following an argument over the music, Dunn opened fire, killing the teenager. Dunn tried to justify the killing by claiming that the teenagers were armed when this was not the case and that he feared for his life.[39] The prosecution claimed that Dunn's fears were "only in his imagination," and he was ultimately convicted of first-degree murder for killing Davis.

It is also suspected that some survey participants deliberately make exaggerated claims about self-defense in order to portray themselves in a positive light or to promote policies favoring armed self-defense. Whether the reason for false claims are imagined threats or a more calculated effort to mislead in a survey, researchers must take respondents' word for what occurred. This situation creates a potential for serious bias as a competent police investigation of such incidents would involve interviews of all parties prior to reaching a conclusion. In fact, researchers Philip Cook of Duke University and Jens Ludwig of the University of Chicago found that more than a third of those claiming a self-defense gun use contradicted themselves later in the survey by saying they had not been attacked, threatened, or injured.[40]

Even if we assume that civilian intentional discharges occur as often as among NYC police officers—a highly questionable assumption—the Kleck and Gertz survey has overestimated these DGUs by close to a factor of 10 (Table 9.1). In that case, we are probably looking at approximately 200,000 DGUs per year, bringing the numbers closer to estimates provided by the largest and probably most credible survey of victims—the NCVS.

The NCVS is an annual survey of about 90,000 households and 160,000 individuals that has been conducted since 1973.[41] It asks respondents about crimes they or household members may have experienced and taps DGUs. The NCVS minimizes bogus self-defense claims by posing questions about DGU only to those respondents who first reported a threatened, attempted, or completed victimization. Thus, in this survey, to claim a DGU, a genuine threat or attack must first occur. Michael Rand, head of victimization statistics at the US Department of Justice's Bureau of Justice Statistics, reported in the 1990s that the average annual number of crime victims over a five-year period who used firearms to defend themselves or their property was 83,000.[42] Just over 62,000 of these victims were fending off a violent attack, while the remainder were using guns to defend their homes, motor vehicle, or other property. These numbers are less than 4 % of the number of DGUs claimed by Kleck and Gertz. Rand also reported that violent crimes by handguns during those years were more than 10 times as common as DGUs against violent offenders.

The FBI's Uniform Crime Reports collect information on the types of weapons used in violent crime. Data for 2013 showed that firearms were used in 69.0 % of the nation's murders, 40.0 % of robberies, and 21.6 % of aggravated assaults.[43] The NCVS revealed that, in 2012, 6.7 % of all violent victimizations involved a firearm and, in 2013, 5.4 % were committed with guns.[44] By contrast, an analysis of the NCVS for 1992–2001 by Jongyeon Tark and Gary Kleck of Florida State University found that in less than 1 % (.9 %) of violent crimes did the victim use a gun in self-defense. Thus, guns are used many times more frequently by the perpetrators of violent crime than they are used to defend against violent incidents. Tark and Kleck further found that using a gun was not more likely to prevent further injury to the victim relative to other protective actions (threats, use of other weapons) they took.[45]

The findings above are not surprising as offenders committing a violent crime are more likely to be armed than their victims. The offender also chooses the timing of an attack, and victims may own a gun but not have one in their possession when attacked or may not be able to use it. Another indication that the criminal uses of firearms outnumber defensive uses by a wide margin can be seen in a comparison of criminal and justifiable homicides. For every justifiable homicide between 2006 and 2010 in which firearms were used, there were 44 criminal homicides with a firearm.[46]

Two national polls commissioned by Harvard University's Injury Control Research Center in 1996 and 1999 have helped to shed light on how inflated results, claiming millions of DGUs each year, are generated by surveys.[47] The Harvard surveys were unique in that they were more detailed and contained open-ended items in which respondents could discuss gun-related incidents and their reactions. The surveys examined the prevalence of self-defense with guns and did not include questions about the defense of property. When the results of the two surveys were combined, 3.5 times as many respondents reported being victims of hostile gun displays as those reporting a DGU.

One issue that raised a concern about the legitimacy of some of the self-defense claims was the finding that, in the 1996 survey, three respondents claimed 74 % of the total incidents of self-defense and, in the 1999 survey, one respondent reported 50 self-defense uses over the previous five years. Such findings naturally lead one to ask whether these reported incidents were genuine acts of self-defense.

To examine this issue, the researchers presented descriptions of the reported incidents to five criminal court judges from California, Pennsylvania, and Massachusetts. The judges were told to assume that the respondent had a permit to own and carry the gun and had provided an honest description of the event. In over half the cases, a majority of the judges rated the purported acts of self-defense as "probably illegal."

Following examples are from the 1999 survey of incidents that the judges unanimously considered as "probably illegal"[48]:

A 62-year-old male said that at 6 pm "the police called. My alarm at my business went off so I went there to shut it off. Two men were outside my building, so from my car I shot at the ground near them." The respondent said the men were trespassing.

A 58-year-old male was inside his home at 2 pm. "I was watching a movie and [an acquaintance] interrupted me. I yelled that I was going to shoot him and he ran to his car." The respondent said his acquaintance was committing a verbal assault. The respondent's gun, a .44 Magnum, was located "in my holster on me."

The many claims of defensive uses by a small fraction of respondents are either outright falsehoods by respondents seeking to exaggerate the number of protective uses of firearms or suggest a high-risk lifestyle rather than legitimate acts of self-defense by individuals who are genuine victims of threats or attacks. Exaggerating protective uses of firearms may be a strategic response by gun owners who are aware of the scientific debate on DGUs and who may wish to inflate DGUs as a way of ensuring that laws allowing for such uses are retained. With around four million NRA members and millions of other owners, a sizable number of gun owners would be found among respondents to such surveys.

The authors of the Harvard surveys conclude:

Certainly some self-defense gun uses are legal and in the public interest. But many are not. The possibility of using a gun in a socially useful manner— against a criminal during the commission of a crime—will rarely, if ever, occur for the average gun owner. By contrast, at any other moment, the use of a gun against another human is illegal, and socially undesirable. Regular citizens with guns, who are sometimes tired, angry, drunk or afraid, and who are not trained in dispute resolution or on when it is proper to use a firearm, have many opportunities for inappropriate gun use.[49]

With regard to property crime, NCVS data show that the use or threatened use of firearms by victims was even more rare. In the five-year period from 2007 through 2011, of a total of 84,495,500 property crime victims, just 103,000 of these victims (1 in every 820 cases) resisted the offender with the help of a gun.[50] By comparison, data from the Department of Justice shows that an average of 232,400 guns were stolen each year from US households from 2005 to 2010.[51]

In an Atlanta study, police reports of home invasions were reviewed for a four-month period by Arthur Kellermann and his colleagues of Emory University. The researchers identified 198 cases of unwanted entry into a single-family dwelling when someone was home.[52] In 32 instances, at least one of the offenders was known to have carried a gun. In 6 of the 198 cases, an invader obtained the victim's gun. In just three cases (1.5 %) was a victim able to use a firearm in self-defense. Thus, the risk of being armed appeared to outweigh the benefit for victims. In just a fraction of cases was the victim able to use a firearm for self-protection. Philip Cook and Kristin Goss of Duke University calculate that just 1 in every 3,500 gun-owning households use a gun against an intruder each year.[53]

In another study headed by Arthur Kellermann, all fatal and nonfatal gunshot injuries involving guns kept in the home were analyzed for a 12–18-month time frame in Memphis, Tennessee, Seattle, Washington, and Galveston, Texas. For every incident in which a gun in the home was used in a self-defense or legally justifiable shooting, there were 22 assaults or homicides, self-inflicted shootings, or unintentional injuries involving a gun in the home.[54] In an earlier study in Seattle in which only fatal shootings were considered, there were 43 homicides, suicides, or fatal accidents for every killing in self-defense.[55]

The body of research on the impact of keeping guns in the home suggests the following: (1) These guns are rarely actually used for self-defense against intruders, and (2) they are far more likely to be used against someone in that home than against an intruder.[56]

Switzerland provides another illustration of how the defensive uses of firearms can be exaggerated. The country has among the highest levels of gun ownership in Europe as firearms are kept in the home as part of military service. According to an international survey of firearm ownership conducted in 2007, Switzerland ranked third in the world with 46 guns for every 100 people.[57] Swiss researchers Martin Killias and Nora Markwalder examined homicides in their country from 1980 to 2004. Just 6 of 1276 homicides (.5 %) were found to be legitimate acts of self-defense by civilians.[58] Thus, in a country with one of the most armed civilian populations, the authors concluded that more than two decades of data showed that "guns kept in Swiss households were virtually never used to kill an assailant."[59]

In addition, Swiss crime victimization surveys conducted in 1998 and 2000 asked gun owners whether they had used (although not necessarily shot) their guns in self-defense during their lifetime (the 1998 survey) or over the last five years (the 2000 survey). A total of 1.9 % reported using a gun for defensive purposes in their lifetime and 1.7 % in the previous year.[60] The authors noted that acts of self-defense with a firearm are extremely rare in Switzerland and that the numbers would be even smaller if illegitimate uses and false claims were taken into account.

John May, medical director of Atlanta's Fulton County Jail, and his associates conducted a survey of jail inmates in a Washington, DC, detention facility.[61] One in four detainees had been shot prior to their incarceration. Most were shot when they were victims of robberies, assaults, and crossfire. Virtually none report being wounded by one of their victims, including homeowners defending themselves from intruders.

The Danger of Merely Counting Defensive Gun Uses

Apart from counting DGUs, there is another issue that merits consideration. Advocates of arming the citizenry assume that all uses of guns for defense of a person or property are equally justifiable and beneficial to society. However, where property rather than lives are being protected, it can be argued that the gun use may result in outcomes that are worse than those that would have occurred had a gun not been available. According to the National Survey of Private Ownership and Use of Firearms, a theft or trespass is the most serious crime reported in one of every five cases in which guns are used for defensive purposes. In such instances, it is legitimate to ask whether society is better off when someone uses a gun as opposed to dialing 9-1-1.

In addition, researchers Philip Cook and Jens Ludwig state that tallying the number of DGUs may be a poor measure of the benefit of guns to society.[62] First, surveys rely on the respondent's version of events, and, as mentioned, people may claim that they have used a gun defensively against threats that are perceived rather than real. People claiming self-defense may also have initiated an altercation and drew a gun when the other party responded in a threatening manner. In addition, the number of DGUs tells us little about the extent to which crime is reduced as a result of the deterrent effect of gun ownership and the carrying of firearms. On the other hand, gun ownership may entice those wishing to steal guns to commit more burglaries and may lead to the escalation of conflicts as offenders arm themselves and use pre-emptive violence believing victims are armed. The number of DGUs therefore tells us little about the many adverse effects on crime of widespread gun ownership. The chapter that follows discusses the adverse effects on public safety of gun ownership and carrying.

The Logic of Armed Self-Defense Advocates

The belief held by the gun lobby and armed self-defense advocates that guns are more likely to protect than to threaten us is flawed in its logic. Let us start with a definition of armed self-defense as the discharging, displaying, or pointing of a firearm at a person who is attacking, making threats, or unlawfully entering the victim's home. This definition does not include those situations in which people carry a firearm *in case* it is needed.

Suppose we ignore all the documented flaws of Kleck and Gertz's survey and, for the moment, accept their claim that there were five DGUs per year for every criminal use (2.5 million DGUs vs. 500,000 criminal uses) when the survey was conducted in the 1990s. On the face of it, this would suggest that guns provide a net benefit to society as they are more often used as a protective tool than as a threat to public safety. An immediate question that comes to mind is: How can there be more defensive than offensive gun uses? When someone is defending himself or herself with a gun, isn't there another person wielding a gun in an offensive or criminal fashion?

Armed self-defense advocates who rely on this study are in effect saying that there are about 2.5 million DGUs a year and there are just half a million armed attacks with a gun, leaving two million cases each year in which a firearm is discharged or pointed at an offender who is *unarmed*! In most countries, one would be hard pressed to justify the use of a firearm against an unarmed individual, even if that person is an aggressor. Apart from questioning the version of events provided by the survey respondents, should we be reassured that citizens are taking steps to protect themselves or should we be concerned that citizens are meting out disproportionate justice on the street or in private spaces against unarmed individuals with whom they are having a dispute?

In fact, judges have found that many claimed DGUs would not be considered to be legal. While a right to self-defense is widely accepted in law, the notion that an individual's actions must be proportional to the threat is recognized internationally as a necessary condition of justified self-defense.[63] Gunning down an unarmed individual does not usually qualify as a proportional action to a general threat. The discharge of a gun aimed at another qualifies as the use of lethal force and the principle of proportionality would appear to require credible evidence of an imminent threat to one's life, something that is hard to demonstrate in the case of an unarmed assailant.

However, states such as Florida are permitting the use of armed self-defense that extends well beyond what a proportional response by a victim would involve. In 2005, Florida passed its version of a "Castle Doctrine" law, which establishes the presumption that a person breaking into a home intends to cause death or great bodily harm and allows occupants to use deadly force, without a duty to retreat, against the intruder.[64] In reality, very few burglars cause serious bodily harm to victims; therefore, the presumption allowing for the use of deadly force is false. To illustrate, analysis by the Bureau of Justice Statistics found that 7 % of all household burglaries involve some violence and the majority of these acts are assaults, usually simple assaults.[65] In addition, in 2014, there were 77 murders during the close to three million household burglaries, or one case in every 39,000 incidents.[66,67] In Florida, no proportionality in the use of force is required as the homeowner can kill the intruder in the absence of any threats or violence.

Bottom Line

The principal reaction to mass shootings and gun violence in general by the gun lobby and gun-rights advocates has been to arm a larger segment of the population. According to their simplistic and fictitious narrative, gun violence is the act of predators ("bad guys") who are ready at any moment to kill, rape, mug, and assault innocent victims ("the good guys"). In reality, most violence occurs among intimate partners and others who are acquainted with one another. Arming women at risk of abuse, for example, creates the risk that their abusers will seize the gun to intimidate, threaten, and even kill these women.

There are many other downsides to widespread gun ownership and gun carrying to be discussed in Chap. 10. This chapter was devoted to the question of the number of DGUs relative to criminal uses. In the mid-1990s, several researchers argued that DGUs outnumbered harmful uses, thereby making the case for arming the public at large. The best known study, conducted by Gary Kleck and Marc Gertz, claimed between 2.2 and 2.5 million DGUs per year, well in excess of the 1.3 million criminal uses reported by crime victims in 1993.[68]

The Kleck and Gertz survey findings are seriously flawed. Many claimed acts of self-defense were cases in which the individual was not threatened or attacked and most adversaries were unarmed. The researchers also did not examine the number of alleged acts of self-defense in which violent encounters were instigated by the respondent. In addition, in some cases, the person claiming a DGU merely referred to a gun rather than brandishing or firing it. Kleck and Gertz acknowledge that if only those cases were considered in which respondents believed their lives were in serious danger, the national estimates of DGUs would range between 340,000 and 400,000.

Even these numbers are likely to be highly inflated. According to the Kleck and Gertz survey, gun owners, many of whom do not even carry their guns, were almost ten times as likely to fire a gun defensively than armed police officers, who regularly encounter dangerous situations as part of their job. Their figures claim more DGUs during burglaries than the total number of burglaries occurring annually in the USA. Their estimated number of self-defense shootings is twice the total number of people who are treated for gunshot wounds in emergency rooms of American hospitals.[69]

The most credible figures are yielded by the largest and most rigorous survey of crime conducted in the USA—the Department of Justice's NCVS. The NCVS, an annual survey conducted for over 40 years, estimated in the early 1990s that there are about 83,000 cases a year of DGUs in response to attacks against persons or property. This number is dwarfed by the 1.3 million annual crimes with guns estimated by the NCVS. Studies of burglary and sexual assault also show that DGUs are relatively rare. A close examination of the number of DGUs certainly does not support the contention that defensive uses outnumber harmful ones and lend little support to the idea that increasing gun ownership enhances public safety.

Notes

1. McIntire M. Selling a new generation on guns [Internet]. The New York Times. 2013 Jan 26. Available from: http://www.nytimes.com/2013/01/27/us/selling-a-new-generation-on-guns.html?smid=nytcore-ipad-share&smprod=nytcore-ipad&_r=0
2. Diaz T., Making a killing: the business of guns in America. New York: The New Press; 1999. P. 185.
3. Federal Bureau of Investigation. Uniform Crime Report 2013, Expanded Homicide Data Table 10 [Internet]. Washington, DC: US Department of Justice. Available from: http://www.fbi.gov/about-us/cjis/ucr/crime-in-the-u.s/2013/crime-in-the-US-2013/offenses-known-to-law-enforcement/expanded-homicide/expanded_homicide_data_table_10_murder_circumstances_by_relationship_2013.xls
4. Violence Policy Center. When Men Murder Women: An Analysis of 2012 Homicide Data. Washington, DC: Violence Policy Center; 2014. P. 3.
5. Truman J, Langton L. Criminal Victimization, 2013. Washington, DC: US Department of Justice; 2014. Table 7.
6. Robles F. Shooter of Trayvon Martin a habitual caller to the cops [Internet]. Miamiherald.com. 2012 Mar 20. Available from: http://www.palmbeach-post.com/news/news/crime-law/shooter-of-trayvon-martin-a-habitual-caller-to-c-1/nLhmX/

7. Briggs B. Terrible tally: 500 children dead from gunshots every year, 7,500 hurt, analysis finds [Internet]. NBC News. 2013 Oct 27. Available from: http://www.nbcnews.com/health/terrible-tally-500-children-dead-gunshots-every-year-7-500-8C11469222

8. Richter N. American vigilante Justice: When amateurs play sheriff [Internet]. Sueddeutsche.de. 2013 Jul 13. Available from: http://world-meets.us/sueddeutsche000043.shtml#.Ueb6vubD-70

9. Verhovek S. States seek to let citizens carry concealed weapons [Internet]. The New York Times. 1995 Mar 6. Available from: http://www.nytimes.com/1995/03/06/us/states-seek-to-let-citizens-carry-concealed-weapons.html

10. Federal Bureau of Investigation. 2014 Crime in the United States, Region [Internet]. Washington, DC: Department of Justice. Available from: https://www.fbi.gov/about-us/cjis/ucr/crime-in-the-u.s/2014/crime-in-the-u.s.-2014/offenses-known-to-law-enforcement/browse-by/region

11. Pew Research Center. Gun ownership trends and demographics [Internet]. 2013 Mar 12. Available from: http://www.people-press.org/2013/03/12/section-3-gun-ownership-trends-and-demographics/

12. Dahlberg L, Ikeda R, Kresnow M. Guns in the home and risk of a violent death in the home: findings from a national study. Am J Epidemiol. 2004; 160(10): 929–936.

13. Wiebe D. Homicide and homicide risks associated with firearms in the home: A national case-control study. Ann Emerg Med. 2003; 41(6): 771–782.

14. Rothman E, Hemenway D, Miller M, Azrael D. Batterers' use of guns to threaten intimate partners. J Am Med Wom Assoc. 2005; 60(1): 62–68.

15. Hemenway D. Risks and benefits of a gun in the home. Am J Lifestyle Med. 2011; 10: 1–10.

16. Hoskin A. Household gun prevalence and rates of violent crime: a test of competing gun theories. Criminal Justice Studies. 2011; 24(1): 125–136.

17. Hemenway D. Risks and benefits of a gun in the home. P. 7.

18. Diaz T. Making a killing: the business of guns in America. New York: The New Press; 2000. P. 108.

19. Diaz T. Making a killing. P. 109.

20. New York City Police Department. Annual Firearm Discharge Report 2011. Executive Summary. New York: NYPD; 2012.

21. Smith T. 2001 National Gun Policy Survey of the National Opinion Research Center: research findings. Chicago: National Opinion Research Center, University of Chicago; 2001.

22. Kleck G, Gertz M. Armed resistance to crime: the prevalence and nature of self-defense with a gun. J Crim L Criminology. 1995; 86(1): 150–187.

23. Kleck G, Gertz M. Armed resistance to crime. P. 163.

24. Kleck G, Gertz M. Armed resistance to crime. P. 185, Table 3.

25. Kleck G, Gertz M. Armed resistance to crime. P. 176.

26. Department of Justice Canada. Bill C-26 (S.C. 2012 c. 9) Reforms to self-defence and defence of property: technical guide for practitioners [Internet]. Available from: http://www.justice.gc.ca/eng/rp-pr/other-autre/rsddp-rlddp/p2.html

27. Kleck G, Gertz M. Armed resistance to crime. P. 177.

28. New York City Police Department. Annual Firearm Discharge Report. P. 22.

29. Smith T. 2001 National Gun Policy Survey of the National Opinion Research Center.

30. Cook P, Ludwig J, Hemenway D. The gun debate's new mythical number: how many defensive uses per year? J Policy Anal Manag. 1997; 16(3): 463–469.

31. Hemenway D. Private guns, public health. Ann Arbor: University of Michigan Press; 2004. P. 67.

32. Kellermann A, Westphal L, Fisher L, Harvard B. Weapon involvement in home invasion crimes. J Am Med Assoc. 1995; 273(22): 1759–1762.

33. Henigan D. Lethal logic: exploding the myths that paralyze American gun policy. Washington, DC: Potomac Books; 2009. P. 119.

34. Hemenway D. Private guns, public health. P. 68.

35. Annest J, Mercy J, Gibson D, Ryan G. National estimates of nonfatal firearm-related injuries: beyond the tip of the iceberg. J Am Med Assoc. 1995; 273(22): 1749–1754.

36. Beaman V, Kresnow M, Pollock D. Lethality of firearm-related injuries in the United States population. Ann Emerg Med. 2000; 35(3): 258–266.

37. Federal Bureau of Investigation. Crime in the United States, 2009. Expanded Homicide Data Table 15 [Internet]. Washington, DC: US Department of Justice. Available from: http://www2.fbi.gov/ucr/cius2009/offenses/expanded_information/data/shrtable_15.html

38. Hemenway D. Private guns, public health. P. 68.

39. Dahl J. "Loud music" shooter gets life in prison [Internet]. CBS News. 2014 Oct 17. Available from: http://www.cbsnews.com/news/michael-dunn-loud-music-shooter-gets-life-in-prison/

40. Cook P, Ludwig J. Defensive gun uses: new evidence from a national survey. J Quant Criminol. 1998; 14(2): 111–131.

41. Bureau of Justice Statistics. National Crime Victimization Survey [Internet]. Washington, DC: US Department of Justice; 2014. Available from: http://www.bjs.gov/index.cfm?ty=dcdetail&iid=245

42. Rand M. Guns and Crime: Handgun Victimization, Firearm Self-Defense, and Firearm Theft. Washington, DC: Bureau of Justice Statistics; 1994.

43. Federal Bureau of Investigation. Uniform Crime Reports 2013, Expanded homicide data table 7, Robbery Table 3, and Aggravated Assault Table [Internet]. Available from: http://www.fbi.gov/about-us/cjis/ucr/crime-in-the-u.s/2013/crime-in-the-US-2013/offenses-known-to-law-enforcement/expanded-offense/expandedoffensemain_final

44. Truman J, Langton L. Criminal Victimization, 2013. Washington, DC: US Department of Justice; 2014.

45. Tark J, Kleck G. Resisting crime: The effect of victim actions on the outcomes of crime. Criminology. 2004; 42(4): 861–910.

46. Violence Policy Center. Firearm justifiable homicides and nonfatal self-defense gun use. Washington, DC: Violence Policy Center; 2013. P. 2.

47. Hemenway D, Azrael D, Miller M. Gun use in the United States: results from two national surveys. Inj Prev. 2000; 6(4): 263–267.

48. Hemenway D, Azrael D, Miller M. Gun use in the United States. P. 265.

49. Hemenway D, Azrael D, Miller, M. Gun use in the United States. P. 266.

50. Violence Policy Center, Firearm Justifiable Homicides and Nonfatal Self-Defense Gun Use, P. 8.

51. US Department of Justice. Firearms stolen during household burglaries and other property crimes 2005–2010. Washington, DC: Bureau of Justice Statistics; 2012.

52. Kellermann A, Westphal, L. Fischer L, Harvard B. Weapon involvement in home invasion crimes.

53. Cook P, Goss K. The Gun debate: what everyone needs to know. New York: Oxford University Press; 2014. P. 21.

54. Kellermann A, Somes G, Rivara F, Lee R, Banton J. Injuries and deaths due to firearms in the home. J Trauma. 1998; 45(2): 263–267.

55. Kellermann A, Reay D. Protection or peril? An analysis of firearm-related deaths in the home. New Engl J Med. 1986; 314(24): 1557–1560.

56. Henigan D. Lethal logic. P. 124.

57. Karp A. Small Arms Survey 2007: Guns and the City. Geneva, Switzerland: Graduate Institute of International Studies; Annex 4.

58. Killias M, Markwalder N. Homicide and firearms in Europe. In: Liem M, Pridemore W, editors. Handbook of European homicide research: patterns, explanations, and country studies. New York: Springer Science and Business Media; 2012. P. 261–272.

59. Killias M, Markwalder N. Homicide and firearms in Europe. P. 270.
60. Killias M, Markwalder N. Homicide and firearms in Europe. P. 270.
61. May J, Hemenway D, Oen R, Pitts K. When criminals are shot: a survey of Washington DC jail detainees. Med Gen Med. 2000; 2(2): E1.
62. Cook P, Ludwig J. Guns in America: national survey on private ownership and use of firearms. Washington, DC: National Institute of Justice; 1997.
63. Uniacke S. Proportionality and self-defense. Law Philos. 2011; 30: 253–272.
64. Florida Statutes, Chapter 776. Justifiable Use of Force [statute on the Internet]. Available from: http://www.leg.state.fl.us/Statutes/index.cfm?App_mode=Display_Statute&URL=0700-0799/0776/0776.html
65. Catalano S. Victimization during household burglary. Washington, DC: Bureau of Justice Statistics; 2010.
66. Truman J, Langton L. Criminal Victimization, 2014. Washington, DC: US Department of Justice; 2015. Table 3.
67. Federal Bureau of Investigation. 2014 Crime in the United States. Expanded Homicide Data Table 10 [Internet]. Available from: https://www.fbi.gov/about-us/cjis/ucr/crime-in-the-u.s/2014/crime-in-the-u.s.-2014/tables/expanded-homicide-data/expanded_homicide_data_table_10_murder_circumstances_by_relationship_2014.xls
68. Zawitz M. Guns used in crime. Washington, DC: Bureau of Justice Statistics; 1995.
69. Annest J, Mercy J, Gibson D, Ryan G. National estimates of nonfatal firearm-related injuries.

10

Armed Self-Defense II: Protection or Hazard?

Unlike other countries (e.g., Australia, Canada, and the UK) in which gun regulation has become tighter in response to large-scale mass murders, there has been a growing gun rights movement in the USA over the last 30 years even as mass murders and school massacres have become more commonplace and more lethal. To many observers from other countries, it is illogical to try to solve gun violence with more guns. It is like dealing with rampant alcoholism by making alcohol more accessible or fighting a communicable disease by encouraging more people to expose themselves to the virus or bacteria responsible.

Nevertheless, over the last quarter of a century, US states have passed numerous laws to lessen controls over firearms and to increase the circumstances in which they can be used by private citizens. With the strong encouragement, financing, and pressure exerted by the gun lobby, we have:

- Laws permitting citizens to carry concealed guns in all states. As of September 2015, 44 states required a concealed-weapons permit, while 6 states did not.[1] There is a push to increase the number of states not requiring a permit.[2] The vast majority of states requiring a permit leave little discretion for authorities to deny the issuance of such

© The Author(s) 2016
T. Gabor, *Confronting Gun Violence in America*,
DOI 10.1007/978-3-319-33723-4_10

permits. As of December 2015, just nine states made it easier for an official to reject an application if, for example, it was thought that the person was not of good character or failed to provide a good reason for carrying a gun. In general, these laws constitute a departure from policies that historically banned or severely restricted concealed carry, including many frontier towns like Dodge City, Kansas.

- As of August 2015, just three states and the District of Columbia prohibited the open carrying of any firearm. Three states allow the open carrying of a handgun but not a long gun, and two states allow the open carrying of a long gun but not a handgun.[3]
- While federal law prohibits the possession of a gun in a school zone, there are exceptions to this prohibition where someone is licensed to possess or carry firearms, or where the firearm is unloaded and locked up. As of December 2015, nine states prohibited colleges and universities from banning firearms from at least certain areas within campuses.[4] Another 16 states leave it up to the institutions to determine their weapons policy.
- Aside from schools, recent legislation is permitting guns in places formerly considered out of bounds. In 2014, Georgia passed a "guns everywhere" law, allowing licensed gun owners to bring guns to schools, bars, churches, and some government buildings.[5] Loaded guns in bars are now allowed in about a half dozen other states, and both federal and some state laws now allow the carrying of firearms in national and state parks.[6]
- As of July 2013, 27 states had adopted Stand Your Ground (SYG; also known as Shoot First) laws that have expanded a person's right to self-defense. Specifically, these states permit the use of deadly force in self-defense in public places, with no duty to retreat. Seven additional states permit the use of deadly force in self-defense in public with no duty to retreat through a combination of statutes, judicial decisions, and/or jury instructions.[7]
- Federal law mandates that licensed gun dealers only sell long guns to individuals 18 and older and handguns to individuals 21 and older. However, less than half the states have a minimum age for long gun possession and for sales from unlicensed dealers. In 20 states, an eight-year-old can both legally buy a shotgun and possess it.[8]

- As of December 2012, 17 states prohibited employers from preventing their employees from bringing guns to work and keeping them locked in their vehicles, even if these vehicles are on the employer's property.[9]

Extent of Gun Carrying

A survey in the mid-1990s, funded by the Police Foundation, estimated that 7.5 % of adults carried a gun for protection in the previous year, but this figure was 5.4 % when those carrying for work only were excluded.[10] Two Harvard-based surveys in the 1990s found that about 3 % of adults have carried guns on their person over the previous month and just over half of these carried for protection from humans.[11] Another survey conducted by the National Opinion Research Center found that 8.9 % of adults carried a gun for protection at least once in the previous year; however, this survey illustrated that the majority of those carrying guns do not do so regularly. The survey found that about 10 % of those carrying did so daily and over half carried once or just several times a year.[12] As of 2014, there were approximately 11 million Americans with permits to carry guns, about 3 % of the nation's population.[13] The number of gun carriers will be somewhat higher than this total, as some states do not require a permit to carry a gun. These figures indicate that gun carriers likely do not exceed 5 % of the population and just a fraction of these individuals carry daily or several times a week.

The Risks versus Benefits of Gun Ownership and Carrying

In 1998, John Lott, then a University of Chicago economist, gave the concealed carry movement some credibility with the publication of his book *More Guns, Less Crime*.[14] Lott conducted statistical analyses from 1985 to 1992 that purported to show that states with *Shall Issue* concealed carry laws (i.e., carry laws with few restrictions) experienced substantial declines in homicides, rapes, and aggravated assaults. Lott's interpretation of this finding was that offenders were deterred from committing crimes in places where they were more likely to encounter an armed victim.

Lott's data have been reanalyzed, and his conclusions have been subject to harsh criticism by a number of highly regarded researchers from the public health, legal, public policy, and criminal justice fields. One study found that, if anything, *Shall Issue* concealed carry laws have been accompanied by increases in adult homicide rates.[15] The National Research Council conducted an analysis with an extended time frame to 2000, and 17 of 18 panel members concluded that the existing research was inadequate to conclude that right to carry laws increased or decreased crime.[16] Further extending the analysis to 2010, researchers from Stanford University and Johns Hopkins found that these laws actually are "associated with substantially higher rates of aggravated assault, rape, robbery and murder."[17]

Dennis Henigan, formerly with the Brady Campaign to Prevent Gun Violence, pointed out that, in Lott's analysis, it was peculiar that the concealed carry laws showed the greatest effect in relation to crimes more often committed by intimates and acquaintances and little or no impact (depending on who conducted the analysis) in relation to robbery, which is far more often a predatory crime involving strangers. It is precisely in relation to crimes like robbery that the effect of gun carrying is expected to have the greatest effect.[18] Such findings suggest that the violent crime rates seemed to have little to do with the concealed carry laws. Another research team concurred with this conclusion, saying that inferences based on Lott's analysis are inappropriate and that Lott's results "cannot be used responsibly to formulate public policy."[19]

Philip Cook and Kristin Goss of Duke University add that we cannot expect much of an effect of concealed carry laws when just a small proportion of the population—their estimate is 3.6 %—has a permit to carry.[20] The number carrying at any given time is fewer as some with permits don't carry or just do so occasionally. Cook and Goss add that the actual change in the number of people carrying is smaller than the number of permits issued would indicate as some of those with permits were already carrying guns in public.[21] In addition, they note that permits to carry tend to be concentrated in rural and suburban areas where crime rates already tend to be relatively low and licensees are most often white, middle-aged, middle-class people who tend to have relatively low victimization rates. Thus, the small proportion of individuals with permits, along with the lower-risk population that carries firearms, are unlikely to lead to more than a modest effect on crime rates.

The notion that offenders are deterred by armed victims has weak empirical support. In fact, street gang members and drug dealers who are more likely to carry guns are also far more likely to be murdered. Gary Kleck of Florida State University reports that gang members are almost 9 times more likely to own guns than other youth and are 19 times more likely to be homicide victims.[22] Drug dealers are almost four times more likely to own a handgun than nondealers and six times more likely to be homicide victims. Rather than serving as a deterrent, it may also be the case that offenders will arm themselves and use preemptive force if they believe their victims will be armed. A survey of offenders in fact indicates that they consider whether the victim is armed in their decision to carry a weapon.[23]

David Fortunato of the University of California tested the idea of whether permissive concealed carry laws ("Shall Issue" laws) have the potential to deter people from committing crimes.[24] He argued that for these laws to deter crime, people in states with more permissive gun laws must believe that there are more people there who carry a gun. Fortunato asked a national sample of Americans how many people out of 1000 in their state carried a gun. Their responses indicated that those in states with more permissive gun laws did not believe that more of their fellow residents carried a gun than those living in states with tougher, more restrictive gun laws. Fortunato concludes that deterrence cannot happen if potential assailants in states with more permissive gun laws are not aware that more people are carrying. It is similar to the idea that people will not be deterred by more police officers on the street or by other security measures if they are not aware of these measures. Fortunato adds that while his findings indicate that deterrence cannot happen, the adverse consequences of more gun carrying, including the escalation of altercations and accidental shootings, will increase with more carrying.

David Hemenway of Harvard University and Sara Solnick of the University of Vermont examined the effectiveness of self-defense gun use in preventing injury and property loss. Using data from the National Crime Victimization Survey for 2007–2011, they focused on violent and property crimes in which there was personal contact between the offender and victim. In over 14,000 incidents, a gun was used in self-defense in just 127 (.9 %) of cases. Victims sustained an injury in virtually an identical proportion of cases, regardless of whether or not a gun was used in self-defense. Property loss was not less for those using a gun as opposed to another weapon as the means of protection.[25] The authors concluded that their findings provided little evidence that defensive gun uses reduced the likelihood of injuries or property loss.

Effect of Gun Carrying Laws on Specific Crimes

Lisa Hepburn and her colleagues at Harvard University's School of Public Health analyzed the effect on homicide of changes in state-level gun carrying laws for all 50 states from 1979 to 1998.[26] The study found that there was no statistically significant association between changes in concealed carry laws and state homicide rates.

Advocates of gun ownership have also argued that high ownership levels will reduce the number of residential burglaries, especially "hot" burglaries (those occurring when someone is at home) as it is thought that burglars will seek out unoccupied dwellings to avoid being shot. The available evidence, however, does not support these purported benefits of gun ownership.

Victimization surveys in 11 developed countries revealed that the USA (with the most guns) ranked in the middle with regard to its attempted and completed burglary rates and that, overall, burglary rates did not show a decline as gun ownership rates increased.[27] In addition, a study of US counties showed that residential burglary rates, including hot burglaries, actually increased, rather than declined, where gun ownership levels were higher when factors such as income and alcohol consumption were statistically controlled.[28] It may be that rather than having a protective effect, guns make a home more attractive to burglars due to their financial value, and the value of stolen guns to individuals who prefer to use stolen guns to commit crimes so the user cannot be traced.

The Justice Department's Bureau of Justice Statistics reports that from 2005 through 2010 an average of 232,400 firearms were stolen each year in the USA, the majority during burglaries.[29] Jim Kessler, formerly a research director with the Americans for Gun Safety Foundation (now a policy institute called Third Way), found that gun thefts were most prevalent in states with the highest rates of gun ownership and the least regulation of gun storage.[30] One study by the Orlando Sentinel found that close to a third of all stolen guns in Orange County, Florida, were taken from parked cars, indicating the consequences of bringing guns to work and other venues that are accessible to the public.[31]

Crimes by Individuals with Concealed Carry Permits

Aside from the inherent risks and benefits associated with carrying firearms, there are questions related to the manner in which these laws are implemented. That is, how thorough is the screening of permit applicants? While procedures vary from state to state, the number of permit holders who have committed serious crimes is troubling. The evidence suggests that many concealed carry license holders do not fit the NRA's description of "law-abiding, upstanding community leaders who merely seek to exercise their right of self-defense."

An analysis by the *Sun-Sentinel* newspaper in South Florida found that, in the first six months of 2006, 216 concealed carry weapon holders had active arrest warrants, 128 individuals had domestic violence restraining orders against them, and 1400 people pleaded guilty or no contest to felony charges. Those receiving licenses to carry a gun included individuals convicted of manslaughter, aggravated assault, burglary, and sex crimes.[32]

In first three years of Texas' concealed carry laws, those with permits were arrested for over 2000 crimes, including homicide, kidnapping, rape, and other types of violent as well as property crimes.[33] Furthermore, the Violence Policy Center (VPC) has reported that during the first six months of 1997, the weapon-related arrest rate of concealed permit hold-ers was more than twice that for the general adult population of Texas eligible to own handguns.[34] A more recent report by the VPC has found that 722 people, including 17 police officers, were killed by concealed carry permit holders between May 2007 and February 2015. During the same period, the VPC reports and provides evidence to the effect that 28 mass shootings were committed by these permit holders.[35]

These casualties are likely the tip of the iceberg as data are not routinely collected on crimes committed by concealed-weapons permit holders. The Brady Center to Prevent Gun Violence provides examples of indi-viduals with concealed-weapons licenses who have committed serious crimes[36]:

Miami, Florida

Lyglenson Lemorin, 32, an accused terrorist alleged to have ties to al-Qaeda, retained his CCW license after two domestic violence arrests in 1997 and 1998. The first time he allegedly threw a beer bottle at his girlfriend's neck. The second time he allegedly punched a pregnant for-mer girlfriend, flashed his gun, and warned her, "I'll kill you." His CCW license was suspended in February 2000 for carrying a weapon with a restraining order against him, but was actually reinstated a month later. It was finally suspended again in 2006 when Lemorin was arrested and ulti-mately indicted in a terrorist plot to destroy the Sears Tower in Chicago.

Manatee County, Florida

Edward Caldwell, 33, a registered sex offender since 1997, got a con-cealed weapon license in 2004. He served seven months in jail and five years probation for threatening to shoot a woman. Caldwell had also amassed an even longer criminal record since 2001: acquitted on a charge of lewd conduct toward a child under 16; a domestic violence restrain-ing order between 2002 and 2003; and a warrant issued against him for failure to report his sex offender status. Caldwell had also made references to committing "suicide by cop." The state of Florida finally moved to suspend his license again in 2006.

Vancouver, Washington, October 3, 2006

Jon W. Loveless, unemployed for ten years, daily marijuana smoker, and father of two children, said that he shot "until my gun was empty" at Kenneth Eichorn, because Eichorn had "a weird look" on his face. Loveless also claimed that Eichorn held a handgun, but Eichorn's family disputes the claim. Loveless was charged with one count of second-degree murder.

Fort Lauderdale, Florida, January 1, 2006

Rogelio Monero, 49, allegedly shot and killed Victor Manuel Villanueva, 17, during a New Year's altercation as Moreno tried to stop a fight between Villanueva and a third party. Moreno was charged with manslaughter.

Orange County, California, August 1, 2005

Raymond K. Yi, an Orange County "sheriff's reserve deputy" was arrested for brandishing a firearm at a golf course. Reserve deputies are honorary and have no police power. Reportedly, a golfer ahead of Yi hit Yi's ball out of the fairway. Yi confronted the man with his badge and gun, and after some escalation, allegedly pointed his weapon at him and said, "I will kill you."

Greenacres, Florida, January 13, 2004

It was reported that James Anthony Settembre, a vocal gun advocate, shot his wife Debra twice and then shot himself in the head.

Bethesda, Maryland, November 24, 2003

A man threatening to commit suicide was taken to the hospital after police seized from his apartment: "17 rifles, 10 handguns, a homemade silencer, two stun guns, two blowguns, two concealed-weapons permits, more than 1,300 rounds of ammunition, 48 knives, and six samurai swords in sheaths."

Davie, Florida, April 30, 2003

Michael Pecora walked into his business partner's office, sat down, and shot him twice in the head. He then shot himself.

Tucson, Arizona, October 29, 2002

Robert Flores, Jr., shot and killed three professors, and then himself, in a rampage at the University of Arizona School of Nursing, where he was a failing student. Reportedly, he had told classmates about a year before that he had obtained a CCW permit.

One of the most highly publicized recent shootings was that of Jordan Davis, a 17-year-old African-American teen by Michael Dunn, a 45-year-old white man.[37] Dunn pulled into a gas station and parked next to an SUV containing four black teenagers, including Davis. Dunn was bothered by the volume of the music coming from the teens' vehicle and asked them to turn it down. The teens initially complied and then Davis turned it back up and apparently used some offensive language. A verbal exchange occurred. Dunn subsequently shot nine rounds into the SUV, mortally wounding Davis. Prosecutors argued that Dunn was angry because he was disrespected by a young black man. Dunn's fiancé at the time testified that he told her, "I hate that thug music."[38] This case illustrates how a spontaneous argument can quickly escalate to a homicide when firearms are present.

A team of Harvard University researchers conducted a telephone survey of 790 licensed drivers in Arizona that examined the relationship between firearm carrying and hostile behavior on the roadway. Respondents were asked whether they had carried a gun while driving in the 12 months prior to the survey and whether they had personally made obscene gestures, cursed or shouted at other drivers, impeded another driver's progress with their vehicle, aggressively "followed another driver too closely," or brandished a gun at another driver. The study found that self-reported hostile behavior while driving was significantly more common among men, young adults, and individuals who carried a firearm in their car. Thus, having a firearm in the car was a predictor of aggressive and illegal behavior behind the wheel.[39] A subsequent nationwide survey of 2,400 drivers also found that individuals who were in a vehicle with a gun were more likely to display some form of road rage.[40]

The National Opinion Research Center's 2001 survey on gun policy found that individuals who carry guns for protection are more likely to have an arrest history (for a nontraffic offense) than nongun carrying adults.[41]

Gun Carrying and Stand Your Ground Laws

Certain laws may inadvertently promote violent acts among concealed weapon permit holders. As of 2014, 33 states have adopted SYG (also known as "Shoot First") laws.[42] While they vary, these laws allow an individual to use deadly force in self-defense, either at home or in public, without a duty to retreat. These laws have been a departure from traditional legal principles that require a person to retreat when he or she feels threatened in a public place. In the Florida version, lethal force is permissible, without a duty to retreat, if a person reasonably believes that he will prevent death, bodily harm, or a forcible felony.[43]

Judge Krista Marx, of the 15th Judicial Circuit of Florida, sums up the manner in which SYG changed the law: "It used to be, 'Did they have a duty to retreat?' It was a much more limited circumstance where justifiable use of deadly force would come into play. And now the door's been flung wide open to almost any situation where a person will assert that they were in imminent fear of death or great bodily harm."[44]

The Law Center to Prevent Gun Violence refers to SYG laws and weak concealed weapon laws as a "deadly combination," as these laws both legitimize the use of lethal force when a person feels threatened and, at the same time, make it more likely that people will have lethal weapons at those times.[45]

In the previous section, we have seen that a significant number of concealed weapon permit holders may have a history of criminal behavior or may commit crimes once they obtain a permit. In a growing number of states, no permit is required at all. Having a gun on one's person may lead some individuals to exercise less caution than he or she may otherwise show. Conversely, not having weapons at the ready may require us to try to resolve disputes in nonviolent ways, including retreating from dangerous situations. With a gun at the ready, people may make fatal errors in judgment with no opportunity to pull back once the trigger is pulled. In addition, research indicates that one of the main reasons offenders choose a gun for a crime is that potential victims may be armed.[46]

John Timoney, former police chief of Miami, made the following prediction just before SYG took effect: "Whether it's trick-or-treaters or kids playing in the yard of someone who doesn't want them there or some drunk guy stumbling into the wrong house, you're encouraging people to possibly use deadly physical force where it shouldn't be used."[47] An analysis by the *Tampa Bay Times* provides support for this prediction as it found that the number of justifiable homicides in Florida tripled following the introduction of SYG in 2005, from an average of 34 per year in the first half of the 2000s to an average of 100 per year from 2007 to 2009.[48]

In 2012, the *Tampa Bay Times* conducted another, comprehensive analysis of about 200 SYG cases and their outcomes based on media reports, court records, and interviews with prosecutors and defense attorneys in Florida.[49] Among the findings are the following:

- Nearly 70 % of those invoking SYG to avoid prosecution were successful.
- Defendants claiming SYG are more likely to be successful if the victim is black.
- The number of cases is increasing as defense attorneys are using the law in unanticipated ways (e.g., in cases with minor or no injuries).
- In nearly a third of the cases analyzed, defendants initiated the fight, shot an unarmed person, or pursued their victims—and still went free.
- In 79 % of the cases the shooter could have retreated to avoid the confrontation.
- 60 % of the defendants had been previously arrested.
- Drug dealers have successfully invoked SYG despite the fact they were in the middle of a deal when the shooting started.

The absurdity of the law was illustrated by Leon County (Florida) Circuit Judge Terry Lewis, who wrote, "Each individual on each side of the exchange of gunfire can claim self-defense," saying the law "could conceivably result in all persons who exchanged gunfire on a public street being immune from prosecution."[50]

Cheng Cheng and Mark Hoekstra of Texas A&M University conducted a nationwide study of the impact of SYG laws.[51] They noted that over 20 states have passed a version of SYG from 2000 to 2010. They found that homicide rates in states with an SYG law increased by an average of 8 % over states without it. This translates to roughly 600 additional homicides per year. The researchers found that Florida provides a useful case study for the more general pattern. Homicide rates in Florida increased by 8 % from the period prior to passing the law (2000–2004) to the period after the law (2006–2010). By contrast, national homicide rates fell by 6 % during the same time period. Cheng and Hoekstra also did not find that SYG laws deter crimes such as burglary, robbery, or aggravated assault.

Chandler McLellan and Erdal Tekin, two Georgia State University economists, also found that SYG laws that removed a duty to retreat in threatening situations were associated with higher homicide rates.[52] They note that these laws may lead more people to carry guns in public and that some people may be emboldened by the fact that they do not need to retreat. These researchers further found that the rise in homicide was primarily found among white males.

John Roman, a Senior Fellow at the Urban Institute, analyzed data from the FBI Supplemental Homicide Reports to conduct a comparative analysis of justified homicide rates from 2005 to 2010 in SYG and non-SYG states.[53] Although racial disparities are also found in states without SYG laws, these disparities were significantly greater in SYG states. In SYG states, a white shooter who kills a black victim is 350 % more likely to be found to be justified than if the same shooter killed a white victim. In these states, justifiable shooting rulings ranged from 3 % to 15 % for white-on-white, black-on-white, and black-on-black killings. When the shooter was white and the victim black, 36 % were ruled justified.

Robert Spitzer, a political scientist at the State University of New York at Cortland, notes that the combination of expanded SYG laws with escalating civilian gun carrying increases unnecessary violent confrontations and deaths.[54] He adds that we need policies that defuse confrontations in public places, especially with the 11 million or so Americans now possessing licenses to carry concealed firearms.

Referring to America's past, Spitzer writes:

We've learned this lesson before, in our own violent past, when strict regulation of concealed gun carrying was the near-universal and successful response to gun violence. As early as 1686, New Jersey enacted a law against wearing weapons because they induced "great Fear and Quarrels." Massachusetts followed in 1750. In the late 1700s, North Carolina and Virginia passed similar laws. In the 1800s, as interpersonal violence and gun carrying spread, 37 states joined the list. Tennessee's 1821 law fined "each and every person so degrading himself" by carrying weapons in public. Alabama's 1839 law was titled "An Act to Suppress the Evil Practice of Carrying Weapons Secretly." Why must we relearn a lesson we codified centuries ago? How dumb are we?[55]

The American Bar Association's National Task Force on SYG laws writes that SYG states experienced an increase in homicide and that the application of these laws is unpredictable and uneven and results in racial disparities.[56] The task force notes that an individual's right to self-defense was protected prior to SYG laws. It adds that victims' rights are undermined in states with statutory immunity from criminal prosecution and civil suit as a result of SYG laws. It recommends that states repeal SYG laws or at least amend provisions that prevent victims and/or innocent bystanders and their families from seeking compensation and other remedies for injuries sustained.

Inaccurate Shooting and Inadequate Training

Experiments with mock school shootings have shown that armed students will often freeze or be shot trying to confront the attacker. Commenting on these studies, Canadian journalist Jonathan Kay writes: "When pro-gun activists and politicians make their case, they often regress into adolescent fantasy worlds—where ordinary Joes and Janes are transformed into heroic commandos. In real life, ordinary people faced with a mass-shooter situation are more likely to wet their pants."[57]

Joseph Vince, an agent with the ATF for 27 years and Director of the Criminal Justice Program at Mount St. Mary's University, is an internationally recognized expert on firearms and gun-related crime. In a report prepared for the National Gun Victims Action Council, Vince and his collaborators, Timothy Wolfe and Layton Field, underscore the lethality of firearms and the importance of a full vetting of those seeking a license to carry a gun:[58]

Since a firearm has immense lethality, the act of carrying one cannot be taken lightly. It should be given to those who have demonstrated good judgment, as well as mastered the necessary skills to handle this awesome responsibility. Legislators need to strengthen the vetting process of persons who are authorized to carry a firearm outside a residence. A simple criminal record check is not sufficient. Preventing criminal or accidental tragedies with firearms begins by allowing only those who have been properly trained initially and ongoing—and are known to be non-violent law abiding citizens to carry in public. Likewise, no one who has anger, mental, or drug/alcohol issues should be permitted to carry a firearm. Certainly, an extensive law enforcement investigation of an applicant's background should be required to detect unsuitable candidates.

Vince and his associates found that for a citizen to carry and, perhaps, use a firearm for protection in a stressful situation, training should include mental preparation, knowledge of the law, judgment, as well as expertise, skill, and familiarity with firearms. They recommend basic initial training to receive a permit and biannual recertification to maintain the permit. Both training and recertification should consist of decision-making during real-life scenarios, shooting accuracy in stressful situations, and firing range practice.

The above-recommended standards are in stark contrast with actual requirements in the states. As of September, 2015, six states required no permit to carry a firearm at all, some states had no training requirement (e.g., Georgia), and many other states were extremely vague in terms of their requirements (e.g., they do not specify the amount of instruction required or the score required in written and field proficiency tests).[59,60]

To illustrate the importance of training and experience in using firearms when threatened, retired Army Sergeant Rafael Noboa y Rivera, who led a combat team in Iraq, states that soldiers generally only function effectively following exposure to fire on several occasions. Unlike gunplay in the movies, he told Joshua Holland of *The Nation* magazine: "When I heard gunfire [in Iraq], I didn't immediately pick up my rifle and react. I first tried to ascertain where the shooting was coming from, where I was in relation to the gunfire and how far away it was. I think most untrained people are either going to freeze up, or just whip out their gun and start firing in that circumstance."[61]

Pete Blair, associate professor of criminal justice at Texas State University and director of the Advanced Law Enforcement Rapid Response Training Center, trains law enforcement personnel to respond to active shooter situations using live-fire exercises with real firearms that are modified to fire "soap rounds" that leave only welts when they hit. Real-world scenarios prepare officers for high-stress situations. Blair notes that one would expect people without training to "freeze up or not know what to do, and to have difficulty performing actions correctly."[62]

David Chipman, a former agent with ATF who spent several years on the agency's SWAT team, says, "Training for a potentially deadly encounter meant, at a minimum, qualifying four times a year throughout my 25-year career. And this wasn't just shooting paper—it meant doing extensive tactical exercises. And when I was on the SWAT team we had to undergo monthly tactical training."[63] Tactical officers receive training in "judgmental shooting," which includes knowing when it is wise to hold their fire, and "blue-on-blue awareness," which reinforces the importance of considering whether other officers are present.

Research and police records show that even trained police officers miss their targets more often than they hit them during stressful combat situations. Measuring shooting accuracy is complex as it varies due to a number of factors, including the distance to the target, visibility (day or night), and the level of the threat. Greg Morrison, a former police officer and firearms instructor, states that there is some agreement among practitioners and researchers that in real-life crime situations, officers hit the mark once in every six shots. This is a proficiency level of 17 % in combat situations. Morrison adds that the limited research in this area indicates that the average adversary (criminal) shoots at 10 % proficiency.[64]

Records of firearm discharges indicate that the New York City Police Department (NYPD) has a 34 % hit ratio (proficiency level) and the Los Angeles Police Department has a 29 % hit ratio.[65] Another analysis, published by the RAND Center on Quality Policing, found that in the years 1998–2006, the average hit ratio for NYPD officers involved in a shooting in which the subject does not fire back was 30 %. However, this rate falls to 18 % where the target is shooting at officers.[66] Another study by the Police Policy Studies Council found that NYPD officers were hitting their targets just 15 % of the time when confronted by an armed suspect.[67] Therefore, several analyses show that, in combat situations, trained officers miss the mark more than 80 % of the time.

We would logically expect the average civilian gun owner to do much worse. Civilian gun owners receive little or no marksmanship training, and they are not required to undergo continued training as is the case with police officers. Ordinarily, civilian gun owners do not receive training in judgment and are less knowledgeable about the law, that is, those circumstances in which lethal force is permissible. Judgment refers to an armed person's ability to make appropriate "shoot/don't shoot" decisions in a stressful situation. The goal is to minimize errors, that is, shooting when not necessary and failing to shoot when one's life is in danger. Many police departments use firearms training simulators that expose officers to a number of high-risk scenarios for training purposes. The aim is to achieve the best judgment possible during threatening situations.

The lack of training of gun carriers in most states is reflected in the many examples of catastrophic errors by individuals who are frightened and have guns in their possession or nearby. Humans will always misperceive threats; however, the presence of guns and a lack of restraint in using them make fatal errors far more likely. Consider the following cases:

- A 21-year-old Iowa woman was killed after she, along with her younger sister, tried to surprise her fiancé by hiding in a closet in his home. He heard a noise and saw the closet door open. When the girls jumped out of the closet, he fired and killed his fiancé with a handgun he kept for protection.[68]
- A seven-year-old boy was in critical condition after his grandmother mistook him for an intruder and shot him. She and her twin grandsons were sleeping after their father went to work. When she heard the bedroom door open, she assumed it was an intruder, grabbed the loaded revolver she kept by her bed, and fired one shot toward the door. As it turned out, she shot her grandson in the upper body.[69]
- A 20-year-old mother was watching television in her parents' home when she heard noises outside the bedroom wall. She had heard stories of recent burglaries in the neighborhood. Though she had no weapons training, she picked up a semiautomatic pistol. She clumsily fired a number of shots and hit her eight-month old son in the head. He died several hours later.[70]

Literally hundreds of these tragedies occur each year in the USA. Humans will always make errors in judgment. However, these errors will be more frequent and are more likely to have a fatal outcome where guns are accessible and individuals lack training in assessing threats and in the proper handling of firearms.[71]

Joseph Vince and his colleagues add:

> *The average violent attack is over in 3 seconds. They are "blitz" attacks, designed to blindside and overwhelm us. We must be able to comprehend what's happening, orient ourselves to that attack, draw, and begin fighting back within that 3 second window, or else there's a very good chance we'll be defeated before we have a chance to even draw our weapons. The problem is, our bodies don't only choose between Fight and Flight, but instead between Fight, Flight, and Freeze. And without specific training, many (if not most) of us are prone to freezing for 3 or more seconds when confronted with a sudden, psychologically and physically overwhelming attack. We need training that will allow us to avoid violence whenever possible, but overcome, defeat, and survive violence when we can't avoid it.[72]*

FBI Study Illustrates the Challenges of Armed Self-Defense

An FBI study of "active shooter" incidents from 2000 to 2013 illustrates the reality of using guns for self-defense.[73] The FBI defines these incidents as those in which a shooting is in progress and law enforcement personnel and citizens have the potential to affect the outcome of the event. An additional aspect of the definition was that "an individual is actively engaged in killing or attempting to kill people in a confined and populated area."

The study examined 160 active shooter incidents that occurred in the USA between 2000 and 2013. The findings are as follows:

- A third of the incidents ended in two minutes or less, and over two-thirds ended in five minutes or less.
- In 45 (28.1 %) of the incidents, law enforcement and the shooter exchanged gunfire. Of these incidents, the shooter was killed at the scene in 21, killed at another location in 4, wounded in 9, committed suicide in 9, and surrendered in 2.

- Law enforcement suffered casualties in 21 (46.7 %) of the 45 incidents where they engaged the shooter. This resulted in 9 officers killed and 28 wounded.
- In 3 (1.9 %) of the 160 incidents, armed, nonsworn security personnel were killed. In 2 additional incidents, 2 unarmed security officers were killed and 2 were wounded.
- In 21 incidents (13.1 %), the situation ended after unarmed citizens successfully restrained the shooter, occasionally with the help of off-duty law enforcement officers. Over half of these incidents involved unarmed principals, teachers, other school staff, and students who confronted shooters (most of these shooters were students).
- In 5 (3.1 %) of the incidents, the shooting ended after armed individuals who were not police officers exchanged fire with the shooters. *Just one of these cases involved a citizen with a valid firearms permit.* In the other four cases, armed security guards confronted the shooter.

Thus, the incidents unfold quickly and the shooter has the advantage as he or she selects the time and place of the attack. Police casualties were almost as common as those among the shooters. In just one of 160 cases did an armed civilian, who was not a security guard, intervene. The number of police casualties shows the danger involved in confronting shooters even by the best trained and equipped officers. Also, this study shows that few armed civilians intervene in active shooter situations, and these cases were selected because they were those in which intervention by civilians and the police was most likely to occur.

Guns and Perceptions of Safety

Do we feel safer when we and others around us own and carry guns? Even if concealed weapon laws and other legislation that encourages the arming of civilians for self-defense do not actually increase our safety, it may appear logical that owning guns for self-protection can make us *feel* safer.

Two national surveys, conducted in 1996 and 1999 on behalf of the Harvard Injury Control Research Center, show that the community at large does not feel more secure when more citizens carry guns. These surveys revealed that 59 % of Americans would feel less safe and 12 % more safe if the number of people carrying guns in their community rises. For women only, 70 % indicated that they would feel less safe. In addition, by margins of at least 9–1, Americans do not believe that ordinary citizens should be permitted to bring their guns into restaurants, college campuses, sports arenas, bars, hospitals, or government buildings.[74] This said, certain groups within the population—whites, men, conservatives, and gun owners—are more likely to view firearms as having a protective value.[75]

More recent surveys have found that the public may be more evenly divided on the issue of gun ownership and safety. However, as illustrated in Chap. 13, the view that guns promote feelings of safety tends to erode when people are asked specifically about gun carrying in their community as opposed to gun possession in the home.[76]

While it is just the story of one individual, Heidi Yewman's story, while perhaps not representative of how the average owner responds to gun ownership, illustrates some of the anxieties and insecurities that may be associated with gun possession.[77] Yewman, an author who attended Columbine High School in Littleton, Colorado, the site of one of America's worst school massacres, decided to experiment with gun possession and carrying for one month. Her experience also indicates some of the risks associated with these activities, even where the owner is a responsible individual.

> *Only two days into my experiment … I put my purse on the counter and then spent the next hour out on the back deck. Walking into the kitchen to refresh our drinks, I noticed my purse with the 9mm Glock still inside it. … Panic set in as I realized my teen son was playing video games just 10 feet away.*
>
> *Since having the gun I've had two repairmen, a carpet cleaner, and a salesman in my home. If the gun's for self-protection, it's not going to do any good in the safe, but it's not really practical to have the gun pointing at them as they work. How else would I eliminate the element of surprise if I were attacked?*
>
> *I was late for a meeting and barely noticed the large man enter [a parking garage] behind me. … "Should I pull the gun out? Should I point it at him?" I realized the gun wouldn't do me any good because he was behind me. My heart racing, we finally got to the lobby door where the man simply passed by me.*

All I felt was fear. Physically taking the gun out of the safe and putting it in a holster on my hip literally reminded me that I was going out into a big bad scary unsafe world.

Bottom Line

Despite numerous high-casualty mass shootings over the last 10–15 years, many states have continued to adopt laws that have expanded the rights of gun owners and increased the circumstances in which guns can be used by private citizens. Despite such changes in legislation, gun carriers do not exceed 5 % of the population and just a fraction of these individuals carry on a daily or biweekly basis.

The idea that the concealed carry laws that have been passed in many states beginning in the 1980s have reduced crime has been discredited by a National Research Council panel, as well as researchers from Stanford University and Johns Hopkins University. In fact, a study assessing the impact of these laws up to 2010 found that they are associated with substantially higher rates of aggravated assault, rape, robbery and murder.

Aside from being counterproductive, laws that enable gun carrying appear to have other side effects and limitations. An FBI study of active shooter incidents have found little evidence of interventions by armed civilians in stopping actual or potential mass killings. Also, studies in Florida and Texas have revealed many crimes committed by concealed carry holders. In addition, laws permitting gun carrying do not seem to be making citizens feel more secure.

Law enforcement and military instructors who have experienced combat note that the training requirements under state concealed and open permitting laws are seriously inadequate in preparing civilians for the actual deployment of weapons in threatening situations. These experts point out that even trained police officers often perform poorly when under fire.

Over half the states have adopted some version of SYG laws. The American Bar Association's National Task Force on SYG laws is highly critical of these laws. The task force writes that SYG states have experienced an increase in homicide and that the application of these laws is unpredictable, uneven, and results in racial disparities.[78] The task force notes that an individual's right to self-defense was already protected prior to SYG laws.

Notes

1. Law Center to Prevent Gun Violence. Concealed weapons permitting policy summary [Internet]. Smartgunlaws.org. 2015 Sep 10. Available from: http://smartgunlaws.org/concealed-weapons-permitting-policy-summary/
2. Spies M. The push to allow Americans to carry concealed guns without a permit [Internet]. The Trace. 2016 Mar 7. Available from: http://www.thetrace.org/2016/03/permitless-carry-states-west-virginia/
3. Law Center to Prevent Gun Violence. Open carry policy summary [Internet]. 2015 Aug 21. Available from: http://smartgunlaws.org/open-carrying-policy-summary/
4. Armed Campuses. Guns on campus laws for public colleges and universities [Internet] Available from: http://www.armedcampuses.org/
5. Copeland L, Richards D. GA. Governor signs "guns everywhere" into law [Internet]. USA Today. 2014 Apr 23. Available from: http://www.usatoday.com/story/news/nation/2014/04/23/georgia-gun-law/8046315/
6. Lee S. Seven craziest gun laws in America [Internet]. Salon.com. 2012 Dec 18. Available from: http://www.salon.com/2012/12/18/7_craziest_gun_laws_in_america/
7. Law Center to Prevent Gun Violence. Stand your ground policy summary [Internet]. Smartgunlaws.org. 2013 Jul 18. Available from: http://smartgunlaws.org/stand-your-ground-policy-summary/
8. Matthews D. The six craziest state gun laws [Internet]. Washington Post. 2012 Dec 16. Available from: http://www.washingtonpost.com/blogs/wonkblog/wp/2012/12/16/the-6-craziest-state-gun-laws
9. Matthews D. The six craziest gun laws.
10. Cook P, Ludwig J. Guns in America: results of a comprehensive national survey on firearms ownership and use. Washington, DC: Police Foundation; 1996.
11. Hemenway D. Private guns, public health. Ann Arbor, Michigan: University of Michigan Press; 2004. P. 97.

12. Smith T. National Gun Policy Survey of the National Opinion Research Center findings. Chicago: National Opinion Research Center: 2001. Tables 13 and 14.

13. CBS DC, Report: Number of concealed carry permits surges as violent crime rate drops [Internet]. CBS. 2014 Jul 10. Available from: http://washington.cbslocal.com/2014/07/10/report-number-of-concealed-carry-permits-surges-as-violent-crime-rate-drops/

14. Lott J. More guns, less crime. Chicago: University of Chicago Press; 1998.

15. Ludwig J. Concealed gun-carrying laws and violent crime: evidence from state panel data. Int Rev. Law Econ. 1998; 18(3): 239–254.

16. Aneja A, Donohue J, Zhang A. The impact of right to carry laws and the NRC report: lessons for the empirical evaluation of law and policy. Am Law Econ Rev. 2011; 13(2): 565–632.

17. Aneja A, Donohue J, Zhang A. The impact of right to carry laws and the NRC report: the latest lessons for the empirical evaluation of law and policy. Stanford, CA: Stanford University; 2014.

18. Henigan D. Lethal logic: exploding the myths that paralyze American gun policy. Washington, DC: Potomac Books; 2009. P. 133.

19. Black D, Nagin D. Do right-to-carry laws deter violent crime? J Legal Stud. 1998; 27(1): 209–219.

20. Cook P, Goss K. The gun debate: what everyone needs to know. New York: Oxford University Press; 2014. P. 22.

21. Cook P, Goss K. The gun debate. P. 26.

22. Kleck G. Targeting guns: firearms and their control. New York: Aldine; 1997. P. 244.

23. Wright J, Rossi P. Armed and considered dangerous: a survey of felons and their firearms. New York: Transaction Publishers; 1986. P. 150.

24. Fortunato D. Can easing concealed carry deter crime? Soc Sci Quart. 2015; 96(4): 1–15.

25. Hemenway D, Solnick S. The epidemiology of self-defense gun use: Evidence from the National Crime Victimization Surveys, 2007–2011. Prev Med. 2015; 79(3): 22–27.

26. Hepburn L, Miller M, Azrael D, Hemenway D. The effect of nondiscretionary concealed weapon carrying laws on homicide. J Trauma. 2004; 56(3): 676–681.

27. Hemenway D. Risks and benefits of a gun in the home. Am J Lifestyle Med. 2011; 5(6): 502–511.

28. Cook P, Goss K. The gun debate. P. 22.

29. Bureau of Justice Statistics, About 1.4 million guns stolen during household burglaries and other property crimes from 2005 through 2010. Washington, DC: DOJ Press release, November 8, 2012, http://www.bjs.gov/content/pub/press/fshbopc0510pr.cfm

30. Locy T. States with high crime see more guns stolen [Internet]. USA Today. 2002 Dec 17. Available from: http://usatoday30.usatoday.com/news/nation/2002-12-17-guns-usat_x.htm

31. Curtis H. OPD thefts put rifles on street, spur new policy [Internet]. Orlando Sentinel. 2007 Jan 30. Available from: http://articles.orlandosentinel.com/2007-01-30/news/STOLENGUNS30_1_rifles-police-department-patrol-cars

32. O'Matz M, Maines J. License to carry: a Sun-Sentinel investigation [Internet]. Sun-Sentinel. 2007 Jan 28. Available from: http://articles.sun-sentinel.com/2007-01-28/news/0701270316_1_gun-licensing-system

33. Glick S, Langley M. License to kill and kidnap and rape and drive drunk: an update on arrests of Texas concealed handgun license holders. Washington, DC: Violence Policy Center; 1999. P. 1.

34. Violence Policy Center. License to kill: arrests involving Texas concealed handgun license holders. Washington, DC: Violence Police Center; 1998. P. 6.

35. Violence Policy Center. Concealed Carry Killers [Internet]. Washington, DC: Violence Policy Center; 2015. Available from: http://www.vpc.org/ccwkillers.htm

36. Brady Center to Prevent Gun Violence. No gun left behind. Washington, DC: Brady Center to Prevent Gun Violence; 2007. Appendix A.

37. Muskal M. Michael Dunn convicted on four of five charges in loud music murder case [Internet]. Los Angeles Times. 2014 Feb 15. Available from: http://www.latimes.com/nation/nationnow/la-na-nn-michael-dunn-loud-music-verdict-20140213-story.html#axzz2todjb8tt&page=1

38. Hsieh S. Jury fails to reach verdict on murder charge in Michael Dunn trial [Internet]. The Nation. 2014 Feb 15. Available from: http://www.thenation.com/blog/178370/jury-fails-reach-verdict-murder-charge-trial-michael-dunn#

39. Miller M, Azrael D, Hemenway D, Solop F. Road rage in Arizona: armed and dangerous? Accid Anal Prev. 2002; 34(6): 807–814.

40. Hemenway D, Vriniotis M, Miller M. Is an armed society a polite society? Guns and road rage. Accid Anal Prev. 2006; 38(4): 687–695.

41. Smith T. National Gun Policy Survey.

42. National Task Force on Stand Your Ground Laws. Preliminary report and recommendations. Chicago: American Bar Association; 2014.
43. Florida Statutes 776.012. Use or threatened use of force in defense of person [Internet]. Available from: http://www.leg.state.fl.us/Statutes/index. cfm?App_mode=Display_Statute&URL=0700-0799/0776/0776.html
44. Kam D. Florida's Stand Your Ground panel: keep self-defense law intact [Internet]. Palm Beach Post. 2012 Nov 13. Available from: http://www. palmbeachpost.com/news/news/state-regional-govt-politics/stand-your-ground-panel-keep-self-defense-law-inta/nS5yj/
45. Law Center to Prevent Gun Violence. Stand your ground policy summary [Internet]. Smartgunlaws.org. 2013 Jul 18. Available from: http://smart-gunlaws.org/stand-your-ground-policy-summary/
46. Wright J, Rossi P. The armed criminal: a survey of incarcerated felons. Washington, DC: US Department of Justice; 1985. P. 24.
47. Montgomery B, Jenkins C. Five years since Florida enacted "stand your ground" law, justifiable homicides are up [Internet]. Tampa Bay Times. 2010 Oct 15. Available from: http://www.tampabay.com/news/public-safety/crime/five-years-since-florida-enacted-stand-your-ground-law-justifiable/1128317
48. Montgomery B, Jenkins C. Five years since Florida enacted "stand your ground" law, justifiable homicides are up.
49. Hundley K, Martin S, Humburg C. Florida "Stand Your Ground" law yields some shocking outcomes depending on how law is applied [Internet]. Tampa Bay Times. 2012 Jun 1. Available from: http://www.tampabay.com/news/publicsafety/crime/florida-stand-your-ground-law-yields-some-shocking-outcomes-depending-on/1233133
50. Hundley K, Martin S, Humburg C. Florida "Stand Your Ground" law yields some shocking outcomes depending on how law is applied.
51. Cheng C, Hoekstra M. Does strengthening self-defense law deter crime or escalate violence: evidence from expansions to Castle Doctrine. J Hum Resour. 2013; 48(3): 821–854.
52. McClellan C, Tekin E. Stand your ground policies and homicides. Cambridge, MA: National Bureau of Economic Research; 2012.
53. National Task Force on Stand Your Ground Laws. Preliminary report and recommendations. P. 21–22.
54. Spitzer R., Stand your ground makes no sense [Internet]. The New York Times. 2015 May 15. Available from: http://www.nytimes.com/2015/05/04/opinion/stand-your-ground-makes-no-sense.html?smid=nytcore-ipad-share&smprod=nytcore-ipad&_r=1

55. Spitzer R. Stand your ground makes no sense.

56. National Task Force on Stand Your Ground Laws. Preliminary report and recommendations. P. 10.

57. Kay J. More guns aren't the answer. For Canadians, America's gun cult looks like a collective suicide cult [Internet]. National Post. 2016 Jan 8. Available from: http://news.nationalpost.com/full-comment/jonathan-kay-more-guns-arent-the-answer-americans-are-likelier-to-wet-their-pants-facing-a-mass-shooter

58. Vince J, Wolfe T, Field L. Firearms training and self-defense. Chicago: National Gun Victims Action Council; 2015. P. 4.

59. Law Center to Prevent Gun Violence. Concealed weapons permitting policy summary [Internet]. 2015 Sep 10. Available from: http://smartgunlaws.org/concealed-weapons-permitting-policy-summary/

60. United States Government Accountability Office. Gun control: states' laws and requirements for concealed carry permits vary across the nation. Washington, DC: GAO; 2012.

61. Holland J. Tactical experts destroy the NRA's heroic gunslinger fantasy [Internet]. The Nation. 2015 Oct 5. Available from: http://www.thenation.com/article/combat-vets-destroy-the-nras-heroic-gunslinger-fantasy/

62. Holland J. Tactical experts destroy NRA's gunslinger fantasy.

63. Holland J. Tactical experts destroy NRA's gunslinger fantasy.

64. Morrison G. Police firearms training survey: preliminary findings. Paper presented at the annual meeting of the Academy of Criminal Justice Sciences; 2002 Mar; Anaheim, CA.

65. Baker A. 11 years of police gunfire in painstaking detail [Internet]. New York Times. 2008 May 8. Available from: http://www.nytimes.com/2008/05/08/nyregion/08nypd.html?pagewanted=all&_r=1&

66. Dahl J. Empire State Building shooting sparks questions about NYPD shot accuracy [Internet]. CBS News. 2012 Aug 29. Available from: http://www.cbsnews.com/8301-504083_162-57502545-504083/empire-state-building-shooting-sparks-questions-about-nypd-shot-accuracy/

67. Aveni T. Officer-involved shootings: what we didn't know has hurt us. Spofford, NH: The Police Policy Studies Council; 2003.

68. Anderson J. Iowan who wanted to surprise fiancé dies in accidental shooting. Omaha World-Herald. 2002 Jun 12. P. 1A.

69. Associated Press. Woman shoots grandson, mistook him for intruder [Internet]. 2014 Aug 19. Available from: http://www.huffingtonpost.com/2014/08/19/woman-shoots-grandson-florida_n_5690820.html

70. Moxley R. I shot my son [Internet]. Orange County Weekly. 2000 Jul 13. Available from: http://www.ocweekly.com/2000-07-20/news/i-shot-my-son/full/

71. American Psychological Association. Expertise improves shoot-no shoot decisions in police officers and lessens potential for racial bias [Internet]. Science Daily. 2007 Jun 4. Available from: http://www.sciencedaily.com/releases/2007/06/070603215445.htm

72. Vince J, Wolfe T, Field L. Firearms training and self-defense. P. 19.

73. Federal Bureau of Investigation. A study of active shooter incidents in the United States between 2000 and 2013. Washington, DC: US Department of Justice; 2014.

74. Hemenway D, Azrael D, Miller M. U.S. national attitudes concerning gun carrying. Inj Prev. 2001; 7(4): 282–285.

75. Cook P, Goss K. The gun debate. P. 27.

76. Quinnipiac University Poll [Internet]. 2015 Dec 23. Hamden, CT: Quinnipiac University. December 16–20, 2015. Available from: http://www.quinnipiac.edu/news-and-events/quinnipiac-university-poll/national/release-detail?ReleaseID=2312

77. Yewman H. "Stupid," "immoral," "dangerous," "coward": My month with a gun [Internet]. The Daily Beast. 2013 Jun 22. Available from: http://www.thedailybeast.com/articles/2013/07/22/stupid-immoral-dangerous-coward-my-month-with-a-gun.html

78. National Task Force on Stand Your Ground Laws. Preliminary report and recommendations. P. 10.

Part IV

Obstacles to Gun Violence Prevention Efforts

11

The Firearms Industry: Guns as a Business

The American firearms industry can be traced back to the founding in 1777 of the Springfield Armory in Springfield, Massachusetts. The armory was established as a safe place for the revolutionary forces to make and store arms.[1] It produced military weapons used by Union soldiers during the Civil War and the M-1 Garand, the standard infantry rifle used in World War II. Scores of firms followed the Springfield Armory in making western Massachusetts and Connecticut a hub for gun manufacturing. Iconic companies, such as Colt, Sturm Ruger & Co., Smith & Wesson, and the Winchester Repeating Arms Co. eventually set up in "Gun Valley." These companies developed products like the revolver, semiautomatic pistols, and various models of rifles, including the M-16 assault rifle.

Following World War II, manufacturing firms were established in other parts of the country (e.g., California) and foreign manufacturers began to penetrate the US market. In some cases, foreign firms bought out established American firms but kept their original names to facilitate sales.[2] Regulation of the firearms industry was minimal until the late 1960s, when the Gun Control Act of 1968 was passed. The act was prompted by the assassinations of President John F. Kennedy in 1963

© The Author(s) 2016
T. Gabor, *Confronting Gun Violence in America*,
DOI 10.1007/978-3-319-33723-4_11

and Senator Robert F. Kennedy and Rev. Martin Luther King in 1968, as well as increases in violent crime and the proliferation of handguns. The act represented the first comprehensive national firearms law.

The Business of Guns

The firearms industry often portrays itself as a champion of individual rights, self-reliance, and the Second Amendment. However, Tom Diaz, a lawyer, a former NRA member, and competitive shooter who became an advocate for regulating the firearms industry, has made the following observation:

> *The ultimate fact is that the gun industry is simply a business, and nothing more. It is neither a national trust nor a repository of American values. Although the people who make, import, and sell guns often wrap themselves in ideological and nostalgic symbols of early America, they are not latter-day founding fathers. They are businessmen. They are in the game because they want to make money, and as much of it as possible.*[3]

The firearms industry is very secretive and most companies are privately owned rather than publicly traded. A number of companies active in the USA are subsidiaries of foreign companies. Detailed data are not available on the number of different types of firearms made and imported into the USA. Nor are industry data kept on product defects, remedial action (if any), and resulting product liability litigation.[4] Despite this lack of transparency of the industry, it has been estimated that guns and related equipment sales total about $5.3 billion per year and that the total economic impact of the gun and ammunition market is approximately $32 billion.[5]

The Failure to Regulate Guns Like Other Consumer Products

Although over 100,000 people are killed or injured by gunfire each year in the USA, the firearms industry is not scrutinized or regulated to the same degree as industries that are associated with far fewer losses of life and serious injuries. The Consumer Product Safety Commission (CPSC) is the federal agency that ensures that consumer products are safe. However, unlike virtually every consumer product manufactured and sold in the USA, the CPSC has been expressly forbidden by Congress from regulating firearms or ammunition.[6] Lawmakers in the House of Representatives in the 1970s feared that allowing the CPSC to regulate guns would create a slippery slope culminating in the disarming of Americans. As a result, no federal agency has the authority to oversee the design of firearms to ensure they are safe and operate as intended.

The CPSC regulates flammability standards for mattresses, and it estimates that 270 lives are thereby saved each year. It also regulates hair dryers (43 reported injuries over a 20-year period), children's toys, appliances, and all sorts of household products in order to protect the public from harm. Yet, Congress has prohibited the CPSC from regulating firearms in any way.[7] No federal agency has the power to ensure that guns are designed and manufactured in such a way as to minimize their danger to humans. One of the most dangerous and ubiquitous products in American homes, the firearm, goes untested and unregulated. One perverse example is that toy guns are subject to consumer protection laws but real guns are not.[8] In addition, due to The Protection of Lawful Commerce in Arms Act, a law signed by President George W. Bush in 2005, gun manufacturers are protected from liability and cannot be sued when their products are used to commit acts of violence.

Regulations might require equipping guns with trigger locks and chamber indicators, as well as personalizing guns so that only lawful owners can use them. Such measures could help prevent crimes by unauthorized users, accidental deaths, and suicides by family members of gun owners. In addition, regulation can ensure that firearms are made with high-quality materials so they are reliable and meet minimum safety standards. Gun safety standards are set by the Sporting Arms and Ammunition Manufacturers' Institute; however, compliance with these standards to ensure that weapons do not explode or discharge when dropped is voluntary.[9]

As most firearm fatalities are due to suicides or stem from arguments among those known to one another, Tom Diaz has argued that a good deal of firearms violence is not a criminal problem, but "stems rather from the virtually unregulated distribution of an inherently dangerous consumer product."[10] Therefore, Diaz notes that a focus on denying access and punishing those using guns in criminal acts misses much of the public health problem stemming from firearms.

Instead of making safer products, the gun industry is producing increasingly dangerous products. Diaz noted in 1999:

> *Over the last two decades, at least, the gun industry has deliberately enhanced its profits by increasing the lethality—the killing power—of its products. Lethality is the nicotine of the gun industry. Time and time again, the gun industry has injected into the civilian market new guns that are specifically designed to be better at killing—guns with greater ammunition capacity, higher firepower in the form of bigger caliber or power, increased concealability, or all three—and created demand for these new products with the collaboration of the "gun press" and the entertainment media.*[11]

In 2011, the ATF reported that more than 8.5 million guns were manufactured in the USA, with an even split between handguns and long guns.[12] Gun makers range from large firms that produce hundreds of thousands of guns to individual operations that make just one gun that is often a prototype or a custom weapon. Despite the large manufacturing operations in the USA, almost as many guns are imported into the country as are made here. According to the ATF, as many as five million guns are imported each year into the USA, with Brazil, Austria, Germany, and Italy being the principal source countries.[13]

It is ironic that, due to more stringent laws in other countries, foreign manufacturers are often unable to sell to their own civilian population and export most of their products to the USA. In the 1990s, for example, just over 1 % of Japan's gun production stayed in Japan and 80 % of the production of its three leading gun manufacturers came to the USA.[14] America's permissive gun laws relative to other countries have promoted gun tourism, and it has been said that the USA has become "a kind of underdeveloped moral Third World, a place where the rest of the world can indulge its gun lust."[15] By contrast with other developed countries, virtually any American adult can buy a firearm unless he or she is a convicted felon or judged to be mentally defective. In addition, the residents of most states can carry concealed weapons unless they are in one of a few specified prohibited categories.

Given the gap in regulation, lawsuits are potentially among the most powerful means through which individuals who have been harmed can seek redress and hold the gun industry accountable. At the same time, these legal cases allow members of the public to gain insight into the harmful practices of the industry. Aside from compensating victims of violence, civil litigation can contribute to positive change in the gun industry, including improvements in product design (e.g., features that prevent a gun from discharging when dropped).[16]

In 2005, this avenue was removed for victims of gun violence. Several cities, including New York and Chicago, had filed lawsuits against gun makers and dealers, claiming that their actions had compromised public health and created huge financial obligations for the municipalities. The Protection of Lawful Commerce in Arms Act gave the gun industry unprecedented immunity from negligence-based lawsuits. Specifically this act shields the industry from lawsuits relating to the use of firearms and ammunition, when "the product functioned as designed and intended." The act provides broad protection to companies in the gun industry that make unsafe products and engage in distribution practices that result in easy access by criminals. No other industry benefits from such protection.

Gun Dealers and Gun Shows

The source of many of the guns used in crime is licensed dealers. Often, purchases are made through "straw purchasers," individuals with clean criminal records who buy guns on behalf of those who would be ineligible due to a felony conviction or some other disqualifying condition. It appears that some dealers are especially prolific in selling guns that are eventually used in crime. A 2000 report by the ATF revealed that just over 1 % of federally licensed firearm dealers sold 57 % of the guns later traced to crime.[17] For example, in 2005, 447 guns used in crime were traced to a sporting goods store outside of Oakland, California. An astounding one of every eight guns sold in that store were later found to be used in a crime or were seized from an individual involved in crime.[18]

In another case described by the Brady Center to Prevent Gun Violence, a gun dealer in Dayton, Ohio, sold 87 Hi-Point pistols to a straw buyer in a single transaction. That sale contributed to a crime wave in Buffalo, New York.[19] In another approach documented by the Brady Center, four individuals made multiple purchases of the same model of gun (Hi-Point pistols) from the same Oklahoma dealer and many of the close to one hundred guns purchased were sold on the streets of Baltimore.

Gun shows are another major source of crime guns. According to the ATF, 30 % of guns involved in federal gun trafficking investigations have a gun show connection.[20] New York City investigators visited seven gun shows in Nevada, Ohio, and Tennessee.[21] They conducted integrity tests of 47 sellers, both licensed dealers and private sellers. Nearly two-thirds of private sellers approached by investigators failed the integrity test, as they sold to a purchaser who said he probably could not pass a background check. Some private sellers failed this test more than once at different shows. While private sellers are not required to conduct background checks they are committing a felony if they know or have reason to believe they are selling to a prohibited purchaser.

More than nine out of ten licensed dealers failed the integrity test by selling to apparent straw purchasers. In all, 35 out of 47 sellers approached by investigators completed sales to people who appeared to be criminals or straw purchasers. Investigators also learned that some private sellers were in the business of selling guns without a license. For example, one seller sold to investigators at three different shows and admitted to selling 348 assault rifles in less than one year.

Licensed dealers have been found to be the largest source of guns for the illegal market.[22] Thus, a focus on dealers in enforcement efforts can be highly beneficial in reducing the number of guns diverted to the illegal market. A number of states have their own requirements for dealers, although they vary by state. States may require a separate dealer's license, background checks of employees, security measures to prevent thefts, and the reporting of thefts or losses of firearms.

Major flaws in federal gun laws impede the ATF from preventing the illegal diversion of firearms from licensed firearm dealers. The agency is limited to one unannounced dealer inspection per year, and it faces an uphill battle in convicting dealers of wrongdoing. In criminal cases, it must show that the dealer *willfully* engaged in wrongdoing, and, to revoke a license, a pattern of wrongdoing over many years must be demonstrated.[23]

Missing records can hide illegal sales that can compromise public safety; however, serious recordkeeping violations usually go unpunished. Since 1986, recordkeeping violations are classified as misdemeanors rather than felonies. As Federal prosecutors generally do not tend to spend their limited resources prosecuting misdemeanors, most recordkeeping violations escape punishment.[24]

The ATF lacks the workforce to monitor thousands of gun dealers across the country. The Department of Justice's Office of the Inspector General concluded that it would take the ATF over 22 years to inspect all federally licensed dealers.[25] A more recent report by the inspector general found that 58 % of dealers had not been inspected within the past five years due, in part, to a lack of resources.[26] A *Washington Post* investigation found that, due to inadequate staffing, ATF inspected fewer than 10 % of federally licensed dealers in 2009, and, on average, dealers are inspected just once a decade.[27] The paper reported that there are only about 15 license revocations in a typical year.[28]

Moreover, the inspector general's 2013 report found that some license revocation processes took over two years to complete,[29] allowing scofflaw dealers to legally continue selling firearms during that time. The report also found that, between 2004 and 2011, licensed gun dealers reported 174,679 firearms missing from their inventories, a major concern as these guns may end up being used in crime.

The actions of wholesalers can be critical with regard to the trafficking of firearms as selling to one rogue dealer can prove disastrous. In one case, a dealer in Southern California diverted thousands of handguns to street gangs in just one year.[30]

It has been said that the USA once had more gun dealers than gas stations. While the number of dealers has declined, as of 2011, there were 129,817 federally licensed gun dealers as opposed to 143,839 gas stations, 36,569 grocery stores, and 14,098 McDonald's restaurants in the USA.[31] From 1968 to 1993, virtually anyone who was not prohibited from owning firearms and had a location from which they could conduct business, including a home or office, could obtain a federal firearms license.

A three-year license cost all of $30, allowing the licensee to ship, transport, and receive firearms in interstate commerce and engage in retail sales. License holders are exempt from many of the restrictions on the sale and transfer of firearms that private citizens are subject to.

The relaxed licensing requirements undoubtedly contributed to a sharp increase in dealerships from the mid-1970s to the early 1990s. The majority of the licensees were "kitchen-table" dealers operating out of homes and small offices rather than sporting goods stores. Some of these small dealers obtained a license to benefit from lower prices, while others recognized that licenses could be exploited to facilitate high-volume gun trafficking.

The Clinton administration in the 1990s responded to the widespread abuse of federal firearms licenses by strictly enforcing the federal statute requiring that licensees be engaged in the business of selling firearms. Licensing fees were increased, applicants had to submit photographs and fingerprints, and they had to provide a number of certifications (e.g., that their businesses complied with all state and local laws).[32] These new licensing requirements were thought to be largely responsible for the decline in dealers.

Gun shows are another weak link in the firearms marketplace. According to a report by the ATF, there are about 4,000 such shows a year in the USA, as well as numerous other public markets (e.g., flea markets) at which firearms are sold or traded.[33] Currently, under federal law, private sellers are not required to find out whether they are selling a gun to a felon or other prohibited person. If these firearms are recovered at a crime scene, it is very difficult to trace them back to the purchaser. The ATF report notes:

> *The casual atmosphere in which firearms are sold at gun shows provides an opportunity for individual buyers and sellers to exchange firearms without the expense of renting a table, and it is not uncommon to see people walking around a show attempting to sell a firearm. They may sell their firearms to a vendor who has rented a table or simply to someone they meet at the show. Many non-licensees entice potential customers to their tables with comments such as, "No background checks required; we need only to know where you live and how old you are." ... Although the majority of people who visit gun shows are*

law-abiding citizens, too often the shows provide a ready supply of firearms to prohibited persons, gangs, violent criminals, and illegal firearms traffickers.[34]

Collectively, ATF investigations paint a disturbing picture. Although they are prohibited from acquiring firearms, felons are able to purchase firearms at gun shows. Felons buying or selling firearms were involved in nearly half of the investigations involving gun shows. In more than a third of the investigations, the guns involved were found to have been used in subsequent crimes. The offenses included drug crimes, assault, robbery, burglary, and homicide. The two largest investigations covered in the ATF report involved up to 7,000 and 10,000 firearms, respectively. Violations observed in the investigations included straw purchases (purchase by a lawful buyer on behalf of one prohibited from buying a gun), out-of-state sales by licensed dealers, transactions by licensed dealers without background checks, engaging in the business without a license, and the sale of kits that modify semiautomatic firearms into automatic ones.

Pursuing New Markets

The last few decades have seen a dramatic change in the US firearms market, from supplying hunters and sport shooters to more lethal handguns and military-style long guns.[35] The handgun share of the market rose sharply over the last half century. The boom in handgun sales in the 1960s and 1970s eventually led to a glut in the late 1970s. In addition, fewer young people were interested in participating in the traditional activities of hunting and sport shooting. Rural populations, the traditional mainstay of the industry, were declining. Moreover, some large retailers have discontinued their sales of guns as they have concluded they are harmful to their image and therefore bad for business.

As in any other industry, the goal is to keep producing and selling new products. This is especially challenging to an industry that makes products that tend to last longer than most consumer goods. More guns are concentrated in the hands of fewer consumers.[36] In this context, innovation becomes necessary to keep sales going, to attract new markets, and to find new uses for the same market. Faced with a crisis, gun makers concluded that they must create new products and establish new markets. New products could render older guns obsolete and could entice existing gun owners to purchase more firearms.

William Ruger Sr., chairman of Sturm, Ruger & Co. of Southport, CT, a leading manufacturer of handguns and rifles has stated: "We've woken up to the fact that these guns are not wearing out, and used guns are competing with our new production. People are buying guns for half the money. I think that hurt sales of a lot of companies in the 1980s."[37]

Ruger argued that one aspect of the solution to a saturated market was to develop innovative designs that would appeal to every gun owner. The goal was to generate a demand for products through advertising and by making guns that were more lethal, more compact, and thereby more concealable.[38] In the 1990s and beyond, sales of semiautomatic pistols grew while the rest of the market stagnated, and these weapons encouraged "spray and pray" shooting techniques due to high-capacity magazines. These guns are capable of producing mass casualties. In recent years, we have also seen the rise of pocket rockets, concealable but highly lethal guns in higher calibers. These weapons were intended as a stimulus to a lethargic market rather than due to market demand or legal reforms, such as the assault weapons ban of 1994.

Marketing to Women

Apart from injecting more lethal weapons into the market, the other strategy pursued by the firearms industry to revitalize the business has been to cultivate new markets. Market research conducted in the 1980s by Smith and Wesson, one of America's iconic manufacturers of both handguns and rifles, revealed that all but a small fraction of men who were interested in owning a firearm already had one, whereas less than half of all women interested in gun ownership had purchased one.[39] Such knowledge convinced manufacturers that there were still large untapped markets for the industry. Gunmakers have designed firearms for women knowing that they are now often the economic head of the household, as well as responsible for protecting members of the family.

The industry and the gun lobby rely relentlessly on fear tactics and the necessity of acquiring guns as a means of protection from rape and other forms of violence. The industry and the gun lobby frequently present themselves as champions of women's safety. They portray gun control as a means of undermining the empowerment and freedom of women.[40] The fear tactics of the industry tend to assume the following theme: A woman who is alone is attacked by a stranger, most often to commit a rape. The police are not there when she needs them. Following the victimization, she empowers herself by obtaining a gun.

In the 1980s and 1990s, following a surge of marketing aimed at women, gun manufacturers developed a number of handguns for the anticipated deluge of women they thought would purchase them. However, just 10 % of US women own guns, and the level of ownership among women has not increased from the 1980s.[41] Women on the whole may have an aversion to guns due to a fear that guns pose a danger to the safety of their household. If this is the principal reason for their reluctance to purchase guns, they are supported by a wide body of research showing that guns in the home elevate, rather than diminish, the danger to women living there.

There is strong evidence that women are more likely to be murdered, to commit suicide, or to die from gun accidents where firearms are more available. On an international level, in a study using data from the late 1990s, among high-income countries, American women accounted for less than one-third of all women but 70 % of all female homicide victims and 84 % of all female gun homicide victims. The US female homicide rate during that period was five times that of other high-income countries combined and the gun homicide victimization rate was 11 times higher than that of the other countries.[42]

In the USA, Matthew Miller and his colleagues at Harvard University found that women residing in states with the highest levels of gun ownership were four times more likely to be victims of gun homicide than those living in states with the lowest gun ownership levels.[43] A major study of homicide in the home in three metropolitan counties found that the presence of a gun in the home was a major and significant risk factor for homicide, after factors such as age, race, neighborhood, and mental illness were taken into account.[44] So much for the idea that more guns in an area or in the home protects women.

In addition, the gun industry's portrayal of violence against women as primarily involving attacks by strangers is a distortion of the real picture of violence experienced by women. The Centers for Disease Control and Prevention's 2010 National Intimate Partner and Sexual Violence Survey revealed that the vast majority of rape victims were assaulted by their current or former intimate partners or by acquaintances. Less than 15 %of rape victims were attacked by complete strangers.[45] In fact, nearly two-thirds of all nonlethal violence (rape, assault, stalking) is intimate partner violence.[46] With regard to lethal violence, the overwhelming majority of women who are murdered are victimized by persons they know. An analysis of the FBI's Supplementary Report for 2010 revealed that 94 % of women killed in single victim/single offender incidents in which the victim–offender relationship could be ascertained were murdered by a male they knew.[47] Two-thirds of these incidents involved an intimate partner.

Intimate partner violence is why a gun in the home may be a bad idea, serving as more of a threat to women than a means of protection. Women are also at an increased risk of suicide and unintentional death in states where gun ownership is higher.[48] Thus, the entire premise that women need to own guns and to have easy access to them to ensure their safety is contradicted by what we know about violence and other tragedies involving guns. The primary motive for the campaigns to arm women was to increase the bottom line of gun manufacturers, retailers, and other businesses in the gun industry. Evidently, the failure of most women to respond to these campaigns suggests that this key demographic group remains unconvinced.

Marketing to Minorities

The firearms industry has also recognized the enormous potential of marketing its products to minority groups. However, to do so successfully, industry analysts assert that it must shed its racist image. In a 1997 article entitled "Gun Industry Must Become Less Racist to Survive in the 21st Century," analyst Bob Hausman wrote:

All of the usual customers the industry reaches (people of Northern European descent) who wanted a gun, now have one. … A major effort needs to be made to include those groups who are presently referred to as America's racial and ethnic minorities, but who are rapidly becoming the majority. And there is tremendous potential within this largely untapped market.[49]

Hausman was referring to comments such as those of Ted Nugent, an NRA board member. When commenting on change in South Africa in 1990, Nugent stated:

Apartheid isn't that cut and dry. All men are not created equal. The preponderance of South Africa is a different breed of man … I say that with great respect. … They are still people of the earth, but they are different. They still put bones in their noses, they still walk around naked, they wipe their butts with their hands. … These are different people. You give'em toothpaste, they f—ing eat it … I hope they don't become civilized. They're way ahead of the game.[50]

Also contributing to the image of the gun industry as hostile or, at least, unwelcoming, to minorities is the frequent appearance of Nazi memorabilia at gun shows. At one show in San Francisco, one could find translations of Adolf Hitler's "Mein Kampf," swastika arm bands, tapes of marching songs from the Third Reich, and t-shirts with images of Nazi soldiers striking heroic poses.[51]

Aside from cleaning up the industry's image among visible minorities, there are serious questions as to the reception minority communities are likely to give to firearm marketing campaigns aimed at them. African-Americans, on the whole, are far more supportive of gun control efforts than are whites. A Pew Research Center poll in December 2012 found that blacks as a group favored gun control over gun rights by a margin of 68–24 %.[52] Among whites, the situation was reversed as protecting gun rights was viewed as more important than controlling ownership by a margin of 51–42 %. In addition, the poll found that African-Americans, by a wide margin (53–29 %), believed that gun ownership compromises public safety rather than protecting people from crime. Furthermore, 83 % of those surveyed thought that allowing citizens to own assault weapons makes the country more dangerous.

The views of African-Americans are likely influenced by the toll guns have taken in their communities. Black males are nine times as likely as white males to die of a firearm homicide.[53] While national surveys indicate that black youths are not more likely to be physically assaulted than white youths, they are more likely to report being threatened with or shot at with a firearm.[54] Given the higher gun violence victimization rates of African-Americans, the idea of exposing this segment of the population to more guns as a way of enhancing public safety is not likely to gain much credibility or traction.

Marketing to Children and Youth

The Police Foundation Study, *Guns in America*, revealed that almost everyone owning a gun in the 1990s had some experience with a gun as a youth, either from growing up with guns in the home or due to military service.[55] The gun lobby and industry believe that immersing young people in the gun culture is essential to maintaining the political clout of the lobby and the financial health of the firearms industry. A study for the firearms industry concluded that new first-time shooters must be encouraged on a continuing basis and their entry into shooting sports must be facilitated.[56]

Faced with a general societal decline in the shooting sports, Marion Hammer, the NRA's first female president, stated at the organization's 1995 Annual Meeting that reaching out to America's youth was of paramount importance:

> One [mission of the NRA]is to build an NRA bridge to America's youth. The other is being fiscally far-sighted to provide for bold new programs that will teach America's children values to last a lifetime. … If we do not successfully reach out to the next generation, then the freedom and liberty we've lived for—and that many of our ancestors have died for—will not live beyond us.[57]

In 2000, Wayne LaPierre, then executive vice president of the NRA, echoed those comments in the organization's *American Guardian* magazine:

The battle over gun control is no longer about crime and criminals. The battle is about kids—our kids—stepping into an America dominated by the anti-gun media and politicians.[58]

Marketing campaigns include the design of lighter firearms for children and recreational programs established by sports shooting organizations. For example, the National Shooting Sports Foundation operates a number of programs for youth, including clay target championships, marksmanship for youth, and financial as well as other support to promote the formation of college shooting teams.[59]

The long-term value of cultivating the ownership and uses of firearms by young people is certainly debatable. The risks are clear as illustrated by America's troubling record with regard to the harms experienced by its children and youth as a consequence of gun violence, self-inflicted injuries, and accidents.

According to the Centers for Disease Control and Prevention, in 2010, there were 2,711 infant, child, and teen firearm deaths in the USA, about seven such fatalities daily. Between 1981 and 2010, 112,375 infants, children, and teens were killed by firearms. These fatalities exceed the combined deaths of soldiers in Korea, Vietnam, Iraq, and Afghanistan.[60] More than four out of five youths (ages 10–19) murdered in 2010 were killed by a firearm, and almost half of the teens (ages 15–19) who committed suicide in 2010 used a firearm.[61]

As shown in Chap. 2, the USA has the highest civilian gun ownership levels in the world and several times more firearms for every 100 people than most industrialized countries. Rather than serving to protect young people, the volume of guns appears to undermine their safety and sense of security. According to the Children's Defense Fund, US children and teens were 32 times more likely to die from a gun homicide and 10 times more likely to die from a gun suicide or gun accident than their peers in the other high-income countries combined.[62]

Researchers at Harvard University's School of Public Health have found, in a study spanning ten years (1988–1997), that in states where more households owned guns, more children died of homicides, suicides, and accidents with firearms.[63] This statistical association held up even after state levels of poverty, education, and urbanization were taken into account. When the states with the highest and lowest gun ownership levels were compared, children between 5 and 14 years of age were 2.7 times more likely to be victims of a gun homicide, 8 times more likely to be a gun suicide victim, and 24 times as likely to suffer a fatal gun accident if they lived in a high-gun as opposed to a low-gun state.[64]

The *Youth Suicide by Firearms Task Force* (1998), a group that included representatives from a wide variety of organizations, including the American Medical Association, National Shooting Sports Foundation, and Centers for Disease Control and Prevention reported:

- Firearms are the most common method of suicide by youth.
- Guns in the home, especially loaded guns, are associated with an increased risk of suicide by youth.
- Where a gun is used in a suicide attempt, a fatal outcome occurs 78–90 % of the time.[65]

The evidence suggests that young people are most likely to carry guns when they are afraid of gun violence. Fear leads to more gun carrying which, in turn, promotes even more fear and gun carrying. Most youth would prefer to live in a world of fewer guns in the hands of teens.[66]

Connections Between the Gun Industry and Lobby Groups

The NRA, currently one of America's most formidable political lobby groups, was formed in 1871 as Union veterans Colonel William Church and General George Wingate were troubled by the lack of marksmanship shown by their troops. According to Church, the principal goal of the NRA would be to "promote and encourage rifle shooting on a scientific basis."[67] The NRA established a rifle range in Sea Girt, New Jersey, for annual competitions and promoted the shooting sports among America's youth through the establishment of rifle clubs at major colleges, universities, and military academies. By 1906, the NRA's youth program was in full swing with more than 200 boys competing in matches at Sea Girt that summer. Today, more than one million youth participate in NRA shooting sports events and affiliated programs. In addition to youth, the NRA has been active in providing education and training to hunters and law enforcement personnel. The organization publishes several magazines, including *The American Hunter* and *The American Rifleman*.

The NRA formed its Legislative Affairs Division in 1934 in response to a number of firearm bills. It did not lobby directly at that time but mailed out information and analyses to members so they could take action on their own. In the mid-1970s, following the enactment of the Gun Control Act of 1968, a more militant NRA emerged, with more aggressive leadership and lobbying activities.

More recently, the NRA has morphed into more than an aggressive advocate for the rights of gun owners and in defense of the Second Amendment. It has been revealed that the firearms industry is playing an increasingly influential role in shaping the activities of the organization. David Keene, former president of the NRA, acknowledged in an interview with CNN that the organization is receiving more money from the industry than it used to and is seeking to increase these funds. The Washington-based Violence Policy Center has found that, from 2005 to 2011, corporate donations to the NRA have totaled between $20 million and $53 million.[68] While claiming that it is independent of firearm and ammunition manufacturers and other businesses involved in the firearms industry, the reality is that a number of companies, including those making the weapons used in the Sandy Hook Elementary School and Aurora, Colorado, theater shootings, have contributed million dollar gifts to the NRA.

In addition, there is a new gun industry-sponsored NRA membership program in which industry members pay the annual dues for new members. Some NRA board members are executives of gun manufacturing firms. For example, NRA board member Pete Brownell, owner of Brownells, which claims to be the world's largest supplier of firearms accessories and gunsmithing tools, wrote on his website: "Having [NRA] directors who intimately understand and work in leadership positions within the firearms industry ensures the NRA's focus is honed on the overall mission of the organization. These individuals bring a keen sense of the industry and of the bigger fight to the table."[69]

The contributions received by the NRA from the gun industry are very significant, as they explain the extreme antiregulation stance of the organization. Like all industries, the firms that make and sell firearms wish to sell as much product as possible with a minimum of interference. If gun owners' organizations like the NRA become dependent on industry funding, they will use their leverage with lawmakers to promote gun sales regardless of the human toll. This helps explain the gun lobby's opposition to even the most basic, commonsense legislation, such as the requirement that all sales, including private sales, be subject to criminal background checks. This policy would mean that a segment of the market would be lost to the industry, that of people with prior felonies who would no longer be able to get around the background checks by purchasing guns through other than licensed dealers. It is thought that about 40 % of all gun transfers occur in the unregulated market.[70]

The mutually dependent nature of the NRA and the gun industry helps explain the NRA's support of policies that favor gun manufacturers over gun owners. While cultivating the image that the organization is a champion of the rights of ordinary gun owners, the NRA has supported legislation that limits the legal rights of gun owners killed or injured by defective firearms. For example, a number of states have limited the liability of gun range owners for injuries sustained by customers of the range.[71] The NRA claims that its positions are motivated exclusively by a concern for the interests of gun owners, never mentioning its own interest in protecting the profits of its gun industry financiers.

Bottom Line

The gun industry is like any other business, aiming to maximize its sales. Unlike other industries, however, it is largely exempt from liability for the damage produced by its products and laws that would protect consumers from its lethal products. In addition, oversight of the industry (e.g., dealers) by the ATF is limited by law. Furthermore, nearly half of all gun sales and other transfers occur in the unregulated private market. Over the last three decades, the industry has gained increasing influence with political organizations like the NRA, a situation that provides insight into the gun lobby's uncompromising stand against the most basic gun regulations.

The limited regulation of the industry, coupled with the saturation of its traditional market (white males who hunt and engage in shooting sports), has prompted the industry to produce more lethal products and to reach out to new markets, such as women, minorities, and young people. Would these groups be well served if their members acquired guns in greater numbers?

Women overall have not responded to the industry's appeal. Women in the USA and in states with high-gun ownership levels are at higher risk of homicide and violence than women in countries and states with lower ownership levels. Also, women are more likely to be harmed by intimate partners than by strangers. Therefore, guns in the home may be more of a threat to them than a source of protection.

Minorities, especially African-Americans, are already at a substantially elevated risk of gun violence. Similarly, young people in America are far more likely to be killed and injured with a firearm than their peers in other countries. This situation raises serious questions about the morality and wisdom of the gun lobby's and industry's quest to introduce more young people and minority group members to guns.

Notes

1. Diaz T. Making a killing: the business of guns in America. New York: The New Press; 1999. P. 19.
2. Diaz T. Making a killing. P. 21.
3. Diaz T. Making a killing. P. 3.
4. Diaz T. Making a killing. P. 5.
5. National Shooting Sports Foundation. Firearms and ammunition industry economic impact report 2014. Newtown, CT: NSSF; 2015.
6. Bettigole C. Guns, public health, and the Consumer Products Safety Commission [Internet]. Washington, DC: National Physicians Alliance; 2013 May 25. Available from: http://npalliance.org/blog/2013/05/25/guns-public-health-and-the-conumser-products-safety-commission/
7. Bettigole C. Guns, public health, and the Consumer Products Safety Commission.

8. Henigan D. Lethal logic: exploding the myths that paralyze American gun policy. Washington, DC: Potomac Books; 2009. P. 18.

9. Li O. Cars, toys and aspirin have to meet mandatory safety standards. Guns do not. Here's why [Internet]. The Trace. 2016 Jan 19. Available from: http://www.thetrace.org/2016/01/gun-safety-standards/

10. Diaz T. Making a killing. P. 9.

11. Diaz T. Making a killing. P. 15.

12. Bureau of Alcohol, Tobacco, Firearms and Explosives, Firearms Commerce in the United States. Annual Statistical Report 2014. Washington, DC: US Department of Justice; 2015.

13. Bureau of Alcohol, Tobacco, Firearms, and Explosives. Firearms commerce in the United States. Exhibit 5.

14. Diaz T. Making a killing. P. 31.

15. Diaz T. Making a killing. P. 32.

16. The Educational Fund to Stop Gun Violence. Justice denied: the case against gun industry immunity. Washington, DC: The Educational Fund to Stop Gun Violence; 2013.

17. Bureau of Alcohol, Tobacco, Firearms, and Explosives. Commerce in Firearms in the United States. Washington, DC: US Department of the Treasury; 2000.

18. D. Henigan, Lethal logic. P. 174–175.

19. Brady Center to Prevent Gun Violence. Shady dealings: illegal gun trafficking from licensed gun dealers. Washington, DC: Brady Center to Prevent Gun Violence; 2007.

20. Bureau of Alcohol, Tobacco, Firearms, and Explosives. Following the gun: enforcing federal law against firearms traffickers. Washington, DC: US Department of the Treasury; 2000.

21. The City of New York. Gun show undercover: report on illegal sales at gun shows. New York: The City of New York; 2009.

22. Bureau of Alcohol, Tobacco, Firearms, and Explosives. Following the gun.

23. Siebel B, Haile E. Shady dealings: illegal gun trafficking from licensed dealers. Washington, DC: Brady Center to Prevent Gun Violence; 2007. P. 24

24. Siebel B, Haile E. Shady Dealings. P. 25

25. Office of the Inspector General. Inspections of firearm dealers by the Bureau of Alcohol, Tobacco, Firearms, and Explosives. Washington, DC: US Department of Justice; 2004. P. iii.

26. Office of the Inspector General. Review of ATF's Federal Firearms Licensee Inspection Program. Washington, DC: US Department of Justice; 2013. p. ii.

27. Horwitz S, Grimaldi J. ATF's oversight limited in face of gun lobby [Internet]. Washington Post. 2010 Oct 26. Available from: http://www.washingtonpost.com/wp-dyn/content/article/2010/10/25/AR2010102505823.html?sub=AR

28. Fallis D. Virginia gun dealers: small number supply most guns tied to crimes [Internet]. Washington Post. 2010 Oct 25. Available from: http://www.washingtonpost.com/wp-dyn/content/article/2010/10/24/AR2010102402221.html.

29. Office of the Inspector General. Review of ATF's Federal Firearms Licensee Inspection Program. P. 30.

30. Diaz T. Making a killing. P. 41.

31. ABC News. Guns in America: A Statistical Look [Internet]. ABC News. 2012 Aug 25. Available from: http://abcnews.go.com/blogs/headlines/2012/08/guns-in-america-a-statistical-look/

32. Violence Policy Center. An analysis of the decline in gun dealers: 1994–2005. Washington, DC: Violence Policy Center; 2006.

33. Bureau of Alcohol, Tobacco and Firearms. Gun shows: Brady checks and crime gun traces. Washington, DC: Department of the Treasury and Department of Justice; 1999.

34. Bureau of Alcohol, Tobacco and Firearms. Gun Shows. P. 6.

35. Diaz T. Making a killing. P. 83.

36. Diaz T. Making a killing. P. 93.

37. Eckholm E. Ailing gun industry confronts outrage over glut of violence [Internet]. The New York Times. 1992 Mar 8. Available from: http://www.nytimes.com/1992/03/08/us/ailing-gun-industry-confronts-outrage-over-glut-of-violence.html?pagewanted=1

38. Diaz T. Making a killing. P. 96.

39. American Rifleman. Smith & Wesson's Ladysmith revolvers. American Rifleman. 1989 Mar P. 40.

40. Sugarmann J. Every handgun is aimed at you. New York: New Press; 2001. P. 87.

41. Tavernise S, Gebeloff R. Share of homes with guns show 4-decade decline [Internet]. The New York Times. 2013 Mar 9. Available from: http://www.nytimes.com/2013/03/10/us/rate-of-gun-ownership-is-down-survey-shows.html?pagewanted=all.

42. Hemenway D, Shinoda-Tagawa T, Miller M. Firearm availability and female homicide victimization rates among 25 populous high-income countries. J Am Med Women's Assoc. 2002; 57(2): 1–5.

43. Miller M, Azrael D, Hemenway D. Firearm availability and unintentional firearm deaths, suicide, and homicide among women. J Urban Health. 2002; 79(1): 26–38.

44. Kellermann A, Rivara F, Rushforth N, Banton J, Reay D, Francisco J et al. Gun ownership as a risk factor for homicide in the home. New Engl J Med. 1993; 329(15): 1084–1091.

45. Black M, Basile K, Breiding M, Smith S, Walters M, Merrick M. et al. The National Intimate Partner and Sexual Violence Survey (NISVS): 2010 summary report. Atlanta, GA: National Center for Injury Prevention and Control, Centers for Disease Control and Prevention; 2011.

46. Tjaden P, Theonnes N. Full report of the prevalence, incidence, and consequences of violence against women. Washington, DC: US Department of Justice; 2000.

47. Violence Policy Center. When men murder women: an analysis of 2010 homicide data. Washington, DC: Violence Policy Center; 2012.

48. Hemenway D. Private guns, public health. Ann Arbor: University of Michigan Press; 2004. P. 120.

49. Hausman B. Gun industry must become less racist to survive in the 21st century. Shooting Sports Retailer. 1997 Jan P. 86.

50. Noriyuki D. Ted Nugent grows up? Detroit Free Press Magazine. 1990 Jul 15.

51. Martin G. Nazi items sold at gun show/Hitler's Mein Kampf, swastikas sold at Cow Palace [Internet]. San Francisco Chronicle. 1995 Feb 13. Available from: http://www.sfgate.com/news/article/Nazi-Items-Sold-at-Gun-Show-Hitler-s-Mein-3045137.php

52. Pew Research Center. After Newtown, modest change in opinion about gun control. Washington, DC: Pew Research Center; 2012 Dec. 20.

53. Hemenway D. Private guns, public health. Table 6.4, P. 125.

54. Hemenway D. Private guns, public health. P. 126.

55. Cook P, Ludwig J. Guns in America: results of a comprehensive national survey on firearms ownership and use. Summary Report. Washington, DC: Police Foundation; 1996. P. 31.

56. Violence Policy Center. Joe Camel with feathers: how the NRA with gun and tobacco industry dollars uses its Eddie Eagle Program to market guns to kids. Washington, DC: Violence Policy Center; 2000.

57. Violence Policy Center. Joe Camel with feathers.

58. LaPierre W. Standing guard. American Guardian. 2000 Mar P. 6.

59. National Shooting Sports Foundation. Youth programs [Internet]. Newtown, CT: National Shooting Sports Foundation; 2016. Available from: http://www.nssf.org/shooting/youth/

60. Children's Defense Fund. Protect children, not guns: Overview. Washington, DC: Children's Defense Fund; 2013. P. 2.
61. Centers for Disease Control and Prevention. Injury prevention & control: data & statistics (WISQARS™) 2012 [Internet]. Available from: http://www.cdc.gov/injury/wisqars/fatal_injury_reports.html
62. Children's Defense Fund. Protect children, not guns.
63. Miller M, Azrael D, Hemenway D. Firearm availability and unintentional firearm deaths, suicide, and homicide among 5–14 year olds. J Trauma, 2002, 52(2): 267–275.
64. Hemenway D. Private guns, public health. P. 109–110.
65. Berman A. Consensus statement on youth suicide by firearms. Arch Suicide Res. 1998; 4(1): 89–94.
66. Hemenway D. Private guns, public health. P. 117.
67. National Rifle Association. A brief history of the NRA [Internet]. Available from: http://www.nrahq.org/history.asp
68. Violence Policy Center. Blood money: how the gun industry bankrolls the NRA. Washington, DC: Violence Policy Center; 2011. P. 1.
69. Violence Policy Center. Blood money. P. 4.
70. Masters K. Just how many people get guns without a background check: fast-tracked research is set to provide an answer [Internet]. The Trace. 2015 Oct 21.Available from: http://www.thetrace.org/2015/10/private-sale-loophole-background-check-harvard-research/
71. Law Center to Prevent Gun Violence. State immunity statutes, 2012 [Internet]. San Francisco, CA: Law Center to Prevent Gun Violence; 2015. Available from: http://smartgunlaws.org/category/state-immunity-statutes/

12

The "Guns Everywhere" Movement

As of September 2015, every state allowed the carrying of concealed firearms in some form and 47 states allowed the open carrying of long guns, handguns, or both.[1, 2] With these successes, the next frontier for the gun lobby appears to be the promotion of laws that will allow guns to be carried in virtually every setting.

Perhaps the most sweeping pro-gun bill in America was HB 60, passed in Georgia in April, 2014.[3] Dubbed the "guns everywhere" law, the measure allows Georgia residents with a carry permit to bring their weapons into bars, school safety zones (when authorized), and certain government buildings. The law also gives religious leaders the option of allowing guns in places of worship and grants permit holders the right to carry guns into airports. In addition, the law forbids police officers from asking an individual to produce a permit when they see a gun being carried unless a crime has been committed.

The bill passed with opposition from a majority of the state's citizens, the police chief's association, restaurant association, Episcopal and Catholic churches, and the Transportation Security Administration.[4] It is consistent with the mantra of gun rights advocates that gun violence tends to occur in "gun-free zones," settings in which people are easy prey

© The Author(s) 2016
T. Gabor, *Confronting Gun Violence in America*,
DOI 10.1007/978-3-319-33723-4_12

to armed criminals. Interestingly, Georgia legislators ensured that the reach of the "guns everywhere" law ended at the door step of the State Capitol and other government buildings with security screening. The apparent hypocrisy can also be seen at NRA conventions, as attendees are often barred from carrying operational weapons.[5] The same applies to the US Supreme Court, which screens all visitors for guns.[6] In 2008, the Court for the first time ruled that gun possession was an individual right.

Just one of the many potential side effects of the "guns everywhere" initiative can be found at airports. The Transportation Safety Administration reports that the seizures of guns at security checkpoints have increased virtually every year from 2005 to 2014.[7] In 2014, a record 2,212 firearms were confiscated in carry-on bags and 83 % of these guns were loaded. In 2015, 2,653 guns were intercepted.[8] One can imagine that, had even a fraction of these weapons gotten through the checkpoints and been in the wrong hands, the outcome could have been catastrophic.

Another manifestation of the "guns everywhere" effort, coupled with "open carry," will be the omnipresence of individuals with guns protruding from their holsters. Perhaps we will become inured to this new reality; however, surveys indicate that pervasive gun carrying makes many people feel unsafe.[9, 10] Those parts of the country in which tourism is a key industry may suffer, as foreigners may feel uncomfortable surrounded by gun-toting locals. It is not reassuring that law enforcement has major concerns with "open carry." A Texas survey, for example, found that nearly 75 % of police chiefs in the state opposed "open carry."[11] In Florida, the law enforcement community has been deeply divided on the matter, with the Florida Sheriff's Association vigorously opposing the measure and the police chiefs supporting it.[12]

The Campus-Carry Initiative

One major initiative of the "guns everywhere" push has been the effort to allow guns on college and university campuses. By 2014, ten states allowed permit holders on the campuses of postsecondary institutions.[13] In some states, universities could opt out (e.g., Arkansas), while in other states this is not an option. In other states, guns are only permitted in certainly locations on campus, such as parking lots (North Carolina). In addition, court rulings in four states have overturned policies prohibiting firearms on campus (e.g., Colorado).

Arguments by advocates of arming campuses range from those invoking Second Amendment rights to fear-based arguments. Marion Hammer, former head of the NRA and currently its chief Florida lobbyist, has argued:

> *Too often, college campuses are gun-free zones where murderers, rapists and other violent criminals can commit their crimes without fear of being harmed by their victims. This is not raising "the panic level"—it is a fact ... police do the best job they can, but they are not there when the attack occurs. They only arrive after the rape, robbery or other attack has happened. Police can't stop the crime—only the victim has a chance to actually stop it. Denying the tools of self-defense creates more victims.*[14]

On the face of it, Hammer's argument appears logical enough. Campuses may prohibit guns but those intending to commit crimes on campus can nevertheless carry weapons in violation of the prohibition. It is also true that the police tend to respond to crime only after the crime has been committed. Thus, equipping potential victims with the tools that can counter an attack seems reasonable enough. Hammer's argument, however, offers a misleading portrayal of campus life and omits all the potential adverse effects of arming students and others who use college and university campuses. The remainder of this chapter will be devoted to addressing her position on the issue. Before doing so, a glimpse into Ms. Hammer's background provides insight into the culture wars that appear to be at the root of the battle between gun rights and gun safety advocates.

Marion Hammer first handled firearms as a young child. She recalls:

> *My grandparents raised me. I grew up on a farm. I was five years old. My granddaddy would go off rabbit hunting and squirrel hunting couple or three times a week. It's just what we did. And we ate rabbits and squirrels. And I wanted to go. And I begged him to let me go. ... And before I was six years old, I was shooting rabbits and squirrels. It's a way of life.*[15]

Hammer won dozens of shooting competitions and became a gun rights activist after the enactment of the 1968 Gun Control Act. She founded Unified Sportsmen of Florida (USF)—a state affiliate of the NRA—in 1975 and became the full-time lobbyist for USF and the NRA in Florida in 1978. She explains that she formed USF because northerners who had moved to South Florida were bringing their views on gun control with them.

Hammer acknowledges that she has carried a loaded handgun in her purse before Florida passed its concealed carry law in 1987. She adds: "I'm 4-foot-11. I'm 67 years old. If you came at me, and I felt that my life was in danger or that I was going to be injured, I wouldn't hesitate to shoot you."

Campuses Are Safer than the Community

Hammer's argument for "campus-carry" is based on her characterization of university and college campuses as hunting grounds for sexual and other predators. While campuses have their security challenges, including violent crimes, they tend to be safer than the communities that surround them.

The largest crime survey in the country, the annual National Crime Victimization Survey (NCVS), indicates that college students are less likely to be crime victims than nonstudents of the same age.[16] The survey also found that 93 % of all violent crimes against college students occurred off campus. Further contradicting Hammer's portrayal of college campuses is the finding that homicide rates at postsecondary institutions are a fraction of what they are in the country as a whole. A study by the Department of Education found that the overall criminal homicide rate at postsecondary education institutions was 0.07 per 100,000 of enrollment in 1999. By contrast, the criminal homicide rate in the USA was 5.7 per 100,000 persons overall and 14.1 per 100,000 for persons ages 17–29, making college and university students far safer than the country as a whole.[17] While there were nearly 12,000 gun homicides in the country in 2003, there were just 10 homicides (gun and nongun) on college campuses in the same year.[18] Rather than allowing guns on campus, crime data indicate that communities might consider emulating colleges in being more gun free.

Guns on Campus Is Costly

Another set of issues ignored by Hammer relates to the costs associated with allowing guns on campuses. There are at least three types of costs: financial, safety/health, and learning environment related.

Campus officials say that allowing gun carrying on campus will cost millions of dollars in additional personnel, training, equipment, storage facilities, and technology. The Association of Florida Colleges, for example, estimates the cost to approach $75 million for 28 state colleges, shifting valuable resources from education to security. It has been estimated that it will cost the University of Texas and University of Houston systems almost $47 million to implement a law allowing students to bring guns on campus, according to a fiscal analysis by the Texas state Senate in 2015.[19]

Guns on campus may also have a chilling effect on the learning environment. Higher education involves the testing of novel and sometimes provocative ideas. Arming campuses can adversely affect the free exchange of different viewpoints as both faculty and students may be unwilling to express controversial views fearing they may anger someone who is armed. Faculty members may face an armed student who is angered due to a poor grade. A North Carolina study found that workplaces allowing guns were—five to seven times as likely to experience a homicide as those prohibiting guns.[20] The presence of armed students on campus may also fuel a campus arms race as other students at close quarters (e.g., in a dorm) may feel compelled to arm themselves.

While campus safety can always be improved, there is little credible evidence that gun carrying would improve campus safety. Research by John Donohue of Stanford University and his associates indicates that permissive concealed carry laws tend to increase rather than reduce crime and that these laws actually are "associated with substantially higher rates of aggravated assault, rape, robbery and murder."[21]

Guns are far more likely to be used in crime than for protection. FBI data for 2014 show that there were 229 justifiable homicides by private citizens using a gun compared with 8,124 total gun homicides (35 criminal homicides with a gun for every self-defense killing with a gun).[22] Leading studies show that guns in the home are many times more likely to be used to harm or intimidate a family member than an intruder.[23] Introducing guns onto campuses is likely to have a similar outcome.

The idea that guns would provide a net benefit in foiling crime is contradicted by an analysis of five years of data from the NCVS. In over 14,000 crimes involving a personal contact between offenders and victims, guns were used by less than 1 % of the victims despite the fact that close to 25 % of adults were gun owners.[24] In over 300 sexual assaults, not once did a woman use a gun to protect herself. Victims of personal contact crimes who did use a gun in self-defense were no more likely to escape injury than those taking other protective actions. Even owners use guns infrequently in self-defense because they often know the perpetrator, are not carrying at the time, or are surprised by the attacker.

While the gun lobby portrays campuses as bursting with sexual predators, the truth is that most sex offenses are committed by acquaintances or partners of the victim and with alcohol present.[25] In these circumstances, gun owners would not likely be carrying and the presence of a gun may further endanger the victim. Marion Hammer and other advocates of armed self-defense also do not consider the fact that arming more people means that more campus perpetrators, too, will be armed. A study by Jacquelyn Campbell of John Hopkins University and her associates found that a woman's chances of being killed increase more than seven times when the attacker has access to a firearm.[26]

On campuses, the combination of people at their peak years for violence, stormy romantic relationships and rivalries, academic pressures, and widespread binge drinking is sufficiently volatile without adding lethal weapons into the mix. According to a national survey, almost 60 %of college students of ages 18–22 drank alcohol in the previous month and nearly two-thirds of them engaged in binge drinking during that same time frame.[27] The potential for harm and self-harm—1,100 college students commit suicide each year and another 24,000 attempt suicide[28]–is even greater, given the higher lethality rate of gun-related suicide attempts versus other methods.

Licensees Poorly Vetted and Trained

Marion Hammer states that *"only the victim has a chance to actually stop it [the crime]. Denying the tools of self-defense creates more victims."*

Encouraging victims to resist their attackers is questionable advice. Some evidence shows that actively resisting perpetrators makes serious injury more likely.[29, 30] Using lethal force as a first option, which Hammer seems to be recommending, raises the chances of a number of negative outcomes, including prosecution for using force inappropriately or disproportionately, being shot with one's gun or that of the perpetrator, or shooting a bystander.

Hammer's assertion suggests that permitting victims to use guns for self-defense makes them qualified to do so. In fact, most concealed and open carry laws in the USA do not come close to requiring the training needed to using firearms for protection safely and effectively. Chapter 10 discussed the failure of most states to require rigorous training and continuing recertification in gun safety, marksmanship, judgment, and the law before granting carry permits. Several states require no permits or firearms training at all. As discussed in that chapter, even trained police officers miss their mark more than 80 % of the time in combat situations and can make catastrophic errors during stressful encounters with suspects. Hammer suggests that students with little or no firearms training and no experience in highly stressful combat situations should be turned loose to use guns as a routine response to crime. The tragedies produced through inappropriate uses of force are likely to be compounded by Stand Your Ground laws, such as those enacted in Florida.

Hammer also fails to address the inadequate vetting and lack of continuous screening of those with licenses to carry firearms. Upon issuing permits (in states requiring them), most states do not periodically monitor licensees to ensure their continuing suitability while they hold that permit. Minnesota is one exception as there sheriffs must ensure the continuing eligibility of permit holders through a background check to be conducted at least once a year.[31] In "shall issue" states, applicants must be issued a permit if they meet the requirements, even if police have concerns. The result is predictable: As Chap. 10 has shown, a significant number of licensees have committed serious crimes. As of October 2015, the Washington-based Violence Policy Center has found that these "good guys with guns" have been responsible for 763 killings or suicides in a total of 579 incidents since May 2007—nearly 100 deaths per year.[32]

Community Opposed

The effort led by the gun lobby to introduce guns into virtually every setting, including college and university campuses, has disregarded the wishes of those working and studying in many of these settings. A Harvard nationwide poll found that 94 % of Americans opposed allowing guns on college campuses.[33] College administrators, faculty, and students have seldom been so united in relation to an issue as they have on the "campus-carry" issue. A survey at 15 Midwestern colleges and universities found that 78 % of students opposed allowing concealed handguns on campuses and 79 % said they would not feel safe with concealed handguns on campus.[34] A survey of over 900 college and university presidents found that 95 % of respondents opposed allowing concealed handguns on campus, 95 % said no student had been shot during their time in office, and 91 % indicated that no crimes with guns had been committed on their campus in the previous year.[35] A poll of faculty members at 15 colleges across Ohio, Michigan, Indiana, Illinois, and Wisconsin found that 98 % felt safe on campus and 94 % opposed the carrying of concealed guns there.[36]

Also, most campus police chiefs support expelling students who bring guns to campus. The Board of Directors of the International Association of Campus Law Enforcement Administrators (IACLEA) issued a position statement asserting that allowing gun carrying will not make campuses safer:

> *There is no credible evidence to suggest that the presence of students carrying concealed weapons would reduce violence on our college campuses. ... IACLEA is concerned that concealed carry laws have the potential to dramatically increase violence on college and university campuses that our Members are empowered to protect. Among the concerns with concealed carry laws or policies are: the potential for accidental discharge or misuse of firearms at on-campus or off-campus parties where large numbers of students are gathered or at student gatherings where alcohol or drugs are being consumed, as well as the potential for guns to be used as a means to settle disputes between or among students. There is also a real concern that campus police officers responding to a situation involving an active shooter may not be able to distinguish between the shooter and others with firearms.*

IACLEA is also concerned that campus homicide and suicides will increase and that campus police will be endangered by a policy allowing guns on campus. [37]

Bottom Line

Despite the magnitude of America's challenges with guns, the gun lobby and other gun rights advocates persist in their attempt to introduce guns into virtually every setting. These settings include college and university campuses. The number of states allowing this to occur is growing although the effort is facing considerable resistance. Arguments for such a policy range from the belief that it is simply a right protected by the Second Amendment to fear-based arguments portraying colleges as hunting grounds for predators.

Fear-based arguments ignore the fact that college campuses are safer than the community and that most offenses against students occur off campus. The financial costs of equipping a campus and recruiting as well as training security personnel to deal with an anticipated increase in gun-related incidents and violations are expected to be prohibitive. Allowing guns in the classroom can be expected to intimidate and to inhibit discussions of highly controversial issues.

Permitting guns on campuses also ignores recent research showing that permissive carry laws are associated with increases, rather than reductions, in violence. Also, guns are rarely used by victims to foil crimes. In addition, many sex crimes are committed by intimates and acquaintances of the victim; hence, victims usually will not be carrying a gun when attacked. Furthermore, students are exposed to many stresses and activities that may place them at risk of harm and self-harm. Easy access to lethal weapons and some of the risk-taking associated with campus life creates a potentially volatile combination. Finally, campus-carry imposes on postsecondary educational institutions a solution to a crime problem that most administrators, faculty, and students feel does not exist. There is a significant consensus among those who study and work at universities that guns are not needed and that they will make life on campus more dangerous.

Notes

1. Law Center to Prevent Gun Violence. Concealed weapons permitting policy summary [Internet]. Smartgun.laws.org. 2015 Sep 10. Available from: http://smartgunlaws.org/concealed-weapons-permitting-policy-summary/

2. Law Center to Prevent Gun Violence. Open carrying policy summary [Internet]. Smartgunlaws.org. 2015 Aug 21. Available from: http://smartgunlaws.org/open-carrying-policy-summary/

3. Georgia House Bill 60. A bill to be entitled an Act [Internet]. Available from: http://gov.georgia.gov/sites/gov.georgia.gov/files/related_files/document/hb%2060.pdf

4. Sanchez N. Georgia "guns everywhere" law awaits Governor's signature [Internet]. Newsmax. 2014 Mar 27. http://www.newsmax.com/TheWire/georgia-guns-everywhere-law/2014/03/27/id/562028/

5. NRA Convention: No working guns allowed [Internet]. The Daily Beast. Available from: http://www.thedailybeast.com/cheats/2015/04/08/nra-convention-no-guns-allowed.html

6. Winkler A. Gunfight: the battle over the right to bear arms in America. New York: W.W. Norton; 2013. P. 8.

7. Muskal M. Record TSA airport seizures: loaded guns, grenades, knife in an enchilada [Internet]. The Los Angeles Times. 2015 Jan 23. Available from: http://www.latimes.com/nation/la-na-tsa-record-gun-seizure-airports-20150123-story.html

8. Laing K. TSA intercepted 2,653 guns in 2015 [Internet]. The Hill. 2016 Jan 21. Available from: http://thehill.com/policy/transportation/266588-tsa-intercepts-2653-guns-in-2015

9. Hemenway D, Azrael D, Miller M. U.S. national attitudes concerning gun carrying. Inj Prev. 2001; 7(4): 282–285.

10. Quinnipiac University. Quinnipiac University Poll [Internet]. Hamden, CT. 2015 Dec 22. Available from: http://www.quinnipiac.edu/news-and-events/quinnipiac-university-poll/national/release-detail?ReleaseID=2311

11. Benning T. 75% of Texas police chiefs responding to survey oppose open carry [Internet]. The Dallas Morning News. 2015 Feb 13. Available from: http://trailblazersblog.dallasnews.com/2015/02/survey-of-nearly-200-texas-police-chiefs-shows-that-nearly-75-percent-oppose-open-carry.html/

12. Editorial. Sheriff raises real concerns about open-carry bill [Internet]. The Tampa Bay Times. 2015 Dec 17. Available from: http://www.tampabay.com/opinion/editorials/editorial-sheriff-raises-real-concerns-about-open-carry-bill/2258237.

13. The Campaign to Keep Guns off Campus. State Legislation [Internet]. Available from: http://keepgunsoffcampus.org/state-battles/.

14. Hammer M. Marion Hammer: Sun, other critics of campus gun bill are denying reality [Internet]. Gainesville Sun. 2015 Feb 22. Available from: http://www.gainesville.com/article/20150222/OPINION03/150229995?p=1&tc=pg

15. Lyons D. Face to face: a conversation with the NRA's Marion P. Hammer [Internet]. Sun Sentinel. 2011 Apr 24. Available from: http://articles.sun-sentinel.com/2011-04-24/news/fl-dlyons-outlook-facetoface-marionha 20110424_1_guns-people-firearms

16. Baum K. Violent victimization of college students, 1995–2002. Washington, DC: Bureau of Justice Statistics; 2005.

17. US Department of Education. The incidence of crime on the campuses of US postsecondary institutions. A report to Congress. Washington, DC: US Department of Education; 2001. P. 5.

18. US Department of Education. Criminal offenses: Murder/non-negligent manslaughter 2003 [Internet]. Available from: http://www2.ed.gov/admins/lead/safety/crime/criminaloffenses/edlite-murder.html

19. Campus Safety Staff. Study: Guns on campus will cost Texas universities $47 million [Internet]. Campus Safety. 2015 Feb 26. Available from: http://campussafetymagazine.com/article/study_guns_on_campus_will_cost_texas_universities_47m#

20. Loomis D, Marshall S, Ta M. Employer policies toward guns and the risk of homicide in the workplace, Am J Public Health. 2005; 95(5): 830–832.

21. Aneja A, Donohue J, Zhang A. The impact of right to carry laws and the NRC report: the latest lessons for the empirical evaluation of law and policy. Stanford, CA: Stanford University; 2014.

22. Federal Bureau of Investigation. Crime in the United States, 2014. Expanded Homicide Data Tables 8 and 15 [Internet]. Washington, DC: US Department of Justice. Available from: https://www.fbi.gov/about-us/cjis/ucr/crime-in-the-u.s/2014/crime-in-the-u.s.-2014/tables/expanded-homicide-data/expanded_homicide_data_table_15_justifiable_homicide_by_weapon_private_citizen_2010-2014.xls

23. Kellermann A, Somes G, Rivara F, Lee R, Banton J. Injuries and deaths due to firearms in the home. J Trauma. 1998; 45(2): 263–67.

24. Hemenway D, Solnick S. The epidemiology of self-defense gun use: Evidence from the National Crime Victimization Surveys, 2007–2011. Preventive Medicine. 2015; 79: 22–27.

25. Sinozich S, Langton L. Rape and sexual assault victimization among college-age females, 1995–2013. Washington, DC: US Department of Justice; 2014.

26. Campbell J, Webster D, Koziol-Mclain J, Block C, Campbell D, Curry M et al. Risk factors for femicide in abusive relationships: Results from a multisite case control study. Am J Public Health. 2003; 93(7): 1089–1097.

27. National Institute of Health. College drinking [Internet]. Washington, DC: National Institute of Alcohol Abuse and Alcoholism; 2015. Available from: http://pubs.niaaa.nih.gov/publications/CollegeFactSheet/CollegeFactSheet.pdf

28. Scelfo J. Suicide on campus and the pressure of perfection [Internet]. The New York Times. 2015 Jul 27. Available from: http://www.nytimes.com/2015/08/02/education/edlife/stress-social-media-and-suicide-on-campus.html?_r=0

29. Bachman R, Saltzman L, Thompson M, Carmody D. Disentangling the effects of self-protective behaviors on the risk of injury in assaults against women. J Quant Criminol. 2002; 18(2): 135–57.

30. Kleck G, Tark J. Draft Final Technical Report: The impact of victim self-protection on rape completion and injury. Washington, DC: National Institute of Justice; 2004.

31. Law Center to Prevent Gun Violence. Concealed weapons permitting in Minnesota [Internet]. Smartgunlaws.org. 2015 Aug 26. Available from: http://smartgunlaws.org/concealed-weapons-permitting-in-minnesota/

32. Violence Policy Center. Concealed Carry Killers [Internet]. Washington, DC: Violence Policy Center. Available from: http://concealedcarrykillers.org/.

33. Hemenway D, Azrael D, Miller M. US national attitudes concerning gun carrying. Inj Prev. 2001; 7(4): 282–285.

34. Ransford M. Most college students don't want guns on their campuses [Internet]. Ball State University. 2013 Sep 9. Available from: http://cms.bsu.edu/news/articles/2013/9/students-say-no-to-concealed-weapons-on-campus.

35. Chronicle staff. Overwhelming majority of college presidents oppose guns on campus [Internet]. Chronicle of Higher Education. 2014 Jun 3. Available from: http://chronicle.com/blogs/ticker/overwhelming-majority-of-college-presidents-oppose-guns-on-campus/79081

36. Thompson A, Price J, Dake J, Teeple K. Faculty perceptions and practices regarding carrying concealed handguns on university campuses. J Community Health. 2013; 38(2): 366–373.

37. Sprague L. Position Statement on Concealed Carrying of Firearms Proposal on College Campuses. West Hartford, CT: International Association of Campus Law Enforcement Administrators; 2008 Aug 12.

13

Public Opinion: An Impediment to Reform?

Is the public itself an impediment to gun policy reforms? Does it support gun rights over gun control? What forms of gun control, if any, do most Americans favor? Do members of the public feel more or less safe when they learn that more of their fellow citizens are carrying guns for their protection?

Dozens of surveys show that the public strongly supports a number of measures to regulate firearms, promote public safety, and keep criminals from obtaining guns. The public does not support a general ban on gun ownership.[1] On some fundamental issues, such as whether they believe we should prioritize gun rights or gun control, the American people are deeply divided.

The National Gun Policy Survey, conducted by the University of Chicago's National Opinion Research Center in 2001, found that there has been great stability in public attitudes over 40 years.[2] However, we will see that there has been some shift in emphasis over the last few years.

Much of the research on public opinion with regard to gun policy has been conducted by national polling firms such as Gallup or the Pew Research Center, or on behalf of news organizations like CBS, CNN, and *The New York Times*. The reader should note that the analysis below

© The Author(s) 2016   **229**
T. Gabor, *Confronting Gun Violence in America*,
DOI 10.1007/978-3-319-33723-4_13

is based on surveys conducted since 2012, with the exception of comprehensive, seminal surveys conducted by the National Opinion Research Center (the National Gun Policy Survey) and Harvard University's Injury Control Research Center. The website, pollingreport.com, was used to help identify polls during this time frame after the accuracy of the information on that site was verified. The analysis undoubtedly missed some relevant polls during this period. Surveys commissioned by lobby or interest groups were not considered in this analysis.

It is important to note that public opinion is never static. At best, it is a snapshot of sentiment at one point in time. Polling results will vary due to major events, such as mass shootings. In addition, results will vary according to the questions asked, specific wording and sequence of the questions, the group conducting the poll, and the sampling methodology.

Should Gun Laws Be More Strict or Less Strict, or Should they Be Kept as they Are?

As Table 13.1 indicates, surveys have been quite consistent in showing that 47–55 % of Americans believe that gun laws should be more strict than they are now and 8–14 % believe that they should be less strict. With the exception of one CNN/ORC poll in 2015, about a third of the respondents favored keeping the laws as they are. Thus, of those Americans seeking a change in the laws, those favoring stricter laws outnumber those favoring laws that are less strict by a ratio of about 5:1. When the public is given just the two options of whether they favor or are opposed to stricter gun laws, those in favor outnumber those opposed by a small margin (47–54 % vs. 41–51 %) across the polls posing this question. A CNN/ORC survey in September 2015 and a Quinnipiac University poll in December 2015 found that respondents who said it was too easy to buy a gun outnumbered, by a wide margin, those who said it was too difficult to do so.

Table 13.1 The public's views about the strictness of gun laws

Poll	Finding
CBS/*New York Times*, December 4–8, 2015	51 % believe that laws covering the sale of guns should be more strict, 10 % believe they should be less strict, and 36 % said they should be kept as they are
CBS/*New York Times*, February 19–23, 2014	54 % said they should be more strict, 9 % said they should be less strict, and 36 % indicated they should be kept as they are
Gallup, October 12–15, 2014	47 % said that laws covering the sale of firearms should be more strict, 14 % said they should be less strict, and 38 % kept as they are
Gallup, October 3–6, 2013	49 % stated that laws covering the sale of firearms should be more strict, 13 % stated they should be less strict, and 37 % kept as they are
NBC News/Wall Street Journal, December 4–8, 2013,	52 % said laws governing sale of guns should be more strict, 8 % said they should be less strict, and 38 % kept as they are
AP/GFK Roper Public Affairs & Corporate Communications, April 11–15, 2013	49 % think that gun laws should be more strict, 10 % think they should be less strict, and 38 % kept as they are
ABC News/*Washington Post*, December 14–16, 2012	54 % favor and 43 % oppose stricter gun laws in country
Quinnipiac University, June 24–30, 2014	50 % support stricter gun laws and 47 % are opposed
Quinnipiac University, September 23–29, 2013	54 % support stricter gun laws and 41 % are opposed
CNN/ORC, November 18–20, 2013	49 % favor and 50 % oppose stricter gun laws
CNN/ORC, September 4–8, 2015	41 % said laws make it too easy to buy guns, 10 % said it was too difficult, and 49 % thought the laws were just right
Quinnipiac University, December 16–20, 2015	55 % said it is too easy to buy a gun, 4 % said it was too difficult, and 36 % said it was about right
CNN/ORC, December 17–21, 2015	48 % favor and 51 % oppose stricter gun laws
Quinnipiac University, December 16–20, 2015	47 % support and 50 % oppose stricter gun laws
Gallup, October 7–11, 2015	55 % support stricter gun laws, 11 % less strict, and 33 % favor keeping laws as they are

Should Criminal Background Checks Be Required for All Gun Sales, Including Those at Gun Shows and Those Conducted Privately?

Polls consistently show very strong support for conducting criminal background checks on all buyers of firearms, including purchases conducted in private or at gun shows (Table 13.2). Most surveys show that between eight and nine of every ten Americans favor such checks.

Table 13.2 Views on background checks

Poll	Finding
CBS News, December 4–8, 2013	85 % favor background checks on all buyers
CBS/*New York Times*, October 21–25, 2015	92 % favor background checks on all potential gun buyers
Gallup, October 3–6, 2013	91 % support checks for all sales
Gallup, October 7–11, 2015	86 % favor a law requiring background checks on all gun purchases in the USA using a centralized database across all 50 states
AP/GfK Roper, January 10–14, 2013	84 % support checks for gun show purchases
John Hopkins/GfK KN, January 2–14, 2013	89 % support checks for all sales
ABC News/*Washington Post*, April 11–14, 2013	86 % support background checks for gun show and online sales
Quinnipiac University, September 17–21, 2015	93 % support background checks for all buyers
Quinnipiac University, December 16–20, 2015	89 % support background checks for gun show and online sales
Quinnipiac University, June 24–30, 2014	92 % favor background checks for all gun buyers
Quinnipiac University, January 30–February 4, 2013	92 % support background checks for all gun buyers
Pew Research Center, May 1–5, 2013,	81 % favor checks for sales in private or at gun shows
Pew Research Center, July 14–20, 2015	85 % favor expanded background checks for gun shows and private sales
CNN/ORC, April 5–7, 2013	89 % favor checks for sales in gun stores, 83 % at gun shows, and 70 % in private sales
National Gun Policy Survey, May 8–October 30, 2001	78 % support the requirement of a background check prior to a private gun sale
	73 % support mandatory background checks and a five-day waiting period

Should Military-Style Assault Weapons and High-Capacity Gun Magazines/Clips (That Can Hold Many Rounds of Ammunition, Usually More than Ten) Be Banned?

With the exception of two surveys conducted in December 2015, over half of respondents favor a ban on assault weapons and a half to two-thirds support banning high-capacity magazines/ammunition clips (Table 13.3). Support for such bans may erode somewhat if the government is expected to buy these weapons or feeding devices back from owners at their fair market value.

Should the Ownership or Carrying of Handguns by Civilians Be Banned?

About 7 in 10 Americans oppose banning the civilian ownership of all handguns (Table 13.4). As many as 48–58 % support banning semiautomatic guns or handguns; however, many people may not realize that many firearms today are semiautomatic, which means that the energy used in one shot of the gun is harnessed to load the next shot into the chamber. Perhaps without realizing it, a large segment of the public endorses the banning of many models of firearms produced today. The 2001 National Gun Policy Survey found that slightly more than half the population favored limiting the carrying of concealed weapons to individuals with special needs, such as security guards. This figure may well be lower today due to the emphasis on gun ownership for self-protection.

Table 13.3 Views on the prohibition of assault weapons and high-capacity magazines

Poll	Finding
CBS News/*New York Times*, April 24–28, 2013	50 % favor and 47 % oppose a ban on semiautomatic firearms with detachable magazine that allows rapid firing of a high number of rounds
CBS/*New York Times*, December 4–8, 2015	44 % favor and 50 % oppose a nationwide assault weapon ban
CBS News, February 6–10, 2013	59 % in favor and 38 % oppose a ban on high-capacity magazines
Gallup, January 19–20, 2013	54 % favor and 43 % oppose ban on high-capacity gun magazines
AP/GFK Roper, January 10–14, 2013	55 % favor and 34 % oppose ban on assault weapons; 51 % favor and 37 % oppose ban on high-capacity magazines
Johns Hopkins/ GfK KN January 2–14, 2013	69 % favor ban, but just 56 % favor ban if government must pay owners fair market value for their weapons; 68 % favor ban of high-capacity magazines, but just 55 % favor such a ban where the government must pay owners fair market value for the clips
ABC News/*Washington Post* April 11–14, 2013	56 % support and 42 % oppose assault weapons ban; 56 % support and 41 % are opposed to a nationwide ban of high-capacity ammunition clips
ABC News/*Washington Post*, December 10–13, 2015	45 % support and 53 % oppose nationwide ban on the sale of assault weapons
Quinnipiac University, December 16–20, 2015	58 % support and 38 % oppose nationwide ban on the sale of assault weapons
Quinnipiac University, January 30-Feb. 4, 2013	56 % support and 39 % oppose ban on assault weapons; 56 % support and 40 % oppose ban on high-capacity gun magazines
Pew Research Center, January 9–13, 2013	55 % favor and 40 % oppose ban on assault-style weapons; 54 % favor and 42 % oppose ban on high-capacity ammunition clips
Pew Research Center, July 14–20, 2015	57 % favor ban on assault-style weapons
CNN/ORC International, August 7–8, 2012	60 % favor a ban on sale or possession of both semiautomatic weapons and high-capacity magazines
CNN/ORC International, April 5–7, 2013	51 % favor and 48 % oppose assault weapon ban; 53 % favor and 46% oppose high-capacity magazine ban

Table 13.4 Views on the prohibition of handgun ownership and carrying

Poll	Finding
Gallup, October 3–6, 2013	74 % oppose ban on handguns
Gallup, October 12–15, 2014	73 % oppose ban on handguns
Gallup, October 7–11, 2015	72 % oppose ban on handguns
ABC News/*Washington Post*, December 14–16, 2012	71–27 oppose banning civilians from having handguns
An ABC News/*Washington Post*, January 13–16, 2011	50 % oppose and 48 % favor ban on semiautomatic handguns and 67 % oppose and 31 % favor overall ban on sales of handguns to civilians
National Gun Policy Survey (NORC), May 8–October 30, 2001	11 % favor a total handgun ban; 49 % support restricting handguns to law enforcement personnel only. The difference in how respondents interpreted these two items is unclear
Pew Research Center, January 9–13, 2013	58 % support and 39 % oppose ban on semiautomatic guns
National Gun Policy Survey (NORC), May 8–October 30, 2001	52 % support limiting the carrying of concealed weapons to those with special needs, such as private security officers

Should the Mentally Ill Be More Carefully Screened, Prevented from Buying Guns or Be Provided More Services?

Table 13.5 shows that—eight to nine of ten Americans support measures that prevent the mentally ill from purchasing guns and about eight of ten support mental health screening and additional spending for treatment. According to one poll, there is also strong support for reporting individuals with mental illnesses to a gun registry database.

Beliefs Regarding the Value of Gun Ownership, Guns in the Home, and Gun Carrying

These issues expose the divide among the American public. When asked about the impact of guns in the home, 43–63 % feel that an armed home makes it safer, 29–40 % say guns kept in the home make it more

Table 13.5 Gun rights of and services for the mentally ill

Poll	Finding
CBS News, December 4–8, 2013	77 % believe that mental health screening and treatment would have at least some impact in preventing gun violence
CBS/*New York Times*, December 4–8, 2015	77 % believe that mental health screening and treatment would have at least some impact in preventing gun violence
Gallup, January 19–20, 2013	82 % favor more government spending for mental health programs for young people
ABC News/*Washington Post*, January 13–16, 2011	83 % supported a law that would require that all states reported the mentally ill to a gun registry database; 71 % support federal funding to get drug abusers into such a registry
Quinnipiac University, September 17–21, 2015	88 % support laws preventing people with mental illnesses from purchasing guns
Quinnipiac University, June 24–30, 2014	89 % support a measure to prevent those with mental illnesses from buying guns
Pew Research Center, January 9–13, 2013	80 % support preventing people with mental illnesses from buying guns
Pew Research Center, July 14–20, 2015	79 % support laws preventing the mentally ill from buying guns

dangerous, and 16 % say it depends (Table 13.6). The public appears to be less confident about the benefits of gun carrying, as 59–64 % say they would feel less safe and 9–31 % say they would feel safer if more people in their community carried guns. The public was more evenly split with regard to the impact of gun carrying (44 % felt they would be safer and 44 % less safe) where laws required that gun carriers receive a criminal record check and enroll in a gun safety course. A Pew Research Center survey found that over half the respondents felt that gun ownership protected people from being crime victims as opposed to putting them at risk. On the other hand, a Farleigh Dickinson University poll found that almost twice as many people believe that gun regulation rather than gun carrying is the way to reduce mass shootings.

Table 13.6 Beliefs about the value of gun ownership and carrying

Poll	Finding
Harvard University's Injury Control Research Center, 1996	59 % of Americans say they would feel less safe and 12 % said they would feel safer if they learned that more of their neighbors were carrying guns
ABC News/*Washington Post* April 11–14, 2013	51 % feel that a gun in home makes it safer, 29 % say it is makes things more dangerous, and 16 % say "it depends"
National Gun Policy Survey, May 8–October 30, 2001	43 % consider an armed home as safer, 16 % say it depends or are not sure, and 40 % think guns make it less safe. The 2001 survey was the first one in the series in which a plurality narrowly thought that guns made homes safer
Gallup, October 12–15, 2014	63 % said they think a gun in the home makes it safer and 30 % believe it makes it more dangerous
National Gun Policy Survey, May 8–October 30, 2001	Of those anticipating the number of people carrying guns would increase, 61 % said that such laws would make them feel less safe and 31 % felt they would be safer
	44 % stated that laws allowing adults to carry a concealed gun in public would make them safer and 44 % indicated they would be less safe where carriers were assumed to pass a criminal background check and a gun safety course
National Gun Policy Survey, May 8–October 30, 2001	64 % said they would feel less safe and 9 % said they would feel safer if more people in their community carried guns
Pew Research Center, July 14–20, 2015	54 % say that gun ownership does more to protect people from becoming crime victims, while 40 % say it does more to put people's safety at risk
Farleigh Dickinson University's PublicMind Poll, October 1–5, 2014	59 % stated better gun regulation and 33 % said more people carrying guns when asked which approach would help reduce mass shootings

Should it Be Permissible to Bring Guns into Places Such as Stores, Movie Theaters, and Restaurants?

At least two of every three Americans favor denying access to stores, restaurants, and other places frequented by the public to customers who carry guns (Table 13.7). Seven of ten Americans say they would be more likely to go to businesses that prohibit gun carrying.

Recordkeeping and Registration Requirements for Guns

The public appears open to maintaining a public registry of guns and to good recordkeeping in general, although there is some variation in the results of different polls. As Table 13.8 shows, 44–70 % of Americans

Table 13.7 Gun carrying in specific settings

Poll	Finding
National Gun Policy Survey, May 8–October 30, 2001	About two-thirds (67.5 %) favored limiting access to locations like stores and restaurants to those with special needs (e.g., occupational). By a large majority (79 %), Americans would like owners of businesses, such as stores, movie theaters, and restaurants, to keep customers from bringing guns into their establishments
National Gun Policy Survey, May 8–October 30, 2001	In addition, 69 % stated they would be more likely to go to businesses that prohibited gun carrying
Quinnipiac U. Poll in September 23–29, 2013	66 % agree with Starbucks that it is a good idea to ask customers to not bring guns into stores—23 % think it is bad idea
Harvard Injury Control Research Center, 1999	88 % oppose gun carrying into restaurants, 94 % into sports stadiums, 94 % onto college campuses, 93 % into bars, 91 % into hospitals, and 92 % into government buildings

Table 13.8 Beliefs about gun registration and recordkeeping

Poll	Finding
CNN/ORC International, April 5–7, 2013	66 % favor and 33 % oppose a requirement that gun owners register with state or local authorities
CNN/ORC International, April 5–7, 2013	55 % oppose and 44 % favor the creation of a national registry of gun owners and the guns they own
CNN/ORC International, April 5–7, 2013	81 % favor and 19 % oppose a requirement that all gun owners keep records of gun sales
Pew Research Center, January 9–13, 2013	67 % favor and 30 % oppose a federal database to track gun sales
Pew Research Center, July 14–20, 2015	70 % back the creation of a federal database to track gun sales
National Gun Policy Survey, May 8–October 30, 2001	77 % support the mandatory registration of handguns

favor and 30–55 % oppose a public registry of guns and their owners. More than three-quarters support the mandatory registration of handguns and 81 % favor a requirement that all gun owners maintain records of gun sales.

The Public's Views on Other Preventive Measures

A majority of Americans support armed guards in more schools and even in every school in the country (Table 13.9). Three-quarters of Americans also thought it would be helpful to have more police or armed guards in public places, such as malls and theaters. More than half oppose the arming of teachers and school officials. Just over half support banning online sales of ammunition and 39–56 % believe that stricter gun laws would reduce gun violence. Large majorities (at least three-quarters) support mandatory gun safety courses, the need for police permits prior to purchases, and personalizing guns so they can be fired only by their owners. Nearly seven in ten Americans favor limiting handgun purchases for any buyer to one per month and close to two-thirds support licensing and safety training for all handgun owners.

Table 13.9 Views on preventive measures

Poll	Finding
Pew Research Center, January 9–13, 2013	64 % support armed security guards or police in more schools
CNN/ORC International, April 5–7, 2013	53 % support and 46 % oppose armed guards in every school in the country
CBS News, February 6–10, 2013	75 % thought it would help at least some to have police or armed guards in public places, such as schools, malls, theaters
CBS/New York Times, October 21–25, 2015	38 % favor and 57 % oppose allowing more teachers and school officials to carry guns in schools
Pew Research Center, January 9–13, 2013	40 % support more teachers and school officials with guns in schools
Pew Research Center, January 9–13, 2013	53 % support a ban on the online sale of ammunition
John Hopkins/GfK KN, January 2–14, 2013	77 % support the need for a permit from the local law enforcement agency prior to buying a gun
CBS News, December 4–8, 2013	56 % believe that stricter gun laws would have at least some impact in preventing gun violence
CBS/New York Times, December 4–8, 2015	50 % believe that stricter gun laws would have at least some impact in preventing gun violence
CNN/ORC, June 26–28, 2015	39 % said stricter gun laws would reduce violence in the USA and 61 % said such laws would not reduce gun violence
National Gun Policy Survey, May 8–October 30, 2001	54 % favor stricter gun control laws and the vigorous enforcement of current and new laws
National Gun Policy Survey, May 8–October 30, 2001	88 % support mandatory gun safety courses for gun purchasers
National Gun Policy Survey, May 8–October 30, 2001	79 % support the need for a police permit prior to buying a gun
National Gun Policy Survey, May 8–October 30, 2001	74 % support personalizing all new handguns so they can only be fired by their lawful owners
National Gun Policy Survey, May 8–October 30, 2001	69 % support limiting handgun purchases for any buyer to one per month
National Gun Policy Survey, May 8–October 30, 2001	63 % support the requirement that all handgun owners be licensed and trained

Should the Priority Be to Prevent Violence or to Protect Gun Rights?

An ABC News/*Washington Post* poll, conducted on April 11–14, 2013, found that 52 % of Americans believed that the priority in establishing gun policies should be to prevent violence, while 40 % said it was more important to protect gun rights and 3 % said both were important.[3]

The Pew Research Center has been asking this question since 1993. Their poll in December 2014 found for the first time that more Americans prioritized gun rights than gun control by a margin of 52–46 %.[4] However, in July 2015, Pew once again found that respondents prioritized gun control over gun rights by a narrow margin (50–47 %).[5]

The question about gun control and gun rights was first asked in December 1993, a time when former President Clinton's gun proposals and attempts to curb the influence of the NRA gained wide public support. In that survey, 57 % said it was more important to control gun ownership, while 34 % said it was more important to protect gun rights.[6]

On 11 occasions between 1993 and 2008, Pew found that majorities consistently said it was more important to control gun ownership than to protect the right of Americans to own guns. However, since 2009, public opinion has been more evenly divided. Then, following the school shooting in Newtown, Connecticut, public opinion again tilted in favor of controlling gun ownership over protecting gun rights (49 % vs. 42 %). By May 2013, opinion was again divided (50 % said it was more important to control gun ownership, while 48 % said it was more important to protect gun rights). Then, in December 2014, gun rights prevailed by six points over gun control.

Pew researchers attribute the recent shift to a dramatic change in the attitudes of Republicans since 2007. Since that year, the share of Republicans saying it is more important to protect gun rights has increased by 28 points to 75 %. By contrast, Democratic opinion has remained far more stable.[7]

Leonard Pitts Jr., a nationally syndicated columnist, has written the following on efforts to introduce guns onto American college campuses and on the radicalization of the gun rights movement:

> *As has happened with conservatism generally, the gun rights movement has lurched hard to the right in recent years, has alienated reason, ostracized compromise and fetishized guns and gun ownership to a point that seems psychologically unhealthy. What was once a campaign to ensure the right of people to bear arms has mutated into a campaign to ensure guns at all times for everybody everywhere and to smack down those who would seek to ban them, even from places where banning them makes obvious sense.*[8]

Many Gun Owners Support Gun Regulation

According to a Pew Research Center poll conducted in February 2013, close to half (48 %) of gun owners own guns for protection.[9] Also, this poll found that more than three-quarters (79 %) of all owners say ownership makes them feel safer and just a third (35 %) believe that stricter laws could reduce deaths from mass shootings. In addition, 68 % of gun owners believe that stricter laws would give the government too much power over average citizens and 64 % say such laws would make it harder for people to protect their homes and families. Gun owners overwhelmingly say it is more important to protect gun rights than control gun ownership (70 % vs. 27 %).

Despite these views, nearly eight in ten (79 %) gun owners favor background checks on private gun sales. Even people living in households in which someone is an NRA member overwhelmingly favor (74 % vs. 26 %) making private gun sales and sales at gun shows subject to background checks. Almost half of all gun owners (43 %) favor a ban on assault-style weapons and close to this number (41 %) favor a ban on high-capacity ammunition clips.

The pollster Frank Luntz, who has been known for developing messaging for Republican causes, conducted a survey of 945 self-identified gun owners in May 2012, half of whom were members or lapsed members of the NRA.[10] His poll shows that gun rights and public safety can coexist.

Luntz found that 87 % of non-NRA gun owners and 74 % of NRA gun owners support the need to conduct a criminal background check on any individual buying a firearm. By large majorities, non-NRA and NRA gun owners support bans prohibiting people on the terrorist watch list from purchasing guns.

The following findings from Luntz's poll illustrate that the majority of gun owners who are NRA members support reasonable restrictions on an owner's ability to carry a gun:

- 74 %of NRA members believe that concealed carry permits should only be granted to applicants who have completed gun safety training.

- 68 %of NRA members believe that these permits should be granted only to those who do not have prior arrests for domestic violence.
- 63 %of NRA members believe concealed weapons permits should be granted only to applicants who are 21 years of age or older.
- 75 %of NRA members believe that concealed weapons permits should be limited to those who have not committed any violent misdemeanors.

Harvard University researchers Douglas Weil and David Hemenway analyzed data from a national random sample of gun owners. Gun owners who owned a large number of guns (six or more), as opposed to just one gun, were more likely to be NRA members than nonmembers. While nonmembers of the NRA were more supportive of specific forms of gun regulation, a majority of both member and nonmember gun owners favored a waiting period for the purchase of a handgun (77 % and 89 %, respectively) and the mandatory registration of handguns (59 % and 75 %).[11]

Factors Influencing Public Opinion on Firearms

According to the 2001 National Gun Policy Survey, individuals who personally own guns are consistently more pro-gun (i.e., against regulation) and opposed to gun safety measures than those without guns. Those living in gun households, but not personally owning guns, tend to be intermediate in their attitudes between those who personally own guns and those living in households without guns. Support for gun control measures is also consistently lower among gun carriers than nongun carriers.[12]

Despite the differences in attitude of gun owners and nonowners, support for gun control policies in general is quite high even among owners. A majority of gun owners favored 8 of the 14 forms of regulation and safety measures addressed in the survey, and all 4 of the items barring criminals from purchasing guns. Similarly, a majority of gun carriers supported 7 of 13 general measures and all 4 measures to restrict gun sales to criminals. For example, 60 % opposed gun carrying in restaurants.[13]

Other factors influencing attitudes relating to the regulation of firearms:

- Men are less likely to support regulatory measures and bans on criminals acquiring guns than women.
- Residents of rural areas are least supportive of regulating guns or preventing criminals from buying guns and those living in large cities are most supportive of both.
- Income is not related to general attitudes on firearm regulation, but those with lower incomes are more in favor of keeping guns from criminals.
- Liberals are more supportive of gun regulation in general than conservatives, but they do not differ in terms of their support for limiting gun purchases by criminals.
- Victims of robberies and assaults support more measures to keep criminals from buying guns.
- Individuals with confidence in the police to respond quickly when called are more supportive of gun regulation and for keeping criminals from buying guns.
- Men, white Americans, and those without a college degree were more supportive of gun rights as opposed to controls on gun ownership.
- Marital status, age, and race have no significant impact on attitudes toward gun regulation. The evidence is mixed with regard to education. While the 2001 National Gun Policy Survey did not find a link, a Pew Research Center poll in 2015 found that individuals with higher levels of education were more likely to support a number of gun safety measures (e.g., expanded background checks, assault weapons ban).[14,15]

Duke University's Philip Cook and Kristen Goss conducted a statistical analysis, referred to as multiple regression, to isolate the impact of several factors on attitudes toward different gun control measures.[16] They found household gun ownership to be a strong predictor of gun rights, but party affiliation (Republicans are more pro-gun) and gender are also strong independent predictors of one's position on gun policy. High-profile shootings, such as those at Columbine High School and Virginia Tech, tend to produce a brief surge in support for gun control measures, but this support tends not to last and is dwarfed by an apparent long-term shift toward a greater emphasis on gun rights.[17]

While a number of polls of gun owners show that they tend to support several key gun control measures, owners' misunderstanding of laws pertaining to firearms may help account for some of their opposition to less intrusive forms of gun regulation. For example, the Luntz poll of gun owners found that over half of both NRA and other gun owners believed that all those purchasing a gun must pass a background check. In fact, surveys have indicated that approximately 40 % of gun transfers are not transacted through licensed gun dealers and therefore are not subject to a background check.[18] Thus, many gun owners believe that such basic controls are in place when this is not the case.[19]

Bottom Line

In their book, *The Gun Debate*, Philip Cook and Kristin Goss of Duke University discuss the paradox that most Americans favor many reasonable gun control measures, yet they are often not enacted into law. Large majorities of the American public support measures that promote gun safety, including conducting background checks on all gun sales, preventing the mentally ill and felons from buying guns, imposing waiting periods in purchases, registering handguns, securing weapons by personalizing them, and preventing high-volume purchases of handguns. Cook and Goss attribute the gun control paradox to the lack of knowledge of gun laws and confusion about the different forms of firearms, a diminished trust in government in general, and a growing partisan divide which has seen a dramatic drop in support for gun control by Republicans.[20] Even NRA gun owners support such basic measures as criminal background checks for those purchasing guns privately.

A related paradox is that a strong majority of Americans oppose the carrying of guns into settings such as bars, restaurants, sports arenas, and college campuses, yet most states now allow gun carrying and the settings into which guns can be brought are growing in number.

Yet another paradox is that some segments of the population that are more supportive of gun rights face fewer dangers than segments that are more concerned about gun safety. Rural residents, for example, are more likely to be gun owners and to lean toward gun rights but are less likely to be victims of violence or property crime than are urbanites.[21] Such findings suggest that attitudes about gun ownership have less to do with the objective risks people face than they have to do with tradition, self-reliance, and views about government.

While many attribute the failure to enact laws (e.g., background checks on all gun purchases) that most Americans would support to the power of the gun lobby, I tend to agree with Cook and Goss that deep divisions within the population itself play a pivotal role. While supporting many individual gun safety measures, the public remains deeply divided on fundamental issues, such as the desirability of stricter gun laws, the benefits of gun ownership, and whether our society should prioritize gun rights or control gun ownership.

This said, new research does find that a larger segment of the population would support stricter gun laws if they were aware of the gaps in current legislation. Peter Aronow and Benjamin Miller of Yale University have found that nine in ten Americans who were aware that background checks are not required in all gun transfers favored stricter gun laws, whereas, just seven in ten of those who were unaware of this gap supported stricter gun laws.[22] The lesson here is that raising the public's awareness of existing legislation may facilitate the enactment of potentially effective gun safety measures.

Notes

1. Smith T. 2001 National Gun Policy Survey of the National Opinion Research Center: research findings. Chicago: National Opinion Research Center, University of Chicago; 2001. P. 2.
2. Smith T. P. 5.
3. ABC News/Washington Post Poll. Gun control, immigration, and politics [Internet]. ABC News/Washington Post. 2013 Apr 16. Available from: http://www.langerresearch.com/wp-content/uploads/1148a1GunsImmigr ationandPolitics.pdf
4. Doherty C. A public opinion trend that matters: priorities for gun policy [Internet]. Pew Research Center. 2015 Jan 9. Available from: http://www. pewresearch.org/fact-tank/2015/01/09/a-public-opinion-trend-that-matters-priorities-for-gun-policy/

5. Pew Research Center. Continued bipartisan support for expanded background checks on gun sales [Internet]. 2015 Aug 13. Available from: http://www.people-press.org/2015/08/13/continued-bipartisan-support-for-expanded-background-checks-on-gun-sales/
6. Doherty C. A public opinion trend that matters.
7. Doherty C. A public opinion trend that matters.
8. Pitts L. In Colorado, empty gun dorm sends a message [Internet]. The Tampa Tribune. 2013 Mar 13. Available from: http://tbo.com/list/news-opinion-commentary/in-colorado-empty-gun-dorm-sends-a-message-580009
9. Pew Research Center. Perspectives of gun owners, non-owners [Internet]. 2013 Mar 12. Available from: http://www.people-press.org/files/legacy-pdf/03-12-13%20Gun%20Ownership%20Release.pdf
10. Luntz Global. Gun owners poll [Internet]. 2012 Jul 24. Available from: http://www.joycefdn.org/assets/1/7/law_partnership_polling_data.pdf
11. Weil D, Hemenway D. I am the NRA: an analysis of a national random sample of gun owners. Violence Vict. 1993; 8(4):353–365.
12. Smith T. 2001 National Gun Policy Survey. P. 10.
13. Smith T. 2001 National Gun Policy Survey. P. 11.
14. Smith T. 2001 National Gun Policy Survey.
15. Pew Research Center. Continued bipartisan support for expanded background checks on gun sales.
16. Cook P, Goss K. The gun debate: what everyone needs to know. New York: Oxford University Press; 2014. P. 181.
17. Cook P, Goss K. The gun debate. P. 183.
18. Cook P, Ludwig J. Guns in America. Results of a comprehensive national survey on firearms ownership and use. Washington, DC: Police Foundation; 1996.
19. Luntz Global. Gun owners poll.
20. Cook P, Goss K. The gun debate. P. 178–180.
21. Truman J, Langton L. Criminal victimization, 2014. Washington, DC: Bureau of Justice Statistics; 2015. Table 10.
22. Aronow P, Miller B. Policy misperceptions and support for gun control legislation. The Lancet. 2016; 387: 223. Epub 2016 Jan 15.

14

Slogans Relating to Gun Violence: Fact or Fiction?

The previous chapter showed how public opinion can be influenced by inaccurate information about current laws and policies. Slogans often dominate discussions on gun policy and can play a role in shaping public opinion. Although some of these slogans may sound logical and reasonable, they may be patently false. The power of slogans is that they can be easily remembered and repeated.

Slogans also provide simplistic answers to policy dilemmas for people who are not interested in comparing different policy options. Such people are seeking black-and-white answers that involve few shades of gray. In their view, guns are either lethal instruments or beneficial tools that are only harmful in the hands of "bad guys." This chapter points out some of the contradictions and lack of logic in some of the most common slogans. It is interesting that these slogans usually emerge from the gun rights side.

© The Author(s) 2016
T. Gabor, *Confronting Gun Violence in America*,
DOI 10.1007/978-3-319-33723-4_14

"Guns Don't Kill People, People Kill People"

This is one of the most frequently repeated slogans in the debate over firearms policy. There is an obvious truth here that guns are inanimate objects that do not kill without human intervention, but this superficial truth does not mean that guns play no role in lethal violence. Yes, it is people who design firearms, people manufacture and sell them, and people decide on how they are used. However, while it is people who kill, there is compelling evidence that people who use guns to assault others or even in self-defense are more likely to kill and cause severe injuries than are those who use their bare hands or some other weapon (see Chap. 4). While the intent and capabilities of the individual using a gun to harm another are important factors in the outcome of an attack, the means used by the assailant are also critical factors. In addition, certain forms of violence, such as mass killings and the killings of well-armed or protected targets (police officers, security personnel, political figures) are difficult to contemplate without the help of firearms.

It is precisely the lethality of firearms and their ability to immobilize the target that leads gun rights advocates to promote their use for self-defense. The millions of dollars spent each year by the gun lobby and by gun manufacturers to promote firearm ownership and laws that allow people to carry and use firearms for defensive purposes is an acknowledgment of their superior "stopping power" when compared with knives, clubs, or fists. Gun manufacturers market their products by stressing their precision, lethality, their rate of fire, their ability to accept high-capacity magazines, and their compactness. They have sold ammunition that can pierce armor and cause catastrophic damage upon impact with their human targets.[1] When marketing and evaluating these products, gun makers and the gun press are no longer talking about people killing people or people stopping aggressors; they are commenting on the lethality and efficiency of different models of guns.

It is illogical to argue that guns are the most effective tools available to immobilize an aggressor and, at the same time, to argue that the same tool has no impact at all when used by an individual contemplating a crime or suicide. The gun lobby and industry promote the value of a gun, independent of the intent of the owner, as a deterrent to crime and as an effective tool in preventing criminals from harming their victims. The gun lobby fights tooth and nail to defeat virtually any proposed legislation that aims to restrict gun ownership or the circumstances in which guns can be used in self-defense.

However, when it comes to guns in the hands of aggressors, suicidal teenagers, or victims of accidental shootings, the gun lobby and its supporters resort to the slogan, "Guns don't kill people, people kill people." The narrative changes when guns are used in crime, a suicide, or in a deadly accident. Now, the tool is viewed as replaceable and the criminal is viewed as having the same potential to create carnage without a gun. According to this narrative, the suicidal teenager would have died regardless of the availability of a gun because he would have found some other means to kill himself. And the person who has shot himself accidentally is viewed as an accident prone or reckless individual who would have self-destructed in some other way had guns not been available.[2]

It is an obvious truth that guns do not kill on their own. In his book *Lethal Logic*, Dennis Henigan, former vice president of the Brady Center to Prevent Gun Violence, writes:

*Although guns **alone** do not kill people, they **enable** people to kill people more effectively than other weapons. They more effectively enable those with criminal intent to inflict mortal injury on others; they more effectively enable the suicidal to inflict mortal injury on themselves. They enable mortal injury even when no one intends such injury.*[3]

Henigan quotes rock musician Ozzy Osbourne to illustrate the lack of logic that permeates the thinking of those who subscribe to the slogan, "Guns don't kill people, people kill people." Ozzy states, "I keep hearing this [expletive] thing that guns don't kill people, but people kill people. If that's the case, why do we give people guns when they go to war? Why not just send the people?"[4]

It defies logic that people would form an organization of roughly four million members, like the NRA, which has devoted decades tirelessly fighting for the right of individuals to own, carry, and use a tool that they believe is *ineffective* in intimidating and immobilizing aggressors.

And, if it is an effective tool in preventing attack and harming aggressors, it is as effective in the hands of the aggressors themselves or those who are suicidal.

To illustrate that guns influence the seriousness of injuries independent of the intent of an aggressor or suicidal individual, consider the laws of physics and how they apply to the danger posed by any weapon, be it a gun or a fist. Dr. Arthur Kellermann, formerly an emergency room physician and the founding chairman of Emory University's Department of Emergency Medicine, has been one of the most influential researchers on the risks posed by guns. He also grew up around guns, learning to shoot in his preteen years. Kellermann and his colleagues made the following observations on the factors that make guns and ammunition more or less lethal:

> *The specific capacity of a firearm to cause injury depends on its accuracy, the rate of fire, muzzle velocity, and specific characteristics of the projectile [bullet] … weapons with high muzzle velocities, e.g., hunting rifles, generally cause greater tissue damage than weapons with lower muzzle velocities, e.g., handguns. However, the size, shape, and nature of the projectile also play a powerful role in determining the severity of the resultant injury. … A slower bullet, designed to mushroom or fragment on impact, may damage a much larger amount of tissue through direct trauma, cavitation, and shock wave effects. … Damage also increases in direct proportion to the mass of the projectile. The number of projectiles striking the body also influences the expected severity of injury.*[5]

Kellermann and his colleagues added that some gunshot wounds are so extensive that survival is unlikely. Thus, emergency room doctors who routinely deal with gunshot wounds confirm the commonsense notion that firearms vary greatly in their lethality, independent of the intent of the shooter. The same laws of physics indicate that the danger posed by guns will differ from the hazards associated with other categories of weapons, such as knives, sticks, or fists. Chapter 4 discusses research comparing the lethality of attacks and attempts at self-injury when different weapons are used.

"If Guns Are Not Available, People Will Find Other Ways to Kill"

This belief, referred to as the substitution of means or weapons substitution idea, is simply the notion that people will find a way to harm others or themselves, regardless of the means at their disposal. Therefore, according to this gloomy view, there is no point in limiting the availability and circulation of firearms in the civilian population as those determined to cause harm will do so through other means. This view assumes that all killings and suicides involve sober reflection and a final, irrevocable decision to go forward with the act.

Research shows, however, that the majority of homicides and suicides do not involve careful planning and deliberation. Most legal systems recognize several types of homicide in recognition of the fact that homicides vary greatly with regard to the presence of premeditation and the extent of planning involved. In many homicides, the perpetrator is responding to an insult, sudden provocation, or jealousy. In other cases, a person intends to harm another and instead causes the death of the victim. Still other cases involve killings that stem from negligence and a lack of regard for the safety of others. The legal terms for some of these other types of killings are second degree murder, voluntary manslaughter, and involuntary (negligent) manslaughter.

FBI statistics show that close to half of all criminal homicides in which the circumstances were known occurred in the context of some form of argument involving money, a romantic triangle, or a brawl influenced by drugs or alcohol.[6] A substantial body of research in the field of criminology over half a century shows that many homicides involve a deadly interaction between two individuals and that the behavior of the victim is a critical factor in the outcome.[7, 8] It is precisely in those cases where a violent conflict is spontaneous that people will use the means available to them to defend themselves. In such cases, the presence or absence of lethal weapons can make all the difference in terms of whether the conflict results in a fatality.

While intent is important, the means used are also crucial. Studies consistently show that firearms are the most lethal homicide and suicide method.

For example, a US study that examined all suicide deaths in the country in 2001, as well as emergency room data, found that attempts with guns were lethal in 85 %of attempts, whereas cutting or piercing instruments were lethal in just 1 % of the attempts and the use of poisons or drug overdoses were successful in just 2 % of attempts.[9] An Australian study found that the overall fatality rate for suicide attempts was 12 %; however, for firearm attempts it was 90 %.[10] Thus, there is an enormous difference in the lethality of different methods.

It is hard to argue with the notion that people with an unwavering determination to die will find the time and location to do so when intervention by others is unlikely. Such people have many methods to choose from and, in theory at least, can switch to an alternative method if their preferred approach becomes unavailable. However, there is evidence that some people without a history of suicide attempts or depression may make very serious attempts with little warning or planning. Adolescents are especially prone to such attempts, which may be precipitated by conflicts with parents or boyfriends/girlfriends.[11, 12]

Cases and studies discussed in Chap. 6 illustrate the potential impulsivity involved in suicide and that creating barriers and raising the level of effort or skill required to commit suicide may deter people or give them enough time to get through their suicidal impulses. We cannot assume that reducing opportunities for suicides will merely lead to a substitution of means. The evidence does not support that idea. Rather, it seems to support the notion that increasing the availability of highly lethal suicide methods, including firearms, will increase the number of people who will perish as a result of transient suicidal thoughts.

"If Guns Are Outlawed, Only Outlaws Will Have Guns"

Literally, this means that only the law-abiding will conform to a gun ban and the "bad guys" will still get guns, causing a problematic imbalance of power. More generally, this is the view that gun laws favor criminals because responsible gun owners will obey bans, get required permits, and handle guns safely, while criminals who cause all the problems with guns will ignore them anyway. Thus, those who oppose gun control laws in general believe that such laws create unnecessary hardship for the vast majority of owners, who are responsible anyway, and do nothing to prevent the criminal element from obtaining banned guns and misusing firearms.

Those holding this view see the population as neatly divided between law-abiding citizens and criminals (good guys and bad guys). First, there is much evidence that such a clear division has no factual basis as a large body of research shows that many citizens break a wide range of laws, from cheating on taxes to committing violent acts.[13] For example, a study by the Internal Revenue Service found that, in 2001, Americans short-changed the government by $345 billion. In that year, ten million people who were required to file tax returns did not do so.[14]

Surveys of the general public have shown that most people violate the law at some point. One classic study of 1700 New York City adults without a criminal record revealed that 99 %admitted to at least some law-breaking.[15] Numerous surveys of high school students show widespread lawbreaking and support the notion that humanity cannot be neatly divided into "good guys" and "bad guys."[16]

Even violence is not limited to a small subpopulation of "bad guys." For example, a significant proportion of violent conduct occurs within the context of intimate relationships. The National Violence Against Women Survey has found that nearly 25 %of surveyed women have been raped and/or physically assaulted by a current or previous spouse, cohabiting partner, or date.[17] In addition, over half a million women are stalked by an intimate partner each year. Furthermore, close to a quarter of all violent victimizations of women are committed by intimate partners.[18]

Two-thirds of all gun deaths in the USA are suicides. A further 700 or so gun deaths each year are unintentional. About 15 % of all gun homicides are felony-type killings that occur during the course of a rape, robbery, burglary, or other crime.[19] If these are the bad guys the gun lobby is referring to, their murders account for less than 4 % of all gun deaths, including suicides and unintentional fatalities.[20]

The narrative that criminals are so different from the rest of the population as to virtually constitute a distinct species fits nicely with the focus of the gun lobby and pro-gun activists on a despised group of people (convicted criminals), rather than on all gun owners and their guns when offering remedies for the misuses of firearms. Their focus on a small, hardcore criminal element—I assume this is what the NRA means by "bad guys"—is misguided for the following reasons:

- **Many people who commit violent crimes have no history of violence.** Even the most extreme of offenders, murderers, often have no criminal record. An Illinois study found that less than half of all individuals arrested for murder or manslaughter in 2001 had a felony conviction in the previous ten years.[21] This is not a surprising finding as more than 50 years of research has shown that many homicides occur among family members and acquaintances and arise from some form of dispute (e.g., a domestic dispute, argument over money).[22, 23]
- **A significant number of "responsible" gun owners are lawbreakers.** Data compiled by the *Los Angeles Times* found that five years after Texas' concealed carry law was enacted, over 400 people obtained licenses to carry concealed weapons despite prior criminal convictions and more than 3,000 permit holders had been arrested subsequent to receiving permits.[24] Some of these arrests were for very serious crimes, such as murder, kidnapping, rape, and weapons offenses. A Florida study conducted by the *Sun-Sentinel* newspaper discovered that just in the first half of 2006, more than 1,400 convicted felons obtained concealed weapon permits.[25] Another 216 people had outstanding warrants and 128 had active domestic violence injunctions against them, and there were even 6 registered sex offenders who succeeded in obtaining concealed weapon permits.
- **The largest category of firearm misuses is of suicides and suicide attempts.** Two-thirds of all firearm deaths are suicides, and there is no evidence of a link between criminality and suicide with a firearm.
- **There are usually about 10,000 unintentional (accidental) shootings in the USA per year.** This number includes fatal and nonfatal shootings but does not include cases in which people are shot and do not seek medical assistance and those cases in which injuries have resulted from such things as powder burns and firearm recoil.[26] More than half of all fatal gun accidents involve individuals under 25 years

of age. The highest age group comprises those 15–19 years of age.[27] By definition, accidental shootings are just that and can involve anyone with access to a firearm. The many young children and youth who are involved in gun accidents certainly are not career criminals.

- **Many guns used in crime are purchased from a store rather than in the illegal marketplace.** A study based on interviews with prison inmates found that guns used in crime are three times more likely to come from a gun store as from theft and as likely to come from a gun store as the black market.[28] Other studies show that a significant percentage of guns used in crime have been purchased from stores or obtained from friends, rather than "on the street."[29] They may also be obtained from a family member as is most often the case when children and teens carry guns outside the home.[30] In two recent school mass murders, one in Newtown, Connecticut, and one in Winnenden, Germany, firearms owned by the parents were used by the shooter.[31] The firearms were purchased lawfully.

The above-mentioned facts indicate that the problem of violence and firearm misuse is not confined to a shadowy group of outlaws and that guns used in crime or otherwise misused are often obtained from family members and legitimate sources. Gun violence can arise from any segment of society and much of the misuse involves individuals without a criminal past. Focusing on a mythical group of "bad guys" is a misguided strategy that is destined to fail. It is a diversion from focusing on issues such as the volume of guns in America, the number of people who carry concealed firearms, the inadequate screening of owners, the lack of national standards with regard to the quality of guns, and the lack of regulations regarding the safe storage of firearms.

Furthermore, the argument that gun laws are futile because criminals will disobey them is bogus and a justification for doing nothing about gun violence. One can advance the same argument against any law, as all laws are violated by some people. Should we legalize murder and sex crimes because some people will continue to commit these crimes despite the fact that they are prohibited by law?

"An Armed Society Is a Polite Society"

This slogan suggests that a civil society is best achieved via the threat of gun violence. The notion that civility and mutual respect is attained through the threat and use of force appears to be contradictory. The assumption is that arming more civilians will deter criminals from committing crimes due to their fear of being shot. Advocates of arming the population have been very active in the USA over the past 25 years, promoting concealed weapon laws in most states, introducing laws allowing guns at or around the workplace, promoting the carrying of guns on college campuses, in public buildings, and in parks, and, since the massacre of elementary school children and teachers in Newtown, Connecticut, proposing that we arm school staff nationwide.

The above-mentioned slogan implies that we prevent violence through the threat of and use of lethal force. It is like saying that we prevent hatred by teaching hate or prevent infection by increasing exposure to the agent (bacteria, virus, etc.) responsible. According to this belief, we should provide access to guns to as many people as possible and we should assume that those in possession of guns will use guns only to deter others from misusing them or for other legitimate purposes, rather than to commit crimes or acts of violence themselves.

Arming the maximum number of people in our country raises a concern about our liberties. Gun rights advocates often speak of the importance of their liberty to own the guns they want and to be free of government interference. But wouldn't an armed society take away our freedom to disagree with others on a whole range of matters, from politics to domestic and business matters, or even on such mundane things as who arrived first at the deli counter? If most Americans were armed, would it not be reasonable to fear that, in a dispute, the other may pull out a gun and use it against us? Even if an armed society did produce a superficial politeness, wouldn't this be at the expense of our basic freedom to assert ourselves and engage with others without the fear of lethal force being used against us?

The gun lobby's effort to allow guns on college and university campuses is a case in point. Surveys show that a majority of campus officials, instructors, students, and police oppose such a policy.[32] Apart from the public safety concern, opponents of guns on campus fear that the presence of guns would have a chilling effect on the ability of professors and students to express themselves freely while discussing the many controversial subjects that are addressed on a college or university campus. Campus debates are about reason and persuasion through the force of argument, whereas guns signify power and intimidation through the threat of force. Consider what happened at Utah State University when feminist blogger and media critic Anita Sarkessian was invited. Threats were made promising violence, including one that threatened the "deadliest school shooting in American history."[33] The threats, along with the policy of allowing guns on campus, led Sarkessian to cancel her lecture.

Can the freedom of speech really prevail in a fully armed society? Would people running for political office or the local school board feel free to express their views on contentious issues if most of the audience was armed? Would members of the audience feel free to ask questions and make comments if everybody around them was armed? Common sense indicates that a fully armed society would be at risk of being a very repressive place in which liberty would be a major casualty.

Gun rights advocates also fail to acknowledge that the freedoms enjoyed by gun owners in the USA are well in excess of freedoms accorded in virtually every other advanced society. Advanced societies in Asia and Europe, as well as in Australia, New Zealand, and Canada, have national licensing systems that carefully screen future gun owners, require background checks for all purchasers, have strict requirements relating to the transportation and storage of guns, and rarely allow people to carry guns for their personal protection.[34] Americans already are subject to far less intrusive gun regulations than are residents of other advanced countries.

Bottom Line

As is the case with most bumper sticker slogans, the most common slogans repeated by the gun lobby and gun rights advocates have little basis in fact. Studies over nearly half a century have shown that, while guns do not kill without human intervention, they enable killing and are the most lethal of the objects civilians can use to kill. They also provide the most lethal suicide method. In addition, there is no guarantee that, in the absence of guns, those contemplating an assault or suicide will switch to other weapons. If they do, there is a much lower likelihood of a homicide or successful suicide attempt.

The notion that gun laws will only benefit "outlaws" is based on the fiction that society can easily be divided into "good guys" and "bad guys." Most gun deaths, including victims of homicides, suicides, and fatal accidents, are not the product of the actions of career criminals or reckless individuals. The vast majority of deaths are the result of arguments, personal crises, and catastrophic errors, rather than the premeditated acts of "bad guys." It is during these arguments and crises that the presence of firearms is likely to make the greatest difference.

As for the idea that widespread gun ownership and carrying will create a polite society, it is hard to envision that lethal weapons are the most effective means of promoting civility. Guns tend to make the public feel afraid rather than secure. They are designed to intimidate, injure, and kill, rather than to promote the respect that is the basis for a civil society.

Notes

1. Diaz T. Making a killing: the business of guns in America. New York: The New Press; 1999.
2. Kleck G. Point blank: guns and violence in America. Hawthorne, NY: Aldine de Gruyter; 1991. P. 286.
3. Henigan D. Lethal logic: exploding the myths that paralyze American gun policy. Washington, DC: Potomac Books; 2009. P. 30
4. Henigan, D. Lethal logic. P. 31.
5. Kellermann A, Lee A, Mercy J, Banton J. The epidemiologic basis for the prevention of firearm injuries. Annu Rev. Pub Health. 1991; 12: 17–40.
6. Federal Bureau of Investigation. Crime in the United States 2011 [Internet]. Washington, DC: US Department of Justice. Available from: http://www.fbi.gov/about-us/cjis/ucr/crime-in-the-u.s/2011/crime-in-the-US-2011/tables/expanded-homicide-data-table-11
7. Wolfgang M. Patterns in Criminal Homicide. Philadelphia: University of Pennsylvania Press; 1958.

8. Luckenbill D. Criminal homicide as a situational transaction. Soc Prob. 1977; 25(2): 176–186.
9. Vyrostek S, Annest J, Ryan G. Surveillance for fatal and nonfatal injuries–United States, 2001 [Internet]. MMWR. 2004; 53:1–57. Available from: http://www.cdc.gov/mmwr/preview/mmwrhtml/ss5307a1.htm
10. Elnour A, Harrison J. Lethality of suicide methods. Inj Prev. 2008; 14: 39–45.
11. Tonkin R. Suicide methods in British Columbian adolescents. J Adolesc Health. 1984; 5(3): 172–177.
12. Poteet DJ. Adolescent suicide. Am J Forensic Med Pathol. 1987; 8(1):12–17.
13. Gabor T. Everybody does it: crime by the public. Toronto: University of Toronto Press; 1994.
14. Johnston T. Tax cheating has gone up, two federal studies find [Internet]. The New York Times. 2006 Feb 15. Available from: http://www.nytimes.com/2006/02/15/business/15tax.html
15. Wallerstein J, Wyle C. Our lawabiding law-breakers. Probat. 1947; 25:107–112.
16. Gabor T. Everybody Does It.
17. Tjaden P, Thoennes N. Extent, nature, and consequences of intimate partner violence. Findings from the National Violence Against Women Survey. Washington, DC: Office of Justice Programs; 2000.
18. Department of Justice (press release). Intimate partner violence declined between 1993 and 2004. Washington, DC: Office of Justice Programs; 2006 Dec. 28.
19. Federal Bureau of Investigation. Crime in the United States, 2014, Expanded Homicide Table 11 [Internet]. Washington, DC: Department of Justice. Available from: https://www.fbi.gov/about-us/cjis/ucr/crime-in-the-u.s/2014/crime-in-the-US-2014/tables/expanded-homicide-data/expanded_homicide_data_table_11_murder_circumstances_by_weapon_2014.xls
20. Xu J, Murphy S, Kochanek K, Bastian B. Deaths: final data for 2013[Internet]. National Vital Statistics Report. 2016; 64(2): 1–118 (Table 18). Hyattsville, MD: Centers for Disease Control and Prevention. Available from: http://www.cdc.gov/nchs/data/nvsr/nvsr64/nvsr64_02.pdf
21. Cook P, Ludwig J, Braga A. Criminal records of homicide offenders. JAMA. 2005; 294(5): 598–601.
22. Wolfgang M. Patterns of criminal homicide.
23. Zimring F, Hawkins G. Crime is not the problem: lethal violence in America. New York: Oxford; 1997.

24. Rempel W, Serrano R. Felons get concealed licenses under Bush's "tough" law [Internet]. Los Angeles Times. 2000 Oct 3. Available from: http://articles.latimes.com/2000/oct/03/news/mn-30319/4

25. O'Matz M, Maines J. License to carry. Sun.-Sentinel [Internet]. 2007 Jan 28. Available from: http://articles.sun-sentinel.com/2007-01-28/news/0701270 316_1_gun-licensing-system .

26. Hemenway D. Private guns, public health. Ann Arbor: University of Michigan Press; 2004. P. 30.

27. Hemenway D. Private Guns. P. 27.

28. Beck A, Gilliard D, Greenfield L, Harlow C, Hester T, Jankowski L et al. Survey of state prison inmates. Washington, DC: US Department of Justice; 1991.

29. Wachtel J. Sources of crime guns in Los Angeles, California. Policing: An International Journal of Police Strategies & Management. 1998; 21(2): 220–239.

30. Sheley J, Wright J. High school youths, weapons, and violence: a national survey. Washington, DC: National Institute of Justice; 1998.

31. Isikoff M, Winter T, McClam E. Investigators: Adam Lanza surrounded by weapons at home [Internet]. NBC News. 2013 Mar 29. Available from: http://openchannel.nbcnews.com/_news/2013/03/28/17501282-investigators-adam-lanza-surrounded-by-weapons-at-home-attack-took-less-than-5-minutes?lite;

32. Gabor T. Con: Guns on campuses won't make students safer. Palm Beach Post. 2015 Aug 12. A9.

33. Sinor J. Guns on campus have already curtailed free speech. Chronicle of Higher Education [Internet]. 2014 Oct 27. http://chronicle.com/article/Guns-on-Campus-Have-Already/149663/

34. Gabor T. International firearms licensing: a study of six countries. Ottawa: Public Safety Canada; 2013.

15

The Second Amendment: Is Gun Regulation Compatible with the Constitution?

While this book reports on the impact of guns on American life, the battle over guns is more than just a battle over statistics and other evidence drawn from research. There is an enormous cultural divide between those who are alarmed about the deaths and injuries associated with guns and those who are most concerned about the right of individuals to own and carry firearms without governmental interference. Those who believe that gun ownership is a fundamental right guaranteed by the Constitution will be difficult to sway by research, even if that research demonstrates clearly that gun ownership represents more of a public safety threat than a solution.

Researchers and people who have a more practical bent will say: "Let's see what the data tell us about the best ways to tackle firearm violence." In theory at least, this segment of the population can shift their position depending on research findings. However, those viewing gun ownership as an inalienable individual right often see this right as an absolute and will yield little ground regardless of the annual death toll or other evidence pointing to the harm produced by widespread gun ownership. Therefore, bridging the great divide in this area appears insurmountable when a significant segment of the population is not even interested in evidence.

© The Author(s) 2016

263

T. Gabor, *Confronting Gun Violence in America*,
DOI 10.1007/978-3-319-33723-4_15

To them, gun ownership is a right guaranteed by the Constitution. Case closed.

Gun rights advocates often refer to any proposed measure that would tighten access to guns or limit gun uses as an intrusion on their Second Amendment rights. For example, gun rights advocates in Florida have complained that the failure of the state's legislature to pass bills that would allow people to carry guns openly is a violation of their constitutional rights. This chapter will explore the Second Amendment to the US Constitution and whether it, in fact, precludes the passage of measures intended to prevent gun violence, even if such measures might restrict access of certain people to guns and place certain restrictions on gun owners.

The truth is that no right is absolute.[1] Even the freedom of speech, protected by the First Amendment to the Constitution, has its limits. We cannot make death threats against others, incite people to overthrow the government violently, pass on national secrets to agents from other countries, make false statements that defame others, or disseminate materials deemed to be obscene. Municipalities even limit the noise we can make, especially at night. One individual's rights are limited when they are deemed to encroach on the rights of others or the "general welfare," a term contained in the Preamble to the Constitution. Current judicial interpretations of the Second Amendment recognize the need to balance different rights (e.g., liberties vs. security) by allowing for the regulation of firearms, even where outright gun bans have been overturned.

Purpose of the Second Amendment

The Second Amendment to the US Constitution reads:

> *A well regulated Militia, being necessary to the security of a free State, the right of the people to keep and bear Arms, shall not be infringed.*

Surveys indicate that about three-quarters of Americans believe that the Second Amendment guarantees the right to own a gun.[2] However, as Chap. 13 has shown, the polls show that the American public is split quite evenly on the question of which is more important, gun rights or public safety. A Pew Research Center survey conducted in July 2015 found that, by a small margin (50–47 %), Americans believed that controlling gun ownership was more important than protecting gun rights.[3]

One theme running through American history has been a fairly widespread mistrust of a strong central government. During the revolutionary period, the mistrust of a standing army as a threat to liberty was pervasive.[4] America's first Constitution, the Articles of Confederation (Article VI), placed the responsibility for national defense on the states, requiring each state to maintain a "well-regulated and disciplined militia." Early settlers had formed militias to protect themselves from foreign armies and possible attacks by Native Americans. The articles made no provision for a national standing army. The modern Constitution, adopted in 1787, recognized both state militias and a standing army. The existence of both served as a compromise between advocates of state sovereignty and federalists who believed in an effective standing army.

Many prominent historians indicate that the Second Amendment was designed to address the concerns of anti-federalists who feared that Congress' power to create a standing army would make states vulnerable to federal tyranny.[5] To them, the Second Amendment ensured that the right of states to form an armed militia could not be infringed. Ultimately, by the end of the nineteenth century, the lack of investment in the state citizen militias and their poor performance during the War of 1812 led to their almost total abandonment and disappearance. Thus, those holding the militia view would argue that the Second Amendment became obsolete with the decline of state militias.

In four Supreme Court rulings between 1876 and 1939 and in 37 cases involving challenges to gun laws heard by federal courts of appeal between 1942 and 2001, the courts have consistently set aside these challenges and have viewed the Second Amendment as protecting state militias, rather than individual rights.[6] Thus, with little exception, the first 125 years of rulings by higher courts interpreted the Second Amendment to mean that "The people" collectively have the right to bear arms within the context of a well-regulated militia, rather than for protection against fellow citizens or for other personal reasons. This view of the Second Amendment is consistent with the requirement, in

America's first Constitution, that each state maintain a militia and with the modern Constitution, which provides for both state militias and a standing army.

On the face of it, it is hard to look at the first 13 words of the Second Amendment—"A well regulated militia, being necessary to the security of a free state"—and to be aware of the numerous constitutional debates in America's early years in which federalists and anti-federalists argued for a militia, without recognizing that the Second Amendment was meant to protect citizens from an overbearing federal government rather than from muggers and other assailants. In his influential work on the Constitution, Associate Justice of the Supreme Court Joseph Story took the view that the Second Amendment referred to militias and wrote the following: "The militia is the natural defense of a free country against sudden foreign invasions, domestic insurrections, and domestic usurpations of power by rulers."[7] Saul Cornell, a leading historian specializing in early American and Constitutional history, has argued that the amendment was conceived to allow Americans to fulfill their civic obligation to form militias.[8]

Despite numerous court rulings to the contrary, the NRA began an aggressive campaign in the 1970s of promoting the notion that the Second Amendment protected the individual's right to gun ownership, outside of any service in a militia. Over the last four decades, the NRA has actively promoted research taking the individual rights view of the Second Amendment. It has also lobbied for legislation permitting people to carry guns and opposed virtually every form of restriction on gun owners and ownership, from municipal gun bans to the careful screening of owners and scrutiny of dealers.

Warren Burger, former chief justice of the US Supreme Court, a conservative and a hunter himself, was interviewed in 1991 on the *MacNeil/Lehrer News Hour* about the meaning of the Second Amendment's "right to keep and bear arms." Burger responded that the Second Amendment "has been the subject of one of the greatest pieces of fraud—I repeat the word 'fraud'—on the American public by special interest groups that I have ever seen in my lifetime."[9] In a later speech in 1992, he asserted that the Second Amendment does not guarantee the right to have firearms at all.

The Break with Previous Rulings

A major break with previous rulings occurred in recent cases. In 2008, in *District of Columbia v. Heller*, the Supreme Court held, in a narrow 5-4 landmark decision, that the Second Amendment protects an individual's right to possess a firearm for lawful purposes (e.g., self-defense within the home) in federal enclaves (jurisdictions).[10] Special police officer Dick Heller had filed a lawsuit challenging the constitutionality of a local law in the District of Columbia preventing residents from owning handguns and requiring that all firearms be kept unloaded and disassembled or bound by a trigger lock. Mr. Heller applied to register a handgun he wished to keep at home, but the District refused. He filed this suit seeking, on Second Amendment grounds, to prevent the city from enforcing the ban on maintaining a licensed firearm in the home, and the trigger-lock requirement insofar as it impeded the use of functional firearms in the home. The District Court dismissed the suit, but the DC Circuit reversed it, holding that the Second Amendment protects an individual's right to possess firearms and that the city's total ban on handguns and the requirement that firearms in the home be rendered nonfunctional even when necessary for self-defense violated that right.

The Supreme Court had the last word in the Heller case and held the following:

> *The Second Amendment protects an individual right to possess a firearm unconnected with service in a militia, and to use that arm for traditionally lawful purposes, such as self-defense within the home.*[11]

Equally significant in the Heller case was the following affirmation by the Court:

> *Like most rights, the Second Amendment right is not unlimited.* **It is not a right to keep and carry any weapon whatsoever in any manner whatsoever and for whatever purpose** [my emphasis]: *For example, concealed weapons prohibitions have been upheld under the Amendment or state analogues. The Court's opinion should not be taken to cast doubt on longstanding prohibitions on the possession of firearms by felons and the mentally ill, or laws*

forbidding the carrying of firearms in sensitive places such as schools and government buildings, or laws imposing conditions and qualifications on the commercial sale of arms. Miller's [previous Court ruling] *holding that the sorts of weapons protected are those "in common use at the time" finds support in the historical tradition of prohibiting the carrying of dangerous and unusual weapons.*[12]

Thus, in 2008, even though the US Supreme Court for the first time ruled in favor of an individual's right to possess a firearm for personal self-defense outside of militia service, it clearly stated that this right could be limited by a wide variety of reasonable measures, such as those limiting ownership and the carrying of firearms, as well as laws governing the commercial sale of guns.

The Second Amendment in Perspective

This book does not aim to settle the debate as to the meaning of the Second Amendment. It is important to recognize that the overwhelming majority of rulings by the Supreme Court and federal courts of appeal over more than a century upheld the position that the Second Amendment referred to the right of states to form armed militias. However, more recent decisions have taken the view that the right to keep and bear arms is an individual right. In 2010, in *McDonald v. City of Chicago*, the Supreme Court held that the Second Amendment also applied to state and local laws.[13] In addition, since the early 1800s, the majority of states have enacted laws establishing the right of individuals to own guns outside of militia service.[14]

In any event, the Supreme Court in the Heller case made it clear that, while complete bans of all models would be problematic, many forms of gun control are lawful. Thus, even if we accept recent rulings as the final word and ignore over a century of judicial decisions in which no individual right to bear arms was recognized outside of militia service, the Second Amendment does not impede the adoption of sensible gun laws.

In addition, most Americans support federal laws that restrict the sale of fully automatic weapons and that prevent the sale or disposal of firearms to persons who have committed serious crimes or those deemed to be mentally defective. One indication of where Americans, including gun owners, stand on this matter has been the overwhelming support for universal background checks.[15] These checks are intended to determine whether the purchaser of a firearm has a criminal record. Thus, there is little support in America for selling any firearm to any person— Americans in overwhelming numbers support some basic restrictions on gun ownership.

In the Heller decision, the Court made it clear that the Second Amendment is not a barrier to sensible restrictions, although a segment of the population falsely claims that the amendment precludes all restrictions. Often, the Second Amendment appears to be the refuge of those who have no answer when confronted with the harm associated with firearms and the carnage arising from mass shootings. These people speak of the Constitution as though it is frozen in time. In fact, the Second Amendment was part of ten original amendments (also referred to as the Bill of Rights) to America's second Constitution, ratified in 1791 (America's first Constitution, the Articles of Confederation, was adopted in 1777). Since the modern Constitution's 10 original amendments were ratified, there have been 17 additional amendments, with the most recent, the 27th Amendment, ratified in 1992.[16]

Society also changes. The Constitution tolerated slavery and could not have foreseen the dangers of electronic surveillance. Guns and the problems they present too have changed dramatically. Those framing the Constitution could not have envisioned a civilian entering a crowded movie theater and firing hundreds of rounds of ammunition into a crowd from a semiautomatic, assault-style weapon. Thus, to be too orthodox and inflexible about the Constitution as it was originally written is to be stuck in the eighteenth century. This book is about twenty-first-century America, and we have changed enormously as a society over nearly two and a half centuries. Also changing are the types of guns that exist, the need for guns, the type of threats they create, and the impact of guns on our security.

American society cannot continue to withstand the levels of gun violence and mass shootings without serious damage to communities and the erosion of the very liberties gun rights advocates are seeking to protect. Every successive massacre leads to an increasing focus on security at the expense of our liberties and to higher levels of fear and distrust. There are also major consequences for the economy when people begin to worry about going to restaurants, movie theaters, shopping malls, and other public places due to the fear they may get caught in the middle of the next slaughter. We must confront current threats with twenty-first-century solutions, while balancing gun rights and public safety concerns.

A Note on "Rights"

Many people view the issue of guns exclusively from the perspective of rights. Suppose we accepted the extreme view that every American has an inviolable right to gun ownership. If we ignore the first 13 words of the Second Amendment, which refer to "a well-regulated militia" and "being necessary to the security of a free state," we have: "The right to keep and bear arms shall not be infringed." A literal translation of this phrase is that no authority shall interfere with the acquisition of arms by anyone. The Second Amendment does not mention that we shall exclude children, criminals, or mentally ill persons from gun ownership. Do most Americans support federal law, which prohibits minors, persons under indictment for serious crimes, and mentally "defective" people from owning guns? Of course they do. Why, because it is not sensible to extend ownership to these groups.

Having a right does not mean that an action is sensible or has no adverse consequences. For example, in the realm of health there are many areas where exercising a right is not the wise thing to do, from smoking several packs of cigarettes a day to eating large meals laden with saturated fats, or drinking heavily on a daily basis. Adults have these rights, although these actions can be self-destructive and may have an adverse impact on others, as well as society. A young adult who says, "I can smoke and drink as much as I want," is technically correct. However, by focusing exclusively on the issue of rights, the conversation ends there and never moves on to the issue of whether such behaviors are desirable or harmful.

Bottom Line

Throughout most of American history, the courts viewed the Second Amendment as a collective right to form state militias, rather than the right of individuals to acquire arms. Recent Supreme Court rulings broke with this view and held that individuals have a right to possess firearms for a lawful purpose, unconnected with service in a militia. However, in the landmark Heller case of 2008, the Court held that this right does not extend to anyone and for any purpose. The Court made it clear that bans relating to certain categories of people and weapons, as well as uses in certain settings (e.g., schools), were legitimate forms of regulation. Thus, even with today's more broad interpretation of the Second Amendment, the Constitution is not an impediment to most of the measures being proposed by public health and safety advocates.

Notes

1. Tomasky M. There are no "absolute" rights [Internet] . Washington, DC: The Constitutional Accountability Center; 2013 May 5. Available from: http://theusconstitution.org/news/there-are-no-%E2%80%98absolute%E2%80%99-rights
2. Jones, J. Public believes Americans have right to own guns [Internet]. Gallup. 2008 March 27. Available from: http://www.gallup.com/poll/105721/Public-Believes-Americans-Right-Own-Guns.aspx
3. Pew Research Center. Continued bipartisan support for expanded background checks on gun sales [Internet]. 2015 Aug. 13. Available from: http://www.people-press.org/2015/08/13/continued-bipartisan-support-for-expanded-background-checks-on-gun-sales/?beta=true&utm_expid=53098246-2.Lly4CFSVQG2lphsg-KopIg.1&utm_referrer=http%3A%2F%2Fwww.people-press.org%2F2015%2F08%2F13%2Fgun-rights-vs-gun-control%2F%3Fbeta%3Dtrue
4. Spitzer R. The politics of gun control. 3rd ed. Washington, DC: CQ Press; 2004. P. 20–22.
5. Cornell S. A well regulated militia: the founding fathers and the origins of gun control in America. New York: Oxford University Press; 2006.
6. Spitzer R. P. 28–32.

7. Story J. Commentaries on the US Constitution. New York: Harper and Row; 1833. P. 1890.
8. Cornell S. A well regulated militia.
9. Biskupic J. Guns: A second (Amendment) look. Washington Post. 1995 May 10. P. A20.
10. District of Columbia et al. v. Heller 554 U.S. 570 (2008). Supreme Court of the United States. Available from: http://www.supremecourt.gov/opinions/07pdf/07–290.pdf
11. District of Columbia et al. v. Heller 554 U.S. 570 (2008). P. 1.
12. District of Columbia v. Heller 554 U.S. 570 (2008).
13. McDonald v. City of Chicago, 130 Supreme Court 3020 (2010). Supreme Court of the United States. Available from: http://www.supremecourt.gov./opinions/09pdf/08-1521.pdf
14. Winkler A. Gunfight: the battle over the right to bear arms in America. New York: W.W. Norton; 2011. P. 33.
15. Foley E. Universal background checks maintain high public support: polls [Internet]. Huffington Post. 2013 Mar. 22. Available from: http://www.huffingtonpost.com/2013/03/22/universal-background-checks-polls_n_2931683.html
16. Constitution of the United States. Amendments 11–27 [Internet]. Available from: http://archives.gov/exhibits/charters/constitution_amendments_11–27.html

Part V

Preventing Gun Violence

16

A National Strategy for Preventing Gun Violence

Each year, approximately 100,000 Americans die or are wounded by gunfire. Mass shootings have become a regular feature of American life. Following the San Bernardino, California, mass shooting in December 2015, Dr. Debra Malina and her colleagues at the *New England Journal of Medicine* expressed their outrage and issued the following call to action:

> *If any other public health menace were consistently killing and maiming so many Americans, without research, recommendations, and action by the CDC, the public would be outraged. But in the United States, the National Rifle Association (NRA), the legislators it has funded, and a certain breed of gun owners have stood in the way even of research to determine what policies might help. ... A sad distortion of the American principle of individualism prioritizes one's right to live the way one wants, without any government interference, over other people's right to live at all—a distortion that has found one of its key expressions in firearm-related freedoms. ... An equally fundamental American principle holds that ensuring the public health sometimes requires curbing the rights of individuals in order to benefit and protect the community as a whole.*[1]

© The Author(s) 2016
T. Gabor, *Confronting Gun Violence in America*,
DOI 10.1007/978-3-319-33723-4_16

In an earlier editorial in the same journal, Dr. Jerome Kassirer had expressed bewilderment about America's tolerance for "irrational" policies:

> *In the United States, nearly anyone can get a gun, even one that rapidly fires dozens of bullets. We require universal registration of cars but not of guns. In many places, guns can be carried openly, even in malls, schools, and churches. When household guns are not locked up, they are easy to borrow or steal. Among persons in certain age groups, firearm-related homicides and suicides account for more deaths than do diseases. In some jurisdictions, doctors are forbidden to ask patients whether they are at risk for firearm-related injury. Why do we tolerate such irrational behavior?*[2]

Following the San Bernardino mass shooting, the *New York Times* editorial board called for the banning of military-style weapons and asked rhetorically: "What better time than during a presidential election to show, at long last, that our nation has retained its sense of decency?"[3]

What the Research Shows

Much research needs to be done as congressional leaders influenced by the gun lobby virtually shut down federal funding for gun violence research for two decades, beginning in the mid-1990s. Notwithstanding this significant obstacle, the body of research continues to grow with the help of other funding sources and even self-funded research. Research presented in this book has shown that there is a compelling case for increasing the regulation of firearms in the USA in several areas and for introducing other measures to reduce gun violence. We have seen that:

- Civilian gun ownership levels in the USA are the highest in the world, and gun-related deaths in this country exceed by a large margin those in other high-income countries. If guns were more protective than harmful, we would expect to have fewer, not more, fatalities than other advanced countries.
- States with the highest gun ownership levels and weakest gun laws tend to have much higher firearm mortality rates than the states with low ownership levels and strict gun laws.

- Guns facilitate mass murder, killing at a distance, the killing of armed or well-protected targets, impulsive homicides, and the killing of innocent bystanders. Research consistently shows that attacks with guns are more often lethal than attacks involving other weapons.
- While records are not maintained around the globe on mass shootings by civilians, it appears that these events are far more commonplace in the USA than in the rest of the world.
- Mass shootings in public have increased in the USA, especially in the last decade. Military-style weapons and the use of high-capacity magazines produce more casualties and deaths.
- Guns in the home elevate the risk that a member of a household will die of a homicide, suicide, or fatal accident.
- Guns in the home are far more likely to be used to kill a member of the household than an intruder.
- There are many times more criminal uses of a firearm in a given year than there are protective uses.
- The frequent impulsivity and ambivalence of individuals attempting suicide means that the presence of lethal methods when an attempt is made may be all important in whether an individual succeeds in taking his or her life. Firearms are consistently found to be the most lethal suicide method.
- Fatal gun accidents increase with the availability and accessibility of firearms. Many gun accidents can be prevented through better gun storage practices, as well as improved education and training in gun safety. Accidents can also be prevented through features that can indicate when a gun is loaded and that prevent the discharge of a firearm by a young child or other unauthorized user.
- While the proportion of adults who own guns is declining, guns are becoming more concentrated in the hands of a smaller segment of the population.
- Large majorities of the American public support measures that promote gun safety, including background checks on all gun sales, preventing the mentally ill from buying guns, registering handguns, securing weapons by personalizing them, and preventing high-volume purchases of handguns.

- The public remains deeply divided on fundamental issues, such as the desirability of stricter gun laws, the benefits of gun ownership, and whether our society should prioritize gun rights or control gun ownership.

While much research and evaluation of existing gun violence prevention measures remains to be done and debates persist as to the most effective policies going forward, some consensus among researchers is beginning to emerge. David Hemenway, Director of Harvard University's Injury Control Research Center, surveyed 300 researchers in the field and found that there was a broad consensus that:

1. A gun in the home makes it a more dangerous place, increases the risk of a homicide of a woman living there, and increases the risk of suicide of a resident there.
2. Guns are not used more often in self-defense than in crime.
3. Permissive gun carrying laws have not reduced crime rates.
4. Strong gun laws reduce homicide.
5. Background checks can keep guns out of the hands of a significant number of violent people.
6. Safe storage in the home (where guns are locked and unloaded) keeps the risk of suicide down.[4]

Hemenway points out that many initiatives designed to combat gun violence have had a modest impact due to the easy flow of firearms across state, county, or municipal boundaries.[5] He adds, however, that even a 10 % reduction in gun deaths across the country equates to several thousand people each year.

Aside from reducing the human costs of gun violence, there are the massive financial costs incurred by victims and the criminal justice system. In addition, studies show that violence can adversely affect real estate values. One analysis found that a reduction in a given year of one homicide in a zip code produces a 1.5 % increase in housing values in that same zip code the following year. For a city like Boston, a 10 % reduction in homicides can increase the value of the housing stock by over $4 billion.[6]

These and other findings point to the need for sensible firearm policies. Interpretations of the Second Amendment of the US Constitution by the courts have consistently upheld the right of jurisdictions to regulate firearms. Furthermore, historians recognize that guns have been regulated during the Revolutionary Period, in frontier towns, and in the South, following the Civil War. The idea that frontier towns were riddled by daily gun violence is contradicted by the fact that notorious towns like Dodge City, Kansas, had very few murders.[7] The mythology of towns beset by murder and mayhem was fuelled by Hollywood films and television programs. Constitutional law professor Adam Winkler has noted that, during the Revolutionary period, inspections were conducted and a record was maintained of the firearms held by state militia members. In addition, door-to-door inventories were kept of privately owned weapons. In the nineteenth century, many states banned the carrying of concealed weapons and the firing of guns in certain places.[8]

Fast forward to the present day and we can see that regulating guns is not viewed by most Americans as some form of unwanted intrusion on our freedoms by liberal "gun grabbers." As seen in Chap. 13, far more people believe gun laws should be more as opposed to less strict, 80–90 % support universal background checks, the majority favor banning assault weapons and high-capacity ammunition magazines, and at least two-thirds of Americans feel that guns should not be brought to certain public spaces (e.g., stores, restaurants). Even the vast majority of NRA members and other gun owners support such basic measures as universal background checks.[9]

Therefore, the existing body of research, the legal framework, and the public support reasonable gun regulation. There is no one remedy and no combination of solutions that will eliminate all gun violence and injuries. A realistic goal would be to bring America to the much lower levels of gun violence enjoyed by other advanced countries. The emphasis in the sections below is to present solutions that have been shown to be effective in at least some contexts.

I will leave it to others to focus on the anticipated political resistance to these proposals. I believe that when the American people strongly commit themselves to implementing solutions they already believe in, they will override the influence of the powerful lobby that has, over the last few decades, successfully pursued their own agenda at the expense of public safety.

While I anticipate that some of the remedies I present, such as the licensing of gun owners across the country, will face the criticism that they have little chance of being adopted, I believe that a bold strategy that is more likely to be effective is preferable to incremental or modest measures that will, at best, yield unremarkable gains and merely strengthen the position of those who oppose any regulation whatsoever. Even very nonintrusive actions, such as that of President Barack Obama to clarify the definition of a gun dealer, elicited ferocious resistance on the part of the gun lobby and its surrogates in Congress.

The dogmatic pursuit of the freedoms of a minority of inflexible gun owners—probably accounting for less than a tenth of all adults—comes at the expense of the rights of Americans at large to be safe in their communities, work places, and recreational spaces. Ultimately, the lack of a balancing of gun owners' rights with public safety concerns comes at the cost of the liberties of all citizens. Each successive mass shooting brings with it increasing anxiety and greater investments in law enforcement and surveillance.

For example, the massacre in San Bernardino has produced a court order requiring Apple Inc. to work with the FBI in developing software that would allow law enforcement to break into the perpetrators' iPhone and examine their telephone records.[10] The electronics giant has resisted, arguing that all consumers of their smart phones would have their privacy compromised. Thus, the continuing onslaught of gun violence and mass shootings will not only cost many lives but result in the erosion of many of our freedoms. The public will become increasingly tolerant of intrusions on its liberties as levels of fear escalate. Ultimately, we will sacrifice many of our cherished freedoms in order to appease the gun lust of a dwindling minority.

My focus in the sections ahead is on national solutions, although many of the same measures can be implemented at the state and even local level. National measures have the advantage of avoiding the issue of porous state borders that allow guns to be trafficked from states with weaker to those with stronger gun laws.

A National Licensing System for Gun Buyers and Owners

Americans accept the fact that one should obtain a license to operate certain machinery that may pose a danger to the public (e.g., cars, trucks, heavy equipment) when used without skill, irresponsibly, or by individuals unfit—due to age, physical limitations, or mental disability—to operate it safely. The licensing of drivers was first introduced in Massachusetts and Missouri in 1903.[11] As of 2014, gun deaths have actually surpassed deaths arising from motor vehicle crashes in 21 states and the District of Columbia.[12]

A study of 28 countries in every region of the world by Sarah Parker of Geneva, Switzerland's, Graduate Institute of International and Development Studies indicates that most countries have some form of owner licensing or at least impose some restrictions on ownership.[13] There is no licensing requirement in the USA at the federal level, although about a dozen states require a license prior to purchasing a firearm. Parker's international study found that:

- Most countries impose age restrictions on ownership (usually 18 years of age or older).
- Some countries require mental fitness and some require physical fitness for ownership.
- Some countries refuse licenses if an applicant has a history of alcohol or drug abuse.
- A criminal record is usually grounds for the refusal of a sale.
- Many jurisdictions require prospective gun owners to undertake some form of training or testing before obtaining a firearm. The aim is usually to assess the applicant's knowledge of firearms and their safe handling, as well as of laws governing the use of firearms and of legitimate self-defense.
- Most countries require a person to have a "genuine reason" for acquiring a firearm or they restrict use to certain purposes only. Hunting, target practice, and sport shooting are the primary reasons most countries permit civilian ownership of firearms. Firearm possession is

authorized for certain employment-related or professional purposes (e.g., farming, collections). Countries vary greatly in terms of whether self-defense is viewed as a legitimate reason for obtaining firearms.

- Countries may also examine an applicant's lifestyle, previous misuse of a firearm, whether he or she is living with someone who has a criminal record, whether there are outstanding warrants against him or her, the applicant's military service record, the reputation and integrity of associates, and even the number of firearms already present in the applicant's neighborhood.

Licensing systems are designed to promote responsible gun ownership. The most comprehensive of these require all those purchasing or possessing a gun to obtain a license and to renew it on a regular basis. There ought to be no exceptions where firearms are purchased privately. The loophole that exists in the USA, whereby individuals purchasing guns privately are exempted from any form of screening, is unique to this country.

Other than the conditions of licensing mentioned above, some countries have additional requirements. In Germany, substance abuse (including alcohol), limited legal capacity, mental illness, or the inability to handle weapons or ammunition cautiously and properly are grounds for refusal of a license. Persons under 25 years of age are required to obtain a certificate of mental aptitude from a public health officer or psychologist when applying for a license for the first time.[14] In Canada, current or former spouses or conjugal partners must attach their signatures to an individual's license application and are encouraged to notify the Chief Firearms Officer of any safety concerns presented by the applicant.[15]

Apart from screening prospective gun owners, a firearms licensing system can also prevent gun trafficking, as it becomes more difficult for prohibited persons to obtain guns, especially in high volumes. Universal licensing means that nobody can buy or own a gun without a background check. Licensing usually permits a more thorough vetting of applicants than the US's National Instant Criminal Background Check System (NICS) and also normally requires that applicants visit a law enforcement agency to obtain a permit, a potential deterrent to those who are contemplating crimes or planning to traffic guns. Under the current system, NICS, a background check can be conducted through a dealer within a matter of minutes, with no requirement that the applicant visit a police station.

NICS is designed to respond within 30 seconds; however, in the event that the system does not respond to the dealer within three business days, the transaction may proceed and the applicant gets a pass (i.e., the check is not completed).[16] A delay in response is more likely to occur when some match has occurred with federal databases and further investigation is required. Thus, a perverse aspect of the system is that an applicant is more likely to get a pass and avoid a vetting if he or she is at risk of falling in a prohibited category. The system is clearly designed to prioritize the commercial transaction over public safety.

A comprehensive licensing system involves more than a quick background check. Some of the elements are identified in Parker's international review (above). Renewal of licenses is important to ensure that a person's eligibility to own firearms does not change over time, as a result of an emerging mental illness or evidence of domestic violence. US states with licensing systems to own or carry firearms do not tend to monitor individuals for their continuing eligibility to possess firearms.

By contrast, in Australia, a country with many similarities to the USA—a frontier history, strong gun culture, and states with their own gun laws—a national agreement now empowers police with the discretion to undertake the inquiries they view as necessary in deciding whether to grant a gun license. They can confer with local police, the family doctor, and spouses or intimate partners to uncover red flags, including substance abuse, instability, anger issues, and marital conflicts that are not recorded in automated databases. Another concern is the possibility that gun ownership might make guns accessible to another household member whose own circumstances would place them in a prohibited category.[17]

The evidence is mounting that licensing systems can reduce crime and prevent trafficking. A study by Mayors Against Illegal Guns (now Everytown for Gun Safety) used crime gun trace data to determine which states are most likely to be the source for trafficked guns.[18] A short time interval (usually two years or less) between the original sale of a gun by a licensed dealer and its recovery in relation to a crime is usually considered to be an indication of trafficking. The Mayors' study found that states lacking a requirement of a purchase permit for handgun sales were the sources of crime guns at three times the rate of states requiring such a permit. A 2001 study of 25 US cities led by Daniel Webster of Johns Hopkins University Bloomberg School of Public Health revealed that states with both gun registration and licensing systems have far greater success in keeping guns initially sold in the state from being recovered in crimes than states lacking such systems.[19]

Philip Cook and Kristin Goss of Duke University note, "There is a well-established pattern whereby firearms sold in unregulated states flow to those with stringent regulations."[20] Webster of Johns Hopkins and his associates found that states with permit-to-purchase (PTP) laws for handguns were strongly associated with lower rates of crime gun exportation to other states.[21] Their analyses took into account the impact of gun ownership, proximity to states with stronger gun laws, borders with Canada or Mexico, and migration levels from other states. Webster and his colleagues found that discretionary PTP laws, in which law enforcement had the discretion to refuse the issuance of permits, were the most powerful deterrent to interstate gun trafficking.

In 1995, Connecticut introduced a PTP handgun licensing law requiring the applicant to pass a background check for all purchases. Researchers from Johns Hopkins found that the law was associated with a 40 %reduction in the state's firearm-related homicide rate.[22] Also indicative of the likely impact of the law was that there was no corresponding drop in homicides by other means.

A decade ago, Missouri had one of the toughest measures to keep guns out of the hands of dangerous people. All handgun buyers were required to obtain a gun permit through an in-person background check at a sheriff's office. Legislators repealed this measure in 2007 and, following the repeal of this law, there was more than a doubling of the number of guns with an unusually short time interval between retail sale and crime, an indication of trafficking. The share of crime guns that had originally been sold by Missouri gun dealers also rose sharply. In addition, gun homicides increased by 25 % from the pre-repeal period to the first three years following repeal, while there was a 10 % national decline in gun homicides during the same period. There was no increase in homicides without guns or in neighboring states, and the team took into account other social, economic, and criminal justice policy changes that may have explained the increase in gun homicides. All these findings support the conclusion that the change in policy, including the elimination of the gun licensing requirement, was responsible for the spike in the state's gun homicide rate.[23]

In 1977, Canada established its first general screening process whereby those seeking to own firearms were required to obtain a Firearms Acquisition Certificate. Researcher Etienne Blais and his colleagues from the University of Montreal found that the 1977 reforms, which involved some measures aside from licensing, were followed by a significant drop in the firearm homicide rate.[24]

Public opinion polls demonstrate the strong support of Americans for firearm licensing laws. A national survey conducted in January 2013 found that more than three of every four Americans, including a majority of gun owners, support requiring people to obtain a license from a local law enforcement agency prior to purchasing a firearm.[25] Still more Americans (85 %) favor the licensing of handgun owners, according to a 2001 poll.[26]

Recommendations

- A national licensing system should be established, requiring that any individual intending to purchase a firearm must first obtain a permit to do so.
- To be eligible for a license, the applicant must

    - Be 21 years of age or older;
    - Undergo a comprehensive screening process undertaken by a designated law enforcement agency, including an in-person interview;
    - Complete an application form that is signed by his or her current spouse/conjugal partner or former spouse/conjugal partner, where applicable;
    - Not be convicted of an offense punishable by imprisonment for a term exceeding one year or for a misdemeanor crime of domestic violence, not be a fugitive or subject to a court order for harassing, stalking, or threatening an intimate partner or child of the partner;

- Successfully complete training in the operation, safe use, handling, and storage of firearms; securing and childproofing firearms; and in laws relating to the proper use and transportation of firearms;
- Meet standards of mental fitness as per existing federal law;
- Not be dependent on alcohol or psychoactive drugs;
- Receive a certificate of mental aptitude from a psychologist or other designated professional if he or she is under 26 years of age;
- Demonstrate basic competency in shooting a firearm.

- The law enforcement agency must provide reasons, in writing, for the denial of an application.
- A firearms license would be valid for 5 years.
- Separate permits would continue to be required for those seeking to carry guns.

Universal Background Checks

On April 13, 2015, an examiner at the headquarters of the FBI's NICS was asked to look into Dylann Roof, a 21-year-old resident of South Carolina who had been flagged by the system when he tried to buy a .45-caliber Glock pistol at a gun store in West Columbia, South Carolina.[27] He was flagged because he had been arrested for drug possession on February 28. The records indicating whether Roof had been convicted—which could disqualify him from owning a gun—were missing. Due to clerical errors, the examiner could not locate his file and, after three business days, the purchase proceeded by default in accordance with federal law. Had the police file been located, it would have shown that Roof had confessed to drug possession.

On June 17, 2015, Roof entered Emanuel African Methodist Episcopal Church in Charleston, South Carolina, sat down with a group during Bible Study, participated briefly, and then got up and started shooting the attendees with the Glock pistol. He murdered nine members of the prayer group. This and other cases reveal that the NICS was built for speed rather than thoroughness. A 2009 study shows that sales proceeding by default due to the three-day limit for a check were eight times more likely to involve a prohibited purchaser than sales with background checks that are conducted within 72 hours.[28]

Since the enactment of the Brady Handgun Violence Prevention Act of 1993, criminal record checks have been required in the USA when an individual purchases a firearm through a federally licensed dealer. Given a prospective buyer, the dealer begins a background check by contacting NICS via phone or computer. Several databases are searched to determine a person's criminal history and mental health status and the check is usually completed within a few minutes.

Background checks on all firearm transfers would be the cornerstone of an effective firearm licensing system. Why are they important? It has been estimated that approximately 40 % of all firearms transfers in the USA (6.6 million transfers in 2012 alone) are conducted privately and are thereby exempt from a background check that might uncover a person's ineligibility to buy a firearm due to a serious criminal record, mental illness, substance-abuse problem, or some other disqualifying factor.[29,30] This enormous loophole makes it relatively easy for prohibited persons to acquire guns without a record check, as they can do so at gun shows, where many sellers are private parties,[31] or online so long as the gun is not bought from a federally licensed dealer. (An executive order by President Barack Obama in January 2016 may reduce this loophole somewhat as the definition of who qualifies as a licensed dealer has been expanded and may, therefore, require that more transactions include background checks.)[32]

In fact, a survey conducted by the Bureau of Justice Statistics has demonstrated that more than two-thirds of prison inmates who had used a gun in a crime took advantage of the private sales loophole by obtaining the gun from a source other than a licensed dealer, thereby avoiding a background check.[33] This survey also revealed that 84 % of inmates who used a gun in a crime indicated that they were already prohibited from possessing guns at the time of their offense. Thus, they could not have passed a background check had they attempted to purchase a firearm from a licensed dealer. A 2000 report by the ATF found that 30 % of illegally trafficked guns had a gun show connection at some point in their chain of custody, thereby supporting the idea that people contemplating crimes often obtain guns through other than licensed dealers.[34]

Straw purchases, the acquisition of guns by a legitimate buyer on behalf of a prohibited one, have also proven to be a significant problem and are among the most common means through which criminals obtain guns. The ATF report mentioned above found that close to half of all illegally trafficked firearms involved a straw purchase.

Requiring background checks for all guns transfers would reduce the options available to prohibited buyers dramatically, as they would no longer be able to directly buy guns at gun shows or on the Internet. An investigation by Mayors Against Illegal Guns found that 1 in 30 prospective buyers on Armslist, an online firearms marketplace, is in a prohibited category (many with extensive criminal records), but no background check currently prevents the sale from going forward.[35] A New York City study demonstrated that sellers have little restraint when the law does not require a background check. In that study, investigators posed as buyers who indicated to online sellers from 14 states that they probably could not pass a background check. The study revealed that 62 %of these sellers agreed to make the sale despite the fact it is a felony to sell a firearm to an individual the seller has reason to believe is a prohibited purchaser.[36] Universal background checks would force prohibited online and gun show buyers to acquire guns through the black market or theft as sellers would be legally obligated to ensure that background checks were conducted on all sales.

Despite being weakened by the private sales loophole, the Brady Law, from March 1994 through the end of 2012, prevented more than two million prohibited felons, mentally ill persons, and other high-risk individuals from purchasing a firearm or receiving a permit to purchase or carry a firearm.[37]

Contrary to conventional wisdom, buying guns on the black market is neither inexpensive nor easy. Criminals report paying four to five times as much on the black market as opposed to the legal market and these transactions expose them to danger and the risk of arrest. A study of Chicago's illegal gun markets found that more than one in three attempted purchases ended in failure.[38]

Duke University economist Philip Cook has studied Chicago's underground gun market and has said, "There may be a lot of guns, but there is a shortage of trusted sellers." With greater accountability, it is thought that expanded background checks will choke the supply of new guns in the black market and increase street prices, thereby making guns less available to those contemplating gun crimes.[39]

There is a growing body of data demonstrating the impact of background checks. For example, research has shown that in states with more expansive background check laws—over a dozen states require checks for private handgun sales—38 %fewer women are fatally shot by their intimate partners, 39 %fewer police officers are murdered with handguns, and 49 %fewer suicides are committed with guns.[40] In addition, states without universal background check laws have been found to export 30 %more guns across state lines, guns that were later recovered from criminals.[41] Another study found that states conducting background checks for restraining orders and fugitive status had fewer homicide and suicide deaths.[42]

A study of the impact of gun laws by Eric Fleegler and his colleagues at Harvard University's Medical School and School of Public Health found that states with the strongest gun laws had lower overall firearm fatality, firearm homicide, and firearm suicide rates than states with the weakest laws.[43] Laws strengthening background checks were the only single category of gun laws significantly associated with lower firearm homicide and firearm suicide rates. The study statistically controlled for other factors potentially having an impact on mortality rates, including population composition by age, race/ethnicity, sex, poverty, unemployment, educational attainment, and population density.

Daniel Webster of Johns Hopkins' Bloomberg School of Public Health sums up his own extensive work on the impact of background checks and related state gun laws:

> *Meanwhile, my research has shown that state universal background checks— along with other state laws designed to increase gun seller and purchaser accountability—significantly reduce the number of guns diverted to the illegal market, where ... high risk groups often get their guns.*[44]

Internationally, several countries have mandatory waiting periods in place, meaning that applicants must wait a prescribed number of days before receiving a license or they must wait a certain number of days before they can possess a firearm they have purchased. For example, in Australia, there is a mandatory 28-day waiting period from the application date to the receipt of an acquisition permit.[45] However, just ten states and the District of Columbia have waiting periods in relation to the purchase of all firearms, for handguns only, or for handguns and assault weapons. The waiting periods range from two to ten days.[46]

Waiting periods can allow those bent on committing a homicide or suicide an opportunity to "cool off," to permit the homicidal or suicidal impulses to dissipate. Garen Wintemute of the University of California-Davis and his colleagues compared the death rates of close to a quarter of a million people who purchased handguns in California in 1991 with those of the general population.[47] He found that in the first year after purchasing a handgun, the suicide rate of the handgun buyers was four times that of the general population. More dramatic was the finding that during the first week of the gun purchase, the suicide rate by firearm was *57 times* that of the general population. This study provided compelling evidence that some people buy handguns intending to kill themselves and of the potential value of a cooling-off period for purchases.

Universal background checks have consistently garnered strong public support. The polls reviewed in Chap. 13 indicate that between eight and nine of every ten Americans believe that all firearm sales, whether private or through a licensed gun dealer, should be subject to a criminal background check.

Recommendations

- Even with a national licensing system, background checks should be conducted for all firearm purchases, including transactions among private parties. The enormous loophole that allows high-risk individuals (e.g., violent felons, the mentally ill) to purchase guns privately without a background check should be eliminated.
- To ensure compliance with the background check requirement, consideration should be given to requiring all transactions to be conducted through licensed dealers.
- A mandatory waiting period of ten business days should be imposed for the delivery of any firearm. This increases the time available for

background checks (currently three days) and allows time for reflection on the part of individuals contemplating an attack or self-harm. An exception may be considered for those with a license who can demonstrate that they face an immediate threat to their safety or that of their family which the local law enforcement agency cannot address.
* Ensure that the states have sufficient resources to forward all information relevant to a thorough background check to the FBI's National Criminal Background Check System. The aim is to ensure that the system is as complete as possible so as to prevent gun purchases by ineligible individuals.

Ban on Assault Weapons and High-Capacity Magazines

Assault weapons are not a particular category of firearm. They are firearms with features that make them more suitable for military or criminal purposes than for sports shooting or self-defense. Some of these features include the following:

* Detachable ammunition magazines that may hold up to 100 rounds of ammunition
* Pistol grips on rifles, allowing a firearm's use in different positions
* Threaded barrels for attaching silencers
* Folding rifle stocks for concealment and portability
* Flash suppressors to avoid imperiling the shooter's vision and to keep the shooter's position from being identified in a dark place
* Bayonet mounts

The federal assault weapons ban that was in force between 1994 and 2004 defined a firearm as an assault weapon if it contained two or more of these forms of military-type features.[48] Congress allowed the ban to expire in 2004.

Assault weapons or other semiautomatic firearms equipped with high-capacity magazines (holding more than ten rounds of ammunition) have been the weapons of choice in some of America's most horrific mass murders, such as the Orlando nightclub shooting (49 dead, 53 wounded), the Virginia Tech campus shooting (33 dead, 17 wounded), the Aurora, Colorado, theater shooting (12 dead, 58 wounded), the massacre of children and school staff at Sandy Hook Elementary School in Newtown, Connecticut (26 dead and 2 wounded), and the San Bernardino, California, politically motivated attack (14 dead and 22 injured).

In the 1980s and early 1990s, it was observed that assault weapons and other semiautomatic firearms were involved in some high-profile mass shootings.[49] A study of 133 mass shootings (4 people or more killed, not including the shooter) from January 2009 to July 2015, including family shootings, revealed that 11 % involved assault weapons and/or high-capacity magazines. In these incidents, 155 % more people were shot and 47 % more people were killed than in other mass shootings.[50] Thus, the presence of these weapons and magazines facilitates mass casualty shootings.

Daniel Webster of Johns Hopkins University said the following in front of the US Senate's Committee on the Judiciary[51]:

Assault weapons have features that facilitate criminal use and an assailant's ability to rapidly fire a large number of rounds of ammunition and thereby increase both the likelihood of injury and death as well as the number of injuries and deaths in an attack. Such features include the ability to accept large capacity magazines, pistol grips and folding stocks on rifles (to make the weapon more concealable), and threaded barrels for attaching silencers. These features are unnecessary for legitimate sporting uses or self-defense.

There are mixed findings as to whether the assault weapons ban of 1994 had an effect on violent crime or at least the weapons used to commit crimes. One positive sign was that, following the ban, assault weapons made up a small percentage of firearms that were recovered by police in relation to crimes. In six major cities—Baltimore, Boston, Miami, St. Louis, Anchorage, and Milwaukee—the share of gun crimes committed with assault weapons during the post-ban period declined by between 17 % and 72 %.[52] Nationally, gun traces conducted by the ATF were far less likely to involve assault weapons following the ban.

In 1992–1993 (pre-ban), 5.4 % of traces involved assault weapons, and by 2001–2002 just 1.6 % involved assault weapons—a 70 % reduction.[53]

The reduction in crime by assault weapons was, in part, offset by the substitution of assault-type firearms that technically did not qualify as assault weapons. Also, during the post-ban period, a study of four cities—Baltimore, Anchorage, Milwaukee, Louisville—indicated that guns with high-capacity magazines actually rose as semiautomatics were being equipped with them.[54] This increase offset the declining number of assault weapons in crime. The lack of success in reducing the use of high-capacity magazines was likely due to the enormous stock of pre-ban magazines that were exempted from the ban.

There was no discernible reduction in the amount or lethality of gun violence that could be attributed to the assault weapons ban.[55] For example, the percentage of violent gun crimes that resulted in fatalities did not decline in the post-ban period. The grandfathering provisions of the assault weapon ban, which allowed weapons and high-capacity magazines already manufactured to continue to be bought and sold, severely undercut the effectiveness of the ban. Approximately 25 million of these magazines remained in the country and millions more were available for import from other countries.[56] It would have taken many more years for the existing inventory to dry up. Perhaps, at that point, the potential benefits of the ban would have materialized.

Following expiration of the ban, mortality statistics and criminal prosecutions from 2002 to 2006 showed that homicides, gun-related homicides, and gun crimes increased in Mexican towns located closer to Texas and Arizona ports of entry relative to towns near California ports of entry.[57] California maintains a statewide ban on assault weapons. One research team estimated that the US policy change was responsible for at least 158 additional deaths each year in towns near the border during the post-2004 period—after the ban had expired. The study findings suggest that the policy change (expiration of the ban) in the USA with respect to assault weapons increased the supply of assault weapons and thereby contributed to increasing lethal violence in Mexico.

Recommendations

- A new national assault weapons ban should be enacted.
- Rather than grandfathering weapons already manufactured or in the hands of civilians, firearms prohibited by the ban should be bought back by the federal government. A special tax on firearms would be one way to help offset the costs of a gun buyback.
- Legislation should be designed to make it difficult for manufacturers to circumvent the ban through minor modifications in the design of a firearm. Semiautomatic firearms exempted from the ban should be narrowly defined guns used for sporting and other legitimate purposes.
- High-capacity magazines that can hold more than ten rounds of ammunition should be banned. Individuals owning these magazines should be compensated for turning them in.

Limiting Volume Purchases

Limiting the volume of guns a person can buy at one time can potentially prevent an individual bent on mass murder from quickly acquiring an arsenal of weapons. Such a law can also make it more difficult for those engaged in gun trafficking. Tracing data from the ATF shows that about a fifth of handguns recovered in crime were purchased as part of a multiple sale.[58] Federal law in the USA does not set a limit on the number of firearms an individual can purchase; however, a small number of states (e.g., California) prohibit multiple sales. In those jurisdictions, sales are limited to one gun per month.

Virginia was a leading source of crime guns for other states, especially the Northeast. In 1993, the state introduced a law limiting the purchases of handguns to one during any 30-day period. The law appeared to have a dramatic effect on interstate trafficking as the odds of tracing a gun originally acquired in the Southeast to a Virginia gun dealer dropped by 66 % for guns recovered in New Jersey, New York, Connecticut, Rhode Island, and Massachusetts combined.[59]

While some gun owners may have legitimate reasons for the purchase of multiple firearms, it is the belief of this writer that the public safety benefit of a one gun per month policy should override these reasons. Gun owners can still accumulate multiple weapons, although, more gradually, while the number of mass shootings that lack extensive planning will hopefully be reduced through such a policy.

Recommendation

- A one gun per 30-day policy should be adopted at the federal level, with an exception to those who can demonstrate that they face an immediate threat to their safety or that of their family which the local law enforcement agency cannot address.
- Individuals who are gun collectors may also be exempted if they can prove they are *bona fide* collectors and that the guns have been deactivated.

Prohibiting At-Risk Individuals from Owning Firearms

Certain categories of people are at an elevated risk of engaging in gun violence. Recognizing this fact, federal law in the USA prohibits the sale of firearms to individuals who

- have been convicted of, or are under indictment for, a crime punishable by a prison term of over one year;
- are fugitives from justice;
- are unlawful users of or addicted to a controlled substance;
- are under the minimum age. For sales by licensed dealers, the purchaser of a handgun must be 21 and for a long gun, the buyer must be 18 years of age. Unlicensed persons may sell long guns to persons of any age and are prohibited from selling a handgun or handgun ammunition to persons they have reasonable cause to believe are under 18 years of age (with the exception of certain temporary transfers for specified activities, e.g., employment)[60];

- have been adjudicated as a mental defective or committed to a psychiatric institution;
- are not lawfully in the USA or were admitted under a nonimmigrant visa;
- were dishonorably discharged from the military;
- have renounced their US citizenship;
- are subject to a court order restraining them from harassing, stalking, or threatening an intimate partner or child; or
- have been convicted of a misdemeanor domestic violence offense.[61]

Some states have added other categories of persons to this list (e.g., those committing violent or firearm-related misdemeanors or crimes as juveniles).

Dangerous Individuals

Federal law already prohibits from a gun purchase individuals who have been judged to be mentally defective or who have been involuntarily committed to a psychiatric facility. However, mental illness is involved in just a small fraction of all acts of violence and most mentally ill people are not a threat to the public.[62] Even in the case of the most extreme incidents of violence by civilians—mass killings—very few of the perpetrators could have been disqualified from gun ownership by federal law. According to an analysis of 133 mass shootings by the Everytown for Gun Safety organization, in only one incident was there evidence the shooter was prohibited from possessing guns due to severe mental illness.[63] In 15 other incidents (11 %), concerns about the mental health of the shooter had been brought to the attention of a medical practitioner, school officials, or other authority prior to the shooting.

The limitations of focusing on mental illness that is very narrowly defined have prompted some states to broaden the category of mentally ill persons who are prohibited from purchasing or possessing firearms. California law, for example, includes a list of disqualifying factors relating to mental illness, including the communication of a serious threat of violence against an identifiable person to a licensed psychotherapist during the last six months, or being held for psychological treatment for 72 hours within the last five years.[64]

Other predictors of violence or self-injury identified by research may be useful in determining a person's suitability for gun ownership. Aside from communication of threats, planning or preparation for a violent or suicidal act may be considered. Depression is the mental illness most strongly associated with risk of suicide, and half of completed suicides involve the use of firearms.[65] It has been pointed out by several professional groups that factors associated with dangerousness to self or others may be more valuable as a means of determining suitability for gun ownership than mental illness. The challenge is implementing a system of screening applicants for ownership that is not overly complex and that uses information that predicts violence reasonably well that can be readily included in federal databases.

The Consortium for Risk-Based Firearm Policy, a collection of some of the country's leading researchers, practitioners, and advocates in the area of gun violence prevention, met in March 2013 and advanced some recommendations regarding gun policy. The Consortium identified several key factors that are associated with risk of gun violence—toward self and others—including a history of violent crime, domestic violence, and alcohol and drug abuse.[66] Current federal policies do not adequately reduce access to firearms by individuals who meet these evidence-based criteria for risk of violence. The participants emphasized that many persons with mental illness are not at risk of violence. Rather, there is a subset of people with serious mental illness who are at an elevated risk at certain times, such as the period surrounding a psychiatric hospitalization or a first episode of psychosis. In addition, those with serious mental illness display high rates of co-occurring substance use, an important risk factor for violent behavior.

Jeffrey Swanson of Duke University and his collaborators have found that about 22 million Americans (about 9 % of the population) have impulsive anger issues and easy access to guns. Close to four million of these angry gun owners routinely carry their guns in public.[67] Anger in that study referred to explosive, uncontrollable rage. Angry people with guns are typically young or middle-aged men. The researchers also found that people with six or more guns are more likely to carry their guns in public and to have a history of anger issues. Furthermore, those with more than 11 guns were significantly more likely to say that they lose their temper and get into fights than other gun owners.

In the 1990s, those committing a domestic violence misdemeanor were added to the category of persons prohibited from firearm ownership. This ban excludes individuals in a current or former dating relationship who never lived together or had a child together. Research has shown that violence is at least as common in dating relationships as in other intimate relationships presently covered by federal law. Stalkers who are convicted of misdemeanors and are subject to restraining orders are also excluded from federal gun bans. According to the Centers for Disease Control's National Intimate Partner and Sexual Violence Survey, one in six women have been stalked during their lifetime, and stalkers often use weapons to harm or threaten their victims.[68]

Another gap in federal law is in its failure to provide immediate protection for those being harmed or threatened by current or former intimate partners. In some states, access to firearms may be limited for those subject to temporary restraining orders. Such orders are designed to provide immediate protection for those in danger and may be granted by courts even in the absence of the alleged perpetrator. This is a stopgap measure before a hearing can be arranged to consider a petition by a victim of abuse. In general, it has been found that cities and states with gun restrictions due to restraining orders have lower levels of intimate partner homicides.[69]

On January 1, 2016, a landmark California law went into effect. This law allows police or family members to petition the courts to seize the guns and ammunition of a person they believe poses a threat to others or themselves.[70] This measure was introduced after 22-year-old Elliot Rodger went on a murderous rampage. His parents were aware he was threatening violence but lacked the legal tools to intervene. If the petition is successful, a judge can issue an order requiring the subject to surrender his guns and ammunition within 24 hours.

With the exception of misdemeanor domestic violence assault, federal law and laws in most states prohibit firearm possession of those convicted of a crime only if the convictions are for felony offenses in adult courts. Research has shown that misdemeanants who could lawfully purchase handguns committed violent crimes following those purchases at two to ten times the rate of handgun purchasers with no prior convictions.[71] Garen Wintemute, a professor of emergency medicine at the University of California (Davis), and his colleagues examined the impact of a California law that expanded gun bans to include individuals convicted of violent crimes classified as misdemeanors. They found that the denial of handgun purchases as a result of a prior misdemeanor conviction was associated with a significantly lower rate of subsequent violent offending.[72]

Alcohol

Alcohol abuse is related in a number of ways with the potential for firearm misuse. A number of studies have shown that alcohol abuse increases the likelihood that a person will engage in violent behavior.[73] One experiment showed that alcohol consumption reduced shooting accuracy and impaired judgment relating to the appropriate use of a firearm.[74] Another study found that heavy alcohol use was more common among firearm owners who regularly carry guns for protection and who keep their firearm unlocked and loaded.[75] A study conducted in 2011 found that excessive alcohol consumption was associated with an enormously elevated risk of firearm suicide.[76]

Age

There is a large body of evidence showing that age is a risk factor in violence and that a disproportionate number of mass killers are in their late teens to their mid-20s. As indicated at the outset of this section, federal law is inconsistent as to the age requirements for gun ownership, depending on the nature of the firearm (long gun vs. a handgun) and whether a gun is obtained privately or through a federally licensed dealer. Some observers have suggested that the minimum age for firearm acquisition should be set at 25.[77]

Recommendations

- Gun restrictions relating to at-risk individuals should focus on the dangerous rather than the mentally ill. This said, there is a subgroup of violence-prone mentally ill individuals that must be considered.
- In addition to restrictions specified by federal law, the following categories of people should be prohibited from buying firearms:
  - Those convicted of a violent misdemeanor, for a period of five years at liberty following the offense
  - Those convicted of two or more drug or alcohol-related offenses (including driving offenses) within a five-year period should be prohibited for ten years
  - Those violating a restraining order issued due to a threat of violence
  - Those harassing, stalking, or threatening a dating partner or former partner
  - Those convicted of misdemeanor stalking
  - Those subject to a temporary restraining order. A mechanism should be established whereby family members can petition a judge to temporarily remove firearms from a family member if they believe there is a substantial likelihood that the person is a significant danger to himself or others
  - Those who have recently experienced a short-term involuntary hospitalization should be subject to a temporary ban on gun purchases or possession
  - Involuntary outpatient commitment should disqualify individuals temporarily from purchasing or possessing firearms if there is a court finding of substantial likelihood of future danger to self or others or an equivalent finding
- Law enforcement agencies should be authorized to remove firearms when they identify someone who poses an immediate threat of harm to self or others.
- The age of 21 should be established as the minimum age for the purchase or possession of a firearm.

- The application for a firearm license (see section above on licensing) should require a signature or notification of current and former spouses/cohabiting partners. This step will help identify individuals who are prone to violence but where this violence may have gone unreported.
- The states should provide complete reporting of all people prohibited from possessing firearms because of mental illness.
- Educational institutions should be obligated to report people identified as violent or suicidal to a law enforcement agency or licensing body. These people can then be prohibited from purchasing or possessing guns on a temporary basis until a final ruling is made on the case.

Child Access Prevention

Many gun owners fail to store their firearms properly, thereby increasing the likelihood that a child or unauthorized person will gain access to it. Mark Shuster of the University of California, Los Angeles School of Medicine, and his colleagues analyzed data from the National Health Interview Survey and found that 43 % of American homes with children and firearms had at least one firearm that was not locked in a container and not locked with a trigger lock or other locking mechanism.[78] In 13 % of homes with children and guns, firearms were either unlocked and loaded or unlocked and stored with ammunition. A national survey of gun ownership and use estimated that one in three handguns is kept loaded and unlocked, usually in the home.[79]

Many children under ten years of age—three-quarters according to one study—knew the location of their parents' firearms, and more than a third admitted to handling the weapons. In many cases, the parents were not aware that their children knew the storage location of household guns nor that their children had never handled a household gun.[80] Many young children, including children as young as three years old, are strong enough to pull the trigger on a firearm.[81]

The presence of guns in the home that are unlocked not only raises the risk of unintentional gun injuries but also of intentional shootings. A 1999 study found that more than three-quarters of the guns used in youth suicide attempts and unintentional injuries were kept in the home of the victim, a relative, or a friend.[82] An investigation of 37 school shootings by the US Secret Service and US Department of Education found that in more than two-thirds of the cases, the attacker got the gun from his own home or that of a relative.[83]

In some countries, the safe storage of firearms—storing firearms unloaded and/or in a locked container—is a condition of gun ownership. In the UK, one condition stated on the firearm certificate is that it must be stored securely at all times in order to prevent access by unauthorized persons (including children).[84] In the USA, there is an absence of national requirements relating to gun storage and the majority of states have adopted laws enabling armed self-defense both in the home and in public places (e.g., "SYG," "Castle Doctrine"). Where the primary reason for keeping guns in the home is self-defense, safe storage may be viewed as an impediment to those desiring quick access to a loaded weapon.[85] On the other hand, easy access to loaded weapons also can make it easier for children or youth to access them.

The US General Accounting Office has estimated that close to a third of accidental deaths by firearms can be prevented by the addition of child-proof safety locks and loaded chamber indicators that provide a visual and tactile (for darkness) indication that there is a round in the firearm's chamber.[86] Studies of child access prevention laws, which require gun owners to store their guns so that children and teens cannot access them without supervision, have found that these laws reduce accidental shootings of children by up to 23 % and adolescent suicides by 8 %.[87,88,89]

Gun safety training for adults, teens, and children has been suggested as a way of reducing accidental shootings. However, numerous surveys and experiments show that the majority of programs have not been successful in improving storage practices, the safe handling of guns by teens, or in getting children to not handle guns they come across.[90] In several studies, a police officer taught a group of children to leave an area and inform an adult if they came across a gun. The message was clear that they should avoid touching guns. Through the use of hidden cameras, ABC's 20/20 program documented the fact that children, while verbalizing the instructions they received, consistently handled real unloaded guns, pointed them at other children or themselves, and even pulled the trigger. Parents were horrified to see their children disobeying what they had been taught minutes earlier and the potential consequences should their children encounter loaded guns.[91]

The lesson appears to be that gun safety training should be a very minor part of gun accident prevention for children and youth. In initiatives involving children, too much of an onus is placed on the children and it is evident that guns need to be secured and inaccessible to children. With regard to teens, the American Academy of Pediatrics Committee on Adolescence asserted:

> *Because of these inherent developmental and behavioral vulnerabilities [belief in invincibility, curiosity, immaturity, impulsiveness], educational efforts aimed at teaching teenagers to use guns safely are not likely to be successful in preventing firearm death and injury. No published research confirms effectiveness of gun safety training for adolescents.*[92]

Americans strongly support laws requiring the safe storage of firearms. A national survey conducted in January 2013 found that two-thirds of Americans, including almost half of those owning guns, supported laws requiring gun owners to lock up any guns in the home when not in use in order to prevent handling by children or teenagers without adult supervision.[93]

Recommendations

- The CPSC should be empowered to regulate firearms like other consumer products (see discussion in Chap. 11 concerning the minimal oversight of the firearms industry).
- Federal law ought to set design safety standards on firearms manufactured and sold in the USA. Safety testing (e.g., drop test) should be conducted for each type of firearm.
- All firearms entering the civilian market should be equipped with some form of locking device within a specified period of time and all new firearms should be equipped with a magazine disconnect safety (where applicable) and personalization technology (phased in as such

technology is ready for the broad commercial market—see section below).

- National standards should be established for locking devices and gun safes to prevent their failure.
- A federally funded program should educate Americans about the extent of gun deaths and the need for safe storage, especially around children and teens.
- Pilot programs should examine the effectiveness of providing free gun storage devices and counseling on storage to families.[94]
- Health care providers should ask about guns in the home, advise patients and their families on the dangers of guns, and discuss options regarding secure storage. Physician "gag laws" that aim to keep doctors from asking about and providing advice relating to guns in the home should be opposed and repealed.
- Persons who store firearms negligently, where minors can or do gain access to the firearm, should be held criminally liable when that person knows or reasonably should know that a child is likely to gain access to it.

Enhancing Gun Safety Through Personalization and Other Technologies

According to the National Physicians Alliance, almost 3,800 people died and more than 95,000 people were injured in the USA from unintentional shootings from 2005 to 2010. Nearly half of the victims of these shootings were under 25 years of age.[95] Daniel Webster and his colleagues at the Johns Hopkins Center for Gun Policy and Research have pointed out that while unintentional shootings account for a small proportion of firearm-related injuries and deaths, these injuries and fatalities are highly preventable through the proper design of firearms.[96]

Accidental shootings that could be prevented through improved design include the following well-known scenarios:

- A young man who is joking around with friends pulls the ammunition magazine out of a gun and, believing it is unloaded, holds it to his head and fires. Tragically, the young man dies, unaware the gun could be loaded even without the detachable magazine. Firearms can be equipped with a "magazine disconnect mechanism" that prevents them from discharging when the magazine is not attached. They can also be equipped with a "chamber loading indicator" that indicates whether a gun is loaded.

- A child finds a gun in a night table drawer, thinks it is a toy, and pulls the trigger, killing his sister. A number of safety devices can prevent such an accident. The gun may have a trigger lock engaged when not used by its owner. It may also possess one of a number of personalizing features (see below), which would allow only the lawful owner to fire the gun.

- A woman accidentally drops a gun. The gun discharges, wounding her husband. Poorly constructed guns can fire without the trigger being pulled. This situation is characteristic of cheap, low-quality, or "junk guns" that may be built with inferior materials and are aimed at a less affluent market.

Currently, no federal agency oversees the design of firearms, as the CPSC has been prohibited by Congress from regulating firearms as it does consumer products that are associated with far fewer injuries and deaths. With the exception of a small number of states that impose their own standards, firearm manufacturers are not required to consider the safety of the products they make. By contrast, the laws in states such as California, Massachusetts, and New York require handguns to include certain safety features and to undergo tests to ensure they do not fire when dropped or malfunction in other ways.[97]

Personalizing guns represents a new way of ensuring that unauthorized users, including children and those stealing guns, cannot fire them. Aside from saving lives, personalizing weapons removes the incentive to steal guns. Some of the deaths and injuries arising from the use of stolen guns in subsequent crimes also can be prevented. Stephen Teret and Adam Mernit of Johns Hopkins University have argued that the impressive reductions in highway fatalities have been attributable more to design changes in cars than to changes in driver behavior.[98] They make the case that the same result can be achieved through altering the design of firearms. A number of options are being developed with regard to personalized or smart guns[99]:

1. One approach uses radio frequency identification (RFID) technology, whereby "tags," which can be objects (e.g., wristwatches, bracelets) containing tiny electromagnetic transmitters, communicate with "readers," which are embedded in a gun. RFID is widely used for controlled building access and in library book theft prevention, among other uses. When the reader detects the tag, a mechanical device in the gun can move a blocking mechanism so the gun can be fired. Without the tag being in close proximity to the reader on the gun (e.g., the gun is in the possession of an unauthorized user), the blocking mechanism remains in place and the gun is inoperable.
2. Another approach is to use biometric recognition, whereby the fingerprint or grip of the authorized user is scanned and recognized through some form of scanning or imaging. All of the small arms safety technology is incorporated in the gun itself and there is no external device or tag that can be lost. For example, with grip recognition, the palm configuration of the owner is recognized after a period of use and the gun will work only when held by the authorized user.

A study conducted by Jon Vernick of Johns Hopkins and his associates examined the proportion of unintentional and undetermined firearm-related deaths that might have been prevented had one of three safety devices been in place: personalization devices, loaded chamber indicators showing when a gun is loaded, and magazine safeties that prevent a gun from firing when the ammunition magazine is removed.[100] The study examined all known unintentional and undetermined firearm deaths from 1991 to 1998 in Maryland and Milwaukee County, Wisconsin. Following a detailed examination of each of the 117 deaths, the investigators classified 37 % of the incidents as preventable by a personalized gun and 20 % by a loaded chamber indicator, and 4 % were deemed to be preventable by a magazine safety. Overall, 44 % of the deaths were found to be preventable by at least one safety device. Deaths involving children (17 years or under) were more likely to be preventable. On the basis of this study, the researchers estimated that, projecting the findings to the entire USA, 442 deaths might have been prevented in 2000 had all guns been equipped with these safety devices.

According to researchers at John Hopkins, nearly 60 % of Americans and four in ten gun owners, if they were to buy a gun, would be willing to buy one that operated only in the hands of an authorized user.[101]

Improving the Quality of Guns

Some firearms are poorly constructed and may fire without the trigger being pulled (e.g., the gun is dropped). These "junk guns" are made with inferior materials and designed to reduce the manufacturing costs. In the 1980s and 1990s, several California-based manufacturers, referred to as the "Ring of Fire" companies, produced many cheap and conceal-able handguns referred to as "Saturday Night Specials." Five of the ten crime guns most often traced by ATF in 2000 were produced by these companies.[102] Due to their poor construction, inaccuracy, and lack of reliability, they are generally viewed as inappropriate for personal protec-tion or sporting purposes.

Several states have adopted laws to regulate the quality of guns man-ufactured, transferred, or possessed there; however, junk guns are still widely available for sale in most states. The aim of design and safety stan-dards is to ensure the structural integrity of firearms and to prevent them from malfunctioning. Tests are available to determine whether a gun discharges when dropped (drop test), remains structurally sound after repeated firing (firing testing), and whether the metal components can withstand the high levels of heat generated when a gun is fired (melting point tests).

Children's toys, toasters, and 15,000 other products are overseen by a federal agency, the CPSC.[103] When a manufacturer learns of a defect that can produce a substantial risk of injury, the firm must submit a report within 24 hours. Gun manufacturers are exempt from the oversight of the CPSC and therefore have no such obliga-tions. The lack of such reporting also means that no national data exist on the number of deaths and injuries resulting from defective firearms.

Microstamping

Newer technologies can also be useful in the investigation of crimes. Microstamping is a process whereby a small laser is used to engrave a firearm's make, model, and serial number on the firing pin so that it prints the information on discharged cartridge cases when the gun is fired. The process is an investigative tool that is designed to assist law enforcement in solving crimes and helps identify gun trafficking routes, as information is obtained on the firearm source location and compared with the crime scene location.[104] The code on the cartridge case allows law enforcement to connect the cartridge case to the gun that fired it, just as the license plate on a vehicle allows police to determine the particulars of a vehicle. This technology is potentially a deterrent to gun trafficking. This is the case because a trafficker who purchases a gun is aware that the cartridge case could be used to trace the gun back to him if the gun is used in a crime.

Both the American Bar Association and the International Association of Chiefs of Police have endorsed the use of microstamping technology.[105,106] California was the first state adopting a microstamping law, which went into effect in 2013.

There is strong public support for ballistic identification and microstamping laws. A national poll conducted for Mayors Against Illegal Guns in the spring of 2008 found that 77 % of Americans favor requiring all guns sold in the USA to have a ballistic fingerprint, which allows police to determine what gun fired a bullet.[107]

Predictably, firearms organizations have opposed microstamping, purportedly because the technology is flawed.[108] Researchers at University of California at Davis' forensic science program put the technology to the test and found that results varied by the weapon, the ammunition used, and the type of code examined. Bar codes on the sides of the firing pin transferred more poorly to the cartridge cases than did other codes.[109]

Fred Tulleners, director of the university's forensic lab, estimated that setting up a facility to engrave the firing pins of every handgun sold in California would eventually cost under $2 per firing pin. He said that a larger test, from a wider range of guns, would be required to assess the utility of this technology in the real world.

Todd Lizotte, coinventor of microstamping, has conducted new tests and claims that microstamped markings were transferred accurately 97 % of the time when the appropriate firing pins are used and the cartridge markings are viewed by an Optical or Electron microscope.[110] It is evident that this is a promising technology, but further work is required by independent researchers to confirm that this is a useful method of identifying a gun used in crime. It should be noted that 100 % accuracy is an unrealistic standard as the markings do not need to be readable in every case to be useful at least in some investigations.

Nationally syndicated columnist E. J. Dionne of the *Washington Post* points out that governments at all levels account for about 40 % of gun industry revenues and the federal government alone accounts for 25 % of these revenues. He argues that taxpayers have a right to demand responsibility from an industry that obtains so much of our money. As one of the main customers of the industry, he recommends that the federal government buy weapons only from manufacturers that adopt basic safety measures and implement microstamping technology.[111]

Recommendation

- The federal government should make funds available to enable more research into the development of personalized guns, as well as to assess and refine microstamping technologies.
- The federal government, law enforcement agencies, and governments at all levels should only purchase guns from companies that adopt basic gun safety features and implement microstamping technology.
- A target date should be set for introducing personalized guns into the market.
- National standards should be established to childproof guns (e.g., with loaded chamber indicators and magazine safety locks) and to otherwise enhance public safety by ensuring that guns being manufactured are of high quality. All models of guns entering the civilian market should be certified as safe following testing by independent laboratories.
- The CPSC should be empowered to set standards and to assess the readiness of all new firearm technologies for the civilian market.

Increasing Oversight of the Gun Industry

The oversight accorded most industries and consumer products has been virtually absent in relation to the gun industry and its products. The CPSC has been prohibited by Congress from regulating guns. The Protection of Lawful Commerce in Arms Act shields the industry from deaths and injuries associated with its products. Both federal law and inadequate resources limit the ATF's inspections of gun dealers. Also, nearly half of all gun sales occur in the unregulated private market.

Nicholas Kristof of the *New York Times* points out that the Occupational Safety and Health Administration has seven pages of regulations dealing with ladders, which are involved in 300 deaths per year in the USA. Guns, which are involved in over 30,000 deaths each year, are subject to minimal regulation. Kristof points out that efforts to reduced car accidents have been remarkably successful and the same public health approach should be applied to reducing gun deaths:

> *Over the decades, we have systematically taken steps to make cars safer. We adopted seatbelts and airbags, limited licenses for teenage drivers, cracked down on drunken driving and established roundabouts and better crosswalks, auto safety inspections and rules about texting while driving. … This approach has been stunningly successful. We have reduced the fatality rate by more than 95 percent.*[112]

A landmark study by Mayors Against Illegal Guns found that routine inspections of gun dealers provide law enforcement with more opportunities to detect signs of illegal gun activity, such as improper recordkeeping or a gun inventory that does not match their sales records.[113] The study showed that states that do not allow or require gun dealer inspections tend to export guns used in crime to other states at a rate that is 50 % greater than states that do permit or require such inspections. These states with less regulation of dealers are also more likely to be the source of trafficked guns, as determined by the time it takes for a gun to be used in crime following the initial purchase—two years or less is indicative of trafficking. A 2009 study found that cities located in states that comprehensively regulate gun dealers and where these dealers are inspected on a regular basis have significantly lower levels of gun trafficking than cities lacking such regulation and enforcement.[114]

Nathan Irvin and his colleagues at the University of Pennsylvania found that state laws allowing or requiring inspections of gun dealers were associated with significantly lower firearm homicide rates than states without these regulations.[115]

Law enforcement operations against dealers in New York City illustrate how effective enforcement can alter dealer behavior, thereby reducing the number of guns that are eventually used in crime. The city launched a number of undercover operations and lawsuits. The lawsuits could proceed as one exception to the immunity of dealers afforded under the Protection of Lawful Commerce in Arms Act if the dealer knowingly violated laws dealing with gun sales. In 2006, New York City identified 55 gun dealers in seven states who were supplying guns used in crime in the city. About half of these dealers were caught facilitating illegal sales in an undercover operation and were subsequently sued by the city. Nearly all the defendants settled their case and agreed to modify their business practices. An analysis focusing on ten of these dealers found that the change in those practices was followed by an 84 % reduction in the likelihood that a gun sold by one of these dealers was later recovered in a New York crime.[116]

Recommendations

- The ATF should have the authority and funding necessary to conduct routine inspections of gun dealers at its discretion. The agency should not be limited to one inspection per year.
- Sellers of ammunition should be required to obtain a license.
- The Protection of Lawful Commerce in Arms Act, which grants virtual immunity to the gun industry from negligence-based lawsuits, should be repealed.
- Rather than simply punishing gun makers and dealers for violating laws and compromising public safety, approaches should be developed that reward gun makers and dealers for engaging in behaviors that promote public safety and reduce gun trafficking (e.g., through pub-

licity and the awarding of state or federal contracts). These behaviors include safety features on firearms that exceed federal or state requirements, curbing sales to unscrupulous dealers and refusing to sell guns when it is likely that guns are being purchased for the purpose of trafficking them and/or using them for crime.

• Federal legislation that restricts the release of firearms trace data should be repealed to facilitate criminal investigations and to permit research on gun trafficking patterns.

Repealing or Amending Laws that Encourage Gun Violence

As of 2014, a majority of states have adopted some form of Stand Your Ground (SYG) law. While they vary, these laws give individuals the right to use deadly force when they have a "reasonable belief" that they are facing death or serious injury. Critics are concerned that these "shoot first" laws facilitate deadly confrontations—allowing the aggressor to act with impunity. Recent studies at Texas A&M University and Georgia State University concluded that SYG laws increase homicide rates while resulting in no corresponding reduction in criminal activity. The evidence on SYG laws is reviewed in Chap. 10. Studies show that these laws are associated with an increase in homicide, have been implemented unevenly, and are marked by racial disparities. In addition, there is no evidence they have a deterrent effect on other crimes, such as burglary, robbery, or aggravated assault.

Researchers at the Center for American Progress refer to the combination of permissive concealed carry laws and SYG as a "license to kill."[117] They note that the fatal shooting of Trayvon Martin in Sanford, Florida, by neighborhood watch coordinator George Zimmerman might never have happened had the state of Florida denied Zimmerman a license to carry a gun as a result of his history of violence and domestic abuse. Unlike states with stricter laws, Florida will issue permits to carry unless an individual has committed one of a narrow range of offenses specified under federal law or by state statutes.

In recent years, there has been a remarkable increase in the number of permits to carry guns issued across the country. Advocates of gun rights have hailed this development in state laws and argued that the majority of concealed carry permit holders are responsible, law-abiding citizens. While this may be true, the toll of deadly incidents caused by such individuals is rising, with a deadly shooting occurring almost weekly.[118] Making it easy for people with known criminal records, a history of violence and domestic abuse, or substance-abuse problems to obtain permits to carry firearms compromises public safety.

Recommendations

Any individual with a violent misdemeanor conviction or who has been the subject of a domestic violence restraining order in the past ten years should be denied a permit to carry a gun.

- Citizens seeking a carry permit should receive training in the following areas: mental preparation for stressful situations, knowledge of the law (when lethal force is permissible), judgment (making appropriate "shoot/don't shoot" decisions), as well as expertise, skill, and familiarity with firearms. Basic initial training to receive a permit and regular (annual or biannual) recertification to maintain the permit should be required. Both training and recertification should consist of decision-making during real-life scenarios, shooting accuracy in stressful situations, and firing range practice.
- There should be some discretion in the permitting process, to allow law enforcement to consider all relevant aspects of an applicant's criminal and personal history.
- The permitting system should be administered by a law enforcement agency rather than a regulatory agency, such as the Florida Department of Agriculture and Consumer Services. Such agencies are not equipped to evaluate applications for concealed carry permits.
- States should conduct rigorous evaluations of SYG laws to determine their impact on homicide, their deterrent effect (if any), and whether they are applied in a racially equitable manner. States should consider repealing these laws if they are associated with increases in violence or are implemented in a discriminatory way.

- States should reject more extreme versions of SYG laws. One provision proposed in Florida would shift the burden of proof to prosecutors to demonstrate that the shooter used lethal force inappropriately rather than requiring those using the SYG defense to prove they should have immunity from prosecution.[119]

Deterring Gun Violence

Efforts to reduce gun violence are not limited to the regulation of guns or the firearms industry. Aggressive law enforcement strategies that target high-risk individuals or neighborhoods can be beneficial. So can programs that engage neighborhood youth in positive activities or that teach them to resolve conflicts in a nonviolent way. Efforts can also be made to persuade rival groups who have been involved in a cycle of retaliatory violence to break this cycle. In addition, longer sentences can be meted out for using a gun in a crime as opposed to the use of another type of weapon or no weapon at all.

Focused Deterrence Strategies

Rather than engaging in routine preventive patrol and responding to crimes and calls for service, focused deterrence strategies first assess the nature and dynamics that contribute to a neighborhood's gun violence problems. Then, a strategy that combines law enforcement, community mobilization, and social service measures is implemented.[120]

Once a crime problem such as gun violence is identified, focused deterrence operations adopt the following general approach in the affected area:

- An interagency enforcement group is formed, comprising police, probation and parole agencies, and prosecutors.
- Key offenders and groups/gangs are identified.
- A customized enforcement operation is directed at these offenders and groups to influence their behavior through the use of available legal tools.

- These enforcement operations are complemented by providing services and making appeals to these individuals and groups to refrain from violent behavior.
- In direct communication in the form of face-to-face meetings, at-risk individuals and groups are told what they can do to avoid legal consequences.

First implemented in Boston's Operation Ceasefire project, a working group of criminal justice, social service, and community-based agencies, in partnership with Harvard University researchers, diagnosed the youth gun violence problem in Boston as one of patterned, largely vendetta-like conflicts among a small population of chronic offenders.[121] These groups were responsible for more than 60 % of youth homicides in the city. Law enforcement agencies sought to disrupt street drug activity, focused on low-level street crimes such as trespassing, served outstanding warrants, recruited confidential informants, enforced probation and parole conditions strictly, requested stronger bail terms, and brought potentially severe federal investigative and prosecutorial attention to gang-related drug and gun activity.

At the same time, gang outreach workers, probation and parole officers, and community groups offered gang members services and delivered the message that violence was unacceptable. This message was transmitted in formal meetings between police, correctional, and/or gang workers. The focused deterrence approach simultaneously emphasizes the risk of reoffending and the importance of decreasing opportunities for violence and strengthening communities. It also stresses public perceptions of the legitimacy of police actions. Advocates of focused deterrence strategies argue that targeted offenders should be treated with respect and dignity, reflecting procedural justice principles. Recent studies indicate that citizens are more likely to behave in a law-abiding fashion when they evaluate the legitimacy of the police more highly.[122]

Evaluations of focused deterrence strategies have generally found large reductions in violent crime. For example, Boston experienced a 63 % reduction in youth homicides and Stockton, California, experienced a 42 % reduction in gun homicides.[123]

Recommendations

• Support innovative programs that identify high-risk individuals and communities and that offer a combination of focused deterrence strategies to modify violent norms and support to individuals.
• Strong penalties should be imposed on those using guns in crime, as well as those engaged in firearms trafficking and straw purchases.

Learning Lessons from Abroad: Australia's Experience

In April, 1996, a 28-year-old man with significant intellectual disabilities went on a killing spree in Port Arthur, Tasmania, a former penal colony and popular tourist destination south of Melbourne, Australia. A total of 35 people were killed, and 23 people were wounded in one of the worst civilian mass murders in any country. The shooter was armed with semiautomatic rifles that were legally available in Tasmania but banned in other states.[124] The incident precipitated an enormous outpouring of both grief and outrage.

Australia is a large country with a frontier history and an established gun culture. Prior to the massacre, the gun lobby and some sympathetic legislators frustrated efforts to develop more restrictive gun laws that would apply across the country. The massacre and then Prime Minister John Howard's reaction to it were the turning points. It occurred just six weeks into Howard's term as prime minister. Despite the fact that he headed a conservative party that was a natural ally of the gun lobby and drew much of its support from rural regions with many gun owners, Mr. Howard quickly came to the conclusion that strong national legislation, including a ban on automatic and semiautomatic long guns, was necessary.

When some states resisted his proposed reforms, he threatened to hold a national referendum to alter the Australian Constitution in order to give the federal government power over gun policy.[125] Public opinion was on his side, although opposition to major gun reforms was very vocal and threatening. As a result of the national government's leadership, Australia's federal and state governments agreed to harmonize firearm laws across the country in a series of agreements. The most comprehensive, the National Firearms Agreement (NFA) of 1996, included the following elements[126]:

- A ban of the sale, importation, or possession of primarily automatic and semiautomatic long arms. A buyback scheme was implemented in order to compensate owners for the forfeiture of firearms that were now banned.
- A uniform licensing and registration system in all eight states and territories of Australia, replacing a patchwork that included legal regimes of varying stringency. A 28-day waiting period was established for a license application to allow those bent on violence or self-injury to "cool off."
- A "genuine reason" was now required in order to possess, own, or use a firearm, and self-protection did not qualify as a reason for gun ownership.
- Safety training was required for all first-time license applicants.
- A uniform standard was created for the security and storage of firearms.
- Firearm sales could proceed only through licensed dealers.

Estimates indicate that approximately one million firearms—up to a third of the national inventory of privately held guns—were bought back or surrendered voluntarily between 1996 and 2003.[127]

The majority of studies and analyses indicate that the NFA provided significant public safety benefits. For example, Philip Alpers of the University of Sydney's School of Public Health noted that 100 people died in 11 mass shootings in the decade leading up to Australia's legislative reforms in 1996. Since these reforms were announced and as of January 2013, he noted that there have been no mass shootings in the country.[128] In 2014, there was one family murder-suicide by firearm, 18 years after the new laws were introduced. This compares with 13 mass murders by gunfire in 18 years prior to the legal reforms, resulting in 112 deaths and 52 injuries.[129] The decline in mass shootings is a significant sign that the gun ban has had an effect as the guns prohibited by the policy reforms are often the same type used in mass killings.

Simon Chapman and his colleagues at the University of Sydney compared firearm-related homicides, suicides, and unintentional deaths before and after the legislative reforms and observed the following[130]:

- Total firearm deaths declined from 628 per year from 1979 to 1996 (prior to the announcement of the new gun laws) to 333 per year following the announcement (1997–2003). While the total firearm death rate was declining by 3 % prior to the legislative reforms, this rate doubled to 6 % after the introduction of the new gun laws.
- Firearm suicides declined from 492 per year before the reforms were announced to 247 per year following the introduction of the new laws. Here again, the decline in the firearm suicide rate accelerated from 3 % per year prior to the law reforms to 7.4 % per year following the reforms. Suicides by other methods also declined faster after the legislative reforms than before them, indicating that reducing the availability of firearms did not lead to a compensating increase in suicides by other means.
- Firearm homicides declined from 93 per year prior to the reforms to 56 per year after the reforms. The decline in gun homicides accelerated from 3 % per year before the introduction of the new laws to 7.5 % per year after the reforms. At the same time, homicides by means other than a firearm were stable prior to the new gun laws but declined significantly afterword. Thus, the data did not support the idea that reducing the availability of guns would lead to a compensating increase in homicides using other methods.
- One perplexing finding was that unintentional gun deaths increased following the law reforms; however, this increase amounted to just 1.4 deaths per year.

While interpretations of the evidence vary somewhat, there is a fair amount of consensus among researchers that firearm suicides dropped sharply following the NFA and that this drop was statistically significant. Firearm homicides also dropped substantially, although statistical tests did not find this drop to have been statistically significant.[131,132,133,134] In addition, there was no evidence of substantial method substitution, since nonfirearm death rates also decreased following the NFA.[135] The most comprehensive evaluation study also found that the largest declines in firearm homicides and suicides occurred in the states where a larger number of firearms were bought back.[136]

Australia's reforms have been hailed as "a resounding success."[137] The major exception is the research team of Jeanine Baker and Samara McPhedran,[138] who believe that the NFA has not had an overall effect on public safety. Both researchers play prominent roles with sports shooting organizations. They claim that homicide patterns were not influenced by the law reforms. Their study has been shown to have had a fatal flaw in its forecast of the firearm homicide trends for the post-NFA period.[139] According to this forecast, the firearm homicide rate would have been zero by 2004 and less than zero by 2015 had the reforms not occurred. It is hard for a policy to beat an expected homicide rate of less than zero!

Still, their analysis did concede that firearm suicides may have been reduced by the tightening of gun laws in Australia. An impact of the laws on suicide alone could justify the measures as more firearm deaths are suicides than homicides or accidents.

In 2007, economists Andrew Neill and Christine Leigh (2007) reanalyzed the results of Baker and McPhedran's study. They found that reanalyzing the results with two different statistical techniques strengthened the evidence that the NFA was followed by a statistically significant reduction in deaths due to both firearm homicides and suicides.[140] In a subsequent article, these researchers indicated that the buyback led to an 80 % drop in firearm suicide rates and a similar, although less precise, drop in firearm homicides.[141]

Following the Aurora, Colorado, theater mass shooting in July, 2012, John Howard, the former prime minister who spearheaded Australia's gun reforms, stated in an interview: "There are many American traits which we Australians could well emulate to our great benefit. But when it comes to guns, we have been right to take a radically different path."[142]

It is evident from the title of most of the Australian evaluations that the focus has been on the buyback component of the 1996 legislative reforms. A large body of scientific research would support the conclusion that the impact on public safety is very likely due, at least in part, to a massive decline (up to one third) in firearm availability in Australia. Specifically, the nationwide ban on automatic and semiautomatic long guns may well have contributed to the reduction of mass murders after 1996. The fact that the reductions in gun-related violence and suicides were greatest in states with the highest buyback levels is also suggestive of success.

Like the USA, Australia has a federal system of government, a gun culture, and an influential gun lobby. Australia's reforms occurred due to determined national leadership and an outraged public following the Port Arthur massacre. The reluctance of American politicians to commit themselves fully to major gun law reform, combined with the deep divide in public opinion with regard to the relative importance of gun safety versus gun rights, have been significant impediments to reform.

Recommendations

- American leaders ought to familiarize themselves with the Australian experience, including the process of achieving reforms, the reforms achieved, and the outcome of gun laws passed since the 1996 carnage in Port Arthur.
- Semiautomatic, assault-type weapons and high-capacity magazines that have little use other than to kill a large number of civilians should be banned in the USA. A national program should be created to compensate owners for banned firearms and magazines that have been turned in.

The Need for Research on Gun Violence Prevention

How many guns are there in America? How many guns are sold each year? What types of guns are most likely to be used in crime? Are there more gun deaths in areas with higher gun ownership levels? The answers to these and other questions are imprecise at this time due to the lack of sufficient funding of gun violence research.[143]

All areas of inquiry are characterized by gaps in knowledge and can benefit from further research. What is unique about gun violence is that, despite over 30,000 firearm deaths per year in America, there has been a deliberate strategy to block research because the knowledge revealed by scientific studies was a threat to a powerful interest group.

In the mid-1980s, medical doctors, many of whom were emergency room physicians, and public health researchers began to conduct investigations and publish studies on gun violence. Those working in emergency rooms had personally witnessed the severity of the injuries produced by gunfire. The medical and public health fields brought sophisticated research methods to the study of violence and began to systematically isolate the impact of gun availability on violence when other factors influencing violence were held constant.

One of the first of the highly influential studies from the above fields was that led by Dr. John Henry Sloan, a Seattle, Washington, surgeon, and his collaborators—a group of emergency room physicians, forensic pathologists, pediatricians, and epidemiologists.[144] The researchers compared two West Coast cities, Seattle and Vancouver, British Columbia (Canada), a two and a half hour drive to the north. They found remarkable similarities: the cities were approximately of equal size, they enjoyed a similar standard of living, and their residents shared cultural tastes, including a preference for some of the same television programs. The cities also were similar in relation to their crime problem, as they had comparable rates of burglary, robbery, and assault with knives, clubs, and fists during the seven-year study period (1980–1986).

The authors discovered that Seattle had a far higher gun ownership rate than Vancouver, as 41 % of the Seattle homes owned a gun as opposed to just 12 % in Vancouver. Seattle also had a much higher rate of assaults with firearms. The homicide rate with knives and weapons other than firearms was nearly identical in the two cities. However, Seattle had almost five times the rate of homicide by firearm than Vancouver. The gap in firearm homicides led to an overall homicide rate in Seattle that was 50 % higher than that of Vancouver.

Being similar in so many respects, other than with regard to gun ownership, provided a natural laboratory for isolating the impact of gun availability on homicide with many social and cultural factors held constant. The most obvious conclusion was that the greater availability of guns in Seattle led to their more frequent use in assaults, which in turn produced more homicides due to the greater lethality of guns.

The compelling studies by medical and public health researchers in the 1980s and 1990s reached their zenith in an article published in *The New*

England Journal of Medicine in 1993 by Dr. Arthur L. Kellermann and his colleagues entitled "Gun Ownership as a Risk Factor for Homicide in the Home."[145] Applying a rigorous methodology, Dr. Kellermann's work was reaching an expanding audience. The findings of this study undermined the argument of the gun lobby that guns in the home make people safer as they showed that keeping a gun in the home was strongly and independently associated with an increased risk of homicide. The article concluded that guns were a threat to household members rather than a source of protection. This study was viewed as such a threat to the NRA's message that guns in the home play a protective role that the NRA was determined to stop federal research on gun violence.[146]

The NRA and its congressional allies have much to do with the gaps in quality research on gun violence and the effectiveness of gun laws, such as those prohibiting high-capacity ammunition magazines or requiring background checks in all gun sales. Researchers point out that the amount of money available to conduct research on the impact of guns is a fraction of what it was in the mid-1990s, and the number of active researchers in the field has dropped dramatically.[147]

In the 1990s, the CDC was aggressively funding research on gun-related injuries and deaths as a public health concern. Members of Congress sympathetic to the gun lobby initially tried to shut down the CDC's injury prevention center completely, arguing that the center was pursuing an anti-gun political agenda. When they did not succeed, they stripped funds from the CDC's budget. The funds were later restored but were designated for research on traumatic brain injury. The following language was also included in the CDC's appropriations bill: "None of the funds made available for injury prevention and control at the Centers for Disease Control and Prevention may be used to advocate or promote gun control." No other field of inquiry is singled out in this way.

The CDC has been reluctant to finance research on firearms, remaining fearful of retaliation by pro-gun members of Congress. In 2013, following the massacre of children and staff at Sandy Hook Elementary School in Newtown, Connecticut, President Obama ordered the CDC to once again fund studies on gun violence.[148] Congress has continued to block dedicated funding. President Obama requested $10 million for the CDC's gun violence research and congressional Republicans turned down his request.

Public Health Approach to Prevention

One promising avenue for research on gun violence is the public health approach. According to the CDC, this approach to dealing with a disease or problem behavior involves four broad steps[149]:

1. The nature and extent of the problem are first documented through detailed statistical analysis.
2. Research identifies the factors that place individuals and communities at risk and those that protect people and communities from violence.
3. Prevention strategies are developed and subjected to rigorous testing to determine whether they prevent the problem, in this case gun violence.
4. Strategies determined to be effective are then implemented widely.

David Hemenway, director of Harvard University's Injury Control Research Center, points out some of the advantages and distinguishing features of a public health approach.[150] He states that this approach focuses on prevention and emphasizes shared responsibility rather than on assigning blame. The public health approach tries to create a system in which it is difficult to behave inappropriately and where it does occur, inappropriate behavior, such as violence, does not produce serious injury. Advocates of the public health approach take the position that it is often more effective to change the agent (e.g., the weapon) and the environment in which the problem occurs than to change the individual (e.g., victim and perpetrator). Furthermore, the approach examines all possible interventions, including changing social norms and passing new laws, and it tries to enlist the involvement of as many people and institutions as possible.

One of the most dramatic public health successes occurred in relation to the fatalities arising from motor vehicle crashes. According to the CDC, there has been a 90 % decline in the number of deaths per

100 million vehicle miles traveled from the 1920s to the 1990s.[151] Until the 1960s, the focus was almost exclusively on the driver as the cause of accidents through either carelessness or incompetence. This is remarkably similar to the view by the gun lobby that firearm injuries and deaths are the product of "bad guys." In 1966, the National Highway Traffic Safety Administration was created to regulate to ensure road safety, data were collected on injuries, and safety standards were established. Reducing driving deaths was accomplished through a combination of measures focusing on vehicle design (e.g., safety belts, child safety seats, impact-absorbing features), improving the road environment (medians, improved lighting, and signage), and campaigns stressing that drinking and driving were unacceptable (changing attitudes and stronger enforcement).

Recommendations

Acts of Congress to suppress research have been shameful. It is truly a disgrace to impede our understanding of a leading source of death and serious injuries in this country. Let the research proceed and let policies be based on the best information available rather than on the interests of politicians, lobby groups on either side of the gun debate, or the firearms industry.

- A vigorous research effort is required to identify prevention and inter-vention strategies to reduce injuries produced by firearms, including the impact of current restrictions on ownership.[152] The CDC, National Institutes of Health, and National Institute of Justice should receive adequate funding to study the effects of gun violence on public safety. Access to data should not be restricted.
- A public health approach is a useful way of approaching research in this area as it focuses on all aspects of gun violence: the perpetrator, weapon, victim, and the conditions in which violence occurs.
- The National Violent Death Reporting System should be expanded to all states to provide comprehensive national data on gun violence.
- A current, comprehensive national survey on gun ownership should be conducted with a sample of sufficient size to enable detailed analyses

of the connection between gun availability and firearm deaths and injuries. Such a survey should also provide information on the types and number of firearms in different counties and states, as well as data on gun accessibility and storage.

- Research is required on the factors that place individuals and communities at risk of gun violence as well as factors that protect people and communities from violence.
- Research is required in developing new technologies that can prevent gun deaths and injuries.

Innovative Approaches

Cure Violence Program

Gary Slutkin, an epidemiologist, returned to the USA in the mid-1990s after helping Africans address the spread of tuberculosis, AIDS, and other diseases.[153] After returning to Chicago, he began to study the violence that beset inner-city neighborhoods and discovered that the problem resembled the epidemics he had treated in Africa. As in the case of infectious diseases, maps of gun violence showed the clustering of incidents. In 2000, he founded CeaseFire Chicago (now known as Cure Violence), a program treating violence in one such local cluster as a public health rather than a criminal justice issue. There was a significant decline in gang-related shootings.[154]

The Chicago program was based on the idea that change agents could be mobilized to address some of the immediate causes of violence: violent norms, rapid decision-making by individuals at risk of triggering violence, and the perceived risks of involvement in violence among the targeted population. Joe Nocera of the *New York Times* reports that this approach was replicated in the Crown Heights section of Brooklyn, New York. As in public health, the first step in combating an epidemic is to locate the disease carriers. The program hired "outreach" staff—formerly, at-risk individuals themselves—to identify the people in the community most likely to commit gun violence. The next step is to develop a relationship with them in order to dissuade them from future acts of gun violence.

Another group of staff members are referred to as "violence interrupters." They try to mediate when something occurs that could trigger gun violence. When a shooting does occur, a staffer goes to the hospital to persuade the victim and his family, as well as associates, not to exact revenge.

Nocera reports that in 2010, the first full year the Brooklyn program was in operation, the number of shootings in the 40-block area covered by the program was cut in half. Jens Ludwig, an economist at the University of Chicago, did a controlled study in which one large group of middle and high school students went to a weekly class on changing behaviors while the other group did not attend the class. The group that took the class was 44 %less likely to be arrested.[155]

Changing Norms that Fuel Violence

While the focus of this book is on the role played by guns as an independent risk factor in violence and its consequences, cultural and social norms also play an important role in violence, including gun violence. Intimate partner violence is supported by the view that men have the right to assert their power over women and that a man has the right to "discipline" his wife. Violent street norms include the notion that violence is an acceptable and even expected way of resolving disputes and that reporting violence or bullying is unacceptable. School- and community-based programs, neighborhood mentors, and media campaigns are three vehicles through which messages can challenge norms that encourage violence.

Mass media campaigns have been successfully used to alter attitudes and behavior in relation to eating healthily, exercising, stopping smoking, reducing alcohol consumption, and tackling impaired driving.[156] Among the factors that seem to contribute to the success of mass media campaigns are messages about legal penalties for noncompliant behavior. One aspect of changing norms is reinforcing laws that reduce gun violence and eliminating other laws that encourage violence (e.g., SYG laws).

Initiatives in Chicago

Chicago has a major gun violence problem. It has been said that nothing stops a bullet like a job or a quality education. After school programs, job training programs, mentoring programs with business leaders and community recreational programs, such as Chicago's "Windy City Hoops," can keep kids off the streets and focused on achieving productive lives. Alternatives to violence and nonviolent conflict resolution can be promoted through mentoring programs with former gang members that make young people aware of the perils of gang association.

Initiatives in Chicago have included[157]:

- The Match tutoring program provided nearly 700 at-risk students with intensive one-on-one tutors. Early results showed a drop in student misconduct by 67 %, a decrease in violent arrests by 50 %, and reduced course failures by 37 %.
- Student reengagement centers that have counseled more than 700 disconnected youth, creating customized graduation plans for each student they met. Early results showed that more than 50 % of these students either reengaged or were on track to reengage with school.
- The "Becoming a Man" mentoring program, which reduced violent arrests for participants by 44 %, increased graduation rates and reduced failing grades.
- The One Summer Chicago PLUS summer employment and mentoring program for justice involved youth. A thousand youth received a full-time job, mentoring, skills development, and cognitive behavioral therapy. Preliminary results showed that participants were 51 % less likely to be arrested for a violent crime compared to similarly situated youth who did not join the program.

Promoting The Right Not to Bear Arms

Columnist E.J. Dionne of the *Washington Post* has written that we need to change public attitudes about guns and raise awareness of their dangers, rather than just focus on passing laws. Dionne quotes pollster Guy Molyneux:

We need to build a social movement devoted to the simple proposition that owning handguns makes us less safe, not more. The evidence is overwhelming that having a gun in your home increases the risks of suicide, domestic violence and fatal accidents. … We need a public health campaign on the dangers of gun ownership, similar to the successful efforts against smoking and drunk driving.[158]

Molyneux argues that, in place of bans on gun ownership, the health offensive would try to persuade people to voluntarily give up the idea of having a gun in the home because it is safer to do so. He adds those of us who want to live, shop, attend school, and worship in gun-free spaces also have rights. He asks how freedom is advanced when state laws prevent businesspeople from keeping guns out of their establishments. Molyneux argues that the gun lobby is the enemy of freedom, as it seeks to impose its values on the entire population.

Dionne speaks of a campaign with slogans such as "Not in my house," "Not in our school," "Not in my bar," and "Not in our church." Such a campaign would be asserting our right not to bear arms.

Threat Assessment in Preventing Mass Shootings

The US Secret Service's and Department of Education's study of targeted school attacks and the FBI's study of active shooter incidents leave little optimism for the view that these events can be prevented through the development of a specific profile or set of perpetrator characteristics (e.g., personality, demographic characteristics).[159,160]

In the context of school shootings, the use of static profiles (e.g., white males with a history of behavioral problems) will produce errors of identifying students who will not engage in targeted violence and missing students who may pose a serious risk.[161] As these attacks are so rare, overidentification is a concern. Clinical prediction of dangerousness is problematic because most mental health professionals lack formal training in violence risk assessment and cannot distinguish between assessing risk for general violence and assessing risk for targeted violence. In addition, few school attackers had a history of mental illness prior to their attack. Furthermore, research has not demonstrated that standard psychological tests can predict an individual's risk of engaging in targeted violence.[162]

In contrast with a focus on the individual, researchers with the US Secret Service developed a Threat Assessment Approach, which provides a framework for identifying, assessing, and managing persons who pose a risk for targeted violence.[163] This approach distinguishes between making a threat (expressing an intent to harm the target) and posing a threat (engaging in behaviors that further a plan to harm the target). The researchers further found that prior to most school attacks, other students were aware of the impending attack. In most cases, pre-attack planning was observed by others or was potentially detectable. Attackers rarely directed any threats to their targets.

Nearly all of the attackers had engaged in some behavior that seriously concerned one or more adults in their lives. Many attackers felt bullied or persecuted—bullying often went on for long periods of time and was often carried out by several students. Other students often knew of the planned attack and often encouraged or assisted in some way.

The Threat Assessment Approach combines an investigative process and information-gathering strategies to determine whether the student/situation poses a serious risk of targeted violence. A threat assessment may be initiated by any communication or behavior of concern. The focus of the inquiry is on the student's behavior and whether there is progression toward an attack. The aim is early intervention, as the emphasis is on prevention and the development of effective case management strategies. Threat assessments focus on some of the following:

1. Motivation for the behavior
2. Communication about ideas and intentions
3. Unusual interest in targeted violence
4. Evidence of attack-related behaviors and planning
5. The individual's capacity to carry out an act of targeted violence
6. Feelings of hopelessness or despair or recent losses, real or perceived
7. A trusting relationship with a responsible adult (a protective factor)
8. A belief that violence is a solution to the student's problems
9. Consistency between communications and behaviors
10. Concern by others about the student's potential for harm
11. Factors in the student's life that might increase or decrease the likelihood of attack

The information learned from these questions will indicate whether the student is moving on a path toward violent action. In addition, the answer to Item 11 can inform the development of a risk management plan by highlighting conditions in the student's life that could be monitored for changes, enhanced to provide the student support, and/or reduced to help the student solve a problem.

Recommendations

- Laws that may encourage violence should be evaluated and repealed if they are found to contribute to gun violence.
- Funding should be available for the development and evaluation of innovative gun violence prevention programs.
- Media campaigns should tackle the norms that fuel violent behavior, including gun violence, and should raise awareness regarding the risks of gun ownership and carrying. Such a campaign should also deal with gun safety issues. Cities and other jurisdictions should follow Seattle[164] and consider a tax on guns and ammunition that funds these campaigns and compensates taxpayers for the medical costs associated with gun violence.
- Threat assessment approaches should be adopted by schools, work places, and other venues that are most susceptible to mass shootings.

Rebuilding American Communities

Public mass shootings and other targeted attacks (e.g., on schools and workplaces) account for a small percentage of gun-related deaths and injuries but, due to their scale and the extensive media coverage they elicit, have a disproportionate effect on the public's apprehensions and on the strength of the ties that bind Americans.

James Alan Fox, a Northeastern University criminologist, has written extensively on the subject of mass murder. In an opinion piece written for CNN following the massacre at the Century Theater in Aurora, Colorado, in July, 2012, Fox said: "Mass murder is regrettably one of the painful consequences of the freedoms we enjoy."[165]

I respectfully disagree. No other free, advanced society experiences these slaughters with the regularity seen in the USA. Apart from the accessibility of weapons capable of inflicting mass casualties—a matter of grave concern—certain features of American society appear to be especially conducive to these outbursts of homicidal rage often directed at complete strangers.

Studies of mass shootings, of targeted school attacks, and of active shooter incidents show that social isolation and a breakdown in our social institutions may underlie and enable these incidents. These same factors may also point the way to preventing these incidents. While studies point out that there is no single profile of the mass shooter, there is an alternative to resigning ourselves to the idea that these incidents are simply something we must endure or, on the other extreme, embracing the NRA's vision for our society as one that is armed to the teeth. Resignation breeds hopelessness, and the NRA's vision for America would line the pockets of gun makers while undermining many of our freedoms, as well as our sense of security.

Analyses of mass shootings, active shooter incidents, and targeted school attacks show that:

- Nearly all of these incidents are committed by one individual.[166,167,168]
- 40 % of the perpetrators in the active shooter incidents committed suicide and almost a quarter committed suicide before police arrived. Nearly eight in ten school attackers exhibited a history of suicide attempts or suicidal thoughts prior to their attack and more than half had a recorded history of feeling extremely depressed or desperate.[169,170]
- A quarter of the school attackers socialized with fellow students who were disliked by most students or were viewed as belonging to a "fringe" group. Another third of the attackers were viewed by others or themselves as loners.[171]
- Over a third of the school attackers had been suspended or expelled from school.[172]
- Nearly three-quarters of the attackers felt persecuted, bullied, threatened, or attacked or were injured by others prior to the incident. In several cases, the attackers had experienced severe bullying and

harassment for a long period. There were a number of cases in which the experience of being bullied had a significant impact on the attacker and appeared to be a factor in the decision to launch an attack against a school.[173]

- A quarter of the attackers had a known history of alcohol or substance abuse.[174]

- Virtually all mass murderers or school attackers had experienced or perceived a major loss prior to the attack, including a perceived failure or loss of status, loss of a loved one, a major illness suffered by the attacker or someone significant to him, or the loss of a significant relationship, including a romantic one. The behavior of most attackers showed difficulty coping with the loss.[175]

- In more than three-quarters of the school attacks, at least one person—usually a friend, schoolmate, or sibling—had information that the attacker was contemplating or planning the attack, and, in the majority of cases, more than one person was aware of the impending attack. In addition, before nearly all the school attacks, the perpetrators exhibited behavior that caused others—school officials, parents, teachers, police, fellow students—to be concerned.[176]

- Nearly half of the perpetrators of school attacks were encouraged to undertake the attack or assisted by others in some way (e.g., in obtaining a weapon).[177]

Consider the sense of persecution and seething anger expressed in a diary by Eric Harris, one of the perpetrators of the shootings at Columbine High School in Littleton, Colorado:

> *Everyone is always making fun of me because of how I look, how f____g weak I am ... I will get you all back, ultimate f____g revenge here. You people could have shown more respect, treated me better, asked for my knowledge or guidance more, treated me more like a senior, and maybe I wouldn't have been so ready to tear your f___g heads off [expletives deleted].*[178]

To summarize, analyses of mass shootings, school attacks, and active shooter incidents show that most of these attacks were committed by one person and that the perpetrator frequently had a history of suicide attempts and/or a recorded history of depression and feeling desperate. Many school attackers were members of a fringe group or were viewed as loners. A significant number had a history of suspensions or expulsions from school. Many had been bullied or attacked previously. Nearly all school attackers had suffered a major loss prior to the attack with which they had difficulty coping. Often, others were aware the perpetrator was considering a school attack, encouraged the attack, and/or noticed behavior on his part that was disturbing.

These findings point to many opportunities for intervention and vigilance on the part of schools, community groups, and law enforcement. While most depressed individuals, loners, and members of fringe groups will not launch school or other attacks on civilians, a caring, cohesive, and effective community can intervene positively in assisting those who are experiencing a personal crisis, being bullied, suicidal, or feeling desperate. We need to ask why school officials, family members, and peers who were often aware failed to intervene in some way to avert a mass shooting or school attack. To successfully prevent some attacks, at least, the surrounding community must recognize the signs of danger, care enough to act on those signs, and must have the necessary resources and legal tools to provide support as well as ensure that individuals at high risk do not have access to weapons capable of inflicting mass casualties.

This brings us to the current state of communities in America that allow so many people to feel victimized, isolated, desperate, and unsupported. The combination of the large number of people who find themselves in this situation and who have access to weapons of war is lethal. Robert Putnam, Professor of Public Policy at Harvard University, has analyzed an enormous amount of data to document the breakdown of American communities. In his book *Bowling Alone: The Collapse and Revival of American Community*, Putnam painstakingly demonstrates how social networks have declined over the last few decades in so many areas of community life.[179]

Putnam shows that there has been a decline in

- political participation (e.g., voter turnout, volunteering for a political party);

- civic participation (e.g., fraternal organizations, Parent–Teacher Associations);
- religious participation (e.g., church membership, Bible study groups);
- workplace connections (e.g., union membership, ties with coworkers);
- informal social connections (e.g., meals involving the entire family, visits with friends);
- philanthropy; and
- honesty and trust of fellow citizens.

Putnam attributes the disengagement of Americans from community life to television and electronic communications, generational change (the replacement of the civic-minded generation born before 1946 by their less involved offspring and grandchildren), urban sprawl, and, to a lesser extent, time and money pressures. He states that electronic communications and entertainment have rendered our leisure activities more passive and private. We spend more time watching things and less time doing things with others. *Bowling Alone* was published in 2000. One can only imagine the level of community disengagement and impersonality of communications Putnam would find today with the advent of smart phones and the emergence of social media.

Putnam found that states with high ratings on what he calls Social Capital—states in which residents have higher trust levels, join organizations, socialize more, and participate in the electoral process—have healthier children, fewer high school dropouts, and less juvenile crime. They also consistently have lower murder rates. Better overall health and happiness are also linked to social connectedness.

Putnam examined the impact of the decline of community on such things as health and crime. Between 1950 and 1995, the suicide rate among 15- to 19-year-olds quadrupled and it tripled for young adults between 20 and 24 years of age. Levels of depression have increased dramatically during this period.[180] These trends have coincided with the increasing social isolation of teenagers—they spend far more time alone today—and the breakdown of families, religious, and other institutions that previously were available to provide support when young people faced adversity.[181]

Consider the case of Adam Lanza, the 20-year-old young man who murdered 26 children and staff at Sandy Hook Elementary School in Newtown, Connecticut, on December 14, 2012. This is a textbook case of how a socially isolated individual, a broken and socially disconnected family, and failed educational, mental health, and other systems all contributed to this unspeakable tragedy. Yes, Mr. Lanza had developmental disabilities but, as the report by Connecticut's Office of the Child Advocate pointed out, these disabilities rarely manifest themselves in premeditated violence, let alone a mass shooting on the scale of that experienced at Sandy Hook.[182]

The key findings of the child advocate's report reflect the breakdown of American communities and the lack of a safety net for individuals and families that are troubled in some way. Consider the following from the report's Executive Summary:

- *There were early indications of AL's [Adam Lanza's] preoccupation with violence … that appeared to have been largely unaddressed by schools and possibly by parents.*
- *The district provided little surveillance of AL's homebound status, which lasted an entire school year.*
- *Yale's [the Child Study Center at Yale University] recommendations for extensive special education supports, ongoing expert consultation, and rigorous therapeutic supports … went largely unheeded.*
- *AL and his parents did not appear to seek or participate in any mental health treatment after 2008. No sustained input from any mental health provider is documented in AL's educational record or medical record after 2006.*
- *AL's pediatric records from age 13 to 17 note his obsessive compulsive behaviors, markedly underweight presentation, psychiatric diagnoses, and repeated homebound or independent study, but records … often note during high school years that no medication or psychiatric treatment was being provided.*
- *AL progressively deteriorated in the last years of his life, eventually living in virtual social isolation.*
- *AL became increasingly preoccupied with mass murder, encouraged by a cyber-community—a micro society of mass murder enthusiasts with whom he was in email communication.*

- *AL ... retained access to numerous firearms and high capacity ammunition magazines even as his mental health deteriorated in late adolescence.*
- *In the waning months of AL's life, when his mother noted that he would not leave the house and seemed despondent, it is not clear that any measures were taken to curtail his access to guns or whether the family considered AL's potential for suicide.*
- *This report suggests the role that weaknesses and lapses in the educational and healthcare systems' response and untreated mental illness played in AL's deterioration.*

Americans, Putnam tell us, feel disconnected and long for civil, trusting, and caring communities.[183] He calls for reinventing the civic life that was built in the early twentieth century. He states that we need to get young adults engaged in the political process and in organized activities. Civics education is essential, as is the involvement of young people in community service. Labor law should encourage employers to be family and community friendly. Cities and towns should be designed so as to reduce the time spent commuting to work. Cultural activities that bring people together and transcend our differences need to be emphasized. Putnam asserts that a major challenge is to harness the power of the Internet and social media to encourage face-to-face interactions rather than building an alternative virtual world.

Some of these community-building initiatives would be in the medium to long term. In the near term, rather than merely establishing a Chamber of Commerce, communities throughout America might consider creating neighborhood development councils to welcome new residents, ensure that families are integrated into community life, and lend support when people are under stress. Where a family seems to be overwhelmed, neighborhood services could reach out and make them aware of available support. Such outreach can serve as a form of early warning system, where it is evident that a family is floundering and members are withdrawing from community life, as was the case with Adam Lanza and many other mass shooters.

A number of cities have developed school dropout reengagement centers to identify high school dropouts or chronic truants and work closely with them to provide the mentoring and other support required to complete their degrees and to meet their vocational needs.[184] Another idea would be to establish a form of buddy system in high school to ensure that each student has at least one consistent connection with a peer. A falling out with his only friend was a significant loss that preceded Lanza's actions. In the event of the social withdrawal of one's "buddy," the student would notify school authorities, who would then investigate and offer the appropriate support. The failure of the student to cooperate might lead to a referral of the case to law enforcement who could determine whether the individual has acquired gun permits and should be interviewed.

The Sandy Hook Promise, an organization founded by family members of victims of the mass shooting in Newtown, Connecticut, funds a program that helps students develop the social-emotional skills to reach out to and include those who may be chronically isolated in order to create a culture of inclusion and connectedness in school or the community.[185] Social isolation is a growing problem in the USA and, in its extreme, can foster violent and suicidal behavior. The Sandy Hook program provides training and raises awareness about the impact of social isolation. It is currently examining the role of social media in the isolation of young people.

Recommendations

- Investments should be made to fund research and develop practices throughout the country that will reduce social isolation at all age levels.
- Building community networks can play an important role in reducing violence and self-injury. Governments at all levels should support the establishment of community structures and processes that promote the development of more involved, caring, and inclusive communities.
- Community-building initiatives should aim to prevent violence and to explore how to intervene when confronted with individuals who may be at risk of committing an act of extreme violence.

A Final Word

Many Americans are resigned to the belief that no meaningful solutions to gun violence will be introduced by our political leaders or that no such solutions exist. They point, for example, to the existing gun stock and say that there are too many guns in circulation to have effective regulation. This is indeed a great challenge, as are the political, legal, and cultural impediments to change. When confronted with these impediments to change, I point to Australia, a country that has successfully dealt with similar obstacles—a federalist system of government, gun culture, and strong gun lobby—and surmounted resistance to change with an expression of public outrage and determined national leadership.

While there is no single solution to gun violence, I have tried to show in this chapter that there are many approaches that have been shown to be effective or promising. Confronting violence with bold actions rather than rhetoric or excuses is an imperative. It is an imperative due to the unacceptable number of Americans who die or suffer disabling injuries each year as a result of gun violence. Reducing the toll of gun violence is also essential if Americans are to feel secure. Security is a precondition to thriving communities and a healthy economy. People who are afraid of the next murderous rampage are less likely to spend time in their communities, to interact with and trust others, and to participate in recreational activities.

Gun rights advocates often object to and attempt to delegitimize the most reasonable gun laws, arguing that they are an intrusion on their freedoms and violate the Constitution. They do not, as determined repeatedly by the courts. How does the militarization of schools, the NRA's solution to school violence, make children feel free and secure? How do laws that allow guns on campus and in the classroom promote the freedom of college students and faculty to express themselves openly on controversial topics? How do preemption and other laws that force cities and counties to allow guns in places like public buildings, parks, and bars further liberties in communities opposed to such a policy? How do laws that prevent family physicians and pediatricians from discussing gun safety with their patients promote freedom? About three-quarters of Americans do not own firearms and their desire to live in gun-free settings must also be respected.

America's continuing paralysis in relation to gun policy and our failure to respond effectively to gun violence will mean that the trend of more frequent and extreme acts of violence will continue unabated. The inevitable result will be that people will limit their own activities out of fear, security measures that restrict our freedoms will be stepped up, and our privacy will be increasingly compromised by more surveillance of our movements and communications. These erosions of our freedoms will affect gun owners and nongun owners alike.

Our freedoms and our lives are at stake in our struggle against gun violence. Many promising measures are available to deal with this issue. Meaningful changes in policy will occur when Americans fully appreciate the price we pay for gun violence. How many more slaughters of our fellow citizens must we endure before we demand decisive action?

Notes

1. Malina D, Morrisey S, Campion E, Hamel M, Drazen J. Rooting out gun violence. N Engl J Med. 2015; 374(2): 175–176.
2. Kassirer J. Guns, society, and medicine. N Engl J Med. 2015; 372(9): 874–875.
3. Editorial Board. Ending the gun epidemic. The New York Times. 2015 Dec. 4. P. 1 A.
4. Hemenway D. There's scientific consensus on guns and the NRA will not like it [Internet]. Los Angeles Times. 2015 Apr 22. Available from: http:// www.latimes.com/opinion/op-ed/la-oe-hemenway-guns-20150423-story.html?utm_source=Master+List&utm_campaign=76ab89d940-April_Newsletter5_6_2015&utm_medium=email&utm_term=0_a6832f13ed-76ab89d940-49264525&goal=0_a6832f13ed-76ab89d940-49264525
5. Hemenway D. Private guns public health. Ann Arbor: University of Michigan Press; 2004. P. 166 & 169.
6. Shapiro R, Hassett K. The economic benefits of reducing violent crime: a case study of eight American cities. Washington, DC: Center for American Progress; 2012.

7. Dykstra R. The cattle towns. NY: Knopf; 1968.

8. Winkler A. Gunfight: the battle over the right to bear arms in America. NY: Norton; 2011.

9. Honan E. Poll finds gun owners, even NRA members, back some restrictions [Internet]. Chicago Tribune. 2012 Jul 24. Available from: http://articles.chicagotribune.com/2012-07-24/news/sns-rt-us-usa-shooting-denver-gunsbre86o02o-20120724_1_gun-owners-nra-members-gun-control

10. Brenner K, Lichtblau, E, Wingfield, N. Apple goes to court, and FBI presses Congress to settle iPhone privacy fight [Internet]. The New York Times. 2016 Feb 25. Available from: http://www.nytimes.com/2016/02/26/technology/apple-unlock-iphone-fbi-san-bernardino-brief.html?_r=0

11. Watner C. The precursor of national identification cards in the US: drivers licenses and vehicle registration in historical perspective [Internet]. Voluntaryist.com. Available from: http://voluntaryist.com/articles/119a.html#.VbJGHlJRGK4.

12. Violence Policy Center. Gun deaths surpass motor vehicle deaths in 21 states and the District of Columbia. Washington, DC: Violence Policy Center; 2015.

13. Parker S. Balancing act: regulation of civilian firearm possession. Small Arms Survey 2011. Geneva: Graduate Institute of International and Development Studies; 2011.

14. Gabor T. International firearms licensing regimes: a study of six countries. Ottawa: Public Safety Canada; 2013. P. 19.

15. Royal Canadian Mounted Police. Application for a possession and acquisition licence under the Firearms Act [Internet]. Available from: http://www.rcmp-grc.gc.ca/cfp-pcaf/form-formulaire/pdfs/5592-eng.pdf

16. Federal Bureau of Investigation. National Instant Criminal Background Check System. Fact sheet [Internet]. Available from: https://www.fbi.gov/about-us/cjis/nics/general-information/fact-sheet

17. Peters R. When will the US learn from Australia: stricter gun control laws save lives [Internet]. The Guardian. 2013 Dec 14. Available from: http://www.theguardian.com/commentisfree/2013/dec/14/america-mass-murder-australia-gun-control-saves-lives

18. Mayors Against Illegal Guns. Trace the guns: the link between gun laws and interstate gun trafficking. New York: Mayors Against Illegal Guns; 2010.

19. Webster D, Vernick J, Hepburn L. Relationship between licensing, registration, and other gun sale laws and the source state of crime guns. Inj Prev. 2001; 7(3): 184–189.

20. Cook P, Goss, K. The gun debate. New York: Oxford University Press; 2013. P. 139.
21. Webster D, Vernick J, McGinty E, Alcorn T. Preventing the diversion of guns to criminals through effective firearm sales laws. In: Webster D, Vernick J, editors. Reducing gun violence in America. Baltimore: Johns Hopkins University Press; 2013. P. 109–121.
22. Rudolph K. Stuart E, Vernick J, Webster D. Association between Connecticut's permit-to-purchase handgun law and homicides. Baltimore: Johns Hopkins Center for Gun Policy and Research; 2015.
23. Amos J. Missouri gun murders rose after law repeal [Internet]. BBC News. 2014 Feb 17. Available from: http://www.bbc.com/news/science-environment-26222578
24. Blais E, Gagne M, Linteau I. L'effet des lois en matiere de controle des armes a feu sur les homicides au Canada, 1974-2004. Can J Criminol Crim. 2011; 53(1): 27–61.
25. Barry C, McGinty E, Vernick J, Webster D. After Newtown: public opinion on gun policy and mental illness. N Engl J Med. 2013; 368(12): 1077–1081.
26. Law Center to Prevent Gun Violence. Licensing gun owners and purchasers policy summary [Internet]. Smartgunlaws.org. Available from: http://smartgunlaws.org/licensing-of-gun-owners-purchasers-policy-summary/
27. Yablon A. Why Dylann Roof didn't get a background check [Internet]. The Trace. 2015 July 16, 2015. Available from: http://www.thetrace.org/2015/07/dylann-roof-background-check-fbi-nics/
28. Mayors Against Illegal Guns. A Blueprint for federal action on illegal guns: regulation, enforcement, and best practices to combat illegal gun trafficking, Section I. improving gun background checks (Aug. 2009) [Internet]. Available from: http://everytown.org/documents/2014/10/blueprint-federal-action.pdf
29. Cook P, Ludwig J. Guns in America. Washington, DC: Police Foundation; 1996. Mayors Against Illegal Guns, Felon seeks firearm, no strings attached: How dangerous people evade background checks and buy illegal guns online. Kelly Report: Gun Violence in America. Washington, DC: Office of Congresswoman Robin Kelly, 2014, P. 51.
30. Mayors Against Illegal Guns. Felon seeks firearm, no strings attached: How dangerous people evade background checks and buy illegal guns online. In: Kelly Report: Gun Violence in America. Washington, DC: Office of Congresswoman Robin Kelly; 2014. P. 51.

31. Bureau of Alcohol, Tobacco and Firearms. Gun shows: Brady checks and crime gun traces. Washington, DC: ATF; 1999.

32. Shear M, Lichtblau E. Obama to expand background checks and tighten enforcement [Internet]. The New York Times. 2016 Jan 4. Available from: http://www.nytimes.com/2016/01/05/us/politics/obama-says-he-will-act-on-gun-control-in-coming-days.html?_r=0

33. Gerney A, Parsons C. The gun debate 1 Year after Newtown: assessing six key claims about gun background checks. Washington, DC: Center for American Progress; 2013.

34. Bureau of Alcohol, Tobacco & Firearms. Following the gun: enforcing federal law against firearms traffickers. Washington, DC: US Department of the Treasury; 2000. P. 13.

35. Mayors Against Illegal Guns. Felon seeks firearm. P. 50.

36. Mayors Against Illegal Guns. Felon seeks firearm. P. 52.

37. Mayors Against Illegal Guns. Felon seeks firearm. P. 51.

38. Mayors Against Illegal Guns. Felon seeks firearm. P. 54.

39. Webster D. Guns kill people and if we had universal background checks, they would not kill so many [Internet]. New Republic. 2014 Jun 26. Available from: http://www.newrepublic.com/article/118286/facts-about-gun-control-and-universal-background-checks

40. Mayors Against Illegal Guns. Felon Seeks Firearm.

41. Webster D, Wintemute G. Effects of policies designed to keep firearms from high-risk individuals. Annu Rev. Public Health. 2015; 36: 21–37. Epub 2015 Jan 7.

42. Sen B, Panjamapirom A. 2012. State background checks for gun purchase and firearm deaths: an exploratory study. Prev Med. 2012; 55(4):346–350.

43. Fleegler E, Lee L, Monuteaux M, Hemenway D, Mannix R. Firearm legislation and firearm-related fatalities in the United States. JAMA Intern Med. 2013; 173(9): 732–740.

44. Sargent G. Why expanding background checks would, in fact, reduce gun crime [Internet]. Washington Post. 2013 Apr. 3. Available from: https://www.washingtonpost.com/blogs/plum-line/wp/2013/04/03/why-expanding-background-checks-would-in-fact-reduce-gun-crime/

45. Parker S. Balancing act: regulation of civilian firearm possession. P. 22.

46. Law Center to Prevent Gun Violence. Waiting periods policy summary [Internet]. Smartgunlaws.org. Available from: http://smartgunlaws.org/waiting-periods-policy-summary/

47. Wintemute G, Parmham C, Beaumont J, Wright M, Drake C. Mortality among recent purchasers of handguns. N Engl J Med. 1999; 341(21): 1583–1589.

48. Koper C. America's experience with the federal assault weapons ban, 1994–2004. In: Webster D, Vernick J, editors. Reducing gun violence in America: informing policy with evidence and analysis. Baltimore: Johns Hopkins University Press; 2013. P. 159–160.

49. Kleck G. Targeting guns: firearms and their control. New York: Aldine de Gruyter; 1997. P. 124–126.

50. Everytown for Gun Safety. Analysis of Recent Mass Shootings. New York: Everytown for Gun Safety; 2015.

51. Webster D. Testimony at hearings on proposals to reduce gun violence: protecting our communities while respecting the Second Amendment. Washington, DC: Senate Committee on the Judiciary; 2013 Feb 12.

52. Koper C. America's experience with the federal assault weapons ban, 1994–2004. P. 163.

53. Koper C. America's experience with the federal assault weapons ban. P. 163.

54. Koper C. America's experience with the federal assault weapons ban. P. 164.

55. Koper C. America's experience with the federal assault weapons ban. P. 165.

56. Cook P, Goss K. The gun debate. P. 135.

57. Dube A, Dube O, Garcia-Ponce O. Cross-border spillover: US gun laws and violence in Mexico. Washington, DC: Center for Global Development; 2011.

58. Bureau of Alcohol, Tobacco and Firearms. Youth crime gun interdiction initiative, crime gun trace reports (2000) national report 50. Washington, DC: US Department of the Treasury; 2002.

59. Weil D, Knox R. Evaluating the impact of Virginia's one-gun-a-month law. The Center to Prevent Handgun Violence. 1995; 1: 4–6.

60. Law Center to Prevent Gun Violence. Minimum age to purchase and possess firearms policy summary [Internet]. Smartgunlaws.org. 2013 Oct 1. Available from: http://smartgunlaws.org/minimum-age-to-purchase-possess-firearms-policy-summary/

61. Law Center to Prevent Gun Violence. Categories of prohibited people policy summary [Internet]. Smartgunlaws.org. 2013 Sep 29. Available from: http://smartgunlaws.org/prohibited-people-gun-purchaser-policy-summary/

62. American Psychological Association. Gun violence: prediction, prevention, and policy. Washington, DC: Public and Member Communications; 2013. P. 4.

63. Everytown for Gun Safety. Analysis of recent mass shootings.

64. Law Center to Prevent Gun Violence. Mental health reporting policy summary [Internet]. Smartgunlaws.org. 2013 Sep 16. Available from: http://smartgunlaws.org/mental-health-reporting-policy-summary/

65. Consortium for Risk-Based Firearm Policy. Guns, public health, and mental illness: an evidence-based approach for federal and state policy. Washington, DC: The Educational Fund to Stop Gun Violence; 2015.

66. Consortium for Risk-Based Firearm Policy. Risk-based firearm policy recommendations for Virginia. Washington, DC: The Educational Fund to Stop Gun Violence; 2015.

67. Swanson J, Sampson N, Petukhova M, Zaslavsky A, Appelbaum P, Swartz M et al. Guns, impulsive angry behavior, and mental disorders: results from the National Comorbidity Survey Replication (NCS-R). Behav Sci Law. 2015; 33(2–3): 199–212.

68. Centers for Disease Control (US). National Intimate Partner and Sexual Violence Survey: Highlights of 2010 findings [Internet]. Available from: http://www.cdc.gov/violenceprevention/pdf/nisvs_factsheet-a.pdf   (last accessed April 2013).

69. Vigdor E, Mercy J. Do laws restricting access to firearms by domestic violence offenders prevent intimate partner homicide? Eval Rev. 2006; 30(3): 313–346.

70. Lopez M. Landmark California gun seizure law takes effect 1 January but amid concerns [Internet]. The Guardian. 2015 Dec 31. Available from: http://www.theguardian.com/us-news/2015/dec/31/landmark-california-gun-seizure-law-takes-effect?CMP=oth_b-aplnews_d-1

71. Wintemute G, Drake C, Beaumont J, Wright M, Parham C. Prior misdemeanor convictions as a risk factor for later violent and firearm-related criminal activity among authorized purchasers of handguns. JAMA. 1998; 280(24):2083–2087.

72. Wintemute G, Wright M, Drake C, Beaumont J. Subsequent criminal activity among violent misdemeanants who seek to purchase handguns: risk factors and effectiveness of denying handgun purchase. JAMA. 2001; 285(8):1019–1026.

73. Wintemute G. Broadening denial criteria for the purchase and possession of firearms: need, feasibility, and effectiveness. In: Webster D, Vernick J, editors. Reducing gun violence in America. Baltimore: Johns Hopkins University Press; 2013. P. 77–93.

74. Carr B, Wiebe D, Richmond T, Cheney, Branas C. A randomized controlled feasibility trial of alcohol consumption and the ability to appropriately use a firearm. Inj Prev. 2009; 15(6): 409.

75. Wintemute G. Association between firearm ownership, firearm-related risk and risk reduction behaviors and alcohol- related risk behaviors. Inj Prev. 2011; 17(6): 422.

76. Wintemute G. Alcohol misuse, firearm violence perpetration, and public policy in the United States. Prev Med. Epub 2015 Apr 30.

77. Winkler A, Natterson C. There's a simple way to reduce gun violence: raise the gun age [Internet]. Washington Post. 2016 Jan 6. Available from: https://www.washingtonpost.com/posteverything/wp/2016/01/06/there-a-simple-way-to-fight-mass-shootings-raise-the-gun-age/

78. Shuster M, Franke T, Bastian A, Sor S, Halfon N. Firearm storage patterns in US Homes with children. Am J Public Health. 2000; 90(4): 588–594.

79. Cook P, Ludwig J. Guns in America.

80. Baxley F, Miller M. *Parental Misperceptions About Children and Firearms*, 160 Archives Of Pediatric & Adolescent Medicine, 2006, 160: 542–547

81. Naureckas S, Galanter C, Naureckas E, Donovan M, Christoffel K. Children's and women's ability to fire handguns. Arch Pediatr Adolesc Med. 1995; 149(12): 1318–1322.

82. Grossman D, Reay D, Baker S. Self-inflicted and unintentional firearm injuries among children and adolescents: the source of the firearm. Arch Pediatr Adolesc Med. 1999; 153(8):875–879.

83. Vossekuil B, Fein R, Reddy M, Borum R, Modzeleski W. The final report and findings of the safe school initiative: implications for the prevention of school attacks in the United States. Washington, DC: United States Secret Service and the United States Department of Education; 2002.

84. Parker S. Balancing Act. P. 32.

85. Law Center to Prevent Gun Violence. Shoot first laws policy summary [Internet]. Smartgunlaws.org. 2013 Jul 18. Available from: http://smartgunlaws.org/shoot-first-laws-policy-summary/

86. US General Accounting Office. Accidental shootings: many deaths and injuries caused by firearms could be prevented. Washington, DC: US General Accounting Office; 1991.

87. Cummings P, Grossman D, Rivara F, Koepsell T. State gun safe storage laws and child mortality due to guns. JAMA. 1997; 278(13):1084–1086.

88. Hepburn L, Azrael D, Miller M, Hemenway D. The effects of child access prevention laws on unintentional child firearm fatalities, 1979–2000. J Trauma. 2006; 61(2): 423–428.

89. Webster D, Vernick J, Zeoli A, Manganello J. Association between youth-focused firearm laws and youth suicides. JAMA. 2004; 292(5):594–601.

90. Hemenway D. Private guns, public health. Ann Arbor: University of Michigan Press; 2004. P. 84–85.

91. ABC News. What young kids do with guns when parents are not around [Internet]. ABC News. 2014 Jan 31. Available from: http://abcnews. go.com/2020/video/young-kids-guns-parents-22325589

92. American Academy of Pediatrics Committee on Adolescence. Firearms and adolescents. Pediatrics, 1992, 89(4): 784–787.

93. Barry C, McGinty E, Vernick J, Webster D. After Newtown—public opinion on gun policy and mental illness. N Engl J Med. 2013; 368(12): 1077–1081.

94. Rowhani-Rahbar A, Simonetti J, Rivara F. Effectiveness of interventions to promote safe firearm storage. Epidemiol Rev. 2016; 38: 111–124.

95. National Physicians Alliance. Gun safety and public health. Washington, DC: National Physicians Alliance; 2013. P. 10

96. Webster D, Vernick J, Vittes K, McGinty E, Teret S, Frattaroli S. The case for gun policy reforms in America. Baltimore: Johns Hopkins Center for Gun Policy and Research; 2012.

97. National Physicians Alliance. Gun safety and public health.

98. Teret S, Mernit A. Personalized guns: using technology to save lives. In: Webster D, Vernick J, editors. Reducing gun violence in America. Baltimore: Johns Hopkins University Press; 2013. P. 173–182.

99. Teret S. Key perspectives and insights on personalized guns. In: Kelly R, editor. Kelly Report: gun violence in America. Washington, DC: Office of Congresswoman Robin L. Kelly; 2014. P. 58–61.

100. Vernick J, O'Brien M, Hepburn L, Johnson S, Webster D, Hargarten S. Unintentional and undetermined firearm-related deaths: a preventable death analysis for three safety devices. Inj Prev. 2003; 9(4): 307–311.

101. Wolfson J, Teret S, Frattaroli S, Miller M, Azrael D. The US public's preference for safer guns. Am J Public Health. 2016; 106(3): 411–413.

102. Law Center to Prevent Gun Violence. Design safety standards policy summary [Internet]. Smartgunlaws.org. 2013 Dec 1. Available from: http://smartgunlaws.org/gun-design-safety-standards-policy-summary/

103. Dunn C. Bullets beyond recall: defective guns beyond US government's reach [Internet]. International Business Times. 2015 Dec 17. Available from: http://www.ibtimes.com/bullets-beyond-recall-defective-guns-outside-us-governments-reach-2226935

104. Ohar O, Lizotte T. Extracting ballistic forensic intelligence: microstamped firearms deliver data for illegal firearm traffic mapping-technology. Proceedings of the International Society for Optical Engineering. 2013 Jun. Available from: http://csgv.org/wp/wp-content/uploads/2013/06/LIZOTTE-RESEARCH-PAPER-AUGUST-2009.pdf

105. American Bar Association. Recommendation on microstamping [Internet]. Chicago: American Bar Association; 2010. Available from: http://csgv.org/wp/wp-content/uploads/2013/06/aba-resolution-on-microstamping-sept-10.pdf

106. International Association of Chiefs of Police. Resolution: support the use of microstamping technology. Alexandra, VA: International Association of Chiefs of Police; 2008.

107. Greenberg Quinlan Rosner Research & the Tarrance Group for the Mayors Against Illegal Guns. Americans support common sense measures to cut down on illegal guns [Internet]. 2008 Apr 10. Available from: http://www.mayorsagainstillegalguns.org/downloads/pdf/polling_memo.pdf

108. National Shooting Sports Foundation. Microstamping technology: proven flawed and imprecise [Internet]. Newtown, CT: National Shooting Sports Foundation; 2013. Available from: http://www.nssf.org/factsheets/PDF/Microstamping.pdf

109. University of California at Davis. Corrected: study on microstamping of guns. News and information [Internet]. 2007 May 15. Available from: http://news.ucdavis.edu/search/news_detail.lasso?id=8163.

110. Coalition to Stop Gun Violence and Educational Fund to Stop Gun Violence. Microstamping technology: precise and proven [Internet]. Available from: http://www.efsgv.org/wp-content/uploads/2013/06/Microstamping-Technology-Precise-and-Proven-Memo.pdf

111. Dionne EJ. Let us focus on the gun makers [Internet]. Times-Herald. 2015 Oct 8. Available from: http://www.timesheraldonline.com/opinion/20151008/ej-dionne-lets-focus-on-the-gun-makers

112. Kristof N. Lessons from the Virginia shooting [Internet]. The New York Times. 2015 Aug 26. Available from: http://www.nytimes.com/2015/08/27/opinion/lessons-from-the-murders-of-tv-journalists-in-the-virginia-shooting.html?smid=nytcore-ipad-share&smprod=nytcore-ipad&_r=1

113. Mayors against Illegal Guns. Trace the guns: the link between gun laws and interstate gun trafficking. New York: Mayors Against Illegal Guns; 2010.

114. Webster D, Vernick J, Bulzacchelli M. Effects of State-Level Firearm Seller Accountability Policies on Firearms Trafficking. J Urban Health. 2009; 86(4): 525–537.

115. Irvin I, Rhodes K, Cheney R, Wiebe D. Evaluating the effect of state regulation of federally licensed firearm dealers on firearm homicide. Am J Public Health. 2014; 104(8): 1384–1386.

116. Webster D, Vernick J. Spurring responsible firearms sales practices through litigation. In: Webster D, Vernick J, editors. Reducing gun violence in America. Baltimore: Johns Hopkins University Press; 2013. P. 123–31.

117. Gerney A, Parsons C. License to kill: how lax concealed carry laws can combine with Stand Your Ground laws to produce deadly results. Washington, DC: Center for American Progress; 2013.

118. Gerney A, Parsons C. License to Kill. P. 18.

119. Turner J. NRA-backed expansion of Stand Your Ground law dies in Florida House [Internet]. Palm Beach Post. 2015 Nov 17. Available from: http://www.palmbeachpost.com/news/news/state-regional-govt-politics/nra-backed-expansion-of-stand-your-ground-law-dies/npPtC/

120. Braga A, Weisburd D. Focused deterrence and the prevention of violent gun injuries: practice, theoretical principles, and scientific evidence. Annu Rev. Public Health. 2015. 36: 55–68.

121. Kennedy D, Braga A, Piehl A. The (un)known universe: mapping gangs and gang violence in Boston. In: D. Weisburd D, McEwen J, editors. Crime mapping and crime prevention. Monsey, NY: Criminal Justice Press; 1997. P. 219–262.

122. Tyler T. Enhancing police legitimacy. Ann Am Acad Polit SS. 2004; 593(1): 84–99.

123. Braga A, Weisburd D. Focused deterrence and the prevention of violent gun injuries. P. 63.

124. Peters R. Rational firearms regulation: evidence-based firearm regulation in Australia. In: Webster D, Vernick J, editors. Reducing gun violence in America: informing policy with evidence and analysis. Baltimore: Johns Hopkins University Press; 2013. P. 195–204.

125. Howard J. I went after guns. Obama can too [Internet]. The New York Times. January 16, 2013. Available from: http://www.nytimes.com/2013/01/17/opinion/australia-banned-assault-weapons-america-can-too.html

126. Australian Institute of Criminology. Legislative reforms [Internet]. Available from: http://www.aic.gov.au/publications/current%20series/rpp/100-120/rpp116/06_reforms.html

127. Alpers P. The big melt: how one democracy changed after scrapping a third of its firearms. In: Webster D, Vernick J, editors. Reducing gun violence in America. Baltimore: The Johns Hopkins University Press; 2013. P. 205–211.

128. Alpers P. The big melt. P. 208.
129. Chapman S, Alpers P, Agho K, Jones M. Australia's 1996 gun law reforms: faster falls in firearm deaths, firearm suicides, and a decade without mass shootings. Inj Prev. 2006; 12(6): 365–372.
130. Chapman S, Alpers P, Agho K, Jones M. Australia's 1996 gun reform laws.
131. Neill C, Leigh A. Do gun buybacks save lives? evidence from time series variation. Curr I Crim Justice. 2008; 20: 145–162. .
132. Leigh A, Neill C. Do gun buybacks save lives? evidence from panel data. Am Law Econ Rev. 2010; 12(2): 509–557.
133. Reuter P, Mouzos J. Australia: A massive buyback of low-risk guns. In: Cook P, Ludwig J, editors. Evaluating gun policy: effects on crime and violence. Washington, DC: Brookings Institution; 2003. P. 121–156.
134. Neill C, Leigh A. Do gun buybacks save lives?
135. Neill C, Leigh A. Do gun buybacks save lives?
136. Leigh A, Neill C. Do gun buybacks save lives? P. 530.
137. Peters R. Rational firearm regulation: evidence-based gun laws in Australia. In: Webster D, Vernick J, editors. Reducing gun violence in America. Baltimore: The Johns Hopkins University Press; 2013. P. 202.
138. Baker J, McPhedran S. Gun laws and sudden death: did the Australian firearm legislation of 1996 make a difference? Brit J Criminol. 2006; 47(3): 455–469.
139. Hemenway D. How to find nothing. J Public Health Policy. 2009; 30(3): 260–268.
140. Neill C, Leigh A. Weak tests and strong conclusions: a re-analysis of gun deaths and the Australian firearms buyback. Canberra: Australian National University Center for Economic Policy; 2007.
141. Leigh A, Neill C. Do gun buybacks save lives?
142. Matthews D. Did gun control work in Australia [Internet]? Washington Post. 2012 Aug. 2. Available from: https://www.washingtonpost.com/news/wonk/wp/2012/08/02/did-gun-control-work-in-australia/
143. Dunn C. Even as guns proliferate in the US, official data on firearms remain scarce [Internet]. International Business Times. 2015 Dec 5. Available from: http://www.ibtimes.com/even-guns-proliferate-us-official-data-firearms-remain-scarce-2212590?rel=rel1
144. Sloan J, Kellermann A, Reay D, Ferris J, Koepsell T, Rivara F et al. Handgun regulations, crime, assaults, and homicide: a tale of two cities. N Engl J Med. 1988; 319(9): 1256–1262.

145. Kellermann, Rivara F, Rushforth N, Banton J, Reay D, Francisco J et al. Gun ownership as a risk factor for homicide in the home. N Engl J Med. 1993. 329(15): 1084–1091.
146. National Physicians Alliance. Gun safety and public health. Washington, DC: National Physicians Alliance; 2013.
147. Luo M., N.R.A. stymies firearms research, scientists say [Internet]. New York Times. 2011 Jan 25. Available from: http://www.nytimes.com/2011/01/26/us/26guns.html?pagewanted=all
148. Frankel T. Why the CDC still is not researching gun violence, despite the ban being lifted two years ago [Internet]. The Washington Post. January 14, 2015. Available from: http://www.washingtonpost.com/news/storyline/wp/2015/01/14/why-the-cdc-still-isnt-researching-gun-violence-despite-the-ban-being-lifted-two-years-ago/
149. Centers for Disease Control and Prevention, The public health approach to violence prevention [Internet]. Atlanta: National Center for Injury Prevention and Control; 2013. Available from: http://peacealliance.org/cms/assets/uploads/2013/05/CDC-Public-Health-Approach-to-Violence-Prevention.pdf
150. Hemenway D, Miller M. Public health approach to the prevention of gun violence. N Engl J Med. 2013; 368(21): 2033–2035.
151. Centers for Disease Control and Prevention. Morbidity and mortality weekly report [Internet]. Volume 48. 1999 May 14. Available from: http://www.cdc.gov/mmwr/PDF/wk/mm4818.pdf
152. Leshner A, Altevogt B, Lee A, McCoy M, and Kelley P. Priorities for Research to Reduce the Threat of Firearm-Related Violence. Washington, DC: National Academy of Sciences, 2013.
153. Nocera J. Unlearning gun violence [Internet]. The New York Times. 2013 Nov 12. Available from: http://www.nytimes.com/2013/11/12/opinion/nocera-unlearning-gun-violence.html?hp&rref=opinion&_r=1&mtrref=undefined&gwh=C3BAC7525D1300826D11AC00B4CAE9A9&gwt=pay&assetType=opinion
154. Skogan W, Hartnett S, Bump N, Dubois J. Evaluation of CeaseFire-Chicago. Washington, DC: National Institute of Justice; 2009.
155. Nocera J. Unlearning gun violence.
156. World Health Organization. Violence prevention: the evidence. Geneva: World Health Organization; 2009.
157. Emanuel R. In: The Kelly report 2014: gun violence in America. Washington, DC: Office of Congresswoman Robin L. Kelly; 2013. P. 14–15.

158. Dionne EJ., The right to be free from guns [Internet]. Saratogian. 2015 Jun 27. Available from: http://www.saratogian.com/opinion/20150627/ej-dionne-the-right-to-be-free-from-guns

159. Vossekuil B, Fein R, Reddy M, Borum R, Modzeleski W. The final report and findings of the Safe School Initiative: implications for the prevention of school attacks in the United States. Washington, DC: United States Secret Service and the United States Department of Education; 2002.

160. Federal Bureau of Investigation. A study of active shooter incidents in the United States between 2000 and 2013. Washington, DC: Department of Justice; 2014.

161. Randazzo M, Borum R, Vossekuil B, Fein R, Modzelewski W, Pollack W. Threat assessment in schools: empirical support and comparison with other approaches. In: Jimerson S, Furlong M, editors. The handbook of school violence and school safety: from research to practice. Mahwah, NJ: Lawrence Erlbaum Associates Inc.; 2006.

162. Borum R. Assessing violence risk among youth. J Clin Psychol. 2000; 56(10): 1263–1288.

163. Randazzo M, Borum R, Vossckuil B, Fein R, Modzelewski W, Pollack W. Threat assessment in schools.

164. Seattle City Council. Gun safety package [Internet]. Available at: http://www.seattle.gov/council/Burgess/attachments/Gun-Safety-Package.pdf

165. Fox J. Gun control or carry permits won't stop mass murder [Internet]. CNN Opinion. 2012 Jul 20. Available from: http://www.jfox.neu.edu/Columns/CNN%20Aurora.html

166. Follman M, Aronsen G, Pan D. A guide to mass shootings in America. Mother Jones. 2012 Sep 28. 2012.

167. Vossekuil B, Fein R, Reddy M, Borum R, Modzeleski W. The final report and findings of the Safe School Initiative.

168. Federal Bureau of Investigation. A study of active shooter incidents.

169. Federeal Bureau of Investigation. A study of active shooter Incidents. P. 12.

170. Vossekuil B, Fein R, Reddy M, Borum R, Modzeleski W. The final report and findings of the Safe School Initiative. P. 22.

171. Vossekuil B, Fein R, Reddy M, Borum R, Modzeleski W. The final report and findings of the Safe School Initiative. P. 20.

172. Vossekuil B, Fein R, Reddy M, Borum R, Modzeleski W. The final report and findings of the Safe School Initiative. P. 20.

173. Vossekuil B, Fein R, Reddy M, Borum R, Modzeleski W. The final report and findings of the Safe School Initiative. P. 21.

174. Vossekuil B, Fein R, Reddy M, Borum R, Modzeleski W. The final report and findings of the Safe School Initiative. P. 22.

175. Fox J, Levin J. Extreme killing: understanding serial and mass murder. Thousand Oaks, California: Sage, 2014.

176. Vossekuil B, Fein R, Reddy M, Borum R, Modzeleski W. The final report and findings of the Safe School Initiative. P. 25–26

177. Vossekuil B, Fein R, Reddy M, Borum R, Modzeleski W. The final report and findings of the Safe School Initiative. P. 26–27.

178. Dutton D, White K, Fogarty D. Paranoid thinking in mass shooters. Aggress Violent Beh. 2013; 18(5): 548–553.

179. Putnam, R. Bowling alone: the collapse and revival of American community. New York: Simon & Schuster; 2000.

180. Putnam R. Bowling alone. P. 261.

181. Putnam R. Bowling alone. P. 264.

182. Office of the Child Advocate. Shooting at Sandy Hook Elementary School. Hartford, CT: State of Connecticut; 2014. P. 106.

183. Putnam, R. Bowling alone. P. 403.

184. Moore A. Chicago dropout reengagement centers part of a growing national trend [Internet]. National League of Cities. 2013 Aug 8. Available from: http://www.nlc.org/media-center/news-search/chicago-dropout-reengagement-centers-part-of-a-growing-national-trend

185. National Education Association. Combating social isolation: it starts with hello [Internet]. 2016 Feb 18. Available from: http://www.learningfirst.org/combatting-social-isolation-it-starts-hello

Index[1]

---

[1] Note: Page number followed by "n" refers to endnotes.

© The Author(s) 2016
T. Gabor, *Confronting Gun Violence in America,*
DOI 10.1007/978-3-319-33723-4